GATHERING TOGETHER, WE DECIDE

Critical Issues in Indigenous Studies

Jeffrey P. Shepherd and Myla Vicenti Carpio
Series Editors

GATHERING TOGETHER, WE DECIDE

Archives of Dispossession, Resistance, and Memory in Ndé Homelands

EDITED BY
Margo Tamez, Cynthia Bejarano, AND Jeffrey P. Shepherd

THE UNIVERSITY OF ARIZONA PRESS
TUCSON

The University of Arizona Press
www.uapress.arizona.edu

We respectfully acknowledge the University of Arizona is on the land and territories of Indigenous peoples. Today, Arizona is home to twenty-two federally recognized tribes, with Tucson being home to the O'odham and the Yaqui. The University strives to build sustainable relationships with sovereign Native Nations and Indigenous communities through education offerings, partnerships, and community service.

ISBN-13: 978-0-8165-5593-2 (hardcover)
ISBN-13: 978-0-8165-5592-5 (paperback)
ISBN-13: 978-0-8165-5594-9 (ebook)

Cover design by Leigh McDonald
Cover photograph from a video by Mia Boccella
Typeset by Sara Thaxton in 10.5/14 Warnock Pro with Squatina (designed by Louise Sansoldi, Anaëlle Turc, and Julia Veljkovic, XCicero) and Apparat Extra Cond

Publication of this book is made possible in part by financial support from the New Mexico State University College of Arts and Sciences Stan Fulton Endowed Chair, and the University of British Columbia Scholarly Publication Fund.

Library of Congress Cataloging-in-Publication Data
Names: Tamez, Margo editor | Bejarano, Cynthia L., 1973– editor | Shepherd, Jeffrey P., 1970– editor
Title: Gathering together, we decide : archives of dispossession, resistance, and memory in Ndé homelands / edited by Margo Tamez, Cynthia Bejarano, and Jeffrey P. Shepherd.
Other titles: Critical issues in indigenous studies
Description: [Tucson] : University of Arizona Press, 2025. | Series: Critical issues in indigenous studies | Includes bibliographical references and index.
Identifiers: LCCN 2025003787 (print) | LCCN 2025003788 (ebook) | ISBN 9780816555932 hardcover | ISBN 9780816555925 paperback | ISBN 9780816555949 ebook
Subjects: LCSH: Apache women—Texas—Social conditions | Lipan Indians—Texas—Social conditions | Mexican-American Border Region—Social conditions
Classification: LCC E99.A6 G274 2025 (print) | LCC E99.A6 (ebook) | DDC 305.897/250721—dc23/eng/20250729
LC record available at https://lccn.loc.gov/2025003787
LC ebook record available at https://lccn.loc.gov/2025003788

Printed in the United States of America
♾ This paper meets the requirements of ANSI/NISO Z39.48-1992 (Permanence of Paper).

To Eloisa García Taméz

"They took my land. They can't take my voice."

Thank you for saying "no";
for knowing the land's history;
for knowing the oral history;
for being steadfast in the face of violence and destruction;
for standing determined against the dispossession and oppressors;
for showing that a different way is possible;
and for insisting on the truths of your ancestors.

May your voice continue to ignite and illuminate the path
to Indigenous justice and self-determination
for many futures to come.

Contents

PART IV. BÉNÁOŃZI̲I̲NÍ | EMBODYING INDIGENOUS RECOGNITION

PART V. EPISTEMOLOGICAL AND METHODOLOGICAL INTERVENTIONS FOR DECOLONIZED FUTURES

Opening Protocols and Land Acknowledgment

NDÉ LAND ACKNOWLEDGMENT: (Visitors and non-Indigenous residents on Ndé ancestral territories, please use this suggested land acknowledgment at any event or gathering on the unceded Kónìcą̀ą̀hį́į́ Gòkíyàà):

"I/We acknowledge that I am an [invited/uninvited] guest on Ndé Dene ancestral and unceded lands and territory, and that the land on which I/we gather is the ancestral home to Ndé [pronounced 'endéh'] peoples, since time immemorial. I/we acknowledge that this land continually has gifted and nurtured Ndé ancestors for millennia and is needed by Ndé peoples for present-day and future restoration of Ndé health and well-being. I/We acknowledge that throughout Texas we are in customary and known places to Ndé, who contributed to the Treaties of Peace and *never ceded or surrendered to European monarchs, or their successor states, republics, and nations.* While a guest in these lands, I/we acknowledge Ndé *isdzáníízháá* and relative Indigenous kinship governance systems, based in familial and culturally embedded knowledge into the present day. To be in good relations, I/we acknowledge that all Ndé women and girls *must* be respected and honored, and I/we acknowledge their roles as the protectors of Ndé lands, waters, medicines, foods, education, exchange, and laws. I/We acknowledge that Ndé peoples have been forced over centuries to live in subordination to Texans, and still struggle in forced diaspora, in exile, or otherwise separated from the Ndé homelands and kinship. I/We acknowledge the resilience of the Ndé Rancherías, Nation, Bands, Clans, Villages, and Communities residing in and beyond current-day borders of 'Texas,' and recognize that my/our acknowledgment is a necessary step for Ndé peoples to return home safely and live among their relatives leading healthy and restored lives."

Background to Protocols

Ndé Dene (Lipan Apache–Athapaskan) peoples of Kónìcą̀ą̀hį́į́ Gòkíyàà (Big Water People's Homeland) rancherías, villages, and towns along the Lower Rio Grande River and within the interior of the Rio Grande Valley belong to the land as Indigenous peoples who have customary, traditional, and intimate deep-time relationships with place, governance, territory, treaties, and international law. Ndé Dene people continue to carry out their responsibilities, practices, and determination as Indigenous people of the region, prior to and still continuing long after the bordering of Kónìcą̀ą̀hį́į́ Gòkíyàà lands, waters, and resources.

As such, as free, autonomous, and self-determining peoples, the Ndé Dene always freely determined where and how Ndé Dene peoples lived, governed, and existed side by side with the diverse multitudes of Indigenous peoples throughout Kónìcą̀ą̀hį́į́ Gòkíyàà. As a result of enacting self-determination in governance, the Kónìcą̀ą̀hį́į́ Gòkíyàà of the Ndé Dene became one of the most culturally diverse and multipolar cultural nexuses of the Americas. The abundance of the land's gifts to Indigenous peoples created dynamic, mutually thriving societies in which cross-cultural marriage created unity, co-governance mechanisms, and economic benefits for all. The European invasions and occupations of the Kónìcą̀ą̀hį́į́ Gòkíyàà of the Ndé Dene were a man-made catastrophe that plunged the Indigenous pluriverse that had developed for millennia into centuries of disruption, displacement, depletions, and death of a kind previously not experienced in the Americas.

However, the Ndé Dene of Kónìcą̀ą̀hį́į́ Gòkíyàà survived, adapted, and remained over the course of and throughout multiple colonial and settler-colonial phases of economic development and resource plundering, into the present day. Due to the Ndé Dene ancestral governance and anticolonial strategies to maintain the Indigenous world system at any level possible, the system of encouraging Indigenous-to-Indigenous coexistence survived, at least in part. Today, the Ndé Dene peoples are culturally and politically diverse thanks to intermarriage and political alliances with Indigenous and multiracial Indigenous peoples from throughout the Americas. This culturally based geopolitical adaptation is not limited to the Ndé Dene of Kónìcą̀ą̀hį́į́ Gòkíyàà; the Dene Nation peoples of Canada, Mexico, and the United States demonstrate a high diversity of intercultural and interracial alliances as an Indigenous adaptation strategy for long-term survival of colonization and beyond.

Traditionally and historically, Indigenous peoples in our respective customary places, homelands, and territories have had ways of knowing and being within our places of belonging, and we have had ways, or methods and approaches, in which we conveyed our intergenerational and ancestral connection to our homelands, broadly. The familial locations where our lineal relations were born, grew up among extended families, received teachings and knowledge from our Elders, aunties, uncles, cousins, and parents, and received spiritual and land-based learning provide the people a land-emplaced curricular system of Indigenous knowledge "sister" systems, reflecting a high propensity in Kónìcą̀ą̀hį́į́ Gòkíyàà for Indigenous peoples to have Dene, Uto-Aztekan, and related Indigenous linguistic and philosophical systems co-operating simultaneously. In the last three centuries, the colonizers and settlers preempted, expropriated, criminalized, and deeply violated our lands, food systems, water, medicines, religious sacred knowledge systems, languages, ceremonies, rituals, kinship systems, burial places, families, spirits, minds, and bodies. The "sister" curricular systems have worked to counter and resist complete annihilation of the larger operating systems of complementary indigeneity paradigms within extended families, clans, and communities to the present day.

As a result, the colonizer and settler societies could *not* take our spirits, our ways of critical thinking, our voices, our memories, or our resistance. Prior to 2007, the Ndé territorial land acknowledgments and familial and extended-family place-based protocols were always done orally, through intimate kinship rituals that have continued up to the present day. Our protocols—humble and intimate, shared between our people and close relations known to us over generations, who share historical lineages, histories, a belonging consciousness, foods, medicines, and traditions in our lands, which span the entirety of Texas, eastern New Mexico, and northern Mexico—connect us to our Dene Ndé ancestors since time immemorial. Our protocols never left us; they had become normalized as "good, traditional manners" that were embodied, in the flesh, instinctual, not written by outsider anthropologists. Our indoctrination by colonizer education systems prevented the Ndé from receiving a K–12 and post-secondary education that complemented our home- and hearth-based kinship ways of knowing, doing, and being in our world. Since the late 1990s, Ndé peoples took up legal actions that asserted Ndé rights to question and reclaim Ndé belonging, political presence and recognition, and spatial justice on our hereditary and customary land base.

Given the forces of White supremacy, militarism, settler colonialism, and anti-Indigenous racism obstructing Ndé from enjoying our political, social, economic, and spiritual rights in our ancestral places, we were losing knowledge and understandings with each passing generation of Elders whose teachings and experiences have not been comprehensively documented. While settler colonialism and settler dispossession are nefarious, they have never been absolute. Settlers never actually eliminated Ndé; instead, it has been and still is the settler narratives and discourses of Ndé disposability, foreignness/alienness, unrecognizability, and elimination that are germane to the settler-colonial necropolitics of erasure and disavowal.

Protocols: Before Land Acknowledgment . . .

Today, many yearn to do the Indigenous land acknowledgment. And this is good. It is necessary. And it is long overdue. But before this can happen, a space of clarity of mind and purity of heart must be created. Indigenous peoples do this through ceremony, reverence (prayer), song, and dance. This is the protocol.

To clarify, Indigenous peoples do not do a land acknowledgment on our own territory. We are the territory.

We are conducting a protocol of our belonging to territory, to our homeland, to our home, demonstrating how we determine who is invited, who is welcomed, where, for what purpose, and for how long.

Protocols of Indigenous Acknowledgment and Acknowledging: Who Is This For? Who Is Being Acknowledged? Who Is Doing the Acknowledgment? What Is Your Role?

We encourage everyone to acknowledge Ndé peoples all the time, every day, wherever you are, and to please also acknowledge all related Indigenous nations interconnected to these lands who carry our complex systems of ancestral knowledges and revere our ongoing existence.

We still thrive here on our traditional and customary unceded territories. As invited or uninvited visitors, you will be working, creating, breathing, and relating to carry out your existence in these lands.

However, at a formal event, on our territory, there are specific acts that one must take to acknowledge Ndé unceded territory.[1] This is an opportunity for official leaders, representatives, speakers, politicians, and decision-makers to enact and embody crucial steps of decolonization. That is, they recognize that the land acknowledgment is an act of formally acknowledging the understanding that, first and foremost, the Indigenous peoples belong to this land and always will in perpetuity. It is an act of acknowledging that Indigenous peoples have not, and will never, surrender or cede, voluntarily or nonvoluntarily, their collective belonging to the land.

This formal and irreversible act demonstrates that you are a human being coming into critical consciousness and responsibly engaging the enactment, requested of you by Indigenous peoples, of recognition and respect.

It demonstrates that the Ndé struggles, survivorship, resilience, resistance, and ongoing resurgence—past, present, futurity—are not a one-sided process; they are a relationship with members of the colonial institutions and settler-colonial society.

A proper Ndé land acknowledgment demonstrates that you are on a contemporary relational path of recognition and of reconstructing responsibility on the terms understood by current-day Ndé peoples. This is founded in Indigenous relationality, governance, survivance, self-determination, and rights as currently understood and mobilized by Indigenous peoples in international law and upheld by the United Nations Declaration on the Rights of Indigenous Peoples.[2]

This suggested acknowledgment guide ensures that all visitors and guests to Ndé customary territory, invited or uninvited, are informed about the protocols of respectful engagement here. As decolonization knowledge spreads, more and more non-Indigenous and Indigenous visitors to Ndé customary homelands will be engaging in decolonization *in the present*, and will be acknowledging the present-day challenges *rooted in the past* and yet maintained in ongoing ways. Becoming ambassadors for truth, justice, and historical clarification, writers, creators, and academics play a vital and critical role in right relations with Ndé peoples and the Ndé nation.

To acknowledge Ndé unceded territory in (current-day) Texas (in addition to crucial sites of Ndé cultural significance in current-day New Mexico, Chihuahua, Coahuila, Nuevo León, and Tamaulipas) demonstrates that you are on the good relationship road to a social, intellectual, epistemological, ontological, and methodological partnership with Ndé peoples, who are staunch protectors and defenders of Indigenous peoples' self-determination—in Texas and globally. Acknowledgment is an essential and necessary step toward reestablishing healthy futures for all humans and sentient nonhumans in Indigenous territories connected in a web of relationality.

Acknowledging Ndé unceded territory is only part of the path toward reparation, reconciliation, and creating a stronger, healthier relationship with Ndé peoples, who have been dispossessed by settler-colonial institutions in Ndé homelands. Please understand that true decolonization doesn't begin with a reverent and meaningful land acknowledgment, nor does it end there.

Territorial acknowledgments "should not simply be a *pro forma* statement made before getting on with the 'real business' of the meeting; they must be understood as a vital *part* of the business."[3] In fact, to reframe the permission and right to conduct business in Indigenous unceded territory as being an invited "guest," or to acknowledge that one is an uninvited guest by the same token, is to begin to comprehend Indigenous survivors' historical perspectives and futurity. We strongly discourage the use of Indigenous acknowledgment without the understanding that Ndé peoples seek justice through land reclamation and just economic compensation for stolen lands. Land acknowledgment is a step toward meaningful transitional justice. It is not to be confused with reparations. This is due to the fact that Ndé never relinquished Ndé customary and ancestral territory to Mexico, the United States, Texas, or New Mexico. The hold of White supremacy over Ndé peoples of Texas has been profound, yet in spite of this genocidal force and its destructive practices, Ndé have been a continuing force in ongoing self-determining practices in the pursuit of justice for *all* Lipan Apaches in the *gòkíyàà*—homeland.

Ndé (Lipan Apache) are part of a diverse Dene people who are currently in mobilization, and who claim belonging to a larger cultural homeland spanning the continent, from the sub-Arctic to Mexico.

For Non-Ndé Individuals and Groups

Land acknowledgments are done by those who are not Indigenous to a specific territory; these are customary protocols for recognizing that they are entering, traveling through, moving to, settling in, relocating to, or taking up temporary or permanent living inside Indigenous peoples' unceded territories. For settlers and visiting Indigenous peoples, they are a vital form of engaging with the histories of violent colonization, dispossession, displacement, and forced removal of Indigenous peoples. This often involved militarized force, rape, incarceration, and cultural destruction. Land acknowledgment recognizes that there is an ongoing process of Indigenous peoples' refusal to accept this erasure, and, in terms of decolonization, it insists that U.S. society recognize the erasure, suppression, and denial of its genocidal history.

As Ndé belong within our territorial spaces, Ndé do not do land acknowledgment: we already belong. Land acknowledgment is for guests—invited and uninvited.

At the start of this section is our suggested acknowledgment of Ndé Territory. We strongly encourage visitors to research and respectfully enact kindness and sensitivity when approaching Indigenous peoples—who are the living, intergenerational genocide survivor communities—

about their respective land acknowledgment protocols. To enact land acknowledgment is an important step, but just one, in decolonizing one's personal relationship and power relationship with Indigenous peoples in whose territories one takes up space and place. We encourage respectful dialogues with the many diverse Indigenous peoples, tribes, bands, and nations with ancestral connections to Indigenous territories throughout current-day Texas, and we encourage all in their journeys of decolonizing their understanding of the past, in order to see the present with more clarity.

Margo Tamez

NOTES

1. The qualifier "unceded" is a critical element in acknowledging Ndé territory. Therefore, Ndé acknowledgments *must not* be lumped or bundled erroneously into acknowledgments of other Indigenous territories and peoples of, from, or belonging in Texas. This is especially crucial if those Indigenous peoples being acknowledged evolved into federally recognized tribes of the United States, which historically subjugated their customary lands and territories beneath U.S. Congress, federal trust, or other relevant mechanisms. To date, Ndé have retained unceded and nonsurrendered (though continually unrecognized) Indigenous title to Ndé homelands through crucial and strategic Treaties of Peace (i.e., mechanisms for protecting and defending Ndé continuing Indigenous sovereignty; these did not legally subjugate or sever Ndé beingness and belongingness from Ndé homelands).
2. Relevant declarations and conventions include the United Nations Declaration on the Rights of Indigenous Peoples; the International Convention on the Elimination of All Forms of Racial Discrimination; the International Covenant on Civil and Political Rights; and the ILO Convention 169 (1989), which recognizes Indigenous peoples' right to self-determination within a nation-state and consists of forty-four articles delineating the minimum standards of Indigenous peoples' rights.
3. "Guide to Acknowledging First Peoples and Traditional Territory," Canadian Association of University Teachers, https://www.caut.ca/content/guide-acknowledging-first-peoples-traditional-territory.

Foreword

"I Didn't Give Them Permission"

I'm Eloisa Taméz, and I'm one of the landowners who had the misfortune of being one of those selected to have the border wall built across my land. And I wanna tell you that the land that we're standing on is a remnant of the San Pedro de Carricitos Land Grant, which was awarded to my family in 1767. At that time, it was over 12,600 acres. I have three acres here, but it is just as special as if it were 12,000 acres. And it's just as sacred to me and my family as if it were 12,000. The size doesn't matter; it's what it represents.

This is the land that—where my father and my grandfather carved a life for us by farming and raising stock so that we would have good nutrition and a good lifestyle. So, in spite of the poverty that we were experiencing, it didn't seem like poverty to us because we had all the natural foods that were available to us through their efforts. And my father and my grandfather farmed this part of the land grant plus another several acres that went all the way to the river's edge. So I got the news about the wall that would be constructed across my land on August the 7th, 2007. And apparently the government didn't have the courage to face me face-to-face, so they had two Border Patrol agents call me at my office.

I'm a professor at the University of Texas in Brownsville, and I was called [by the government] at my [university office] desk. So they got my number. And I was called directly to my extension by them in which they—at that time, there were two of them and they were on speakerphone, and they told me that—they wanted to know what my name was—if I was Eloisa Taméz, and I said, "Yes." And so then they said, "Well, I am so-and-so from the Border Patrol," and then the second one introduced himself. And so they told me that they needed to tell me that the land that I owned would be affected by the border wall, had I heard about the border wall.

I said, "Well, yes, I've heard about the border wall." And so they said that they wanted me to agree to sign a—to give them permission to come and do a survey of my land.

And I said, "For what purpose?" They said, "Well, we need to do the survey to determine if the land is appropriate for the building of the wall." And I said, "And what will that mean?" "Well, we'll come in and we'll punch a few holes in your property and then we'll determine after the analysis what—whether the land is appropriate or not." And I said, "And you need how much time for that?" "Well, we need at least a year." And I said, "But you said it was only gonna take you a few hours. Why do you need a year?" And so I said, "Well, you know what? You know, we don't need to continue this conversation because I don't do business over the phone. So if you wanna do business with me, you have to come and see me face-to-face." And so that's the way it started.

So it took two more contacts with the same Border Patrol agents, plus some members of the Corps of Engineers, to finally get to the point where they came to see me in my office. Because they would call me on a Saturday evening. More than once. And so I said, "No, you need to come to me and show me the document." Well, they finally came after contacting [me] more, two or three times. And so, then when I wouldn't agree to sign the authorization for the initial survey, I then was told that, "Haven't you heard about eminent domain?" And I said, "Yes, I've heard of eminent domain. I know what it is," and I said, "But I'm still not going to be in favor of this." So I didn't sign—I didn't give them permission to come and do the survey.

Eloisa García Taméz, testimonial
El Calaboz Gathering, June 24–26, 2011
Filmed by Mia Boccella

Acknowledgments

Margo acknowledges the fortitude, persistence, and commitment of Eloisa García Taméz (Lipan Apache, professor, activist, and her mother) to justice, Indigenous rights, Indigenous belonging, and Ndé community voice and empowerment. I acknowledge the significant contribution of our beloved front-line Elders and agitators, now ancestors, who passed on to the spirit realm and whose roles as illuminators in my pursuit of truth, clarification, and justice lit the path for our collective liberation: Teresa Leal (Ópata-Mayo), John Bruno (lifelong supporter and "grandpa" to the community), April Cotte (activist and lifelong friend of Jumano and Lipan Apaches, self-identified as "settler"), and Peter Schey (lawyer, activist, mentor, comrade, and friend). I also give deep appreciation and thanks to Amberley John (Haudenosaunee) for her contributions and service to this project while a graduate student at the University of British Columbia, Okanagan Campus.

I also wish to thank and acknowledge the following for support of this project: the Seventh Generation Fund for Indigenous Development; the Canada Tri-Council Social Science and Humanities Research Council; the Ford Foundation; and the UN Voluntary Fund for Indigenous Peoples. I thank the University of Texas School of Law Immigration Clinic and Human Rights Clinic, faculty, and students, whose bravery and determination alongside the Lipan Apache Women's Defense disrupted coloniality. As well, I thank the Center for Human Rights and

Constitutional Law, and principal partners Peter Schey (in memoriam) and Carlos Holguin, whose prowess defending extremely peripheralized Indigenous women land protectors and fearlessly confronting the state was unsurpassed and changed the practice of U.S. constitutional law with and alongside Indigenous women from the Lower Rio Grande River.

I acknowledge family members who inspired my work and effort: my children, Hawk Mendoza, Milpa Mendoza, Maura Tamez, Myst Tamez-Hrabovsky, and Justin Kassise. I extend deep appreciation and gratitude to the family members and friends of April Cotte, Teresa Leal, and María de Jesús García (de Esparza) Atkinson, who lovingly supported and guided us in our careful editing of their work. A special acknowledgment must go to Pablo Stayton, who facilitated a crucial bridging for our Elder Enrique Madrid, which provided access to participation and ensured the inclusion of his contributions from the militarized digital divide of the traditional Jumano Apache homeland in the Big Bend canyonlands. Thank you to my students for your interest, enthusiasm, curiosity, and conversations, which kept me motivated and encouraged through the pivots and challenges along the journey of this project. Cassidy Acheson, thank you for going above and beyond your role as a graduate student and for all the generosity you extended to me, which increased my capacity to research and write. To Dr. Shirley Chau and Dr. Neha Gupta, thank you for the warm meals, conversations, laughter, critical analysis, and feedback, which helped keep me focused, grounded, and on track under many challenging circumstances!

I offer my gratitude to Erik Kristofer Hrabovsky, Cynthia Bejarano, Jeffrey P. Shepherd, and L Heidenreich, who selflessly gave extensive mental, emotional, and physical energy to supporting me while I devoted many hours and many years traveling away from home and family, enduring hostile international border-crossing encounters and injustices relative to my research topic, in order to immerse myself in Ndé protocols, relationship building, documenting, cataloging, organizing, supporting, listening, writing, thinking, and aching with, for, and alongside the Ndé: iheedn (thank you). As always and until freedom, your relational devotion made it possible for me to persevere in the most difficult times.

Lastly, I wish to thank, honor, and show my eternal love and gratitude to one of my most crucial teachers, Aunt Paco (María de Jesús García de Esparza Atkinson). She guided me in putting my first embroidery thread through a needle, from early childhood, with patience, care, and kindness. She was the first familial female historian and herstorian, using the methodology of "big show, little tell," an Indigenous method of showing through examples, stories, analogy, metaphors, dancing, and acting out the peoples' oral history (embodiment), and she purposefully wrote to make strong points. Aunt Paco taught me the importance of family history, collective memory, and family document collections. When I was a young girl she instructed me in the art of the home- and hearth-based curatorial practices of organizing the everyday objects of the family to instill memories and knowledge of peoplehood and place. She enacted Indigenous women's epistemic roles as creators of worlds, as those upholding, maintaining, and preserving family archives and their meanings. She modeled gender for me as judiciously steadfast and detail-oriented, stressing attention to each story's thread and its location and role in the larger family weaving representing the past, the present, and our worldview of tomorrow.

Cynthia and Jeff would like to thank the Albuquerque Center for Peace and Justice for providing us space in 2009 to orchestrate a press conference during a critical moment in the condemnation of Dr. Eloisa Taméz's ancestral lands while we were attending a conference with Dr. Eloisa and Dr. Margo Tamez. We want to thank Nora Martinez, our developmental editor, for her meticulous work preparing our manuscript for publication, and the entirety of the University of Arizona Press staff for their care of our book, especially Kristen Buckles, acquisitions editor, for her patience and support, as well as copyeditor Matt Gleeson. We would like to thank Cynthia Bartow for her assistance with receipts, as well as GMRS Transcription Services for their transcribing of documents. Cynthia would like to thank New Mexico State University's College of Arts and Sciences for the Stan Fulton Endowment funding, which helped toward funding this book publication, and the Business Center staff, particularly Lucille Casas, Kellie Cooper, and Anessa Roberts. She would also like to thank her program, Gender and Sexuality Studies, and the Department of English. Thanks also to Zaira Martin and Fatima Oliveros for their incredible assistance in preparing this manuscript. Jeff would like to thank Dr. Michelle Hall Kells, University of New Mexico Chicana/o studies professor, for the Writers-in-Residency Fellowship through the National Consortium of Environmental Rhetoric and Writing. Jeff would also like to thank the Department of History at the University of Texas at El Paso, and his students Freddy Cabral, Rick Quezada, Ben Shultz, Sam Reitenour, Nicole Gonzales, and Diana Lopez, as well as everyone in his spring 2025 course Indigenous Peoples of the U.S.-Mexico Borderlands. Cynthia and Jeff would like to thank their son, Joaquín Félix Bejarano-Shepherd, for his love, patience, and beautiful nature as we completed this work. Ultimately, we want to thank Enrique and Ruby Madrid for introducing us to Dr. Margo Tamez and setting us on the path to this collection. We especially want to thank Dr. Eloisa Taméz for her bravery and courage in confronting impunity and injustice, and Dr. Margo Tamez for entrusting us to walk this journey alongside her.

We honor and cherish the strength, passion, and perseverance that Teresa Leal, April Cotte, and María Jesusita García de Esparza Atkinson contributed to this project and which inspired us since the beginning of our journey in 2011. They each stressed the importance of collective struggle for justice and equality, and an unwavering commitment to paving the path for our future generations. We honor their spirits and stories and we uplift their worldviews. In gratitude, we are inspired by their legacy.

A Note on Ndé Mizaa (Ndé Language)

Ndé Mizaa, part of the Dene "k" language group, is utilized in this collection in an ongoing effort to promote its use, strengthen community identity, promote intergenerational learning, raise awareness about challenges (assimilation policies, limited resources, English-only enforcement) contributing to language loss, and document and revitalize it. My personal journey in the identification of traces of Indigenous languages within my family's spoken Spanish started in high school, when my Spanish teacher unsubtly informed me in front of the whole class that people from my background spoke an "improper" version that was riddled with inaccuracies and "mixed" with "Indian words." Her goal was to expunge those from my mouth and speech with the purpose of acquisition of "proper" Spanish. By shaming me, she nearly achieved the opposite of this purpose. I effectively shut down to speaking Spanish in class and elsewhere. Many years after, my personal research in poetry, language, and community history provided me tools to recognize that what I heard in my parents' speech communicated a place-specific Indigenous worldview. Their speech conveyed the opposite of Indigenous erasure, disappearance, and extinction. Indigeneity burst through the pavement of Spanish. Unfortunately, this reality was never acknowledged in Texas K–12 schools, college or university textbooks, or wider society. I learned that there were two language walls that violently enclosed Indigenous peoples of the Texas-Mexico region: the first was Hispanicization, and the second was Americanization. In both cases, those transmitting the colonizer's language to the Indigenous people were of the working class as well as the Roman Catholic clergy. (The colloquial English we learned at home had healthy doses of working-class-adjacent Scottish and Irish slang.) In Indigenous peoples' spoken Spanish, there are many taken-for-granted traces of an Indigenous language pluriverse of South Texas, West Texas, and the Lower Rio Grande Valley. The way we speak the colonizers' languages has been punished far too often and too long. The fact that Indigenous languages survived in any form is to be celebrated as a form of resisting genocidal processes. "Roots" and "stems" of Uto-Aztekan language groups, Dene Athapaskan language groups, and other Indigenous language groups coexist. We celebrate their steadfast determination to return.

Here and there, throughout this collection, readers will encounter these. As far as the sources used for Ndé Mizaa, a "k" Dene language historically spoken in the Kónìcą̀ą̀hį́į́ Gòkíyàà (Big Water People's homeland), the terms "Kónìcą̀ą̀hį́į́ Gòkíyàà" and "Kónìcą̀ą̀" are faithful to Harry Hoijer's original orthographic system for the Ndé Mizaa "k" language group, documented in "The History and Customs of the Lipan, as Told by Augustina Zuazua," *Linguistics* 161 (1975): 5–38. These crucial terms of Ndé homeland and Ndé peoplehood, specifically in the "Big Water Country," do not appear in any other reference on Ndé Mizaa. With the exception of the oral transmission of the terms "Ndé" (Chairman and Hereditary Chief Daniel Castro Romero Jr.) and "hadndín" (Dr. Inés Talamantez), all other "k" dialect references in this collection were carefully researched in, and are attributed to, the *Dictionary of Jicarilla Apache / Abáachi Mizaa Iłkee' Siijai*, by Wilhelmina Phone, Maureen Olson, and Matilda Martinez, edited by Melissa Axelrod, Jule Gómez de García, and Jordan Lachler (Albuquerque: University of New Mexico Press, 2007), which follows the current-day, U.S.-based orthographic conventions for the Ndé "k" dialect. Any errors or omissions are solely mine. In addition to the Dene "k" dialects that spread through the Rio Grande River region, the Dene "k" language group is spoken, preserved, and revitalized in communities in New Mexico, Saskatchewan, Alberta, Manitoba, and the Northwest Territories. I acknowledge there may be questions among Dene "k" linguistic experts about the exact pronunciation of these terms, given distinct differences in diacritical marks used in Hoijer's and Phone et al.'s systems. A major objective of this collection is to spark new dialogues and innovative methodologies that will support decolonial Ndé life, aspirations, and futures. Ndé participatory access to Ndé Mizaa revitalization and decolonization, in respectful and equitable relationships with linguistic experts, is part of that objective.

I gratefully acknowledge Dr. Inés Talamantez (October 31, 1930–September 27, 2019) and Chairman and Hereditary Chief Daniel Castro Romero Jr. (October 9, 1962–April 18, 2022) for their encouragement and support of the Ndé Mizaa language recovery and revitalization expressed here, and for their important contributions to my learning. Again, any errors in the transmission are mine alone.

Margo Tamez

Timeline

Indigenous Place, Dispossession, and Resistance in El Calaboz

1760: Indigenous place in El Calaboz was not incorporated into or governed by Spanish imperial land grant administrative authority.

1761: The king of Spain approves the San Pedro de Carricitos Land Grant of 12,730.58 acres (three leagues) to ancestors of Eloisa García Taméz and relatives in El Calaboz, El Ranchito, and La Encantada, confirmed in 1784. Confirmed by Mexico in 1833. Confirmed by the Texas Legislature in 1852 after the Bourland Commission investigation. Decreed in Cameron County, Texas, 1872.

1848: The Treaty of Guadalupe Hidalgo officially establishes the U.S.-Mexico border and bisects the lands of many Indigenous peoples, such as the Lipan Apache. The treaty normalizes dispossessions en masse, disregard for Indigenous customary place and use rights, and administrative erasures of Indigenous peoples' continued existence along the Rio Grande River.

1924: Indian Citizenship Act and creation of the U.S. Border Patrol.

1935 (March 2): Eloisa García Taméz is born in El Calaboz.

1936: Large levees are built to protect settlements and towns along the Rio Grande from flooding. This facilitates the development of large-scale agriculture with controlled irrigation, complicating Indigenous farming families' access to the river and reducing wetlands, riparian systems, and indigenous fish and bird populations.

1994: Operation Hold the Line, Operation Gatekeeper, Operation Safeguard, and Operation Rio Grande Valley send billions of dollars to increasingly militarize the U.S.-Mexico border.

1997 (May 20): U.S. Marines murder eighteen-year-old Esequiel Hernández (Jumano Apache) in Redford, Texas, while he is herding his family's goats. The Marines were conducting mission no. JT414-97A, a Joint Task Force Six (JTF-6) observation post operation within the village, while concealing themselves from village clans. The Indigenous youth's death due to a U.S. military operation on the Texas border triggers traumatization.

2006: U.S. Congress passes and President George W. Bush signs into law the Secure Fence Act in connection with the U.S. War on Terror. The act further militarizes the border and facilitates construction of physical barriers along the international boundary. Numerous federal environmental laws are waived, and it negatively impacts undocumented migrants and Indigenous peoples disproportionately.

2007 (November 11): First attempt by the federal government to contact Eloisa García Taméz and to seize the Tamez lands in El Calaboz.

2007 (November 14): Margo Tamez leads and submits the first Lipan Apache and border-wall-focused submission to the United Nations Committee on the Elimination of Racial Discrimination, 71st Session.

2008 (January 29): The United States sues Dr. Eloisa Taméz (*United States v. Eloisa G. Tamez et al.* [2008]) for refusing to relinquish her land for the construction of the border wall.

2008 (February 6): Eloisa García Taméz countersues the secretary of the Department of Homeland Security, Michael Chertoff (*Eloisa Garcia Tamez et al. v. Michael Chertoff, U.S. Department of Homeland Security, et al.* [2008]), challenging the relinquishment and condemnation of her land.

2008 (October 22): The Tamez family, represented by Margo Tamez and the University of Texas Working Group on Human Rights and the Border Wall, take the case to the Inter-American Commission / Organization of American States.

2009 (April 16): A federal judge in South Texas signs the possession order allowing the federal government to condemn lands in El Calaboz and begin constructing sections of the wall on the Tamez family land, while Eloisa García Taméz is out of state at an academic conference.

2009: During the fall and subsequent winter, the federal government demands more land along the border, including land from the Tamez family. Eloisa García Taméz refuses further condemnation, but the government proceeds to take her land and construct more of the border wall.

2011 (June 24-26): The El Calaboz Gathering on Indigenous Peoples' Knowledge, Lands, and Human Rights convenes in El Calaboz, Texas.

2012: The UN Committee on the Elimination of Racial Discrimination's Early Warning Urgent Action Special Procedure mechanism receives a report submitted by Margo Tamez and Ariel Dulitzky.

2015: UN Committee on the Elimination of Racial Discrimination, 88th Session, Review of the Holy See. Margo Tamez, India Reed Bowers, and Lorraine Garcia submit a comprehensive intervention.

2016: UN Committee on the Elimination of Racial Discrimination, 89th Session, Review of Spain. Margo Tamez, India Reed Bowers, and Lorraine Garcia submit a comprehensive intervention.

2021: UN Human Rights Committee, 139th Session. Margo Tamez and India Reed Bowers submit an intervention addressing Lipan Apache dispossession and international political status.

GATHERING TOGETHER, WE DECIDE

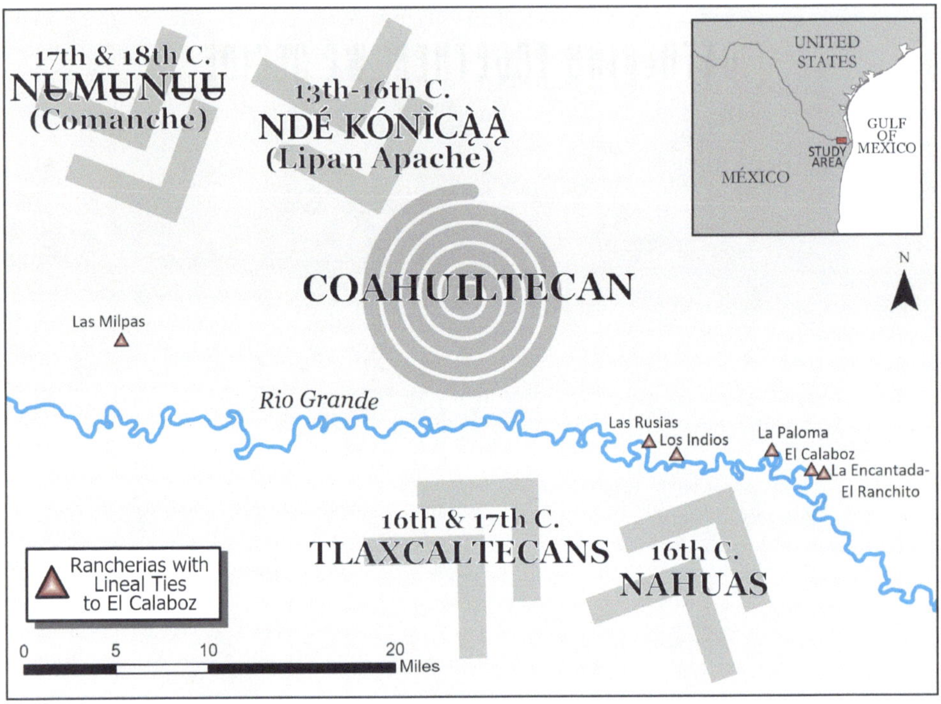

MAP 1 Graphic representation of Indigenous peoples living in and around El Calaboz before and after initial Spanish invasion of the region. Arrows indicate approximate patterns of movement, with general time periods, into the present-day Lower Rio Grande Valley. The map additionally represents the Indigenous lineal ties to specific rancherías in the study area. Illustration by Malinalli X. Leyva, PhD.

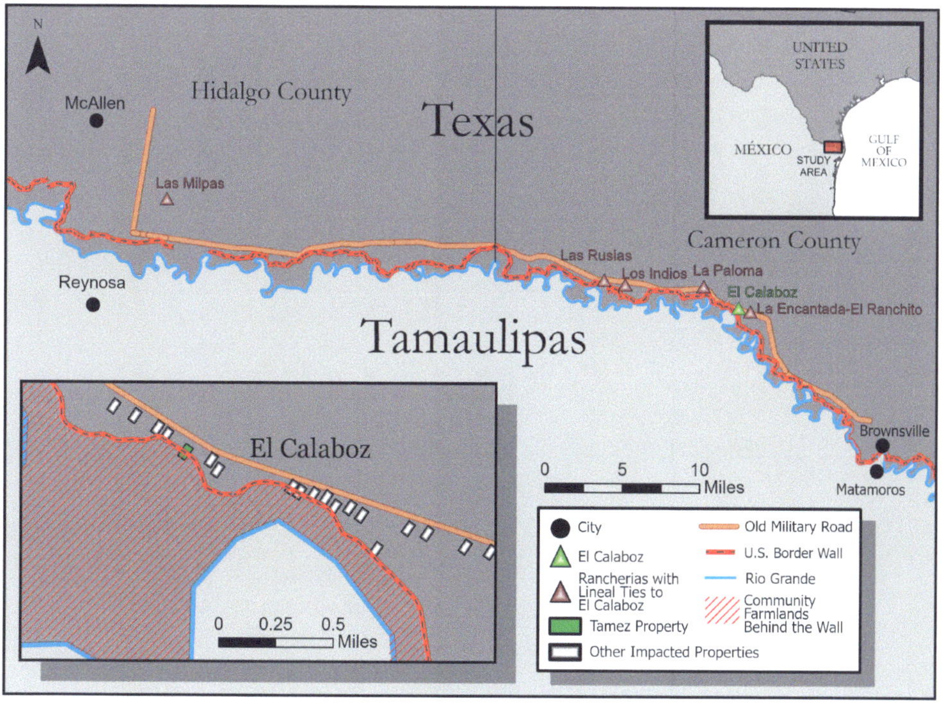

MAP 2 Graphic representation of the contemporary border wall and international boundary in relation to El Calaboz, the Tamez property, and rancherías in the study area. The map includes the Old Military Road through the rancherías, the properties impacted by the construction of the border wall, and the traditional community farmlands sequestered between the wall and the Rio Grande and international boundary. Illustration by Malinalli X. Leyva, PhD.

Introduction

MARGO TAMEZ, CYNTHIA BEJARANO, JEFFREY P. SHEPHERD

On November 11, 2007, my colleague Seánna Howard and I were driving from West Texas to Tucson, Arizona. Seánna, an attorney with specialization in human rights and Indigenous rights and affiliated with the University of Arizona at the Indigenous Peoples' Law and Policy Program, was working with me to document testimonies of Jumano Apache peoples in their farming village, El Polvo / Redford, located on the Rio Grande River in the Big Bend. We had just completed in-depth interviews with the Jumano Apache elder Enrique Madrid, who related the long history of state-sanctioned violations in their community located within a heavily militarized sector of the U.S.-Mexico border. We were approaching the town of Marfa when my phone got reconnected, and I promptly received a phone call from my mother. Her voice sounded off. Something terrible was happening. She informed me that men representing the DHS, CBP, and Army had been going house to house in the village, demanding that the El Calaboz community members sign forms to waive their rights to their ancestral lands. These men, armed, had intimidated them by threatening them that the government was going to take their lands regardless. She said she refused to sign anything, and told them "no" numerous times, and demanded that they leave. They didn't leave

> *immediately. They kept insisting that she sign the document on the spot, coercively bullying her to compel her to sign. Her refusal to do so and their threatening behavior put her into a horrible state of shock. With an urgency in her voice, she asked me to help her find legal support right away, and I assured her that I would.*
>
> —Margo Tamez, journal entry, field notes, November 12, 2007

In the spring of 2011, Kónìcą̀ą̀ Ndé Dene (Big Water People, Lipan Apache, Athapaskan) women called out across physical and virtual space for a gathering in El Calaboz, a small ancestral village situated in a remote region of South Texas, in the Lower Rio Grande Valley, within a few yards of the recently constructed U.S.-Mexico border wall. The women invited Indigenous and non-Indigenous people to gather in June 2011 to listen, observe, witness, and contribute their understanding, stories, testimonies, and histories of dispossession vis-à-vis the U.S. border wall, colonization, settler colonialism, militarization, racism, classism, gender discrimination, and the organized and state-sanctioned cultural and physical removal of Indigenous peoples from customary and traditional places.

When Ndé Dene women called for the gathering, Dr. Eloisa García Taméz, a community leader, U.S. veteran, and nursing professor at the then University of Texas at Brownsville, was involved in resisting the government's demands to relinquish her lands to construct the U.S. border wall.[1] The demands began on November 11, 2007, and they evolved into legal processes on January 29, 2008, when the United States sued to condemn her land (*United States v. Eloisa G. Tamez et al.* [2008]). On February 6, 2008, Eloisa García Taméz countersued the secretary of the Department of Homeland Security, Michael Chertoff, as the point person for the attempt by the federal government to build a portion of the border wall on Taméz's land, which sat along a small stretch of the Rio Grande. These lawsuits commenced her two-year standoff against the U.S. Army Corps of Engineers and agencies within the U.S. Department of Homeland Security including the U.S. Border Patrol.

Between 2008 and 2011, two international human rights legal forums formally heard the legal case made by Lipan Apaches and Taméz, and, within those cases, learned about the effects of the U.S. wall on other Indigenous peoples in the Texas-Mexico border region. *Tamez v. Cher-*

toff (2008) rose to national and international prominence, stimulating excitement and hope as well as heated national debates inflected with anti-Indigenous racism, xenophobia, anti-Mexican racism, misogyny, class discrimination, and dehumanization. As the case dragged on, the federal government dispossessed over one hundred economically insecure and disenfranchised families along the Texas-Mexico border of their lands, via condemnation proceedings enacted through the U.S. Federal Declaration of Taking Act (40 U.S.C. §3114). A significant number of these lands had been secured by Indigenous and multiracial ancestors in the eighteenth century, at a time when Indigenous peoples gained title to their lands in the Spanish colonial legal system. Indigenous and multiracial communities along the Lower Rio Grande River with ancestral lands protected under Spanish Crown legal titles, and some within the geopolitical and historical treaty areas of Lipan Apaches, questioned the authority of the United States to compel them to surrender lands to armed government agents for the construction of a wall across them. It became clear to Taméz and other Lipan resisters that they had to organize against the ensuing state violence and militarization directly related to Eloisa's refusals and her countersuit, which illuminated Indigenous land tenure and identity in this remote place with a long history of Indigenous politics. Considering the Lower Rio Grande Valley's longer history of imperialist, colonial, and settler militarist land dispossessions against Indigenous and racialized peoples, Dr. Eloisa Taméz and her daughter, Dr. Margo Tamez, called for a gathering at El Calaboz to examine the U.S. border wall through the lenses of Indigenous peoples along the Texas-Mexico border.

Their call for a gathering in 2011 emphasized the need to be heard, seen, understood, and witnessed in their concerns. The meeting focused on a range of issues related to Indigenous rights, human rights, land rights, recognition, self-determination, state-sanctioned discrimination, Indigenous youth, women, culture, and education. The activists, academics, traditional leaders, mentors, youth, and Elders collectively investigated the many weaponized narratives in which the state legitimates violence against Indigenous women; used constitutional law, civil rights, and international law to confront U.S. dispossession; and critiqued how the state frames Indigenous land protectors and Indigenous rights as a threat to Americans, to U.S. sovereignty, and to U.S. territorial borders and security. The Ndé Dene women land protectors from El Calaboz gathered together people with relevant skills, knowledge, training, life experiences, and analysis of the colonial abuses, and resistances to these, that Indigenous peoples in the remote areas of Texas had experienced across the generations. Gathering together on community lands was crucial to sustaining the endurance required to process the scope and depth of trauma the wall imposed on the people, and to developing collective analysis that included Elders, youth, community leaders, activists, and academics. Centering stories, this community drew together courageous thinking from multiple perspectives, offered mutual empathy and hands-on collective support, and created resiliency-building practices and tools that provided inspirational ideas for contesting the wall construction and determining how to persevere in the aftermath of traumatizing dispossession of the community's lands. The stark reality of the impact upon future Indigenous landholders, specifically the youth, in El Calaboz, and more broadly along the entire stretch of the international boundary, remained as a daily reminder of the necessity to resist despair. The gathering sought to create a truth and justice space to confront harms stemming from intergenerational colonization. Listening to community testimonies helped to create a collective memory on-site. The desire to heal from the mental, physical, spiritual, and emotional fatigue that resistance to state violence produces, urgently expressed in the youth testimonies, framed the deliberations on the work required to achieve justice for generations to come.

Eloisa and Margo's call was distributed through the internet and across multiple platforms, and twenty-four people answered it and gathered in El Calaboz on June 24–26, 2011. Over three days we listened, heard, and witnessed Indigenous people sharing personal testimonials, firsthand accounts, photographs, oral history, legal analysis, video documentaries, and artwork. The women enacted local Ndé governance and self-determination by structuring the event through a blend of the traditional and current protocols that constituted life in El Calaboz. Some people cohabitated in the Tamez home, some pitched their tipis, some camped in tents, and some stayed in local lodging accommodations. People took turns cooking breakfast during the pre-gathering preparation days. A local family from El Calaboz prepared all the meals for the gathering at the community hall at the St. Ignatius Oblate Immaculate Church in the neighboring village of El Ranchito–La Encantada, a few miles from El Calaboz. The women invited individuals to serve as the gathering's rapporteurs—to remember, document, observe, witness, and disseminate the knowledges and testimonials shared throughout the event. The rapporteurs were Chief and Chairman Daniel Castro Romero Jr. (Ndé; Lipan Apache Band of Texas), Teresa Leal (Ópata-Mayo), Dr. Shannon Speed (Chickasaw, then at the University of Texas at Austin), Dr. Cynthia Bejarano (New Mexico State University), and Dr. Jeffrey P. Shepherd (University of Texas at El Paso), who together represented the Ndé leadership, an Indigenous Elder, and activists / human rights experts / academics. Together participants contributed to a deeper understanding of the evidence amassed in El Calaboz of the U.S. government's human rights abuses against this community, which it attempted to maintain hidden in the shadow of the wall.

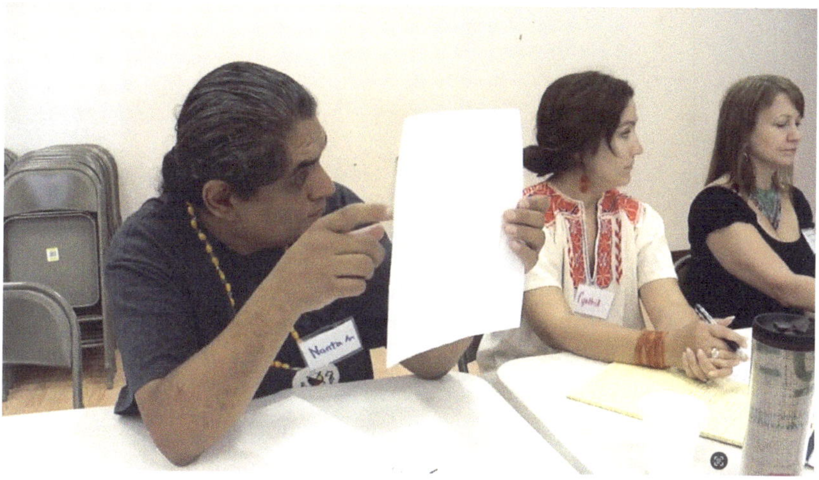

The rapporteurs Chief Daniel Castro Romero Jr., Dr. Cynthia Bejarano, and Dr. Shannon Speed (*left to right*), at the first listening session with the Indigenous Youth Caucus. Chief Romero (*left*) is holding and discussing the pencil drawing of the separation wall created by one of the youth delegates in attendance. The drawing was submitted by the youth delegation to the rapporteurs for discussion and for the memory archive. The drawing, the youth testimonies, and the supportive responses from the assembled representatives of Indigenous peoples from territories across Texas, New Mexico, and Arizona energized a dynamic dialogue with the rapporteurs. June 23, 2011, San Ignacio Catholic Church Community Hall, La Encantada–El Ranchito village, Lower Rio Grande Valley, Texas.

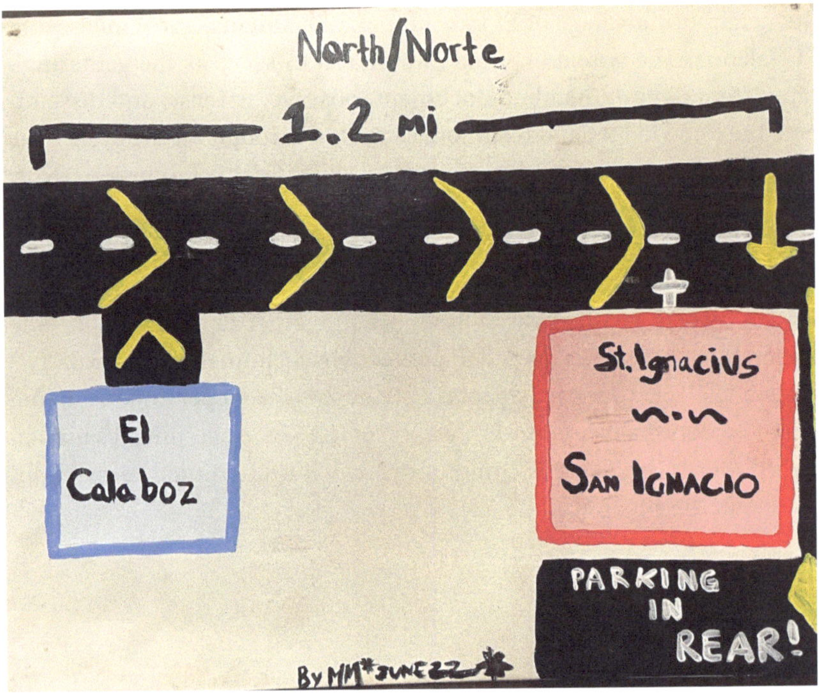

Map showing directions from El Calaboz to San Ignacio church in El Ranchito–La Encantada, by Milpa Mendoza.

Gathering together to defend local Indigenous peoples' rights to being, belonging, and homelands, the gathered placed emphasis on the local Indigenous understanding that the land is not merely the place where local Indigenous peoples live; rather, they *are* the land. We focused our efforts on (re)collecting Indigenous knowledge about dispossessions over time and space through the local lens of the long memory of braided Indigenous peoples' belonging, which predated colonization and which still remains. We concentrated on individual and community memory and the oral history of sites of crisis, which has been collected and handed down over two centuries of multiple settler-colonial occupations. These histories of violence predate the secretary of the Department of Homeland Security Michael Chertoff's predatory attack on Indigenous peoples in a region known for extrajudicial violence. Thus, the Indigenous resistance to massive dispossessions in the Lower Rio Grande Valley did not begin when the U.S. Congress passed the Secure Fence Act of 2006.

Indigenous mass resistance to Texas and U.S. dispossessions, forced removals, and ethnic cleansings began more than 150 years earlier during significant waves of Anglo settler colonization in the region.

The name of the village where we gathered, El Calaboz, which translates to "the dungeon," is a continuous reminder of the colonial violence Indigenous people have endured for centuries.[2] Spanish imperialism discursively articulated European carceral place-making as a territorial act of enclosure in a larger campaign to unground Ndé symbolically and legally from the expansiveness and fluidity of Ndé belonging and power. The Spanish imposition of an imagined political-geographical concept called "La Gran Apachería" was, on the one hand, a sign of Europeans' recognition of Ndé collective embodiment of belonging, place-making, social structures, and territorial defense systems, which communicated "Apache"-ness (people, culture, laws, cosmovision, metaphysics, territory, and influence). On the other, it was a historically significant act of European domination that attempted to impose a Western imperialist reconnaissance lens of "Apaches" (a term popularized by Europeans). For the Ndé, European carceral place-making is rooted in large-scale enclosure projects such as La Gran Apachería, which were obsessed with surveilling, renaming, and containing Ndé homelands while simultaneously demonizing, dehumanizing, and evicting the pluri-Indigenous worldviews the Ndé co-created alongside many Indigenous nations in their homeland. In the *calaboz*, colonial authorities aimed to transform Ndé indigeneity into a tool of state control by characterizing Indigenous resistance as deviant behavior emanating from an Indigenous ungovernable "savage"/"wild" state of being, a trope that was weaponized to criminalize legitimate Ndé anticolonial defense against Western imperialist invasions. The Spanish Camino Militar (Military Road), which people use to this day, connected El Calaboz and surrounding Indigenous villages with numerous presidios and villas throughout La Gran Apachería and La Gran Comanchería. Despite this early militarization, El Calaboz remained an Indigenous enclave, and its inhabitants established it as an important point of exchange of horses, goods, arms, refuge, and knowledge.

Drawing upon this long history of resisting militarization, in the twenty-first century Ndé women refused the modern border wall, which we characterize as a megaproject linked to massive dispossession of Indigenous and racialized peoples throughout the border region. In the process, Ndé women confronted numerous threats to their lands, water, foods, medicines, burial sites, culture, and right to self-determination. They also experienced physical, mental, psychological, and emotional harm from these threats enacted by numerous actors. In a heavily militarized, post–Patriot Act "no-constitution" zone, in a state in which many uphold an ideology propagated by the ruling elites from the oil and extractive industries, and in a settler society with deeply held beliefs about the "Indians" in and from Texas, the dominant public sentiment in Texas and across the United States deemed their actions to be unpatriotic, threatening, and extremist.[3]

The underlying and widespread anti-Indigenous attitude in Texas underscores the courage of Eloisa García Taméz in her stand against a nation and a state that continue to deny the legacy of genocide, mass enforced displacements, and ethnic cleansing practices at the foundation of Texas and connected Mexican states along the 1,254-mile length of its border. While the El Calaboz Gathering reflected concerns at the local level, it also connected El Calaboz to larger struggles of Lipan, Dene, and Indigenous peoples throughout the hemisphere. Through Eloisa's public refusals to bend to Secretary Chertoff's aggressions against her community and ancestral lands, the Tamez women strengthened and expanded their circle. The gathering was more than a symbolic moment in a larger movement; the gathering evolved as part of the transition to an organized way of thinking and organizing based in pluri-legal justice—that is, in El Calaboz, a space was created where local Indigenous justice and governance systems connected to Indigenous peoples' relationships with sentient land, water, sky, and animals, with laws held in stories, songs, dance, and oral traditions, and with family or clan customs embedded in land were positioned to counter, correct, and critique the state, national, and international systems. Eyewitness, embodied, and documented narratives offered positionalities that challenged how U.S. elites used the wall to recolonize and recontain the multitudes of Indigenous peoples in the colonial calaboz—that is, a perpetual asymmetric containment by colonial Western legal traditions and material realities. The gathering reflected the organic and dynamic analytical change generated by front-line resisters and land protectors in El Calaboz and their Indigenous perspectives, and it reflected the transition of the movement from a hive network of justice workers surrounding and protecting and being informed by a matriarch during her two-year standoff, built across multiple global time zones, to an in-person gathering at the wall itself.

Women-led Indigenous processes emphasized organizing, strategizing, and thinking in a collective manner for their families, bands, and nations. Their objective was to share their stories, expand the network of storytellers, and stimulate energetic co-sharing of Indigenous models that upheld community-driven values, community-based practices, ethical research protocols, and collaborations across nontraditional alliances. The gathering also revealed theoretical frameworks and traditions of Indigenous women's laws and justice. By selecting a group of individuals spanning diverse sectors of society, Ndé mothers and daughters sought and created a new justice space that respected and took seriously Indigenous peoples' perspectives and claims. In the process of creating a new space to center Indigenous peoples' truths, we collectively reimagined justice. The women shaped the principles and protocols for a collective examination of these truths, which afforded everyone the basic tools to reimagine Indigenous rights, recognition, and responsibility within and across communities all along the Rio Grande River, across Texas, and beyond.

By gathering together, Indigenous women and their kin convened across diverse nations, tribes, clans, and communities. They reclaimed and reestablished the Lower Rio Grande River peoples' rancherías as current sites of ancestral and current place-centered protocols and modes of critical interaction with people from diverse backgrounds, identities, and interests. They reconstructed Ndé women's matriarchal foundations in governance, foregrounding Kónìcą̀ą̀hį́į́ Gòkíyàà (Big Water Country)—the ancestral name of the local people's homeland. Revitalizing and revalorizing the rare Ndé eastern dialect pertinent to local peoples' ancestral migration stories enacted and reasserted linguistic self-determination against the linguistic erasures carried out by violent colonial, patriarchal, assimilative, and oppressive settler colonialism and U.S. militarization. Rejecting the U.S. government's colonial interpretations, uses, and abuses of constitutional law and justice, Ndé women countercontended that Indigenous and multiracial communities had enacted Indigenous human rights and cooperative pluri-legal systems for centuries. They asserted that Indigenous and detribalized racialized peoples harmfully impacted by militarized and bordered zones have extensive knowledge of how borders arose on top of and were built over their disagreement and suffering. The peoples of the Lower Rio Grande River and Kónìcą̀ą̀hį́į́ Gòkíyàà are the story carriers of genocidal violence enacted and hidden at the roots of the origin stories of imperial colonies, nations, and settler states that abused the region. Thus, the underlying colonial violence and oppressive discourses and laws of "liberty" and a "constitutional" society have been culturally, artistically, and politically subverted by Indigenous and racialized peoples by means of their collective struggle against colonial brutalism.

Indigenous women tied the border wall dispossession to a larger U.S. project that involved draining domestic resources and militarizing the already deep divides between the federal government and elected lawmakers, on one hand, and the disproportionately racialized working poor who are most people in the region, on the other. In El Calaboz, Indigenous women declared that at some point there would be a reckoning with their stories of struggle and survival. The United States could not continue to plunder and violate Indigenous peoples while simultaneously using the trope of a "border in crisis" to hide state-sanctioned crimes against these peoples. Indigenous women were connecting these issues in dialogue with the communities in which the government was constructing the wall on the Rio Grande River. These dialogues in small community centers, churches, parking lots, protests, and marches reckoned with the fact that walls, at the most granular level, are tools of suppression implemented and enacted against local communities with histories of colonial and decolonial resistance.

Ndé women held numerous press conferences at key stages of the movement to dismantle the wall and expose the lies and injustices. They spoke directly to those who struggled against the national intolerance for Indigenous peoples from a bordered region in Texas and their calls for fundamental respect and accountability. Because of their steadfast commitment to creating different spaces, such as the press conferences and listening sessions in conference calls, as well as sessions at UN meetings, their message managed to reach diverse communities in the United States, Mexico, Canada, the Americas, Africa, Europe, and Asia.

The Ndé refused to remain silent as the government chose not to build the wall on the lands owned by certain other property holders in South Texas. They monitored these situations and reported their findings to Secretary Michael Chertoff. It became increasingly clear that Chertoff favored certain individuals seeking relief from the wall construction, such as the owner of the Nye Plantation (formerly the "Old Brulay Plantation," aka "Rio Grande Plantation," established ca. 1870), a historic sugarcane plantation near Brownsville, Texas, and the owner of the River Bend Resort, a local golf course with an adjacent clubhouse and trailer park where "winter Texans" from Canada and northern U.S. states reside. Ndé women saw this as blatant bias at the expense of Indigenous peoples, racialized laborers, and their families, who were caged in cyclical debt and economic insecurity throughout the Lower Rio Grande Valley. The privileges afforded to certain landowners further punctuated the racialized landscape of South Texas, where class differences reflected deeply entrenched and painfully divergent realities.

In this collection, *Gathering Together, We Decide*, we, the editors, return to the 2011 gathering and assess its origins and impact over time by pulling together personal testimonies, interviews, academic articles, legal briefs, artwork, poetry, and other materials that reflect the struggles of Lipan and other Indigenous peoples experiencing the separation wall, border militarization, and state violence. In collaboration with Ndé (Lipan Apache) Elders and Indigenous land-rights protectors, we "re-gather" with the voices, memories, and contributions of Indigenous and non-Indigenous truth-tellers who defend(ed) Indigenous communities in the borderlands. Central to these struggles are the Ndé women's efforts to protect ancestral place, belonging, existence, and distinct perspectives from a bordered, militarized, and walled region of Turtle Island.

Known to their ancestors as Kónìcą̀ą̀hį́į Gòkíyàà (the Big Water Country), the Rio Grande River, since time immemorial, has been home to a tremendous diversity of human, animal, and plant life systems situated at the confluence of desert and river and blessed with life-giving sustenance. European colonization, and with it the subversion and dispossession of Indigenous peoples' intrinsic rights to exist and to maintain self-determined presence and existence in Texas and along the life-giving Rio Grande River, has been a contentious issue for centuries. The histories of Indigenous peoples enacting rights, presence, and continuing existence have been evident in the collective memory of ongoing struggles to protect Indigenous homelands in this region. These struggles have been obscured by overwhelming patterns of anti-Indigenous aggression, indifference, and negation which perpetuate the untenable conditions in the region. Colonization sparked painful experiences of Indigenous subjugation under Euro-supremacy, dispossession, domination, land settlement, cattle ranching, mining, and industrial, agricultural, and petrochemical development. The El Calaboz Gathering held a crucial space for Indigenous storying to clarify and historicize this reality.

This collection offers a rare opportunity to learn about the unique collective that, with Eloisa and Margo, gathered together to make difficult decisions about how to deal with the bone-chilling apathy, repression, and indifference of a powerful group protected by an extremely powerful actor—Michael Chertoff, secretary of the Department of Homeland Security—endowed with unilateral powers to guard their special interests. This collection foregrounds Indigenous peoples' perspectives: the perspectives of those directly impacted, and those who witnessed, firsthand, the U.S. government's wall construction and its punitive and aggressive policies targeting Indigenous peoples and the racialized and economically insecure. After Eloisa García Tamez refused to surrender ("waive") her land rights, and as she countersued Chertoff, the Ndé women utilized social media, cell phones, and telephonic press conferences to convey their perspectives to media across local, regional, and international borders. When plaintiffs including Indigenous and racialized working families, municipalities, wildlife reserves, and utility companies followed the *Tamez v. Chertoff* legal framework, and numerous individual landowners began countersuing the government, the government immediately reacted by utilizing local and national legacy media to conduct smear campaigns against plaintiffs and trying to suppress the popular support for the Tamez standpoint.

In short, Eloisa said, "No!" to Michael Chertoff. She refused. She maintained her position of refusal, and she sued Chertoff based upon her comprehension of her ancestral and inherent Indigenous rights and human rights. Common people, journalists, activists, and Indigenous land protectors around the world heard about her story. Many journalists, civil rights lawyers, scholars, students, artists, activists, and empathetic Indigenous land protectors traveled to El Calaboz to learn more about this Indigenous land protector and rights defender.

This collection offers a critique, and an expanded discussion of settler dispossession, separation walls, border militarization, and transgenerational resistance based on Indigenous knowledge, strategies, and solidarities across borders and international geopolitical regions. This collection embodies a resurgent form of Indigenous standpoints: it articulates Indigenous peoples' grounded connection to ancestry, land, tradition, and memory, anchored in Indigenous culture, family, rancherías, languages, food and medicinal systems, religious practices, healing arts, philosophy, music, science, and law. Through the wide range of material we highlight, we emphasize that reclaiming stolen Indigenous lands and homelands is key to Indigenous struggles across colonial borders. Yet the contexts of place, history, and settler-colonial cultures and erasures—in spaces such as El Calaboz and its sister villages up and down the Rio Grande River—that underlie these struggles have been interpreted primarily, or only, through colonial, national, and state archives, misinformation, or blatant propaganda sanctioned as truth. Indigenous self-determination struggles in sites of resistance like El Calaboz activate the realities and the imaginaries of the dispossessed Indigenous peoples in a bordered and walled homeland. These are not the Indigenous peoples produced in the U.S. mainstream imaginary, nor are they the "Indian Country" that Americans and Native Americans with federal recognition status have come to expect. Rather, they are Indigenous in a vast bordered and walled homeland, and they have embodied oral histories that transcend invading and occupying monarchies, confederacies, republics, nations, states, and settler colonialism. They are not in U.S. national museums dedicated to Indigenous peoples; their knowledge, law, memory, literature, arts, history, and cultures are embedded in the peoples' archives intimately rooted in their lands. These othered Indigenous worlds in the bordered and walled homelands existed long before the hegemonic U.S.–Native American legalized land enclosures, and they keep existing at the far edges of that system and structure—defiantly. Their defiance as an act of self-determination has transcended these enclosures over time.

At these sites, at the hemispheric periphery of national "American Indian history," Indigenous land and freedom struggles expanded the paradigm of the international and hemispheric Indigenous rights movement. Ndé women pushed to expand spaces for Indigenous peoples' critical engagement with and confrontation of the multiple state-sanctioned violent transgressions enacted against Indigenous and racialized peoples—the way their homelands were subjected to being reduced and categorized mechanistically as a walled separation zone—and refused this violence. They called for Indigenous peoples' rights to decide, to determine, and to gather peoples of conscience in Kónìcą̀ą̀hį́į́ Gòkíyàà for change.

Deciding to refuse, and defend and protect against, violent dispossession is a central theme of this collection. In El Calaboz, Indigenous women mobilized ancestral knowledge and decolonial, collaborative strategies to foreground the importance of southern Dene Ndé river peoples' knowing, relationships, kinship-based governance, ethics, and recognition processes beyond the state-centric model. Via interviews, affidavits, oral histories, *testimonios*, legal briefs, poetry, art, and academic reflections and analysis, the contributors manifest cultural revitalization and decolonization methodologies to address crucial local, global, international, and transnational problems through an intercultural Indigenous paradigm offering grounded solutions to the myriad problems we face today.

Additionally, this collection draws attention to complex struggles of Ndé and neighboring Indigenous peoples, who predate and have long histories contesting "Texas" and the "borderlands." While broad in its implications, it offers a painful snapshot of the challenges facing Indigenous peoples living in the increasingly violent and militarized space of the U.S.-Mexico border. During the El Calaboz Gathering, representatives from multiple Native nations, tribes, bands, and communities attended to offer their support and to share their stories of militarization. To name a few, members came from Tohono O'odham, Mayo and Ópata, Diné (Navajo), Chickasaw, and of course multiple Lipan communities. In the aftermath of the gathering, as we continued with our activism, advocacy, research, and teaching, our circle of allies and collaborators grew to include members from several First Nations bands in Canada (mainly as a result of Margo working in Canada), as well as individuals from Coahuiltecan communities throughout Texas. As reflected in the voices of contributors to this volume, the issues of anti-Indigenous violence, militarization, and historical erasure encompass yet extend beyond the geopolitical space of the U.S.-Mexico border wall. Casting this wide net places a focus on the lived and remembered experiences of Elders, community-based activists, filmmakers, artists, and academics who forged crucial alliances between 2007 and 2011 and beyond, and it simultaneously sheds light on a range of issues of importance to Indigenous communities in the Americas.

This collection is grounded in Ndé, Indigenous, and critical methodologies founded in respect and reverence for the interconnectivity between the sentience of earth, sky, water, and Indigenous women frontline land protectors and defenders and their supportive webs of being. It establishes a framework for activists, scholars, and Indigenous peoples broadly to engage with a groundbreaking paradigm of Ndé decolonization and recognition as a model of radically rethinking the legacy of five hundred years of Indigenous resistance to settler-colonial violence and ecological destruction. In this regard, the collection of material gathered here acts like a decolonial road map for speaking back against border walls, state impunity, and anti-Indigenous racism. By weaving together testimonies, essays, art, and analysis by key individuals who gathered in El Calaboz, the collection maps the ongoing and reenergized efforts of Ndé women to protect ancestral lands, to reconnect their existence and belonging to the larger Dene world, and to enact self-determination, critical memory, and a revitalized resistance methodology. In close coordination with the land protectors, collective decision-making was reawoken—*íłahałee dáłe' nahk'éé nahkéyaah 'át'éh béodaazi̱i̱ł*: that is, gathering together, we decide—revitalizing an Ndé framework that began to map a resurgent form of collective analysis between, for, and alongside local Indigenous peoples.

The wide array of voices included in this collection are woven together by a common set of theoretical frameworks and conceptual paradigms, reflecting our deep and unified concern for a connection between theories and real-world impacts, between ideas and social change. Many of the contributors speak from their experiences and worldview(s) as Indigenous people, but, as this collection notes, indigeneity in the contested space of "the Texas borderlands," in which militarization and gulag-style separation walls have heightened critical understandings of U.S. and Texas settler colonialism, is complex and complicated. The contributors draw upon well-known theorists of state power, leading critics of militarization, and internationally recognized legal scholars. They are also drawing upon the theoretical musings of Indigenous and human rights scholars, including Angelique EagleWoman and others.[4]

Alternatively, as residents of the militarized bordered lands are involved in ongoing contestations in current-day international legal courts and systems, many of the contributors theorize and critique the legality of settler-colonial borders. Ndé women have continued to expand the hemispheric and global understanding of the relevance of the analysis of the Texas-Mexico border through the lens of international conventions on decolonization and settler-colonial extra-lethal violence. Since 2007, the Ndé standpoint has been positively received by numerous UN convention bodies. The International Court of Justice's view on the illegality of walls constructed in Indigenous homelands occupied through settler colonialism is an established precedent. In direct response to Margo Tamez's testimony, a jurist of the Inter-American Commission on Human Rights of the Organization of American States thanked her for her courage in confronting the injustices and researching and documenting the harms to those affected, and encouraged her to return to the court with detailed stories from the ground as a necessary collective, pluri-legal formation to confront the specific forms of anti-Indigenous violence and injustice in the walled homelands. This collection is the next pivot and transition to truth, historical clarification, memory, and justice. With, for, and alongside the Ndé and detribalized and racialized peoples in Kónìcą̀ą̀hį́į́ Gòkíyàà, this collection theorizes and implements a new, crucial process of "gathering together."

While anchored in South Texas and rooted in the unique historical conditions of El Calaboz, the theory and praxis of "gathering together" emphasizes a larger international array of spatial and temporal standpoints promoting Indigenous autonomy and self-determination. This critical intervention seeks to contribute to the extensive and inspiring efforts of Indigenous peoples around the world struggling to end the domination and oppression of the land, the earth, the people, and the spirit, with the goal of sustaining the paradigms of truth, clarification, justice, liberation, freedom, peace, and well-being for all. Yet Indigenous peoples in the wall's shadow are living the grave realization that walled separation is becoming normalized. Governments at all levels collaborate with corporations and PACs to normalize separation walls, and Indigenous peoples bear the brunt of arbitrary and indiscriminate violations and denial of justice. Permanent grief is a condition in the shadow of American silence. The contributions in this collection refuse that silence and erasure and seek to shift the debilitating dynamics of trauma into collective grievance.

This collection establishes an archive of Indigenous resistance to racial violence, economic colonization ("poverty"), land dispossession, environmental destruction ("pollution"), community policing, and militarization. Many of the people included in this collection have built their own theoretical paradigms, and they have created extensive archives of text-based documents, material objects, artwork, songs, poetry, and other expressions of culture and knowledge. Rooted in personal experience, family trauma, and intergenerational knowledge, the authors, poets, activists, and community members offer an Indigenous-centered worldview that sits confidently in its power and poignancy alongside scholars who have published numerous books and articles. This decolonial, Indigenous-centered building of theory with community reflects recent trends that speak to Indigenous intellectual traditions and production of knowledge based on Indigenous concerns about space, time, place, culture, and epistemology.[5]

One of the primary theoretical frameworks can also be considered a methodology—it is best epitomized by the simple notion that "gathering together, we decide." Articulated by Eloisa and Margo Tamez to describe the El Calaboz Gathering, this declarative statement announces that Indigenous people—particularly women—came together along the Rio Grande River to make decisions about their lives and futures. Superficially, this phrase describes the common action of like-minded people coming together in common cause to use their knowledge about and perspectives on issues concerning them to chart a future path. Scratch beneath this veneer and one sees a deeply empowering action of Indigenous resistance to power and a reclamation of self-authority and community authority in dialogue, individual and community identity, and collective analysis, voice, and agency. A deeply meaningful action, "gathering together, we decide" reveals an epistemological movement to overcome relocations and dislocations, reject settler-colonial claims, ignorance, apathy, and aggression, and examine and renegotiate the unjust terms of colonization, land dispossession, and militarization.[6]

As a theoretical paradigm, the notion of gathering and making decisions speaks to conceptualizations of decolonization and refusals of settler colonialism. This is indeed what the phrase evokes. The Ndé women had been conducting their entire journey and movement in this manner, and, given severe suppression of their perspectives and voices by powerful government officials, the media, institutions, and special interest groups, it was important to create healthy, supportive spaces where they could express their truths, be heard on their own terms, and be appreciated rather than silenced, as was the pattern in government-run "consultations." The gathering with Indigenous leaders, Indigenous experts, activists, artists, scholars, lawyers, and movement leaders shifted this need and desire in mutually affirming ways into a theoretical framework and methodology. From the community consultation process that Margo developed throughout her mother's case, she developed the idea of weaving Indigenous community-based consciousness, oral history, memory, community analysis of the archives, and critical analysis with scholarly theory to establish concepts anchored in "rivered remembering" and "mother-daughter" models for intrinsic family, kinship, and community strengthening, all crucial in resistance to suppression.[7] She also enacted the concept of the El Calaboz Indigenous listening session, with selected rapporteurs—those invited to be witnesses, listeners, investigators, and "rememberers," who would report back to those who were affected and who mandated them—as part of the methodology. Margo worked alongside legal scholars and Indigenous participants in human rights tribunals and received formal training in truth and justice processes. These taught her the importance of the creation and preservation of the Indigenous memory archive produced in autonomous Indigenous gatherings where independent Indigenous decision-making processes occurred. Gathering, assembling, conserving, and housing the archives in Canada and South Texas, in digital databases, copied on multiple external hard drives, and in temperature-controlled storage units, was crucial to ensure that informed decisions would continue in future gatherings.[8]

Contributions to the Literature

This collection speaks to several trends in scholarly literature as well as the critical work of activists, scholars, legal practitioners, Indigenous leaders, poets, and visual artists. Because the 2011 El Calaboz Gathering grew out of the lawsuit *Tamez v. Chertoff*, one goal of this collection is to encourage legal theorists, human rights and land defenders, scholar-activists, and others to think deeply about how the Tamez case challenged standard assumptions about Indian law, international human rights, and legal decisions about land and property. The roots of this discussion are deeply embedded in legal theories dating back to the Spanish colonial era, particularly because the land held by the Tamez family in El Calaboz was documented as theirs, through a land grant by the king of Spain in 1761, as Indigenous people. Their official land grant held an important and valuable place in Spanish Crown law, and this legal status carried over through the Mexican, Texas, and U.S. eras. One of the most salient elements of this discussion is that the Tamez family, like many Indigenous people in bordered and walled (current-day) Texas, never ceded their lands to Spain, Mexico, Texas, or the United States. In the lawsuit against the Department of Homeland Security, Eloisa and Margo, along with their internationally known attorneys, argued that taking their land not only was unconstitutional but also violated Indigenous rights to the land predating the creation of the United States. After receiving no satisfactory legal resolution within the U.S. legal system, Eloisa Taméz took her grievance to the supranational level. In fact, in testimony to the United Nations and to the Organization of American States' Inter-American Commission and Inter-American Court system, the Tamez family offered arguments and crafted frameworks regarding Indigenous land rights that Indigenous peoples in other countries have employed in their struggles.[9]

In this regard, our collection engages with conversations about Indigenous sovereignty and self-determination, particularly for Native peoples not recognized by the U.S. federal government. It raises important questions about the conceptual location of Indigenous land claims, and it disrupts assumptions about the origins of "Indian law" as a product of settler-colonial jurisprudence. As contributors discuss in this collection, the Tamez case demonstrates how Indigenous law is rooted in the traditions, knowledge, and practice of Indigenous people themselves, particularly women, who frequently hold title to the lands of their families. These women are focused on identifying and defining their historical and present realities through their family's archives within, and retrievals of, memory collections—Indigenous, Spanish, Mexican, Texas, and U.S.—which complicates the U.S. conception of "Indian" and challenges the arbitrary ways the government, institutions, and academe refused to accept the persistent reality of indigeneity along the Lower Rio Grande River, on the Texas-Mexico border, and in southern Texas.[10]

Although *Tamez v. Chertoff* has implications for Indigenous land rights broadly, the fact that the Tamez land sits on the U.S.-Mexico border also speaks to borderlands history and contemporary borderlands studies. Indigenous peoples living in Texas, and particularly along the border, have experienced generations of marginalization, violence, erasure, and genocide. Spanish presidios launched attacks against Lipan, Tonkawa, Karankawa, Caddo, Comanche, and other Indigenous groups during the formal colonial era. The mission system congregated Indigenous peoples into its orbit, where missionaries converted them to Christianity, taught them Spanish, and put them to work as slaves or in slave-like conditions. Hacendados, ranchers, and mining operations pulled people from their communities and forced them into backbreaking labor. The extensive borderlands system of taking captives and forcing them into slavery defined the daily life of groups such as the Lipan. Waves of diseases also killed innumerable Indigenous people. This history of violence, coercion, confinement, and land theft continued through the Mexican Republic, accelerated during Texan independence, and hit unprecedented levels after the United States annexed Texas in 1845.[11]

After the U.S. invasion of Mexico pulled the Mexican north into the United States, the new international border became a contested landscape marked by violence, contraband, militarization, and debates over national identity. Indigenous peoples such as the Lipan moved across the new boundary in both directions and adapted to and intimately interacted with local *fronterizo* cultures and communities, carving out a new identity to remain and resist the multiple types of armed and militarized settler colonies/societies despite the attempts by central states to control this liminal space. U.S. filibusters into Mexico increased, and cross-border vice industries flourished, even as capitalists, railroad magnates, mining firms, and myriad business interests sought to tame the unpredictable region.[12]

By the early twentieth century, new agencies emerged to enforce an increasingly rigid notion of national space and territory. U.S. customs houses dotted the border, and in 1924 the Border Patrol officially began monitoring movement across the international boundary. A growing network of roads, trails, and fences helped these agents of the state catch border crossers outside the official ports of entry. Additionally, large-scale infrastructure projects propelled by the Bureau of Reclamation, the Army Corps of Engineers, and the International Boundary and Water Commission, particularly the damming and channeling of the Rio Grande, altered the landscape, typically to the detriment of Indigenous landowners like the Tamez family. Finally, border control measures after World War II, most notably Operation Hold the Line and Operation Gatekeeper, further militarized the border and increased the culture of surveillance and policing throughout Indigenous communities.[13]

The Tamez case opened a window onto this long history of violence, destruction of Indigenous lands, surveillance, and militarization of Native territory. While the Tamez family pursued their claim and resisted land condemnation, they had to rearticulate this painful history that contradicted the hegemonic Texas mythologies of settler-colonial expansion and rugged individualism. Their activism in the present involved a rewriting of the racist and heroic narratives that buttressed contemporary racial inequities and marginalized Indigenous peoples across the Texas political landscape. After the 2011 Gathering in El Calaboz, more Indigenous groups throughout the borderlands learned about the legal and human rights strategies employed against border militarization and institutional racism. Moreover, the Indigenous people whose current and ancestral lands include the Rio Grande River / Texas-Mexico bordered area have a history of resisting the federal government's normalizing Indian administrative system. Significant scholarship has pointed to the dynamic historical context of this region's cultures, traditions, customs, and practices, and the spirit of the retention of autonomy and independence, as noted and marked by the earliest Spanish colonists and settlers as well as later successor occupiers. Despite centuries of attempts to fully assimilate and dispose of them, Indigenous peoples steadfastly adapted and retained their own histories of the rise and decline of colonial powers.[14]

The Ndé women, members of a notable family of the region with extensive precolonial, colonial, and modern community archives, resolved to generate a greater awareness of their community's knowledge, documentation of their historical struggles, and ongoing, dynamic, contemporary presence. In the El Calaboz oral tradition, the precolonial era to the present is a seamless history relating the encounters, confrontations, victories, and endurances up to the present day. Margo defines this as a historical understanding that centers the transhistorical nature of Ndé worldviews of deep time-space and race. Nowhere in the El Calaboz oral history did the people melt into the generalized Mexican, Mexican American, Hispanic, or Anglo world system. Rather, they were always alive, observing, counternarrating, and adapting to ongoing dispossession logics through continual resistance. New generations of Ndé thinkers and agents of change built upon this richness and utilized newly available technologies to advance Ndé critical consciousness, memory, and determination across borders, languages, and systems.

Indigenous Women's Activism

In addition to magnifying Indigenous voices throughout borderlands studies, the Tamez case speaks to scholarship on Indigenous knowledge, activism, and leadership among Native women. As many of the contributors to this collection will argue, despite the adoption of Euro-American and Christian gender roles in some Native communities, women have played key roles in all aspects of Indigenous life. Lipan Apache women are carriers and cultivators of history, knowledge, and tradition, but throughout multiple colonizations and their responses to them, their central rights and responsibilities with respect to the home, land, food, medicinal plants, children, education, animals, and diplomacy reflect their impressive impact on Indigenous survival. Apache women hold knowledge about medicine as well, thereby ensuring the physical and spiritual well-being of immediate family and extended kin relations. In Eloisa Taméz's case, this knowledge and status as a leader of her family and community shines brightly through her persistent activism and her strength to fight against DHS to protect and preserve her land and culture and to guarantee that these are passed down to her descendants intact. Indeed, a constant theme in the struggles of Indigenous women throughout the borderlands has been retaining access to plants, food, and medicine, and in this case the life-giving waters of the Rio Grande.[15]

As alluded to above, Ndé women are keepers of knowledge, and they nurture methods and processes critical to making important decisions in their families and bands. Just as Ndé knowledge represents a theoretical and conceptual framework for understanding ties to ancestral homelands, the process of making life-altering decisions should similarly attract the attention of scholars and community activists. Ndé women understood and implemented local, Native-centric legal principles and enacted and embodied Indigenous legal practices and procedures. Rooted in building consensus and listening to diverse voices and perspectives, Native women's traditions of leadership rested upon community well-being, not individual aggrandizement or personal advancement. These traditions continue in contemporary activism, whether it takes place in face-to-face meetings, at the kitchen table, or online in chat groups and social media platforms. Collaboration and cooperation are key, as is the positive valuation of diverse opinions and viewpoints.

These themes and practices were evident in the 2011 El Calaboz Gathering, which brought together women from Lipan, Mescalero, Tohono O'odham, Mayo, Yaqui, Ópata, Diné, and Akimel O'odham communities to share their experiences with border militarization, toxic masculinity and gender discrimination, racialized violence and classism, and historical erasure. Procedurally, the gathering involved Lipan expressions of openness, inclusiveness, hospitality, and creativity, and participants collaborated to create supportive spaces with extensive listening sessions, led mainly by women. Participants shared responsibility for taking notes when people gave official testimonies/testimonios, while individuals with vehicles helped with transportation, and everyone helped to cook food and clean up. While the gathering had specific goals in mind associated with resisting land condemnation and militarization, the process of gathering together and collectively deciding embodied participatory practices of shared governance, mutual respect, traditional knowledge, and commitment to justice. These themes of women-led activism, collaboration, land protection, and community advocacy continued after the meeting, particularly as various economic, political, social, cultural, and health pressures challenged many attendees.

As noted throughout this collection, the El Calaboz Gathering was a result of Indigenous resistance, and it was a catalyst for continued activism in the following decade. In South Texas, Lipan and other Indigenous communities coped with surveillance and scrutiny as anti-immigrant sentiment resulted in an array of racist policies. The election of Donald Trump in 2016 emboldened vigilante groups and mainstream politicians to publicly embrace platforms that criminalized human beings seeking refuge from cartels, corrupt governments, and exploitative corporations. Lipan individuals, like people belonging to other Indigenous groups along the border—particularly the Tohono O'odham, as well as the Kumeyaay and Cocopah—found themselves caught in the middle of racist sentiments and violent political rhetoric clamoring for increased border militarization. These high-profile conflicts in the Sonoran Desert included an increase in drug and human trafficking through O'odham lands, which threatened the physical safety of O'odham on both sides of the border. Increased trafficking brought the heightened presence of cartels, which in turn resulted in an expanded Border Patrol footprint. Border Patrol officers harassed and intimidated innocent O'odham, who increasingly feared for their lives as they were caught in the middle of a "drug war" compounded by cartels seeking to gain control of drug trafficking channels. The O'odham, like the Lipan, faced the Trump administration and its accelerated waiving of federal laws along the border to expedite the construction of his wall. While these events unfolded, the Tamez family and the attendees at the 2011 gathering continued fighting against the violent and racist militarization of their homelands across the U.S. borderlands.[16]

As militarization, environmental exploitation, and anti-Indigenous racism accelerated in the 2010s, Indigenous activism gained center stage in the political landscape. The globally televised confrontation between Indigenous land and water protectors and the rapacious Energy Transfer Corporation at Standing Rock illuminated the power of Native activism. Similar resistance to oil and gas production occurred along the U.S.-Mexico border, as Water Protectors protested new pipelines for natural gas fracking. These Indigenous-led efforts to protect land and culture overlapped with the investigative work of the Land Grab U project, which exposed how public "land-grant universities" generated massive profits from the theft of Native lands. Similarly, the Land Back Movement not only pursued a greater awareness of the history behind the largest transfer of land in the Western Hemisphere, it also prodded federal, state, and local agencies to consider how they could return land to Indigenous peoples. All these movements saw women at the forefront, and in this regard the Tamez case and the Gathering at El Calaboz should be assessed alongside these monumental events.[17]

In the decade following the El Calaboz gathering, the Tamez family remained in communication with many participants as they not only continued to struggle against the legacy of the land condemnation and construction of the wall, but also dealt with other challenges presented to them by the settler-colonial society. The effect of these stresses on the lives of participants and community members reveals a lesser-known dimension of activist work. Akin to the intergenerational trauma of violence, the impact of state impunity, economic precarity, surveillance and monitoring, legal obfuscation, gender and racial discrimination, and chronic health disparities needs to be foregrounded in all discussions of activism. This pain rippled outward to family, friends, allies, and students associated with university-based research on militarization and gender-based violence. As is discussed in this collection, participants in the Gathering at El Calaboz endured cancer acquired from toxic industries in border communities, stress-induced mental health problems, unemployment, anxiety, and other harms. Several core contributors to the gathering—Teresa Leal, April Cotte, and Daniel Castro Romero Jr.—have died due to the cumulative health and economic pressures they faced throughout their lives.

Coping with these challenges took many forms for the participants, allies, and people who came into the orbit of the Tamez family, even as they were engaged with their own struggles against racism, violence, and militarization. As scholars have noted, visual art, murals, and even performance art can play a powerful role in resisting violence, but they also provide a catharsis that helps in dealing with the trauma of violence. As demonstrated by contributors to this collection, visual art can reveal sentiments and convey important ideas that activists and scholars may not be able to address in their grassroots efforts or academic articles. Similarly, creative writing and poetry offer powerful messages about trauma, personal grief and loss, and individual or community healing. In form, content, and message, poetry can reach people in direct and visceral ways that can move the reader or listener spiritually, emotionally, and philosophically. Even tattoo artistry helps an individual who has suffered pain to achieve a degree of solace and healing. Tattooing is a common form of bodily adornment that tells the stories of a person or community, reminds them about their place in the world, and marks transitions in life. Inscribed upon the body, tattooing is one of the most intimate and permanent forms of expression of pain and trauma on the one hand, and survival and joy on the other. All these modes of survival are discussed by the contributors to this collection, and because of this, we feel that this project makes an important offering to scholars, artists, activists, community members, and others interested in resisting violence against Indigenous people.

Finally, this collection contributes to themes of Indigenous documentation, witnessing, testifying, remembering, and truth-telling. Indigenous communities have systems for acknowledging and remembering important events and nurturing critical information. Elders train specific individuals as official historians, while parents hand down to their children stories and knowledge that are central to their identities. With the violent disruptions of settler colonialism, and its implementation of the written word, the imperial archive, and exclusionary traditions of historical representation, the actions and perspectives of Indigenous peoples have been marginalized, and in some cases erased, from the dominant collective national consciousness. While Indigenous peoples have furtively maintained their traditions, memories, and practices of knowledge keeping, the hegemonic systems of the occupying nation-states have posed an existential challenge to Native ways of documenting, remembering, and presenting their stories in the public domain.[18]

This collection builds from Indigenous ways of remembering, documenting, and testifying, but it foregrounds Ndé/Apache voices within a highly militarized space. It also pulls from non-Indigenous practices and strategies spanning a diverse range of time and space to provide an Indigenous archive of violence, marginalization, and militarization, as well as resistance and survival. At one end of the spectrum, this collection includes legal rulings and assorted materials associated with the court case *Tamez v. Chertoff*. The Tamez family litigated their case in multiple courts, and these battles yielded important documents, such as affidavits from Indigenous landholders and community members opposing the wall. In these official statements, we learn about Indigenous claims to the land, but we also gain insights into traditional land-use patterns, spatial dispersal of families and bands, and generations of resistance to state violence. Other such material articulates a future-oriented Indigenous land protection strategy that carves out new spaces for international courts to recognize the rights of nonrecognized peoples. Thus, the legal documents include important historical narratives, but they also point to important legal strategies that Indigenous groups around the world can adopt.

Alongside the legal documents, there is the adjacent process of documenting individual testimonies/testimonios outside the framework of settler-colonial law. We include personal interviews, or, as scholars of Latinx, Latine, Mexican, Latin American, and Chicana/o studies would refer to them, testimonios. Such narratives are central to Native American and Indigenous studies because they reveal the experiences of Native people outside of violent institutions such as the Bureau of Indian Affairs, the boarding schools and residential schools, and the church. These oral history interviews cover a range of topics, from personal histories with violence to the contemporary border militarization efforts, as well as specific reflections on the El Calaboz Gathering. These testimonies counterbalance dominant narratives that silence the experiences, thoughts, and observations of people struggling with the quotidian impacts of state-sponsored violence. Some of these individuals are the youth who are uniquely impacted, not only by contemporary upheavals such as land condemnation, but also by the cumulative effect of intergenerational trauma and chronic environmental and mental health problems. These testimonies offer an important documentary trail that can help "set the record straight" and in the process offer an anticolonial narrative that centers Indigenous voices and experiences.[19] As the title of this collection implies, Native people have gathered together to decide not only their futures, but also the ways in which their pasts are remembered, curated, and represented, even if they challenge or subvert some of the most cherished tropes about the nation and its identity. In this regard, our collection seeks to preserve Ndé pasts and protect Ndé futures.

The diverse voices, formats, approaches, and perspectives in this collection follow a common yet diverse set of themes that speak to the central framework of the collection: gathering together, we decide. Part 1, "Memory and Belonging in El Calaboz (The Dungeon): kanánsht'ásh, nádńdáł, náyéskoináh, yénáałni, nahkéyah, nahk'éé, á̱'shi̱gha̱h, ńgoshniłje | I have already returned, you will return, he remembered, she remembered, our country, our relatives, there is my home, punishment," focuses on the themes of memory, kinship, place, protecting, refusing, and dispossession. These chapters offer first-person accounts that reflect on the intimacies of settler-colonial violence as represented in the construction of the wall, from the perspectives of Ndé women. The collection opens with these stories to ground readers in both the deep-time context of Ndé women's struggles and their contemporary acts of resistance, refusal, and remembering.

Part 2, "The El Calaboz Dispossession Tribunal: Community Testimonies and Witnessing," focuses on the 2011 El Calaboz Gathering itself, which was a community-made tribunal informed by Indigenous women and matrilineal knowledge. The selections curated in this chapter reflect the voices of localized Indigenous and non-Native community members from multiple points along the border who have dedicated their lives to anti-violence activism. These voices reflect on the decades-long militarization of Indigenous homelands bifurcated by the international boundary, and they epitomize the grassroots efforts of individuals to protect their communities against environmental exploitation as well as the detrimental impacts of border wall construction. Importantly, this chapter foregrounds the voices of Indigenous youth involved with the El Calaboz Gathering and thus reflects the multigenerational nature of resistance efforts.

Part 3, "Oral History, Remembering, and Documentation as Resistance: Ndé beenahch'i̱haasdziih, náyéskoináh, yénáałni, hishnił, hwiigo | I speak to you about it, he remembered, she remembered, building, vigorously," includes an array of interviews, testimonies, and textual and visual documentation from the El Calaboz Gathering. This chapter focuses on the theme of collectively building common understanding of the origins, course, and legacy of militarization while foregrounding the actions and perspectives of Indigenous activists and non-Native allies. This section expands outward from the gathering itself to include the personal reflections of scholar-witnesses as they consider the larger geography of militarization in the U.S.-Mexico borderlands. Contributors meditate upon their individual and family stories growing up in an increasingly violent social, cultural, and economic landscape impacted by transnational violence and settler-colonial exploitation. The authors in this part also analyze how certain memories are created to silence other memories, particularly the resistance stories of Indigenous peoples, who face profound questions about identity, race, and federal recognition and nonrecognition. This section offers a critical intervention into some of the "canon" of Native American and Indigenous studies scholarship by centering Indigenous lives in Texas, where settler-colonial erasure and borderlands violence crafted specific identities that prompt us to reconsider how we conceptualize indigeneity in the modern world.

Between parts 3 and 4 we have included what we term "Resistance Artwork: didíigo biłgoshni hwiigo | witness tell stories powerfully, strongly, vigorously." Through photography, painting, murals, and other formats, this intervention between sections focuses on visual storytelling, visual witnessing, and using visual representations to offer stories about witnessing state violence, racial violence, and militarization. The artists in this section are actors and activists mobilizing Indigenous knowledge to protect land, water, and rights. They are also concerned with community empowerment and with foregrounding the role of Indigenous digital arts as a powerful means of protecting the environment.

Part 4, "Bénáońzi̱i̱ní | Embodying Indigenous Recognition," focuses on the ways in which contributors have embodied belonging and preserved and re-created kinship ties despite multiple forms of barriers and walls erected in settler-colonial society. In this part, we focus on the ways in which community members, particularly youth and young activists, nurture decolonial practices and re-create their Indigenous identities despite diaspora and marginalization. We foreground youth voices and perspectives as well as nonnormative expressions of identity, as in tattoo art. While the artwork and tattoos are deeply personal, they speak to global trends among Indigenous youth who seek connections between their selves, bodies, and individual experiences, and those of similarly minded youth communities trying to flourish in settler-dominated spaces. This chapter provides visual evidence of youth empowerment, intergenerational trauma, and the nuanced strategies of memory-making in the twenty-first century.

Part 5, "Epistemological and Methodological Interventions for Decolonized Futures: iłego̱zhiish, yiskao, aandahyé | through time, tomorrow, farther (movement into future)," includes a small selection of critical reflections on the significance of the Tamez case and larger questions of militarization, settler-colonial violence, and resistance. These pieces are largely, though not solely, scholarly treatments that emphasize historical context and make important connections between land, history, identity, and the modern militarization of the borderlands. Each selection offers a different point of entry into the larger themes of the book—resistance, archives, history, memory, erasure, and gender—by critically thinking about positionality as defined by place, time, and identity. These chapters collectively weave together the deconstruction of hegemonic historical narratives of Texas exceptionalism, decolonial research methodologies, and reverence for the lands and peoples of the region. This entwining strengthens our understanding of the origins, impact, and legacy of militarizing Indigenous spaces. Finally, a brief conclusion offers a macro-level meditation on where the Tamez case, the El Calaboz Gathering, and the voices in this collection are situated within Indigenous-centered resistance to settler-colonial violence. By asking, "What do you think?" we are inviting readers to sit with and contemplate your reactions to the contributions in this collection, to the collection as a whole, and to the insights and new awarenesses these generate with respect to your understanding of Indigenous peoples' experiences in this complex geopolitical and cultural space of resistance. We wonder what your preconceptions were and are, and we ask, "What do you think now?" This is an invitation to join us in forging a new dialogue and a new direction. In essence, we envision the conclusion serving as a momentary pause that allows us to collectively take a deep breath, exhale, and try to process what it means for Indigenous peoples impacted by the border wall, militarization, racial violence, historical erasure, and patriarchy to *gather together and decide* how we want to remake our future for generations to come.

íłahałee dáłe' nahk'éé nahkéyaah 'át'éh béodaaziił
Gathering together, we [those from the land] decide.

NOTES

1. Dene ("the people") is a word in Dene ("Athapaskan") languages. The Dene Nation has existed for millennia and has persisted into the present day, despite numerous imperialist and colonial occupations. Presently, the Dene Nation actively works to educate and to revitalize Dene relationships and consciousness beyond settler borders. The Dene Nation is a political organization in Denendeh, meaning "the Land of the People," located in Northwest Territories, Canada. The Dene Nation covers a large geographical area—from present-day Alaska to the southernmost tip of North America. See the Dene Nation website, https://denenation.com/. According to John Ives, professor in the Anthropology Department at the University of Alberta, "Dene speakers go from the North

slope of Alaska all the way to northern Mexico." Quoted in Walter Strong, "History, Science, and the 'Year of Two Winters': Uncovering the Secrets of Dene Migration," CBC News, September 24, 2017, https://www.cbc.ca/news/canada/north/dene-migrations-1.4304503. Tamez has utilized "Dene Ndé" in reference to the Ndé peoples in her research and advocacy as a response to Dene Nation leadership's mandates for Dene reunification beyond borders and calls to actively reinstill Dene identity consciousness throughout Dene ancestral territories. Tamez has answered this call in many ways, and specifically does so in her contributions to decolonial Ndé research as an intervention against settler-colonial bordering and long-standing academic devaluation of Ndé peoples, which have contributed to generations of Ndé being politically, socially, economically, and culturally severed from Dene Nation cultural continuity, political unity, empowerment, mutual aid, and sustained relationships. Tamez's intervention helps Ndé to self-determine, reclaim, and reinstate Ndé with the Dene Nation as a present and future in which the Ndé community define Ndé existence, knowing, and power on their own terms.

2. Similar locations in Mexico, El Salvador, Venezuela, and Chile with the place-name "El Calaboz" or "El Calabozo"—a dug-out space of incarceration, for example—are referencing the spatialized establishment of torture chambers by colonial authorities in Indigenous communities. While some of these Indigenous places renamed "Calaboz/Calabozo" by colonizers across the Americas also retained a majority Indigenous population over centuries, a significant number retained the name "Calaboz" or "Calabozo" into the present day. El Calaboz, Lower Rio Grande, Texas, is the only surviving documented case of one of the original Spanish "calaboz" dungeon systems imposed on an Indigenous population along the Rio Grande River.

3. Denise Gilman, "Seeking Breaches in the Wall: An International Human Rights Law Challenge to the Texas-Mexico Border Wall," *Texas International Law Journal* 46 (2011): 257–93.

4. Scholarship on Indigenous theory and methodology is now quite vast, but the following works have been particularly influential: Aileen Moreton-Robinson, ed., *Critical Indigenous Studies: Engagements in First World Locations* (Tucson: University of Arizona Press, 2016); Christine Leza, *Divided Peoples: Policy, Activism, and Indigenous Identities on the U.S.-Mexico Border* (Tucson: University of Arizona Press, 2021); Angelique EagleWoman, "The Eagle and the Condor of the Western Hemisphere: Application of International Indigenous Principles to Halt the United States Border Wall," *Idaho Law Review* 45, no. 3 (2009): 1–18. Though often used as a model for Indigenous methodology, this work offers important theoretical insights: Kathleen E. Absolon (Minogiizhigokwe), *Kaandossiwin: How We Come to Know: Indigenous Re-Search Methodologies*, 2nd ed. (Halifax: Fernwood Publishing, 2022).

5. Though adjacent to our work, Rose Miron, *Indigenous Archival Activism: Mohican Interventions in Public History and Memory* (Minneapolis: University of Minnesota Press, 2024), offers useful insights.

6. Margo Tamez, "áanzho ha'shi 'dał'k'ida,' 'áá'áná,' 'doo maanaashni': Welcoming 'long ago,' 'way back' and 'remember'—as an Ndé Decolonization and Land Recovery Process," *InTensions* 6 (Fall/Winter 2012): 18. Referring to gathering together physically next to the wall in El Calaboz: "It was a major step initiated by Indigenous peoples reclaiming and recovering Ndé ways, memory and remembering in direct connection to 19thc. and 20thc. killing fields, land dispossession, gender violence, lynching, and poverty. . . . The results made it clear that Ndé struggles for future autonomy against state violence rest on the recovery of Kónitsą̨ą̨íí Gokíyaa—Ndé homeland."
7. Margo Tamez, "Indigenous Women's Rivered Refusals in El Calaboz," *Diálogo* 19, no. 1 (2016): 7–21.
8. Some of these issues are covered in Tahu Kukutai and John Taylor, *Indigenous Data Sovereignty: Toward an Agenda* (Canberra: Centre for Aboriginal Economic Policy Research, 2016).
9. See Margo Tamez, "Response to the United States Periodic Report of April 2007 on the United Nations International Convention on the Elimination of All Forms of Racial Discrimination" (letter to Nathalie Prouvez, United Nations Committee for the Elimination of Racial Discrimination, November 14, 2007), https://law.utexas.edu/humanrights/borderwall/communities/indigenous-Lipan-Apache-Report.pdf; Margo Tamez, "Kónitsą̨ą̨íí gokíyaa Ndé: 'Big Water People's Homeland'; A Shadow of Self-Determination in a Bifurcated Traditional Territory" (paper contributed to the 3rd UN seminar, "Strengthening Partnership Between States and Indigenous Peoples: Treaties, Agreements and Other Constructive Arrangements," organized by the Office of the United Nations High Commissioner for Human Rights, Geneva, July 16–17, 2012), https://www.ohchr.org/Documents/Issues/IPeoples/Seminars/Treaties/BP7.pdf; Ariel Dulitzky and Margo Tamez, "The Situation of the Texas-Mexico Border Wall: A Request for Consideration Under the Early Warning and Urgent Action Procedures of the United Nations Committee on the Elimination of Racial Discrimination (80th Session)" (legal brief on behalf of the Human Rights Clinic, School of Law, University of Texas at Austin, and Lipan Apache Women's Defense to the United Nations Committee on the Elimination of Racial Discrimination, May 10, 2012), 1–134, https://www.academia.edu/3830287/The_Situation_of_the_Texas_Mexico_Border_Wall_A_Request_for_Consideration_under_the_Early_Warning_and_Urgent_Action_Procedures_of_the_United_Nations_Committee_on_the_Elimination_of_Racial_Discrimination_80th_Session_by_Ariel_Dulitzky_and_Margo_Tamez_et_al; International Indian Treaty Council, "Indigenous Peoples Consolidated Alternative Report: Updates" (part of report to United Nations Human Rights Committee, 110th Session, 10–28 March 2014, Consideration of the Fourth Periodic Report of the United States of America Under Article 40 of the International Covenant on Civil and Political Rights, February 3, 2014), https://www.iitc.org/wp-content/uploads/2014/02/ICCPR-IITC-Consolidated-Alternate-Report-UPDATES-February-2014_web.pdf; Margo

Tamez, India Reed Bowers, Matthew Babcock, and Lorraine Garcia, "The Holy See and European Dispossession of Apache-Ndé-Nnee Peoples: A Call for Truth, Disclosure, Justice and Redress" (Apache-Ndé-Nneé Working Group shadow report, UNCERD 88th Session: Review of the Holy See, November 2015), https://www.academia.edu/41361264/Apache_Ndé_Nneé_Working_Group_Shadow_Report_The_Holy_See_and_European_Dispossession_of_Apache_Ndé_Nnee_Peoples_A_call_for_truth_disclosure_justice_and_redress_UN_CERD_88th_Session_Review_of_the_Holy_See.

10. Angelique T. EagleWoman and Stacey L. Leeds, *Mastering American Indian Law* (Durham, N.C.: Carolina Academic Press, 2019).
11. The scholarship on the Lipan Apache is significant but of uneven quality. See, for instance, Sherry Robinson, *I Fought a Good Fight: A History of the Lipan Peoples* (Denton: University of North Texas Press, 2013); Thomas A. Britten, *The Lipan Apaches: People of Wind and Lightning* (Albuquerque: University of New Mexico Press, 2009); Nancy McGown Minor, *The Light Gray People: An Ethnohistory of the Lipan Apaches of Texas and Northern Mexico* (Lanham, Md.: University Press of America, 2009).
12. For general histories investigating the intersections of borderlands and Native history, see Gary Clayton Anderson, *The Conquest of Texas: Ethnic Cleansing in the Promised Land, 1825–1875* (Norman: University of Oklahoma Press, 2004); Brian DeLay, *War of a Thousand Deserts: Indian Raids and the U.S.-Mexican War* (New Haven: Yale University Press, 2007).
13. Kelley Lytle Hernandez, *Migra! A History of the U.S. Border Patrol* (Berkeley: University of California Press, 2010); C. J. Alvarez, *Border Land, Border Water: A History of Construction on the U.S.-Mexico Divide* (Austin: University of Texas Press, 2019).
14. Brian DeLay, "Independent Indians and the US-Mexican War," *The American Historical Review* 112, no. 1 (2007): 35–68; DeLay, *War of a Thousand Deserts*; Benjamin H. Johnson, *Revolution in Texas: How a Forgotten Rebellion and Its Bloody Suppression Turned Mexicans into Americans* (New Haven: Yale University Press, 2003); Juliana Barr, "Geographies of Power: Mapping Indian Borders in the 'Borderlands' of the Early Southwest," *William and Mary Quarterly* 68, no. 1 (2011): 5–46; and Juliana Barr, *Peace Came in the Form of a Woman: Indians and Spaniards in the Texas Borderlands* (Chapel Hill: University of North Carolina Press, 2007).
15. Lynn Stephen and Shannon Speed, eds., *Indigenous Women and Violence: Feminist Activist Research in Heightened States of Injustice* (Tucson: University of Arizona Press, 2021); Devon Mihesuah, *Indigenous American Women: Decolonization, Empowerment, Activism* (Lincoln: University of Nebraska Press, 2003). From two dramatically different Indigenous communities, see: Theda Perdue, *Cherokee Women: Gender and Culture Change, 1700–1835* (Lincoln: University of Nebraska Press, 1998); and Brenda Child, *Holding Our World Together: Ojibwe Women and the Survival of Community* (New York: Penguin,

2012). Both echo what this collection argues regarding the roles of Native women as keepers of knowledge and tradition.

16. Leza, *Divided Peoples*; María Josefina Saldaña-Portillo, *Indian Given: Racial Geographies Across Mexico and the United States* (Durham, N.C.: Duke University Press, 2016).
17. Nick Estes and Jaskiran Dhillon, eds., *Standing with Standing Rock: Voices from the #NoDAPL Movement* (Minneapolis: University of Minnesota Press, 2019). The "Land Grab Universities" project is a collaborative effort between *High Country News* and Robert Lee, Tristan Ahtone, Margaret Pearce, Kalen Goodluck, Geoff McGhee, Cody Leff, Katherine Lanpher, and Taryn Salinas; see https://www.landgrabu.org/.
18. Miron, *Indigenous Archival Activism*.
19. Patricia DeRocher, *Transnational Testimonios: The Politics of Collective Knowledge Production* (Seattle: University of Washington Press, 2018); Dolores Delgado Bernal, Judith Flores Carmona, and Rebeca Burciaga, *Chicana/Latina Testimonios as Pedagogical, Methodological, and Activist Approaches to Social Justice* (London: Routledge, 2017).

BIBLIOGRAPHY

Absolon, Kathleen E. *Kaandossiwin: How We Come to Know: Indigenous Re-Search Methodologies*, 2nd ed. Halifax: Fernwood Publishing, 2022.

Alvarez, C. J. *Border Land, Border Water: A History of Construction on the U.S.-Mexico Divide*. Austin: University of Texas Press, 2019.

Anderson, Gary Clayton. *The Conquest of Texas: Ethnic Cleansing in the Promised Land, 1825–1875*. Norman: University of Oklahoma Press, 2004.

Barr, Juliana. "Geographies of Power: Mapping Indian Borders in the 'Borderlands' of the Early Southwest." *William and Mary Quarterly* 68, no. 1 (2011): 5–46.

Barr, Juliana. *Peace Came in the Form of a Woman: Indians and Spaniards in the Texas Borderlands*. Chapel Hill: University of North Carolina Press, 2007.

Bernal, Dolores Delgado, Judith Flores Carmona, and Rebeca Burciaga. *Chicana/Latina Testimonios as Pedagogical, Methodological, and Activist Approaches to Social Justice*. London: Routledge, 2017.

Britten, Thomas A. *The Lipan Apaches: People of Wind and Lightning*. Albuquerque: University of New Mexico Press, 2009.

Child, Brenda. *Holding Our World Together: Ojibwe Women and the Survival of Community*. New York: Penguin, 2012.

DeLay, Brian. "Independent Indians and the US-Mexican War." *The American Historical Review* 112, no. 1 (2007): 35–68.

DeLay, Brian. *War of a Thousand Deserts: Indian Raids and the U.S.-Mexican War*. New Haven: Yale University Press, 2007.

DeRocher, Patricia. *Transnational Testimonios: The Politics of Collective Knowledge Production*. Seattle: University of Washington Press, 2018.

Dulitzky, Ariel, and Margo Tamez. "The Situation of the Texas-Mexico Border Wall: A Request for Consideration Under the Early Warning and Urgent Action Procedures of the United Nations Committee on the Elimination of Racial Discrimination (80th Session)." Legal brief on behalf of the Human Rights Clinic, School of Law, University of Texas at Austin, and Lipan Apache Women's Defense to the United Nations Committee on the Elimination of Racial Discrimination, May 10, 2012. https://www.academia.edu/3830287/The_Situation_of_the_Texas_Mexico_Border_Wall_A_Request_for_Consideration_under_the_Early_Warning_and_Urgent_Action_Procedures_of_the_United_Nations_Committee_on_the_Elimination_of_Racial_Discrimination_80th_Session_by_Ariel_Dulitzky_and_Margo_Tamez_et_al.

EagleWoman, Angelique. "The Eagle and the Condor of the Western Hemisphere: Application of International Indigenous Principles to Halt the United States Border Wall." *Idaho Law Review* 45, no. 3 (2009): 1–18.

EagleWoman, Angelique, and Stacey L. Leeds. *Mastering American Indian Law.* Durham, N.C.: Carolina Academic Press, 2019.

Estes, Nick, and Jaskiran Dhillon, eds. *Standing with Standing Rock: Voices from the #NoDAPL Movement.* Minneapolis: University of Minnesota Press, 2019.

Gilman, Denise. "Seeking Breaches in the Wall: An International Human Rights Law Challenge to the Texas-Mexico Border Wall." *Texas International Law Journal* 46 (2011): 257–93.

Hernandez, Kelley Lytle. *Migra! A History of the U.S. Border Patrol.* Berkeley: University of California Press, 2010.

International Indian Treaty Council. "Indigenous Peoples Consolidated Alternative Report: Updates." Part of report to United Nations Human Rights Committee, 110th Session, 10–28 March 2014, Consideration of the Fourth Periodic Report of the United States of America Under Article 40 of the International Covenant on Civil and Political Rights, February 3, 2014. https://www.iitc.org/wp-content/uploads/2014/02/ICCPR-IITC-Consolidated-Alternate-Report-UPDATES-February-2014_web.pdf.

Johnson, Benjamin H. *Revolution in Texas: How a Forgotten Rebellion and Its Bloody Suppression Turned Mexicans into Americans.* New Haven: Yale University Press, 2003.

Kukutai, Tahu, and John Taylor. *Indigenous Data Sovereignty: Toward an Agenda.* Canberra: Centre for Aboriginal Economic Policy Research, 2016.

Leza, Christine. *Divided Peoples: Policy, Activism, and Indigenous Identities on the U.S.-Mexico Border.* Tucson: University of Arizona Press, 2021.

McGown Minor, Nancy. *The Light Gray People: An Ethnohistory of the Lipan Apaches of Texas and Northern Mexico.* Lanham, Md.: University Press of America, 2009.

Mihesuah, Devon. *Indigenous American Women: Decolonization, Empowerment, Activism.* Lincoln: University of Nebraska Press, 2003.

Miron, Rose. *Indigenous Archival Activism: Mohican Interventions in Public History and Memory.* Minneapolis: University of Minnesota Press, 2024.

Moreton-Robinson, Aileen, ed. *Critical Indigenous Studies: Engagements in First World Locations*. Tucson: University of Arizona Press, 2016.

Perdue, Theda. *Cherokee Women: Gender and Culture Change, 1700–1835*. Lincoln: University of Nebraska Press, 1998.

Robinson, Sherry. *I Fought a Good Fight: A History of the Lipan Peoples*. Denton: University of North Texas Press, 2013.

Saldaña-Portillo, María Josefina. *Indian Given: Racial Geographies Across Mexico and the United States*. Durham, N.C.: Duke University Press, 2016.

Stephen, Lynn, and Shannon Speed, eds. *Indigenous Women and Violence: Feminist Activist Research in Heightened States of Injustice*. Tucson: University of Arizona Press, 2021.

Strong, Walter. "History, Science, and the 'Year of Two Winters': Uncovering the Secrets of Dene Migration." CBC News, September 24, 2017. https://www.cbc.ca/news/canada/north/dene-migrations-1.4304503.

Tamez, Margo. "áanzho ha'shi 'dał'k'ida,' 'áá'áná,' 'doo maanaashni': Welcoming 'long ago,' 'way back' and 'remember'—as an Ndé Decolonization and Land Recovery Process." *InTensions* 6 (Fall/Winter 2012): 1–23.

Tamez, Margo. "Indigenous Women's Rivered Refusals in El Calaboz." *Diálogo* 19, no. 1 (2016): 7–21.

Tamez, Margo. "Kónitsąąíí gokíyaa Ndé: 'Big Water People's Homeland'; A Shadow of Self-Determination in a Bifurcated Traditional Territory." Paper contributed to the 3rd UN seminar, "Strengthening Partnership Between States and Indigenous Peoples: Treaties, Agreements and Other Constructive Arrangements," organized by the Office of the United Nations High Commissioner for Human Rights, Geneva, July 16–17, 2012. https://www.ohchr.org/Documents/Issues/IPeoples/Seminars/Treaties/BP7.pdf.

Tamez, Margo. "Response to the United States Periodic Report of April 2007 on the United Nations International Convention on the Elimination of All Forms of Racial Discrimination." Letter to Nathalie Prouvez, United Nations Committee for the Elimination of Racial Discrimination, November 14, 2007. https://law.utexas.edu/humanrights/borderwall/communities/indigenous-Lipan-Apache-Report.pdf.

Tamez, Margo, India Reed Bowers, Matthew Babcock, and Lorraine Garcia. "The Holy See and European Dispossession of Apache-Ndé-Nnee Peoples: A Call for Truth, Disclosure, Justice and Redress." Apache-Ndé-Nneé Working Group shadow report, UNCERD 88th Session: Review of the Holy See, November 2015. https://www.academia.edu/41361264/Apache_Ndé_Nneé_Working_Group_Shadow_Report_The_Holy_See_and_European_Dispossession_of_Apache_Ndé_Nnee_Peoples_A_call_for_truth_disclosure_justice_and_redress_UN_CERD_88th_Session_Review_of_the_Holy_See.

PART I

Memory and Belonging in El Calaboz (The Dungeon)

kanánshtʼásh, nádńdáł, náyéskoináh, yénáałni, nahkéyah, nahkʼéé, á̱ʼshig̱ha̱h, ńgoshniłje | I have already returned, you will return, he remembered, she remembered, our country, our relatives, there is my home, punishment

ONE

Some Memories Leave a Mark

MARÍA DE JESÚS GARCÍA ATKINSON

Some memories leave a mark on people. These memories are so strong that they cannot be forgotten. Sometimes it's good to go back in time and hear echoes of our childhood. Echoes, like those of hearing your parents or grandparents call your name; of running around outside barefooted; of catching fireflies and putting them in a jar; of laughing and singing; and of trying to count all the stars at night. I hear them time and again.

Today, as I am sitting on my back porch, I hear birds singing in the trees, and I am suddenly taken back to my beloved El Calaboz. My mind is racing back to a very important time in my life's journey. It is the very early 1940s and I find myself in my grandmother Andrea's kitchen.

My grandmother's kitchen is bursting with activity. The kitchen seems so big. There are so many things to see. On the far left I see a chimney where my grandmother does some cooking. It is made of adobe bricks. Next to it is a wood-burning stove. I can see that something is cooking on it. On the stove, a coffee pot is brewing, and I can smell the rich coffee aroma. Hanging on a wall, I see a bundle of fresh garlic. Sitting on the floor is a big tub of lard, a favorite cooking oil at that time. Her cupboard is opened and I can see all her pretty dishes. Her sisters María Cavazos García and Gertrudis Cavazos Rodríguez are there as well. They live in the village nearby and often they get together for cooking and sewing. I have seen the beautiful quilts and embroidery, and their technique, which

FIGURE 1.1 1948, El Calaboz Ranchería. Eloisa García Taméz (*left*), age 13, and María de Jesús García Atkinson (*right*), age 11, standing in the community milpa (maize field). The community's levee (*behind them*) protected the community from the Rio Grande's overflow. In 2009, the United States built the wall on top of the levee, severing human access and restricting traditional maize farming.

my grandmother calls "perfilado," that they all make working side by side. My sister Chata and I are in the mix.[1] We want to help, but we are mostly in the way, though the women don't mind.

The sisters are here today to help my grandmother prepare our corn into masa, or corn dough. I see the dried-up corn kernels, boiling in a pot of water. This is corn that my grandfather Aniceto stores in a shed after harvesting, drying, and shucking it. Everyone in the village does this for our sustenance. My grandmother is explaining that when the kernels soften enough, they will be soaked in lime water, which she calls *cal*. This step must not be omitted, as the cal provides a very essential nutrient called niacin. Without this important step of the process, we could become ill. In the past, people died under harsh conditions.[2]

It's now time to grind the corn in a grinder called a *molino*. My sister and I are begging our grandmother to let us do the grinding. We get tired and soon stop. My grandmother is smiling. The masa must now go through a second grinding. This time a metate is used. They use a family metate, a long, thick, broad stone, carved flat at a downward-sloping angle, with a hand-stone, carved into a tool to crush, mash, and grind the corn finely. The masa is then spiced up and is now ready to be cooked into delicious corn tortillas. My grandmother's sisters who were helping are now leaving, each with a batch of prepared masa. This is a regular part of life in our little village. I am marveling at how well they have worked together, and I even heard them singing. My memory of this widens and I see my grandfather.

My grandfather, Aniceto, is a farmer. He grows many different kinds of crops, tomatoes being one of them. If the tomatoes get too ripe, he will be unable to sell them. Besides our traditional crops, he grows vegetables like tomatoes for people from other nearby villages. My grandfather does not let them go to waste. I see my grandfather outside. He is instructing relatives and neighbors from the village on what is to be done. It is tomato preserving time! Everyone is being assigned a task. All of us children are to wash the bottles that are to be used for the preserved tomato sauce. My grandfather has been accumulating these Coca-Cola, Pepsi-Cola, and other kinds of glass bottles for this event. Two big tubs of water have been placed on a fire pit and the water is now boiling. The adults are taking turns yelling, "Don't get near the fire!" to us children.

The washed red tomatoes are now being placed in one of the tubs of water, and the washed bottles in the other tub. Soon I can hear the popping sounds of some of the bottles breaking. After a while, I see some of the men taking out the tomatoes with some sort of net. The bottles are also being taken out very carefully. When the tomatoes cool off a little it will be time to grind them. I can see the women busy spicing up the tomato puree. They pass the spiced puree to other people who are in charge of filling up the glass bottles with the tomato sauce. The filled-up bottles are then passed to yet another person in charge of capping them. The filled and capped bottles are then thrown back into another tub of boiling clean water. This is the final step. It has been a long and tiring day, but I only see a happy and satisfied look on everyone's faces because of a job well done. The families are all going home with some of the preserved tomato sauce.

It is toward the end of October in 1946. It is fun to watch the grown-ups busy gathering the wreaths or "*coronas*." Some of the wreaths are made by the talented women around the area. They are so beautiful. All imaginable kinds and colors of flowers are being placed in tubs full of water. My grandmother is telling me that soon it will be All Souls' Day or, as she puts it, "Día de los Muertos." "Tonight," she goes on to say, "we will all go to the cemetery and light some candles" for the ancestors. She explains that several volunteers from El Calaboz have been cleaning the cemetery in preparation for this two-day event. They have even washed and brightened the tombs and the bricks around each grave, making them a brighter white, she goes on to say.

It is evening now and we are all gathering together in a group to walk to the cemetery. It seems to me that all the El Calaboz villagers are lined up to go. As we approach the cemetery, I notice how clean it looks. Soon the candles are all lit throughout the place. Somebody starts to pray and soon we all join in. My grandmother's sister, María, then starts to sing some hymns. We all join in the singing too. She has such a lovely voice, I'm thinking all the while. It is a good feeling to honor and remember our loved ones departed. There is so much family history in this small plot of land that still remains with us. It is the next day, and time to take all the flowers to the cemetery. It will be all aglow again, but this time with the vibrant colors of the flowers. Such a pretty sight to see.

Religion is very important to everybody, not only to El Calaboz people, but to all surrounding villages. The nearest church to us is a mile away at El Ranchito, and the Mass is heard only once a month, as we don't have a permanent priest assigned to our community. The church, named Saint Ignatius, must have been built in the early 1930s, although some of our ancestors gave a small plot of land between the villages to the Oblates generations before then. I can still see us getting up very early on the Sundays when Mass was heard. We gather in a group and walk the mile to church. We don't have cars at this time. In spite of this, I am observing so much faith and devotion. I am seeing it in their eyes. This is in 1940 and I am four years old. We would eventually get a permanent priest in the mid-1940s. When I was about eleven or twelve a church choir was formed. My sister and I were members of the choir. It was a fun time.

Everyone, I am observing, has an altar in their homes. Everyone's altar or shrine is slightly different. This is a way to honor the ancestors and saints and to pray as a family in front of the altar. I see figurines of favorite saints, Jesus on the cross, La Virgen de Guadalupe, candles, and fresh flowers from the garden. As I recall this important tradition, I am thinking to myself that I have an altar in my house to this day. This community-wide tradition has made a great impression on me.

My best friend Ida has been absent from school a few days now. We are in first grade at Encantada School. Long ago, one of our maternal Esparza (de Moctezuma) ancestors donated part of the land from the La Encantada–El Ranchito village for our school. In spite of the hate and aggression against our villages long ago, and still in my childhood, our ancestors made it possible for us children, and children in the future, to be educated in the villages and close to home for safety.

It has been very cold lately, as it is around November of 1943. My mother is telling me that I cannot go see my friend just yet, as she is very sick. A few days later my teacher announces that Ida will not be coming back to school. She has passed away. I do not understand. At home that afternoon my mom is trying to explain what happened. I want to go see Ida and my mother is taking me. I walk up to the coffin and start crying. I want her to wake up. I see her mother walking toward me. She is crying hysterically and hugs me tight. I am so glad my mother is right there beside me. It was customary at that time to hold vigils and viewings at one's own house. The whole community would come together. We did everything together in a customary familial way.

Could a doctor have saved Ida? The Elders had been lamenting the fact that we lived too far away from a city and doctors and hospitals. A relative had recently died of tuberculosis and my friend Ida had died of pneumonia. At the time, I didn't understand their concern. My mother, my grandmother, Tía (Aunt) Tules, Tía Juanita, and many others always knew how to cure whatever was ailing me. Teas for stomachaches and other discomforts were made from different medicinal herbs that they grew in their garden or gathered wild on the land. I especially liked the orange leaf tea. Garlic was used for ant and bee stings. They had so many home remedies that doctors were hardly ever needed.

It is December of 1941. My grandfather Aniceto is frantically calling everybody to come and listen to a speech by President Franklin D. Roosevelt on his battery-operated radio. We have no electricity. We all assemble around the radio in silence. I am five years old and am not understanding. After the radio broadcast my grandfather explains the essence of the president's speech. "Japan has bombed Pearl Harbor and we are at war," he is explaining. A lot of the young men around the villages are being drafted. My father is not immediately drafted because he is a farmer, and farmers are needed on the home front. However, as the war progresses, there is a need for more soldiers, and my father is drafted sometime in late 1942 or early 1943 into the U.S. Air Force.

My grandfather takes charge of not only running the farm without my father's help, but also taking care of my mother, my sister, and me. He has become more of a hero to me. Without the help of the young men, I see more women, including my grandmother, helping out with the harvesting. My grandfather is working very hard. He soon becomes very ill and is calling for my father. Leaves are not easily granted at this time. With my mother's persistence and diligence, my father is finally granted a three-day pass. With such a short time granted to my father, when he arrives home, he hurriedly hugs my sister and me and kisses my mom. He then makes his way to his father's side. I had noticed his worried look. Those two are so close, I am thinking. My grandfather had given my father the name Emiliano but would always call him Emilio. My grandfather starts to feel better. All he needed was to see his beloved son. To this day, I do not know the nature of his illness. He would make a full recovery and I would get to enjoy him several more years.

It is now time for my father to return to his military base. He is to catch the train in Harlingen, Texas. My mother, sister, and I go to see him off. My father wants to take us for breakfast, as we are early for his train ride. My father looks so handsome in his uniform. We find a restaurant close to the train station. A waitress soon comes to take our order. I notice her blond hair and blue eyes. My father wants us to order first. We do so without incident. It is now my father's turn to order. He is ordering two scrambled eggs, a cup of coffee with cream, and two biscuits with butter. He is ordering in English. The waitress is saying, "Whaaaaaat?" My father repeats the order. She again says, "Whaaaaaat?" I can see that my father is getting a little irritated, and he is now ordering in Spanish. He is saying, "Yo quiero dos huevos batidos, una taza de cafe y dos bisquetes con flin flan, eso que se le unta al pan." My sister and I are now bursting into giggles. The waitress glares at us and walks over to a picture window and stares out. She then goes and places the order. She understood what my father was ordering the whole time. She had no respect for a non-Anglo serviceman. I would go back time and again to that incident. It has been cause for a lot of laughter and also pleasure.

Education is very important to the Elders. To have somebody graduate from high school is a cause for a celebration. Portraits of those who have graduated and are in cap and gown are often seen displayed in many of the El Calaboz homes. My grandmother Andrea has announced that she will buy a watch for any of her grandchildren who graduate from high school. Not everybody would attend high school, for various reasons. Many would drop out of school because they had to work to help their families. My father's motto is "Your knowledge is your legacy." This he repeats time and again. Was he referring only to school education, or was he in fact telling us to educate ourselves about our ancestral legacy? I am thinking both. Decades later, one of his granddaughters, Maria Rebecca Tamez Drury, would compose a tribute song to honor him. These are some of the lyrics: "And in the words of Emilio, hear them ringing in her ears. Your knowledge is your legacy, you will see." He would be so proud to know his message is alive and well.

"There is going to be a dance tonight," my mother is saying very excitedly. Domingo García and his wife hold dances in the open land behind their house every now and then. Domingo García is the younger brother of my great-grandmother Inocente García Cavazos. Inocente is my grandmother Andrea's mother. We are now getting ready to go to the dance. Everybody goes, young and old, and everybody dances, young and old. As we are nearing the gathering place, I can already hear the music playing. Kerosene lamps are hanging here and there. It is the only light there is besides the moon and stars. In a corner, I spot the record player. It is the crank-up kind. Beside it are a stack of records. Chairs have been placed all around for those wishing to sit. Soon I see dancers on the floor. The floor is just the bare earth; no grass is growing there. My parents soon join in the dancing. There are polkas, *valses, redovas, huapangos,* and *chotises* to dance to. These are the Spanish names for the different dance styles of the people. Some of the names are the Spaniard's ways of saying and spelling Indigenous terms for the dances. Mrs. García goes around after each dance and collects money from the dancers. We children are not left out. We all dance on the sidelines. We try to copy the dance steps of the dancers. It's been a fun night.

I am back in first grade again. Unlike our Elders, we now have a school bus that takes us to school. All the students from El Calaboz attend Encantada School at El Ranchito. The place where the bus picks us up is a structure that looks like a little house, which has been built not far from where I live. This is the designated place for all of us to congregate every morning and wait for the bus. This little structure comes in handy on cold and rainy days. We all huddle in there, and this helps keep us warm. I am thinking of a time when it had rained all night. The next morning, when we arrive at school, there are puddles everywhere. I decide to get on the swings in spite of the puddles of water. I am happily swinging away when suddenly I find myself flying in the air. I land in a mud puddle. Somebody is calling my sister and I see her running toward me. My sister is trying her best to clean me up and console me at the same time. The bell rings and we have to go to our respective classes. I remain wet and muddy until I dry off naturally.

I am learning that speaking Spanish is prohibited in our school. If we are caught speaking Spanish, an older student is saying, we will get a whipping with a rubber hose from the school principal. This can't be so, I'm thinking. I love to speak Spanish just like my grandpa. In our villages, we have a beautiful language.

The Spanish we learned in our places developed from centuries of our Indigenous ancestors' languages influencing the local Spanish that we inherited in El Calaboz. My understanding is that our ancestors learned Spanish to trade with the Spaniards, to teach them local customs and ways, and sometimes to dispute with them when they neglected to follow the rules in our places and lands belonging to our people. The Spanish language we inherited from our Elders and the land and places where we are from is unique to our people's history, and to the villages that kept these Spanish language customs over generations as a way to survive. They learned to speak it from early Spanish colonists and military conquerors, and then they learned from priests, and from many peoples with diverse cultures—some who were Indigenous and others who were from Europe, but not Spaniards—who settled in our region over generations and were exposed to Spanish colonization. To this day, some speak a humble Spanish, similar to us.

From this Spanish brought here, we learned many words from other Indigenous peoples whom the Spaniards made relationships with, such as Nahuatl words, mixed into Spanish. These words became familiar to many of the Lipan Apache and Comanche ancestors here, because some of our Nahua ancestors, traveling to our area with the Spaniards long ago, spoke a Spanish that they learned from them as well. Through marriages between people of the villages of La Encantada, El Ranchito, Las Rusias, and Los Indios, over generations, the Indigenous words and phrases stayed alive and spread across the villages.

In this way, our ancestors with different Indigenous languages handed down a Spanish language that included many words and expressions from different Indigenous peoples and cultures. This makes El Calaboz and its sister rancherías special.

In the past, when Mexico dominated our region, before the United States had a presence here, Spanish became more required, and Indigenous languages were forbidden. Spanish here was given more weight than the Indigenous languages. Our Elders adapted to this. By the time of our generation, our Elders spoke our local Spanish, and if a person listens closely and for a long time, they will hear the many Indigenous words kept in the everyday speech of local *originario* (Native) peoples' spoken Spanish.

They spoke Spanish with their Indigenous words. It sounds beautiful to those of us from here. It is important to keep it alive to preserve our culture and history.

It will soon be lunchtime. I am hoping the ants have not gotten into my lunch bag, or I will simply not eat. It has happened before. Today we are lucky because it's a nice day out. We eat outside regardless of the weather. Somebody is telling me to make sure to hide the flour-tortilla tacos if a teacher approaches. I didn't know I had to feel ashamed of what I ate. Didn't everybody eat flour-tortilla tacos?

As early as third grade I knew I wanted to become a teacher someday. I am not happy with what goes on in my class. We have all been instructed on the correct way to ask permission to go to the bathroom. We must ask, "May I be excused?" Some students forget how to ask correctly and I hear them say, "May I go to the biz cuse?" The teacher is laughing instead of quietly and respectfully correcting them. This same teacher does not correct us if we use the wrong tenses or pronouns.

Skipping on to the fifth or sixth grade (1947–48) in my memory, I am seeing a great teacher, Miss La Madrid. Miss La Madrid is bringing us books that she checks out from a library in Brownsville, Texas. A lot of our teachers at Encantada School come from Brownsville. She brings the American classics, such as *Tom Sawyer* and *Huckleberry Finn, Uncle Tom's Cabin, Alice in Wonderland,* and many more. She allows us to check out the books to read at home. We have a time limit because she has to return the books after a certain time. I read as many as I can within that time. She is exposing us to poets such as Edgar Allan Poe and Alfred, Lord Tennyson, to name a few. She has us memorizing some of the poems; for example, the poem "Annabel Lee" by Edgar Allan Poe. I want to be a teacher like Miss La Madrid, I am thinking.

Encantada School offers classes from the first grade to the eighth grade. It is May of 1951, and I am graduating from Encantada School. I have just finished my eighth-grade class. There will be a ceremony to denote this accomplishment. All the eighth graders are dressing up. My dress is a beautiful white gown that a seamstress made for me. Dignitaries such as the Encantada School trustees and the San Benito School District superintendent are there. Speeches are being made. I myself am giving a speech, since I am the third honor student. It is nerve-wracking, but I am doing it. We as a graduating group are singing a song called "My Happiness." In 1954, Elvis Presley would record this song for his mother.

After graduating from Encantada School, I am now attending San Benito High School. I ride to school in a school bus. Some of the students there look down on me, not only because I'm so-called Mexican American, a strange and foreign term that we learned about as it was directed at us by authorities and the government, but also because I come from El Calaboz, a place with deep Indigenous history. I am not letting that worry me. My father's motto remains steadfast in my mind. He taught us not to allow those people to define us. His method provided a model of strength and resistance for my sister, me, and our many cousins. He taught us that we had to define ourselves, and to know history, geography, and political errors. He often said to authorities who went onto our lands without permission that "the border is a political line, not a cultural line." My father knew who he was. He insisted that we not be confused by them. I felt comforted by his teachings to not be afraid to correct the mistakes they made about our identity. The more the Anglos wanted what we had, the more I heard my father speak bravely on the subject of our land and our places.

Here's another memory: It is 1954 and I am a senior at Brownsville High. It is the second term and I am taking English literature. I am enjoying this class. We have just finished the chapter on medieval times. Our teacher has given us an assignment or project to be turned in in two weeks. She wants us to present an item related to what we just learned and also a write-up about our project. I go home that day and tell my parents all about the project and the fact that I have no idea what to do. My father wants to know all about the project. I tell him I have to construct an item related to medieval times. He says, "Let me see your book." He goes to the chapter I tell him and he starts reading through it. He tells me, "How about a carriage that they used to present plays." They used a carriage on wheels driven by horses and would travel around to present their plays. I tell him that that sounds good but I don't think I could build one. "No," he says, "but I can." So I jump at his suggestion, and then Mother says she can sew up a curtain. She gets very excited and adds that she saw some small dolls at Woolworth, where she works. She will also make little costumes for the dolls to match that era. My father works on the carriage and Mom on the costumes. She buys three dolls in all. Everything is looking so beautiful. I am working on the write-up. My dad says that I will have to paint the carriage. I tell him what colors I want and he gets them for me. Meanwhile Mom is all finished up with the dresses. Everything is coming together and looking beautiful. We glue the feet of the dolls onto the platform so they won't be falling all over the place as I take it to school on the due date. Needless to say, it's a big hit. I am sure the teacher knows I got help with the project. I get an A on both the written part and the physical project. The teacher kept my project, and now I regret not insisting that I wanted it back. Both my parents were always there to help. Education meant a lot to them. They would often read some of the textbooks I would bring home.

I graduate from high school in 1954. My grandmother is giving me a most beautiful watch.

Texas Southmost Junior College in Brownsville, Texas, is in my mind. I enroll for the summer session and then for the fall and spring semesters. Things are going well, but soon I must transfer to a four-year college. I enroll at Southwest Texas State in San Marcos, Texas. My father had been stationed at San Marcos at one point when he was in the Air Force. He would often speak of the college there. It is 1955 now. Some boys at

San Marcos are singing the song "South of the Border" and directing it toward my friends and me. We ignore them, and they soon stop. Because of financial reasons I do not return for the fall semester in 1956.

That summer of 1956, as I am figuring out my next step, I learn that the San Benito School District is experiencing a shortage of certified teachers. They are willing to hire college students without a degree. I apply and am hired right away. I am to teach second graders at Los Indios Elementary School. Los Indios is a village up the river to the west of El Calaboz. We have maternal ancestors and relations there. Like Encantada, it is a rural school not too far from where I live. It is my first day of class. I am somewhat scared. I am seeing my students looking at me with anticipation reflected on their little faces. They are telling me with their expressions that they are ready to learn. I am remembering my elementary school days and Miss La Madrid. I am telling myself, *You can do this.* I smile at my students and say, "Good morning, children, my name is Miss García. Welcome to second grade!"

There was never a doubt that I would return to college and get my teaching degree. It's December 23, 1956, and I am getting married. Two babies later, I have decided to go back to school. This time I am attending Pan American College in Edinburg, Texas. I attend classes on Monday nights, Saturday mornings, and summers. My husband is extremely supportive all this time. It is 1961, and I am receiving my degree in education.

It is now 1964. My husband and I are both teaching at the same elementary school, Garden Park, in Brownsville, Texas. It is after school and I am walking over to my husband's room so we can start going home. He is talking to an elderly man, a Mr. Peña. He lives around the area, and his grandson or great-grandson is in my husband's class. Mr. Peña is looking at me and is saying that I remind him of a relative of his that lives at El Calaboz. That relative is my grandmother Andrea. He is saying that my great-grandfather, José Cavazos, owned a lot of land at one time. "He slowly," he goes on, "lost a lot of his land due to the trickery of the Anglos." He says they were "talking him into" selling the land for much less than it was worth. I find myself asking him if he knows the origin of the name El Calaboz, since he mentioned that he had lived there a long time ago. He is telling us that many years ago there used to be a structure or house where prisoners were kept temporarily. These prisoners, caught by the Texas Rangers, were either Mexicans (meaning poor, displaced Indigenous people of Mexico) or Indians (meaning poor, displaced Indigenous people of Texas). Some of the prisoners, he says, would be killed on the spot. Those not killed would be transported to a jail in San Benito, Texas. He is saying that people would refer to the little village as the place that has a jail. Pretty soon, he is saying, people were just referring to the little village as El Calaboz. *Calaboz* is the Spanish word for jail, or dungeon. This story might not be the only one about El Calaboz, but it is the only version that makes sense to me. Sadly, Mr. Peña passes away before we have more conversations with him.

My teaching days were memorable on so many levels. It was the school year of 1978–79 and I was still teaching at Longoria Elementary. My son Bobby was a senior at Pace High School and a member of the Pace football team. The school colors were green and white. Every Friday, during the football season, I would wear something green. Unknown to me, I

FIGURE 1.2 Chata (Eloisa) and Paquita (María de Jesús) sharing a meal in El Calaboz, 2023. Photo by Rebecca María Tamez, Eloisa García Taméz archive collection.

was being observed by one of my second graders. Christmas came along and I received presents from some of my students. I loved their presents. Soon there was a knock on the door. It was a parent who was carrying a present. She called me outside and explained that her son had taken her all over town because the present just had to be green. He had told his mom that I loved the color green. I invited her in and opened the present. It was the most beautiful green crystal bell. It almost made me cry, but I couldn't show that I liked this present more than the other children's. I still have the bell.

So many memories. So many echoes.

I'm telling myself to always remember my ancestors, to be brave, strong, and unwavering. I am seeing that the sun is going down. Wally, my cat, is meowing. He is trying to tell me it's time to go inside because he is hungry. It will soon be *novela* time for me. I will leave you with one last thought in the form of a favorite poem of mine:

> I am bound to them,
> Though I can't look into
> Their eyes
> Or hear their voice.
> I honor their history.
> I cherish their lives.
> I will tell their story.
> I will remember them.
>
> —Author Unknown

NOTES

1. *Editors' note*: "Chata" is Eloisa García Taméz's nickname, which refers to the "flat" features of her face. "Chata" is a Spanish-Ndé creolization of *che'/chi'* + *ze*, derived from an older northeastern Dene word, *chizazé* (Denesų̂łį̂né) or *chíze* (Birch Narrows Dene), which refers to a cat or lynx with a flat face. The shortened "Chata/Chato" was not an uncommon Indigenous nickname throughout Apache territories before Indigenous peoples experienced forced, compulsory, assimilative domestication imposed by the White settler society, which displaced later generations further and further from living in close connection with the land, and, by virtue of the close connection, from the language they used when living as independent and nonsubjugated peoples. By the mid-twentieth century, nicknames reflected this generation's intimacy with older knowledge, lifeways, and language pathways. Historically, diverse cats, such

as ocelots, jaguarundis, bobcats, and mountain lions inhabited the Lower Rio Grande Valley. Eurocentric agrarian and settler-colonial extractive ecologies reduced their ranges, leading to declining numbers and scarcity.

2. *Editors' note*: A community member originally from the village of Las Rusias, and married into the village La Encantada, died of illness, starvation, and pellagra, a disease caused by a lack of niacin (vitamin B3) among Indigenous peoples with a traditional diet of maize when it was consumed with inadequate nixtamalization processing. Famine-like conditions prevailed during the 1915–16 U.S. military maneuver to the Lower Rio Grande Valley to address mass violence carried out by armed White settlers there. According to community oral history, U.S. military noninterference regarding settler violence against Indigenous peoples was the norm. Under siege-like conditions emanating from the murderous rampages of armed settlers, Indigenous resistance occurred on the north (Texas) and south (Mexico) banks of the river. Both armed and unarmed Indigenous people were forced to defend themselves against well-armed settler militias and the bystander U.S. military. Under these conditions, many did not have time to complete the necessary nixtamalization of their maize harvests. Mariana Montalvo Esparza (de Moctezuma), María de Jesús and Eloisa's maternal grandmother, died of pellagra during the 1915–19 waves of White terror targeting Indigenous lands along the Rio Grande River.

TWO

My Story

A Path to Self-Determination

ELOISA GARCÍA TAMÉZ

I returned to the Rio Grande Valley in August 1999 from an extended sick leave primarily related to the death of my spouse, and to the impacts of long-term employment as a nurse and years of service to the U.S. Army Nurse Corps.

Although my husband, Luis Carrasco Taméz Jr., passed away in 1996, while I was still the chief nurse executive at the Department of Veterans Affairs hospital in Cleveland, Ohio, the loss did not hit me until three years later. My limited energy was invested in my responsibilities and the work required of my position to ensure that the nursing department excelled in meeting accreditation requirements in the provision of optimal health care to our veterans. Once that was accomplished, grief settled in and landed like a rock.

In 1996, the nursing department staff and I were in the process of preparing for a hospital accreditation and focused on health care standards compliance. While the latter is met on a daily basis, what is often missed is the documentation of this important work. My mind and spirit were fully absorbed in tasks rather than attending to personal need. Once I accomplished that mission, there was a void. My personal need immediately filled that space. My energy level was nonexistent; my children and other relatives were distant; my only contacts were my colleagues from the United States Army Reserve Combat Support Hospital in Columbus, whom I saw once a month. This fellowship was significant, as there were individuals among the group with whom I could confide my innermost thoughts without prejudice. I no longer had that in my home on a daily basis.

My emotional stability and strength soon gave way, and I knew it was time to take care of myself. I retired from the Department of Veterans Affairs and returned to the Rio Grande Valley (southeastern Texas) to heal. Being closer to my children, my grandchildren, my mother, my sister, and other extended family members felt wonderful and peaceful.

I went back to El Calaboz, my birthplace, to once again inhabit a parcel of my ancestral land, the birthplace of countless generations. The days were pleasant; the quiet nights lulled my body to a restful sleep. I was back home reigniting relationships with my mother, sister, nieces, nephews, cousins. Spiritually, I was once again attending Mass at San Ignacio Catholic Church, where I had been baptized, confirmed, and married. I soon became involved in teaching catechism to the youth group preparing for confirmation. This took a lot of energy and preparation, which helped to sneak me out of a depression I was experiencing due to the loss of my husband and the giving up of a position caring for our veterans that I really enjoyed, as well as of my military assignment. The joy of teaching catechism thrust me further into healing and recovery, because the youth group was also responsible for incorporating a live portrayal of the appearance of Our Lady of Guadalupe on December 12 as well as one of the Passion during Holy Week. This produced great anxiety, as I have no skills in this field, but it also gave me the drive to produce an accurate and meaningful presentation for our Catholic community. What was most poignant, and still imprinted in my mind, was the faith people demonstrated during the portrayals: during Our Lady of Guadalupe's appearance, love and joy in the faces of the people; during the Passion, tears and sadness when Jesus was crucified. This is what the community living *en la orilla del Rio Grande* is all about.[1]

From Retiree to University Professor

On February 1, 2000, after I retired from the Department of Veterans Affairs and returned home, I sought employment with the University of

Texas–Pan American in the Department of Nursing as an assistant professor in the undergraduate program. In September 2004, I transferred to the University of Texas, Brownsville, as an associate professor of nursing and director of the Graduate Nursing Education Program.

Tamez v. Chertoff (2007)

El Calaboz is where I was born and raised. My father and grandfather were farmers and worked land to the Rio Grande River's edge. My mother, sister, and I would visit them in the field when we took them lunch and fresh water. My grandfather built a hutch, placing palm leaves on the roof for protection from rain and sun, and we would sit inside it while they ate their lunch. I was always looking for the ripened tomatoes, which I enjoyed right off the vine.

But how did this crop give fruit and provide nutrition for all of us? My father had a horse, a plow, and a set of goggles. To plant, he would use the horse and the plow and walk miles up and down planting seeds row after row after row. Then came the drawing of water (*riego*) from the Rio Grande for each row. He would do this at night when it was cooler. Once the plants begin to sprout, then the pests must be dealt with. That is when the goggles came into use.

How stressful it was to see my father come in from a day's work with his eyes red, burning, and in pain. He used a sack full of *azufre* and walked miles up and down each row in an effort to save the crops from the pests. While the goggles offered some protection, it was not enough, as the dust filtered through to his eyes. My mother would make a paste of *golondrina* and apply compresses over his eyes as treatment. The next day, my father was on the field again.

My father did not have money for major farm equipment or to buy pesticides to spray on the crops. He was never overweight. We had fresh, organic food from the vine and were unaware of it!

My grandfather and father sold crops but also shared and exchanged the harvest with our relatives and neighbors. That was life in El Calaboz.

As an adult, I would find out that my grandfather was a land protector and made sure that the property taxes were paid on time, even for properties belonging to my grandmother's siblings. He was shunned by the same for his indigeneity, although they were there to partake of the harvest and his generosity.

It was not long after I returned to El Calaboz that my life would change in ways that I never imagined. Memories of my childhood were threatened by a painful reality.

On August 7, 2007, while sitting at my desk at the University of Texas Brownsville, I received a phone call from Captain Cavazos, a Customs and Border Protection (CBP) agent. Given that my residence is off Camino Militar and about two miles from the Rio Grande, I was unprepared for his message.[2] My first thoughts were that there may have been some problem with my property, since the Border Patrol agents seemed to have occupied the levee, which bisected my property. CBP had converted it into a continuous-use area that resembled a highway, not a levee. In the process, CBP trespassed on my property numerous times, day and night. The levee in El Calaboz is a dense pile of soil that was built in 1936 as a barrier to protect the families from the floods of the Rio Grande. Importantly, the community members had a right-of-way agreement with the U.S. International Boundary and Water Commission. The land under the levee was the property of the community member-owner, never having been ceded or surrendered to the United States government under said agreement. In essence, the community landowners retained Indigenous title, which predated the United States and other successor states or governments of the colonial period.

Indeed, Captain Cavazos had quite a message. He first confirmed my identity as Eloisa Taméz and then he said, "I am calling because I need to inform you that your property is in the path of the plans to build the border fence. We need to let you know that we need to go into your property to conduct a survey."

I said, "I will not conduct business about my land over the phone."

As if he didn't or wouldn't hear me, he continued, "We need your authorization to enter your land."

I said, "Well, you do not have it."

To which Cavazos replied, "You do know about eminent domain."

I said, "Yes, I know about eminent domain, but I am still not conducting this type of business over the phone."

This parley was deeply shocking to me, so much so that I was shaking incessantly and my hands and body felt clammy as I hung up the receiver of my university office telephone.

I felt violated by having been pursued in this manner at my place of employment.

I immediately began to look for someone to talk to for consolation, as I felt threatened and helpless.

I was shaking, breathing rapidly, and at the point of tears.

While I had heard rumors about the building of a border wall, I never believed that it would happen. That reality was here and now. I was devastated.

The land that my parents and my predecessors knew, respected, related to, loved, and worked for our survival was now being sought by the United States government.

My thoughts took me back to just a few months back, when I woke up one morning to find that the fence my father had installed, years back, had been torn down. I went to talk to my *tía* Juanita next door to find out what happened.[3] She told me that the workers from the U.S. International Boundary and Water Commission (IBWC) had torn it down the day before, a Friday. Once again, I thought, the government is wanting to take more of our land. I began to put these two incidents together. They were connected. My tía witnessed the illegal trespassing and destruction of property.

This was frightening. My hopelessness and vulnerability increased!

As I began to think this through, I recalled that what the IBWC did to my property had not gone over well with me. I did not receive notice, nor did I have consultation, nor was free, prior, and informed consent performed. In fact, the very next Monday I called the local office and then the El Paso headquarters and proceeded to take care of business. The IBWC officials argued that they had a three-hundred-foot right-of-way, when my deed had a 1936 notation that the IBWC had a one-hundred-foot right-of-way. The IBWC representatives showed me a 1938 document with a three-hundred-foot notation that was not evident as an amendment in my official deed. I argued that the fence must be replaced immediately. I won that argument.

Remembering this incident gave me the resolve to stand up to the U.S. Department of Homeland Security (DHS) secretary Michael Chertoff with regard to the border wall construction issues in my community, our ancestral land-base. More generally I resolved, as a Lipan Apache woman and land title holder, to defend the rights of my community members to challenge the illegal actions and violations by the DHS and U.S. Congress that were taking place with the purpose of grabbing lands held by Indigenous American citizens in the affected area, and to help educate my community members, especially elder land title holders, to not be afraid to demand equal protection to defend their property against the unlawful processes that were unfolding. I was the first American citizen, and Native Indigenous American, to countersue the DHS, demanding full accountability for and protection against the government's violations of constitutional and civil law. Lipan Apache and related Indigenous peoples in our region have rights that need to be defended, not neglected as is the historical pattern.

After all, what about my human rights and my need to have an explanation as to the purpose of the border wall construction?

So, by the time I was contacted more than once by members of the United States Army Corps of Engineers, I was no longer shaking, having difficulty breathing, or feeling vulnerable. I stood fast and said I would not authorize the government's entry into my property.

Shifting the Terms of Engagement Regarding My Rights

Representatives of the U.S. Army Corps of Engineers (ACE) were involved in the border wall construction from the outset, under the authority of DHS secretary Michael Chertoff. Persistent and true to task, they tried more than once to get me to sign documents to allow them onto my property to conduct a survey. After I countersued Chertoff, they no longer could legally take actions on my property without my knowledge. The ACE wanted my authorization to come onto the property to dig holes and cut down trees and vegetation to determine if the land could withstand the structures planned. They brought equipment onto my land to do all this. According to their statements at the time, it might take a year. Or so the document read! I refused to sign it and was warned again that I would be sued. A letter arrived, dated December 7, 2007, indicating that I had thirty more days to make up my mind or I would be sued. I was sued.

I was summoned to the federal court in Brownsville, Texas, on February 7, 2008. That same day, DHS Secretary Chertoff was speaking at Harvard.[4] In informal remarks, he stated that people who were against the "border fence," as he called it, were militant and only interested in being able to take their cows to the Rio Grande. He got a good laugh on my account. On that same day, I was the only one going to court to address the DHS lawsuits against landowners, and I was the first landowner to take that step to challenge the construction of the "border wall," as I call it.

Due to the fact that Secretary Chertoff failed to allow the landowners consultation time, as the 2008 congressional appropriations bill required, Judge Andrew Hanen ordered the U.S. attorneys to award me that right and privilege. Several other landowners, facing the same loss of land, soon followed the court route.

I Will Not Be Silenced

Although I lost the case in the end—a case brought against me by Chertoff that was, according to legal experts, impossible to win due to the government's numerous manipulations and abuses of power—and the border wall was built across my property, I will not be silenced.

The U.S. government denied me equal protection, and denied this to other landowners of minority descent. According to a race and place spatial study conducted by Dr. Jeff Wilson, Indigenous, Hispanic, and Latinx landowners along the Rio Grande River had radically different experiences from those of landowners residing in the River Bend Resort or the Hunt Plantation along the Camino Militar. No border wall was built in those locations.

NOTES

1. This is a reference to the spirituality of the predominantly Indigenous peoples involved in the historical relationship with San Ignacio church, and their communal and collective experiences of love and joy, as well as tears and sadness, which are annually commemorated and embodied during Our Lady of Guadalupe celebrations. The representation of an Indigenous spiritual and emotional claiming of the Guadalupe signals the adherence to the underlying Nahua history and the deity Tonantzin. The local peoples' projection of Indigenous power upon the Virgin Mary as their Guadalupe of the Indigenous Americas has been

instrumental to Indigenous identity, culture, place, and resistance in El Calaboz and sister rancherías over centuries.

2. The historical significance of the Camino Militar (also known as U.S. Highway 281) to local Indigenous peoples of El Calaboz and related rancherías and Indigenous knowledge keepers along the Rio Grande River is embedded in oral history.
3. *Tía*: aunt, auntie.
4. Stephanie Schorow, "Security Chief Cautions Against Complacency," *The Harvard Gazette*, February 14, 2008, https://news.harvard.edu/gazette/story/2008/02/security-chief-cautions-against-complacency/. *Editors' note*: In his speech, entitled "Why Washington Doesn't Work," Secretary Chertoff uses defensive and politically charged anti-"terrorist" (implied to be a reference to the Islamic world) rhetoric, in defense of building support for purported demands for increased security on the border. Schorow states, "If Michael Chertoff, secretary of the U.S. Department of Homeland Security, was politically wounded by his department's response to Hurricane Katrina, he showed no sign of it during his forceful lecture Feb. 6 at the Kennedy School of Government. Chertoff, a graduate of Harvard College (1975) and Harvard Law School (1978), defended efforts to correctly access and manage the risk of terrorism and other security threats and to move forward with long-term policies that may be unpopular in the short term. In a public address provocatively titled 'Why Washington Doesn't Work' for the Albert H. Gordon Lecture on Finance and Public Policy, Chertoff outlined what he called 'structural obstacles' to improved homeland security." Undoubtedly, Eloisa G. Taméz's countersuit against him stirred up important questions, as well as a counterintuitive Indigenous logic that challenged Chertoff's claims that Americans were complacent about homeland security issues. *Tamez v. Chertoff* reframed "homeland" and "security" firmly within Indigenous decolonial subjectivity and historical memory.

THREE

Ndé Peoples' Resistance Against the U.S. Separation Wall, Dispossession, and Settler-Colonial Erasure

Place, Memory, Rights, and Self-Determination

MARGO TAMEZ

How Are Ndé Doing? We Decide

During the El Calaboz Gathering on Ndé Knowledge, Lands, Self-Determination, and Human Rights on June 24–26, 2011, I witnessed, heard, and voiced deep commitment to continuing the intergenerational advocacy for the recognition of Ndé rights to resist against all forms of organized and state-sanctioned violence. This gathering occurred in response to Eloisa García Taméz's call for an Indigenous-led dialogue in El Calaboz village focusing on Indigenous lands and self-determination.[1] Working with her to create a framework and invitation for the gathering based on her concerns, issues, and key words, we drafted a call prioritizing the knowledge of Indigenous peoples from the Rio Grande River region of the Texas-Mexico bifurcated area where the government constructed the wall. Attending to her goal of building relationships and exchanging knowledge across Indigenous places and historical experiences, we welcomed Indigenous people from throughout the borderlands and beyond who were resisting militarization, racism, and settler-colonial exploitation of their lands and traditions.

Eloisa sought to gain a comparative perspective on the contested border from people all along its length, understanding that there is diversity across the region and that there would most likely be myriad Indigenous experiences in other border sectors. She hoped to bring knowledge and perspectives as gifts and tools to her community in El Calaboz and her extensive kinship community across the old villages in her region. In addition, she sought to create a space of hospitality and reciprocity for storytelling, for memory, for relationship building, for difference and respectful dialogue, for sharing, and for acknowledgment between Indigenous peoples with related histories of multiple levels of colonization by Spain, Mexico, settler territories, settler confederacies, and settler states and nations. She also desired to make a welcome space for connection and dialogue between Indigenous peoples and the legal, academic, activist, and community-based supporters of her federal and international cases challenging the U.S. separation border wall, known nationally as "the border fence."[2] The gathering constructed an independent Indigenous justice space to voice and hear perspectives on truth, experience, memory, knowledge, testimony, aspirations, law, and decision-making that no other mechanism—national or international—provided. The gathering served to build coherence and unity of thought and action in geopolitical spaces that have long separated Indigenous agency in diverse bifurcated communities from decision-making and relevant recognition of the many consequences of ignoring the impacts of successive dispossessions.

We sought a consensus on Indigenous perspectives on settler-colonial violations of the international human rights of Indigenous peoples, and how this could facilitate understandings, education, collaboration, and strengthening of Indigenous self-determination. Unlike the emphasis in many settler institutional meetings and conferences related to Indigenous peoples, which spend exorbitant resources, this gathering stemmed from a foundational epistemological question: *How are Ndé and related Indigenous peoples doing?* That is, anti–separation wall land protectors and human rights protectors resisted the imposed isolation and obfuscation of the struggle we experienced, and instead of sinking into the despair imposed by trolling and extremist media aggression, Ndé women invited testimonies that would share our feelings, our modes of coping and surviving, the stories our bodies tell, the mental and emotional processing after the "event" of construction passed, and the experience of living in "the shadow of the wall."[3] As two leaders respected in our community, as Ndé academics, and as two generations of Ndé women enacting self-determination, Eloisa and I experienced violence connected to our ancestors' refusals. We had been wounded severely. And it took some time for us to heal, in our own ways, from the day neither of us will ever forget—the day Michael Chertoff took our land, to symbolically claim a "victory" in the entire issue of the two-year standoff, and built the wall despite a U.S. federal court's order to pause for an Ndé consultation.

We were honored by a small yet dedicated and committed group who gathered together with our family and small community of land protectors, and who sustained commitment to our struggle. This became vital to sustaining our vision and purpose, especially in light of the reality that a large, vocal, and powerful sector of U.S. society was positioned strongly in opposition to our stand to protect our land, property, civil rights, constitutional rights, and human rights. We experienced harassment, intimidation tactics, threats, stalking, and other forms of social violence intended to silence and stop us. As Indigenous people from a region of the hemisphere in which our ancestors' history of anticolonial struggle against the opposing European monarchy goes back farther than our history with the Texans and Americans, and from a homeland historically divided up by Mexico, Texas, and the United States, we have been peripheralized by many social justice and Indigenous rights movements and land claims processes in (what has come to be known as) North America. Lipan Apaches are dangerously marginalized by the three geopolitical forces that occupy our lands. Therefore, other than the group who gathered together with us in El Calaboz initially, most people, including many Indigenous peoples, sadly, kept their distance—physical and social—from our movement centering Ndéness (Lipan Apacheness). Nonetheless, by establishing an Ndé-focused platform for many complex community-wide issues we disrupted the long-standing suppressive environment imposed upon Ndé families and communities. We shattered a long-standing, deeply conditioned expectation in many settler and Indigenous circles in and outside Texas that Ndé peoples were peripheral, disorganized, and nothing to be concerned about in terms of land claims and Indigenous title action. Our insistence on protecting our remaining lands and drawing attention to Lipan Apache lands held by unceded Aboriginal title, after centuries of dispossession, came to a head in El Calaboz between 2007 and 2011. The relatively swift pace and forthrightness of our movement took many by surprise at the regional, national, and international levels. At the core of the movement was the struggle to center our ancestors' teachings on prioritizing and defending our innate value and health as human beings and as a people. While millions advocated for crushing the Ndé women's land movement and for vilifying and suppressing Lipan Apache presence, we valued our lives, our health, and the future of our people, land, and water. We asked how we were faring under U.S. imperialism, militarization, and unredressed violations by Texas and the United States of our ancestral rights to existence and identity with our lands. We asked how we were feeling about ongoing dispossession as a global network of military contractors lined up to enact land theft and the depopulation of us by means of forced displacement under the guise of the war on terror. We asked, "How are we?" While we insisted on centering how we are doing, I understood that this disturbed and unsettled many people. I learned that so much resistance to us demonstrated that these people believed that we—as surviving Lipan Apaches, the Ndé of Kónìcą̀ą̀hį́į́ Gòkíyàà (Big Water Country)—did not have value, nor the right to defend ourselves against their attempts to extinguish our Indigenous identity, place, belonging, and human dignity.

In the four years between the *Tamez v. Chertoff* lawsuit and the Gathering in El Calaboz, several processes converged that threatened Indigenous peoples' exercise of universal human rights. The intensification of extremist, nationalist rhetoric in favor of building a wall emboldened far-right groups in their real threats and endangerment of Indigenous peoples enacting self-defense against mass land seizures and dispossession. The U.S. government's enforcement of the Secure Fence Act of 2006 instituted a guise of legal authority that extended to the creation of an impunity zone in which it used the cover of sovereign immunity to enact questionable and controversial suppressions of civil, constitutional, and international rights of Indigenous landowners in El Calaboz and other sectors of the Rio Grande River. Denise Gilman has argued that the goal of international human rights law has been "protecting individuals from abuse by the government."[4] When the government granted itself immunity from liability, thus generating an independent state of impunity in the walled zone, this cemented the atmosphere of what Denise Gilman refers to as "unacceptable limitations on human rights."[5]

The state worked to protect itself from legitimate litigation (domestic and international) brought forward by *Tamez v. Chertoff*, and it used tactical narrative warfare—the strategic use of stories and narratives to influence public opinion in order to maintain a specific agenda and goals, in this case related to the corporate economy of military weaponry contracting. The wall was a carceral and punitive weapon that directly impacted Indigenous peoples' lands, cultures, identities, movement, subsistence, and livelihoods. Unsurprisingly, the state apparatus manufactured the old trope of American exceptionalism—that is, the idea that the American state's use of violence and its deployment of sovereign immunity is unquestionable, above criticism, and beyond the reach of law. The use of American exceptionalism to impose a separation wall in unceded Indigenous lands was cloaked in typical heroic and mythic renderings of American righteousness, virtue, and moral superiority. When deployed, the narrative war was a component in a bundle of weapons used to shape the public's cognitive perception in order to convince them to accept and support policies that may not otherwise have been accepted on moral grounds. Importantly, American exceptionalist tropes often posit the threat of an enemy other. Lipan Apaches and Mexican peoples have both been historically defined this way in the U.S. settler-colonial place-making and border-making projects. This weaponization of the enemy other has been deployed so that it is now normalized in the American psyche, and this supports the governing elites' primary aim to purposefully manipulate how the U.S. domestic population makes sense of the world—a significant aim of narrative warfare. This system operated to justify the state's en-masse human rights violations against Indigenous land-title holders along the Rio Grande River and the state-sanctioned impunity zone along the wall that was conducted and operationalized, under the guise of American immunity, to cover up these human rights violations, specifically those in El Calaboz, where Indigenous peoples physically and legally challenged the state's authority to forcibly dispossess, displace, remove, contain, restrain, separate, and commit acts of terror against them. Thus, through the guise of American exceptionalist tropes, the myth of state immunity mobilized the low-intensity conflict narrative war and the creation of state impunity on the ground, all of which operated to thwart Eloisa Taméz's resistance and to quash—through any means—the movement's popular local, national, and international support.

The Secure Fence Act sanctioned and mobilized the widespread low-intensity conflict methods undertaken by Department of Homeland Security, U.S. Army, and U.S. Customs and Border Protection personnel to steal our Indigenous community's lands. Mass psychological and demonization campaigns deployed against those who refused to surrender their lands were normalized by government officials and modeled by Michael Chertoff, secretary of homeland security. These effectively enabled widespread permissiveness across U.S. society toward participation in aggressive dehumanization campaigns imposed upon all non-White and Spanish-surnamed people of the Rio Grande River sector. This was calculated to impact the social behavior of families, clans, bands, tribes, friends, acquaintances, businesses, peers, and co-workers, causing them to distance themselves from the Indigenous land protectors / wall resisters. The government's underhandedness in its planning related to the wall construction was calculated to instill chaos. In turn, this increased the scale of stressors that frontline Indigenous people experienced. Official government descriptions of them as unpatriotic traitors to the nation normalized a widespread passive consent to and condoning of Indigenous peoples' dispossession in El Calaboz. This left El Calaboz enclosed and separated from its community members and lands on the south side of the wall—which was a mile inland from the U.S.-Mexico border. These factors encouraged us to gather together, discuss, and decide how to transition into new forms of resistance and determination to confront the colonial violence, grief, loss, and trauma unleashed upon the Rio Grande River peoples.

We Remain

Ndé (Lipan Apaches) are peoples with ancient connections to *neegosdzan*—mother earth—and to Kónìcą̀ą̀hį́į́ Gòkíyàà—the Big Water Country (also referred to as the Rio Grande or Río Bravo region).[6] We have deep-time relations with many Indigenous peoples, from the sub-Arctic to northern Mexico. The peoples of and from Kónìcą̀ą̀hį́į́ Gòkíyàà, the lands and territories bifurcated by the Texas-Mexico boundary and border wall, conceptualize identity within a pluri-Indigenous relational, temporal, and spatial transhistorical reality where a complex knowledge system of many peoples was always dynamic. We had a well-organized system of stories and experiences that was well understood by our forebears. Ndé deep-time history and herstory has encompassed place-based and intergenerational knowledge systems that created intersections between and shaped our relationships with all living beings and systems on earth and in the cosmos. Ndé are significant actors, throughout centuries of European colonial archives of conquest and domination, in relation to Ndé independence, self-determination, and methodologies of territorial protection and defense. European monarchies, empires, republics, confederacies, nations, and states have attempted to subjugate Ndé peoples, to sever us from our inherent and inalienable personhood as a nation of bands, tribes, and clans, and to convert us into a minoritized and fourth-class "ethnic" group. None of the above entities have legally severed us from our identity as a people with a land.

While collaborating with Denise Gilman, who led the University of Texas School of Law Working Group on Human Rights, we addressed the Indigenous principles that shape the legal frameworks to analyze the border wall and its impact on Ndé people of and from villages along the Texas-Mexico border. At the heart of the matter, Indigenous resistance to and legal actions against the U.S. border wall are connected to the long-standing Ndé commitment to the protection of Ndé people. Moreover, we are concerned with the Ndé inherent rights to protect and defend Ndé unceded lands as Indigenous collective land. Ndé territories are filled with stories, memory, heritage sites, holy sites, language, and cosmologies of the Ndé and related Indigenous peoples. Ndé resistance against imperial, colonial, and settler-colonial dispossession predates the U.S. border wall, as does the long struggle of Ndé peoples against multiple mechanisms of erasure, propaganda, and disinformation. This repression has been structured systemically within Texas and the United States with the intention of instilling forgetting among the beneficiaries—the settler-colonial society.

These principles—the rights of Indigenous peoples to protect and defend ourselves against dispossession, forced displacement, physical separation, erasure, and cultural and heritage destruction—are informed and guided by Ndé women's epistemologies, which shape Ndé denunciations of the wall, refusals, and resistance. Through in-depth, community-led investigations into Ndé Indigenous title and rights, legal mechanisms such as colonial land grants, treaties, and agreements, and Ndé social, cultural, religious, environmental, economic, and political memory, we have revitalized community pedagogies. These are embodied and place-based teachings, practices, philosophies, and laws. We collectively received these from Elders and share them with our relatives.

Indigenous participatory action research, in solidarity with Ndé community members, enacted self-determination as "localized critical theory," "sites of resistance and empowerment," and "resistance and struggle at the local level."[7] Places of Ndé resistance along the border wall brought to light personal and collective narratives and decolonial counternarratives of a history of dispossession that was unknown by civil society, erased by settler government systems, and disputed by many U.S. citizens. Furthermore, Ndé decolonial history and archaeology are underexamined in academic research in the region, nationally, and internationally in Canada and Mexico, where Ndé have ancestral, linguistic, cultural heritage, geographic, and religious connections.

Working against the historical narratives produced by South Texas ranching, petrochemical, and uranium-mining regimes, which are interconnected with the settler capitalist military defense industry, the Ndé and our allies were not surprised by how they marginalized and erased our histories. Despite this erasure, segments of the federal government had to acknowledge our presence in the region. The "Native American Cultural Affiliation Overview" of the U.S. Army Corps of Engineers acknowledges the Lipan Apache as a "federally unrecognized indigenous group," and, as predicted by Ndé Elders and knowledge keepers, the U.S. Army Corps of Engineers' environmental impact assessment "makes the Lipan Apache identity of property owners in the Lower Rio Grande Valley and Coastal Bend region invisible."[8] The U.S. denial of the political personhood and the continuing existence of Lipan Apaches in Texas history is intrinsically tied to the political economy of entrenched settler coloniality occupying Ndé territory, which has been described as ethnic cleansing manifesting in the form of genocidal sprees, mass killing fields, the threat of genocide, and extreme genocidal intolerance against Indigenous peoples throughout Texas.[9]

Ndé Valuing How Things Really Are

Ndé axiology emphasizes how things are in real time. As human beings, Ndé have the intelligence and capacity to process knowledge of the past, present, and future simultaneously. To understand the value that Ndé people placed on Eloisa's and my resistance against dispossession and dehumanization is to consider the value that Ndé people place on knowing how things really are for those who live in and belong to Ndé customary places under settler-colonial rule. Ndé have experienced domination and assimilation for generations, yet, in spite of these forces working to crush our spirits and our culture, we still value our own definitions and descriptions of how things are, and are confident that these are grounded in embodied knowledge and emotional intelligence.

Ndé people value defining ourselves, and we know the power and strength this brings, allowing us to uphold our integrity on a daily basis. Ndé have been taught that valuing ourselves—a self-preserving act of defiance against coloniality—is a necessary form of resistance against colonial and settler-colonial violence, dehumanization, land theft, marginalization, and erasure, all of which stresses the continual devaluing of the Ndé. Ndé people defy the colonial government and anti-Ndé society by valuing Ndé women's insistence on walking with dignity in the struggle against the separation wall. The women's approach centers the struggles of Indigenous women in walled lands and places against systemic injustice, violence, and oppression. Ndé women's struggle against the separation wall confronts historical patriarchy, colonialism, land theft, environmental destruction, racism, discrimination, gender oppression, sexual violence and misogyny, Two-Spirit phobia, nonrecognition, political violence, treaties and land grants, and Indigenous title. Ndé women's critiques of separation walls include a critical carceral lens that values and valorizes Ndé diversity as a contemporary component of Ndé historical solidarity struggles alongside other Indigenous peoples and racialized groups. This carceral lens recognizes the distinct factors of Spanish colonization, Texas settler colonialism, Mexicanization, U.S. militarism, Indigenous geopolitics of place and race, and familial, physical, emotional, psychosocial, and spatial proximity to the Lower Rio Grande River. These constituent details have saturated the carcerality that is an everyday experience of Ndé peoples, who have been the objects of colonial surveillance and persecution for centuries on the basis of culture, race, religion, and an Indigenous political status that has never been addressed formally by any of the state parties. Ndé women extend the carceral lens into bordered and walled understandings of Ndé beingness in the Lower

Rio Grande River region, which can be expressed as, and is often viewed as, the antithesis of traditional, customary, and expected expressions of Apache womanhood and identity as reified in Apache federally recognized communities, as well as in Apache communities in Texas that are geospatially located inland from the Rio Grande River and the walled lands. All of these concerns are instrumental to Ndé people's ongoing decolonization. Ndé women weave these strands into our wall resistance and our confrontation of state violence against us. Ndé people place significance on Ndé women's actions to reestablish grounded community law systems that allow Ndé people to gather together safely, make sound decisions together, and reclaim our unity over the instability, crisis, and oppressive conditions of settler-colonial systems that are deeply invested in the interlocking global genocide and military for-profit industry. In the walled lands, Ndé women from El Calaboz, as Rio Grande River people, have an inherent right to value the prevention of further harms from the oppressive and morally bankrupt settler economic system, and to be valued for taking direct action based on our understanding of who we are, our worth, and our identity in our lands.

Our efforts to foreground Ndé existence and the right to be are a response to the historical and ongoing devaluing of Ndé women by the U.S. government, by the 109th Congress, which passed the Secure Fence Act, and by the U.S. DHS, CBP, and Army Corps of Engineers, which physically carried out an armed operation to dispossess and silence Eloisa and other Indigenous and racialized wall refusers. The colonizer society's disinterest in meaningfully addressing Ndé women's dignified land protection and resistance against the wall and against dispossession is manifested in the unipolar consciousness of the American psyche. This condition actively suppresses the freedom of speech, assembly, and press of Ndé and related land protectors and human rights defenders, who enact a pluri-legal, pluripolitical, and multipolar worldview. The unipolar consciousness was evident in the numerous speeches Michael Chertoff delivered at American Ivy League universities that defamed Eloisa's refusal to permit the United States to take her ancestral lands and to build a separation wall through the middle of her property. Her rebuttal and countersuit were received by Chertoff and the American conservative, far, and ultra-right as an assault on American democracy. The hardened anti-Indigenous bias in the American unipolar consciousness carried an implied response: *How dare she, the peon? the savage!* Challenging this dehumanizing rhetoric, Ndé decided to center voices of diverse Indigenous peoples of the Rio Grande Valley in the Ndé struggle and legal processes. This antihegemonic, decolonial narrative rested on Ndé knowledge, research, and production, which was and is foundational for addressing international human rights violations against Ndé and redressing historical wrongs, including ethnic cleansing and genocide, which are intimately tied to how settlers constructed and normalized borders, border peoples, and the border wall as acts of Indigenous erasure. Ndé women had stories and underlying hidden histories that revealed how things really are.

Ndé Have Deep Knowledge of a Deep-Time Story of Resistance and Proud Land Defense

Ndé Indigenous peoples of the lands violated by the illegal enactment of sovereign immunity and international impunity for the U.S. border wall construction, dispossession, and destruction of cultural heritage confront the presence and influence of older Spanish colonial institutions and systems. In southern Texas, the present-day law system is built upon and intricately embedded in the eighteenth-century colonial land tenure and water rights that the Spanish imposed upon the precolonial Indigenous customary uses and practices. There are remnants of these systems—the Spanish and the Indigenous—still existing in El Calaboz and sister communities along the Rio Grande. These rights to customary use and practices in the small and vulnerable rancherías are quite valuable. As a result, the communities have been affected directly by the anti-Indigenous, vigilante-style repression that has occurred over generations with the purpose of acquiring their lands along the Rio Grande. The current layers of technology contracted to and constructed by Israeli military manufacturers, which perform both surveillance and assimilation of the U.S.-Mexico border region into a global network of militarization, are iterative in that they build upon nearly two hundred years of intensive Texas settler ecologies of barbed wire and checkpoints. An always vigilant and focused settler Texas is heavily invested in border militarization, checkpoint systems, and racial policing throughout South

Texas and the Lower Rio Grande Valley. Indigenous peoples affected by the separation wall are immersed in the omnipresent and dystopic U.S. militarization apparatus separating the Brown and Indigenous poor from White people (of the United States and Canada, predominantly), who largely are not socially, physically, economically, culturally, or politically impacted by the wall in the ways Indigenous peoples of the Rio Grande River region are.

Despite the impacts of these destructive processes, Ndé epistemology continues informing the actions and perspectives of people seeking justice. This epistemology is a fusion of oral history and a shifting oral tradition among the Ndé peoples of the Rio Grande River, which not only includes an oral tradition of warriors and protectors in Ndé antiquity, colonial periods, and the Texas and U.S. periods, but also has transitioned into new conceptualizations of history. These conceptualizations stress attention to Ndé history transcending millennia, with emphasis on cosmology, metaphysics, poetics, and law. They emphasize Ndé reclamations of place and time beyond American and Texan borders. They place the colonizing entities in a larger Ndé temporal and spatial construction that puts primacy on Ndé relationships, cycles, and understandings rather than on linear chronologies stripped of Ndé people. They foreground Ndé reconstructions of genocidal violence that transcend traditional Western chronologies and periodizations. And this, with hegemonic Spanish colonialism (Hispanicism) ongoing, has radically changed Ndé life on the land. The church's presence in the communities, representing dire impositions upon ancestral Indigenous people as well as strategic decisions they made under conditions of persecution, can be a painfully conflicting reminder of significant quantities of stolen Ndé lands predating the American and Texas land thefts.

Paradoxically, it is the Ndé people's epistemology of how settler knowledge systems are used to legitimize dispossession and Indigenous erasure in the context of settler colonialism in Ndé lands that is in a dialectical encounter with Ndé peoples' epistemology of our confrontation with settler society's suppression of our knowledge. At the same time, the settler society and state were unable to quash the Ndé ethos of belonging, remaining, and returning to our separated lands on the other side of the wall. At the root of Indigenous land-based authority, it was never in question who has the authority to directly confront the state apparatus and ongoing forms of land theft: the women title holders do. Indigenous erasure is the process through which the state and settlers obfuscate these realities. This puts the American public's idea of "Apaches" living on a U.S. federal Indian reservation in an antithetical encounter with Ndé women and their title to ancestral lands, never enclosed in the state's recognition and federal lands apparatus, in which a history of refusals of the carceral enclosure of their lands (such as reservations, camps, prisons, checkpoints, detention, walls) and refusals to leave their lands underscores the resistance to the wall. Ndé women seek to deromanticize and decolonize resistance that is required against settler legal and material capture. On a spiritual and physical level, we seek decolonial *redress,* while crucially rejecting the meanings underlying representations of the traditional Apache women's *camp dress,* which I have previously analyzed as a historical by-product of American seizure, imprisonment, and thingification of Apache women, and which has also been reclaimed by Apache women as a visual and physical symbol of cultural survival and resilience.[10] However, from my positionality under the separation wall's presence, and as a member of a people who never have been enclosed in the legal subordination regimes of U.S. federal recognition, I have stressed Ndé women's physical and visual deconstruction of the camp dress. I have deconstructed the camp dress through poetic and intertextual visual resistance to the state's violence against Eloisa, me, and many other Indigenous women along the Rio Grande River who never had the opportunity to voice their dissent.

Thus, the Ndé standpoint and positionality, which is in many ways an element of Ndé protocols of respectful and relational engagement, is a crucial act of self-determination, rejecting centuries of dismal and demeaning tropes of the colonizer's "Lipan Apache" and making a continuing claim of self-definition and refusal to be misdefined by the colonizer society and its government. This then leads to Ndé claiming multiple platforms to discuss the divides in terms of access to resources between academic institutions and the collaborative partnerships of Indigenous researchers and affected Ndé peoples engaged in land protection and human rights defense. The above is and has been inseparable from the broader Indigenous and specific Ndé anti–border wall social movement in response to the human rights crisis that has unfolded. Thus, the Ndé epistemology founded in the historically specific memory, history, herstory, politics, and economic analysis within the community has been censored by settler mythologies and mythohistorical public education.

Ndé epistemology of the reutilization of the land-based resistance of previous generations informed an Ndé women-led politics of resistance. Research into the family and community archives of land title and tenure, and the previous attempts by colonial and settler governments and groups to covertly or overtly expropriate their lands, informed the Ndé refusals and resistance strategies against the present, reoccurring land grab attempt by the federal government. The state-sanctioned violence trumpeted by the state-aligned media and the state's uses of the border policing apparatus to impose the separation wall upon Indigenous title holders had precedents in the affected communities. There is abundant community oral history of the people's many encounters with attempts by White settlers to coerce them into relinquishing their lands, to deceptively manipulate them to sell their lands, or to outright take their lands forcibly. This transgenerational knowledge informed me about how Indigenous peoples owned *porciones* in the Indigenous rancherías, and this became a significant component of my doctoral study to establish an Indigenous-focused river heritage database. Working alongside Eloisa and related female Elders, we became critically aware that the Ndé women's multifaceted and multilevel resistance was motivated by a rich history of Indigenous women's resourceful resistance to these aggressions, and their legacy was a source of motivation for other Rio Grande River communities as well. As I took the case to international legal spaces, this component resonated strongly with many Indigenous peoples in the Global South (West Asia, Latin America, Africa, Asia). We are aware that Ndé women have motivated Ndé people to confront, disarm, and debunk settler discourses, propaganda, and disinformation—and to detect and monitor the subversion tactics of Indigenous people who are aligned with and collaborate with the state, media, and extractive economic interests, or who are aligned with the disinformation wars in their attempt to delegitimize the autonomous ("nonrecognized") Indigenous peoples' movements, and who either wittingly or unwittingly facilitate settler colonialism, state violence, and genocidal policies against Ndé people. Ndé women land protectors and human rights defenders created a different praxis drawing on the cultural and physical politics of place and violence, the maintenance of the liberation oratory of the oppressed over time, and the persistence of agency over generations. According to Denzin, Lincoln, and Smith, "There is an emphasis on critiques of ideology and the development of counterhegemonic forms of discourse and praxis, as well as theories of resistance that presume the historicity of knowledge."[11] The El Calaboz Ranchería, Rio Grande River counterhegemonic discursive praxis apparently is perceived as unsettling to the normalized political relations between U.S.-recognized tribes and the United States. The El Calaboz Ranchería praxis has drawn the United States into a distinct and different set of politics that concerns autonomous and diverse Indigenous peoples in Indigenous lands the United States has never truly "conquered"—that is, expropriated as U.S. property. Such is the case of the Ndé, with radically different historical and legal paths and different political directions being brought to bear on the United States by Ndé women. These Indigenous transitions cannot be erased in the current digital, live-streamed dynamic in which international legal systems are crumbling under the pressure brought by contemporary forms of Indigenous struggle against *all* forms of oppression. In this transition, departing from the normalized, hegemonic, unipolar, Cold-War-esque U.S.(-recognized) Indian monolith, Indigenous peoples still independent of that hegemon must expose all groups participating in, benefiting from, and in alignment with oppression and dispossession of Ndé of the Rio Grande River.

Eloisa Confronted Chertoff, Shattering an American Myth That Men with "Supreme" Power Are Beyond Reach

In 2007, Eloisa García Taméz countersued Michael Chertoff, the secretary of the U.S. Department of Homeland Security, as well as the U.S. Army Corps of Engineers and U.S. Customs and Border Protection. Her case highlighted Ndé peoples' multigenerational struggles to refute and correct settler ignorance about and domination of Indigenous peoples in lands occupied by European settlers in the U.S. South. Behind the scenes when preparing the case, Eloisa, the case support team members, and I expressed frustrations, anger, conflicted feelings, and concerns that the U.S. court system—literally the court of the settler nation and settler state oppressor government—was an illegitimate venue. On the one hand, we felt it was one of the few tools at our disposal—to take Chertoff et al. to court, to contest the wall's legality in U.S. federal law and the human rights violations occurring. But on the other hand, we did not feel much hope that this court would give us justice.

Fearing a miscarriage of justice, Eloisa pursued her case at the international level. Her case in the international legal system was simultaneous with and parallel to the U.S. federal process. It is in international legal spaces that her legal personhood, as an Ndé with inherent personhood within the collective peoplehood, has become a central and groundbreaking facet of the case. In 2008, at the Inter-American Commission on Human Rights of the Organization of American States and at the United Nations, Ndé began documenting human rights violations, land title history, oral history, traditional knowledge, and Indigenous land protection against armed settlers and paramilitary groups, and petitioning international human rights systems against colonizing European monarchs and their settler nations, republics, and states. The U.S. court process made us feel anxious and defensive. The Western legal tradition's positive-law emphasis on "individual" harm and "property" ensured that the history of Ndé Indigenous rights and title would be censored and silenced. In *Tamez v. Chertoff* (2008), the Ndé aimed to challenge U.S. dispossession and the separation wall, to educate attorneys and judges, and to enact a decolonization process.[12]

The legal struggle at the national and international level brought many Ndé community members into contact with new concepts, obstacles, frustrations, and systems that had, in effect, been normalized over time. They may not have "seen" them, but they understood and experienced them. The majority of Ndé are from low-income, working-class backgrounds, and decolonization is somewhat of a new term in the grassroots. It is often an academic term that still does not quite reflect the enormity and complexity of the Indigenous peoples that the United States and Mexico subjugated and separated from Indigenous title and rights but did not assimilate or integrate into the federal sovereignty system—that is, federal recognition. The hostility and aggression by the United States against one Ndé plaintiff and her legal team have brought vicious and violent attacks, coercion, and manipulation in an attempt to fracture and divide the people. It was extremely difficult, but it didn't defeat Eloisa. It made her more determined.

Ndé and Rio Grande River Peoples Value Ndé Women Who Confronted Harmful Forces

Ndé peoples dealing with systemic settler-colonial policing welcomed the renewed possibility for global understanding of and support for Ndé women refusing and resisting violent U.S. state power in their homelands. I believe that what Eloisa, the Ndé people, and I have been recognizing is the way Ndé women's resistance demonstrates that in each generation the average Ndé person must become involved with recovering and reclaiming Ndé autonomy and decision-making. This maintains and retains Ndéness. And we have breathed new life into Ndéness so that it is neither a replica nor an artifact of our ancestors and the past resistances. This movement is not reshaping the past; rather, it is shaping the present and the future. Ndéness in the U.S. anti-Indigenous settler-colonial separation wall period and our beingness are intricately co-constitutive. What this means is that, as the Ndé liberation struggle continues, it is Eloisa and a very small cohort of Ndé people like me who understand that Ndé women can resist the colonial and settler-colonial oppressor, the occupier, the destroyer of life.

How are we doing? Are we allowed to grieve yet? Ndé anticolonial struggles encourage us to see and feel the fundamental beingness and complexity of Ndé women resisting violent reoccupation. We are daughters and granddaughters of people who repelled settler-colonial violence in the nineteenth and twentieth centuries. This hasn't stopped. Our genealogical strands of resistance have shaped this precise moment in which our ancestors' rage and disappointment calls me in. On some level, Ndé women take up our roles in the present, with all their complexity, and I must wonder if (and hope that) the ancestors' grief is being alleviated as we reconnect with their stories, challenges, activism, and knowledge. The colonization of our ancestors and intergenerational trauma inform Ndé women's resistance. Different forms of grief and soul suffering affect how we view, accept, and transform Ndéness in the shadow of the wall. In other words, I have accepted wholeheartedly that my Ndéness as a walled human being is immutable and silenced, is antithetical and othered, is dialectical and abjected. I am a monster slayer, but those who are disturbed by my form of Ndéness think I'm the transgressive monster. While we feel it has been important to be steadfast through the long struggle for justice, the wall instills a type of gulag time of disposability and thingification. In the walled region, there is no warden and no end date for release. There is no adjudicator or review board for appeal. A walled system instills in human beings a clear sense of separateness, difference, and counterexistence. Our healing is a lengthy process with no real sense of resolution; and so our trauma, rage, and pain transfer to the next generation. Healing the deep hurt, terror, and despair would require, like everything else in the walled zones, a parallel world where there is the joy that emerges from walled peoples' creativity maintaining our positionality and history as walled people; our joy is defined by a different set of rules and experiences. What heals the unwalled world will not be the antidote for the walled. A walled Ndéness transfers a new set of rules and counterorders. While we have been strong and steadfast, we have also had to suppress and postpone grief. The silence is not ours; it belongs to the majority of those who demand a wall, yet are aloof to the wall's effects and its transformations of the human beings living in this hemispheric edgy place. Of course this changes Ndé methods. Those who don't live in the walled region, who desired it, and who are benefiting from its existence are violating us as they ignore and forget us. We haven't forgotten. We won't forget.

Ndé Know What We Know Is True, Dignified, Worthy, and Just

Ndé axiology and epistemology are braided with our ontology—that is, what Ndé know and have evidence of through our embodied experience is the true state, relationship, and cause of our being, existence, and survivance. The settler society and settler nation have constructed a system that demands our death, disappearance, and extermination, and Americans participate in all this complicitly and compliantly. Thus, an Ndé ontology of refusal is shaped by forces of colonization and the power of our subconscious, ancestral, dreaming, and liberation-desiring experience as human beings. Ndé ontology is committed to the human experience in all its mysteries, wonderment, tragedy, grief, joy, and awe. These braids are sister strands, they are sister relational logics, and they are crucial to the Ndé anti-wall movement and liberation struggle, and thus to the way we understand indigeneity of the region. Consider that I and four generations of my ancestors before me have only known increasing militarization since 1848, when Mexico and the United States (and global imperial powers) illegally bordered Ndé and many Indigenous peoples' sovereign territories. Sit with that for a moment.

Ontologically, Ndé women questioned the limits imposed via the historical colonial and settler-colonial misrepresentations of Ndé based on biased, racist, discriminatory, and dehumanizing perspectives, infused in the term "Lipan Apache." Ndé resistances have been misdefined by oppressor groups that perpetuated projects and operations of colonization, persecution, imprisonment, abductions, removals, and significant land loss, defining U.S. hegemony and Texas settler domination. Ndé women land protectors have acknowledged these destructive systems throughout the resistance against the separation wall construction, and also refused to give them power or enable them; in their field of analysis, the wall demanded a reexamination of the normalization of "the border" as a process of ongoing colonization. Ndé have had to come to terms with psychological colonization by the surrounding settler society, and with the many Indigenous peoples whose worldviews have been conditioned differently than the Ndé worldview through the U.S. system of blood quantum and federal status (recognition). Ndé storying of Ndé resistance and self-determination history has illuminated and re-created a different and revitalized space for multitudes of Indigenous peoples with different histories of U.S. internal political, social, and economic experiences. The Ndé movement has galvanized the reemergence and resurgence of these Indigenous voices, experiences, and economic-political standing in ways that had not previously been possible at this scale. Ndé women's vocal resistance began to shatter this internal American myth on a national and international stage, revealing that more than four hundred independent Indigenous nations/peoples still exist under the shadow of U.S. hegemonic suppression and censorship of the grim reality. The Ndé legal cases stimulated popular public discussion, debate, and analysis, and many have forthrightly come to the realization that Ndé and potentially many more independent Indigenous nations have unfinished legal matters with Texas, the United States, and Mexico.

Aspiring to foreground Ndé knowledge and to resist construction of the separation wall, we worked with Denise Gilman, of the University of

Texas School of Law, who led the Texas/Mexico Border Wall Working Group. In 2008, Guzman and Hurwitz found that

> the historical lands of the Cúelcahén Ndé people were constituted by the region between the Pecos River and Rio Grande River and most of the Costal Bend Region, but was porous to interaction and mixing with Spanish colonizers, and the result was the transformation of the social spaces of the Cúelcahén Ndé into rancherías, settlements, and buffalo hunting territory.[13]

This amounts to millions of acres in the Texas-Mexico bordered lands. As Gilman stated, Ndé impacted by the wall have been targeted by "abusive government actions." It is important to appreciate Indigenous peoples as decision-makers pushed by myriad forces to consider, as Gilman states, "all possible mechanisms, including human rights and other legal strategies" in an Indigenous decolonial movement to defend human rights, protect land, and challenge the underlying coloniality of power relationships between Texas, the United States, and transnational military contractors.[14] These latter entities benefit financially and economically from this latest iteration of demolition and reinvention of the originary settler myth: terra nullius, bare land, a land without a people and a people without land, disposable people.

Debunking Nativist Worlding, Place-Making, and Definition of Indigenous "Others"

Popular fictions circulating in South Texas's ranching, petrochemical, uranium, and agriculture industries reinforce settler nativist ideas and logics regarding Indigenous peoples of Texas and Mexico. Colonial and nativist settler-colonial place-making always required the majority population of Brown "Others" to remain (according to settlers) rigidly within the confined enclosure of a deficit caricature in the background of the conquerors: as representatives of the "folkloric" trope of quaint vestiges of ancient yet degraded cultures, and as a population that drains and burdens the nativist settler resources. However, this nativist settler logic masks the contrasting reality of generations of Indigenous fluid autonomous place- and world-making, dynamic movement and mobility, uprising, rebellion, and organized collective refusals of the settler values and devaluing that, over the course of settler generations, legally, socially, and physically dispossessed, dehumanized, and erased the Ndé by means of violence. Prior to the wall construction, Ndé shaped transnational and transborder knowledge networks between communities and kinship systems. These have supported the long-standing efforts by Ndé to recover sacred burial sites and related cultural and intellectual heritage property, and have also supported the identification of sites connected to late nineteenth-century massacres.

Ndé storying expressed a territory that was bifurcated by the border in the decades predating the wall's construction, and harassment by U.S. Customs and Border Protection impeding them from moving freely across Texas and Mexico and "being" Ndé openly. Ndé storying dismantled the nativist settler fictions purporting that Brown peoples in South Texas and the Lower Rio Grande Valley are "Hispanic," "Mexican," "Mexican American," or "Latino." These are socially constructed state-imposed identities constituted in settler ecological and economic values and devaluing systems. They served the political-economic interest of a settler society with a high percentage of private landowners and an extractive economy. Reconstructing Ndé and related Indigenous peoples as non-Indigenous, ethnic, minority, fourth-class "populations" is a policy that has served the settler economy. George W. Bush neatly summarized the ingrained Texas settler mind-set when he stated, "There ain't no Indians in Texas."[15] In other words, gaining and maintaining operational control over the land in Texas, a state where over 75 percent of the land is private property, requires "Indians" to be invisible both politically and economically. Fictive ethnic and racial identities are psychologically imposed in order for the unceded and nonsurrendered dispossessed land, cultural heritage, and self-determining governance of Indigenous peoples to be deemed irrelevant to Texas, but also a threat to Texas. Between 2007 and 2009, this system reencountered a real Ndé threat as resistance cracked open the other side of settler memory and place-making. Eloisa García Taméz stated:

> The biggest shock to the journalists . . . and to the average U.S. citizen was that there are Indigenous peoples in the Lower Rio Grande Valley.

> But I think the bigger shock to them is . . . they've been lied to by their own government, who taught them to think in racist ways through school textbooks. When they visit the [Lower Rio Grande] Valley they see the reality . . . Indigenous peoples here are the majority. They assume that because the Spanish-speaking people have been forced into the "Hispanic" mold that this is "real." It's always part of the occupation.[16]

Eloisa García Taméz's observation is shared by many Ndé, whose local oral histories are often minimized in the nationalist histories that propagate a skewed narrative of the "birth" of Texas. The act of Ndé sculpting the present and past is often received with "shock," as Eloisa stated, and this points to the national miseducation of the American public.

This miseducation served a particular purpose by expanding upon the Doctrine of Discovery, papal bulls, and militarization, used by the colonizers to subordinate and subjugate Indigenous peoples for their knowledge and labor in the project of colonization. And yet we are here, still. We remain. We did not disappear. We persisted. We haven't forgotten. We still resist. As Peter H. Russell posits, "These are the peoples of the Fourth World—the Indigenous peoples living in Third World conditions within First World countries, dominated by the descendants of the European settlers and other relative newcomers."[17] Legally, Ndé have not ceded anything, and our political status and identities survive in the territory. Again, citing Russell, "The only home the settlers' descendants know are the New World countries they now inhabit and on which they base their collective identities. The challenge in this context is to work out ways in which descendants of the original occupants and descendants of the settlers can share these countries on a basis of mutual respect and consent, rather than on the force of the majority."[18] In dialogue with these lines of inquiry, Ndé ranchería-based research has found that settler dispossession is the very space and site of crisis where Indigenous peoples enact anticolonial and decolonial processes in the very same place where their lineal predecessors resisted and survived genocidal physical, mental, emotional, and psychological violence. We continue to require an international legal system to sustain and support Ndé ranchería peoples' needs at the site of severe impacts on life, land, health, well-being, culture, language, religious freedom, political freedom, food, water, and security.

Border Wall as Déjà Vu and Catalyst

Ndé peoples in the Lower Rio Grande Valley have histories with European and Euro-American societies and Western legal systems that received scant attention from the academy up to the early twenty-first century. Despite the many structural barriers put in place to discourage Ndé resurgence, Ndé activists, writers, academics, poets, and community voices emerged to challenge our erasure. We developed different pathways to be heard, to contribute to dialogues and debates within and across the communities, and to develop decolonial pathways in the academy. Ndé still retain a strong sense of family oral history, which preserves stories of colonization, anticolonial warfare, ethnic cleansing, genocidal violence, dispossession, assimilation, militarization, and settler penal and legal systems. As well, at the grassroots, and in customary Ndé oratory, history, and storytelling traditions, in specific communities, it is clear that the separation wall triggered illegal and extralegal dispossessions enacted by either local and regional settlers or the U.S. government.

The separation wall is a catalyst that triggered a flood of memory and retraumatization for Elders in Granjeno, El Calaboz, Las Milpas, El Ranchito, La Encantada, and Redford / El Polvo. In interviews with Ndé conducted between August 2007 and May 2010, a repeating narrative emerged from those who were youngsters in the early 1900s. Those in their seventies, eighties, and nineties witnessed forced dispossession and displacement. They saw militias and militarization subjugating clans (families) who refused to be dominated. At the El Calaboz Gathering, Daniel Castro Romero Jr. stated, "The wall and the motivation for it is not new to Ndé, only the technology is recent, the U.S. and Texas did this to our grandparents and great-grandparents, and theirs . . . all across this area."[19] Eloisa García Taméz remarked, "We know from reading court records from my grandmother's time that there were serious harms committed in Cameron County against particular peoples' land rights. The wall is a prison, an open-air prison . . . We already know what that is."[20] It is clear to Ndé that the wall is a *reinforcement* of past dispossessions, separations, and settler projects: it is part of a much longer history of violence against subjugated peoples of a *particular* place.

Indigenous peoples' collective memory provides us with much to ponder, consider, and plan with regard to sustaining and maintaining research supports and collaborations that address our goals in meaningful ways. Ndé people whose families conducted orature including speeches and narrative customs that recalled past violations specific to their families, in their customary places, often were the same individuals who expressed their deepest hope for *Tamez v. Chertoff*.[21] As more human rights and constitutional rights experts learned about the case, I learned that the Indigenous custom of orature in relation to the memory of extralegal and state-sanctioned violence and injustice made a significant impact across the spectrum of academe.[22] The Indigenous separation-wall resisters were viewed by the left as heroically liberatory and avant-garde, and by the far right as traitorous dissidents refusing to stay in their place and submit to U.S. threats of eminent domain. Ndé landowners and their relatives continued to express that their refusal was inextricably braided in a historical genealogy of resistance to colonial dispossession and genocide. The Ndé anti–separation wall movement invited Indigenous peoples to join in dialogue and unite in partnerships and relationships of mutual recognition and respect beyond the settler state and nation's commands of containment. The fact is that Ndé anti–separation wall alliance building—especially at the international level—triggered the far right of the settler society, as the Ndé anticolonial alliance agreements in previous centuries had overtaken, defeated, and dominated European colonials.

This is not to downplay the anxiety, fear, and abuse the government forced upon Elders and women landowners. Hostile and violent tactics promoted a climate of psychological warfare: chaos, paranoia, fear, and distrust between different land-based groups emerged. Unsurprisingly, some anti-wall activists along the Texas border obfuscated Indigenous claims to Crown land grants and treaties in order to promote environmentalist, municipal, and settler heritage claims. U.S. dispossession in the Indigenous Rio Grande River communities bifurcated by the border was also perceived as a *re*assertion of U.S. "sovereignty" vis-à-vis militarization and the construction of superhighway structures enabling north-south commerce. A violent transnational necropolitical order had long been escalating in the Texas-Mexico region, with armed warfare and death regimes dominating physical and psychological space.

Ndé and related Indigenous peoples were aligning resistances in a larger cultural kinship network with Jumano Apaches of Redford, Texas ("El Polvo"), who in 1997 were collective targets of the U.S. low-intensity conflict operations. The execution of clan member Esequiel Hernández, a Jumano Apache goatherder, and the strategies employed by Jumano Apache community leaders for redress informed collective, place-based, and networked decision-making for a unity-transborder "Lipan Apache–Jumano Apache" governance system. Family rights, clan rights, community rights, history, and shared decision-making welded two Texas Ndé border communities' analyses of power, oppression, coloniality, and land-based resistance in two areas of the Rio Grande River overrun and overshadowed by U.S. violence.

While it is true that *Tamez v. Chertoff* has contained and diminished emancipatory frameworks, we should not discount the ways in which Indigenous peoples galvanized social and cultural capital through *Tamez.* Ndé influence how others view the contested history and uneven terrain of Indigenous land claims in the United States, and specifically in Texas, and they unsettle the notion that settler colonialism is a completed project. By continually defining and reframing the meaning of *Tamez* through an Indigenous anticolonial lens, we disrupted the unipolar consciousness (the government framed *Tamez* as merely a "compensation" issue), projecting Ndé memory narratives as a counterarchive challenging settler place-making, memory, and records of history. Decolonizing Texas is core to Ndé conceptions of a new paradigm and its cultural alignments.

Ndé Women's Documentations

The border wall in El Calaboz and the Lower Rio Grande River is part of a narrative about the United States' incremental and steady expropriation and dispossession of Indigenous peoples' collective rights and self-governance, as well as about the Indigenous resistance led by Ndé women supported by a diverse Ndé community and a solidarity alliance of Indigenous peoples, activists, academics, and artists both regionally and globally. The suppression of the Southern Athapaskan language and knowledge systems in the Texas-Mexico region is a direct consequence of settler place-making, extractive ecologies and industries, and systematic exclusion of Ndé from accessing culturally significant places and managing them according to an Ndé worldview. In the Lower Rio Grande region, as it experiences escalating economic, environmental, political, and cultural crisis, Elders' memories have been operating and informing efforts to protect Indigenous knowledge systems.

The reality of Indigenous women's extensive documentation of land tenure and collection of genealogies, testimonies, news clippings, letters, photographs, and oral histories situated not only Ndé epistemologies, but also details about White organized violence. Indigenous peoples insisted all along that the border wall must not be corralled in twenty-first-century periodizations. The genealogies of harms by settlers who participated in the dispossession and killings of the late nineteenth and early twentieth centuries were being traced by Ndé to structural relationships, forces, and actors shaping the dispossession produced by the wall.

Memory "with, alongside, and for" Ndé Peoples

Research conducted, as Linda Tuhiwai Smith argues, "with, alongside and for Indigenous peoples" privileges the periodizations of Indigenous peoples' frameworks to make meaning of the present and the past, in specific lands, with the protection of Indigenous principles undergoing decolonization.[23] This philosophy supports Indigenous peoples' autonomy to enact self-determination and to decolonize research, which, Smith argues, is "implicated in the worst excesses of colonialism [and] remains a powerful remembered history for many of the world's colonized peoples."[24] I was conscious of this in the process of recovering Ndé history related to how Ndé Elders born in the early twentieth century viewed academic history as a weapon of *los gringos, na'inda' mangáání*—enemy White people. Ndé felt empowered to talk about their existence in the United States as a condition of being in between and invisible: of being Indigenous peoples with U.S. third-class citizenship imposed upon them as the people already on the land, who didn't immigrate, and who claim the river and the lands on both sides as an ancestral homeland. Living as colonized peoples without recognition is an untenable form of existence. Due to dominant systems of racialization, Indigenous people were marked as "Indians"/"Apaches"/"Comanches," "Mexicans," and "peon" laborers across myriad sites of contact with the settler state and its systems of industrialization. The South Texas settler society rendered Ndé peoples nationless and stateless in their own lands. Women's narrative remembrances demonstrate how Ndé resistance against the wall is rooted in their refusal to cede collective kinship conceptions of peoplehood and territories, known as *herencia* (heredity, inheritance, legacy), homeland, and Kónìcą̀ą̀hį́į́ Gòkíyàà, or Lipan Country.

El Calaboz Ranchería—A Weapon (of Colonization) and a Tool (of Decolonization)

El Calaboz Ranchería (Cameron County) is the site of a four-hundred-year Indigenous crossroads of Ndé, Tlaxcaltecas, Nahuas, Comanches, and other Plains and coastal peoples. In the case of Eloisa García Taméz, born in El Calaboz, we delve into a kinship network spanning the Tlaxcala *señoríos*, the direct lineal bloodline of Moctezuma Xocoyotzin, and Ndé buffalo hunters.[25] Women have been community advocates, transmitting knowledge systems across nineteen generations, and have incorporated generations of Indigenous peoples' knowledges to *unsettle* settler societies.

I borrow from historian Patrick Wolfe, who argued that settler societies "destroy to replace."[26] Destroying to replace on the Texas-Mexico border was narrated to Eloisa through the historiographies of Ndé ancestors and relatives, and she observed continual forms of violence from early childhood. Her family nurtured women's legal and physical challenges to dispossession in everyday songs, *cuentos*, memorials, genealogies, photographs, and marks on the land itself. In El Calaboz, the resistance against erasure was regenerated in collective action organized by women, set in a larger collective weaving of Ndé, Nahuatl, and Tlaxcalteca cultural convergence.

By the mid-sixteenth century, the Ndé lived along the Texas coast, along the Rio Grande River, and in (current-day) Matamoros, Saltillo, Morelos, Monclova, and Ojinaga. By the late eighteenth century Ndé engaged in diverse commerce and settled spaces in mountain, desert, plateau, and valleys between southern Chihuahua and San Antonio. By the early nineteenth century, Ndé established significant trans-river, transborder, and transnational (i.e., between Indigenous "nations") kinship networks with Tlaxcalteca and Nahua peoples across (current-day) Tamaulipas, Coahuila, Nuevo León, and Texas. These intimate contacts enlarged the cultural, social, and political-economic spaces of the Tlaxcala Nation (situated in current-day central Mexico) and expanded the trade economies of Ndé.[27]

Along the Texas-Mexico border, women recount stories of militarized gender violence as a tactic to simultaneously subordinate and appropriate Indigenous peoples' knowledge. Ndé women's bodies, memories, and experiences of El Calaboz Ranchería are sites, texts, and archives that disrupt assumed settler epistemic truths and favor their own ways of being, knowing, remembering, and narrating Ndé rivered axiologies (values) and ontological truths (of how Ndé women's experiences and worldview accurately reflect the properties of their existence in the real world).[28] Ndé women's perspectives inform the multiple iterations of rights and identities of Ndé multicultural/multinationed Indigenous families, such as those of Ndé-Tlaxcalteca/Ndé-Nahua land protectors in the surrounding settler ecologies of violence. In El Calaboz Ranchería, kinship knowledge and shared resources between women maintained land-tenure rights under the Spanish colonial land-grant system and the Anglo-Texan settler-nationalist regime. The exercise of traditional decision-making advantaged women's matrifocal and matrilocal *jacalitas*—women's "home sites"—where thriving, interwoven Indigenous economies anchored Ndé families to land and community. Knowledge streams flowed from women, exchanging models for pushing back.[29]

El Calaboz women have undoubtedly drawn upon their rich heritage while transmitting Indigenous principles regarding land ownership. One figure was Mariana Leonor de Moctezuma (ca. 1505–ca. 1562), older daughter of Moctezuma Xocoyotzin, and the maternal thirteenth great-grandmother of Eloisa García Taméz. Mariana's legal philosophies, used against the Spanish Crown, tapped deeply into Nahuatl principles of land tenure and set forth narratives for women in El Calaboz, as well as across northeastern Mexico, to animate collective rights of Indigenous families, as well as Indigenous women's rights to inherit land and territories in connection with land grants.[30]

To briefly illustrate the land rights philosophies transmitted between Indigenous women in El Ranchito and La Encantada, I turn to Francisca (de Moctezuma) Reyes Esparza (1901–80). Francisca challenged the Esparza family's dispossession in the United States' and Mexico's legal systems on Indigenous-originated principles to protect *comunitario* and *originario* land grants given to her families in 1749–67, and she also sought to reclaim mineral and riparian rights bound to her family's lands. The Esparza (de Moctezuma) cartographies of Indigenous land tenure were shaped between lineal descendants of Moctezuma II, Tlaxcalteca hidalgos, Tlaxcalteca agriculturalists, and Ndé buffalo societies, which the settler state flattened into "Mexicans."

Eloisa Taméz's Nahuatl foremothers transmitted a consciousness of challenging colonial elites and courts while fighting to sustain Indigenous principles of extended family and women's inherent rights to lands and territories. In addition, her paternal Ndé ancestors from the deserts, mountains, grasslands, and coastal watersheds modeled an intimate knowledge of place and a food system shaped over centuries based in bison hunting, hunter-gatherer subsistence, and commerce. Ndé conceptions of Indigenous title with First Foods underlie the Ndé principles of Kónìcą̀ą̀hį́į́ Gòkíyàà, or "Lipan Big Water Country."[31] Taméz and others refer to this knowledge as "my living history book," a reference to her paternal Ndé-Tlaxcalteca grandmother, Andrea Cavazos García. Taméz's "encyclopedia" was an accumulation of violent invasions and physical resistances she witnessed while under her grandmother's tutelage.

Ndé Human Rights in Direct Dialogue with International Law

Ndé ancestors have been struggling with clashing paradigms of rights since the sixteenth century: the Ndé principles and protocols of collective responsibilities, obligations, and duties, and the colonial presuppositions of possession, title, and positive rights, which are paternalistic and destructive. Ndé conceptions of Indigenous peoples' rights to lands, territories, self-governance, and self-determination—beyond borders—have continued to be in motion and in dialogue with relevant cases related to Aboriginal title. At the time of this writing, Ndé are working in coalition with Indigenous scholars in the United States and Canada who are linking landmark cases, such as *Delgamuukw v. British Columbia* (*Delgamuukw III*) in Canada and *Mabo v. Queensland (No. 2)* in Australia, to applications of Indigenous human rights and Indigenous proprietary title in the United States. Ndé rights analysts are aware that these two cases set forth important models that go beyond theorizing; they clarify, articulate, and calculate the rights of Indigenous peoples in settler states as central to transformative human rights approaches that excavate the disturbing foundations of neoliberal and neocolonial dispossession projects, such as the wall. There is much more research to pursue and to recognize as ontologically relevant and accurate relating to Ndé refusals of and resistance to the U.S. militarization of lands seized historically through extralegal methods, the "border wall," and the current-day structural impediments that the separation wall imposes upon Ndé people's physical, cultural, social, spiritual, economic, and political rights to their lands, their cultural heritage, their traditional food systems, and their livelihoods. The separation wall is not gender-neutral, as it regulates Indigenous women's bodies and social-political movement differently from men's, and disproportionately impacts women's access to water, soil, Indigenous plant-based food and medicines, wild game, seasonal community harvests, economic development, and political and legal rights to defend the above. The wall heightens generational injustices, such as the unlawful nonrecognition of Indigenous peoples' political status in the Texas-Mexico bordered region. The separation wall didn't begin in 2006; it was built upon a history of occupation, colonization, and militarization that constructed racial difference between colonizers and colonized, as reified in Texas nativist constructions of Apaches, Mexicans, Indians, migrants, and terrorists.[32] In future work, connecting the past to the present will inform Ndé research that gets to the roots of the problem, which is a mandate that emanated from the 2011 El Calaboz Gathering. It will be prudent for Indigenous peoples of the Rio Grande River to understand the relationship between the Secure Fence Act of 2006, Israel's separation wall implemented by Ariel Sharon in 2002, and the International Court of Justice's notable findings on the latter regarding the illegality of separation walls and related human rights violations. The continuing existence of the U.S. separation border wall in El Calaboz is a haunting reminder that Ndé women fought so that the resistance against the wall and its many human rights violations would be remembered, but not merely as a set of motions, pleas, and demands held by international legal repositories. Rather, the struggle for justice in El Calaboz is a lived and known body, site, and text reactivating the memories of front-line defenders to be transmitted to the land protectors of tomorrow. Dynamic, embodied resistance experiences cannot be isolated from sites and texts; they seek out space and place to educate us about the body's, the land's, and the community's evidence of crimes past. Memories cry out to be an ongoing repository of trauma and suffering, analysis, and intergenerational defiance connecting both personal and collective memory and preserving Ndé presence, which colonization through militarization attempts to obscure and subvert.[33] Annually active in multiple international treaty bodies, Ndé women are there to ensure jurists remember that the U.S. border wall is an ongoing, unresolved legal and political matter with a documented historical past. Ndé women continue advancing legal precedents to correct the settler-colonial politics, policies, propaganda, and disinformation at play in shaping the geopolitical erasure and destruction of Ndé as inconvenient and disposable enemy others.

In decolonization processes, Indigenous peoples must put primacy on recovering memory, archives, collections, history, knowledge, lands, language, ethical principles, philosophies, and self-governance—with recognition and territories that are detethered from normative "Native" "recognition." The process leads to the exposure of preconditions underlying contemporary megaprojects such as the separation wall and the settler state's prisons, checkpoints, drones, surveillance, and biometrics. Each one of us must engage with our role in either reinforcing colonial power relations or resisting the state-sanctioned violence and making the herstory of refusal to surrender to the plots of the ruling elites. For Ndé, the wall is literally on killing fields. These are holy and crucial sites of resistance to the attempts to fragment and fracture communities and to disband and disunify our collective consciousness, memories, and research traditions. The Ndé investigation of memory is integral to confronting genocidal, nativist histories and to reclaiming Ndé rights to self-determination and respectful relations.

By elevating the Ndé historical perspective in dialogue with critical Indigenous methodologies, Indigenous memory, and Indigenous women's documentations, I reaffirm the importance of research by, with, for, and alongside all Indigenous peoples of the Rio Grande River. Ndé peoples' indigenization of a human rights approach to the border wall and desire to advance this at the Inter-American Commission on Human Rights of the Organization of American States represents the most recent and concentrated expression of a much longer history of Ndé peoples' struggles for international recognition and redress. The preconditions underlying the wall and Ndé peoples' intentions for ongoing human rights legal approaches will undoubtedly sustain pressure upon the United States and Texas. As Indigenous peoples dismantle social, legal, psychological, and physical bricks, and rupture myths, fictions, and ideological barriers, we will continue to interrogate the intersections between academic research and Indigenous struggles for autonomy. These relationships are continually foregrounding partnerships as part of local decolonial methods firmly situated in an Ndé-Texas-Mexico-U.S. and international nexus that Dene peoples, hemispherically, never voluntarily surrendered.

The Texas-Mexico border wall and the fierce opposition it engendered function as an illustrative microcosm of long-standing struggles—in Texas, the United States, and internationally—between competing visions of borders, sovereignty, property, law, rights, autonomy, and dignity. In the dispute over the border wall, a multiplicity of civil society actors, municipalities, and settler interest–based advocates crafted collaborations and strategies to deploy against government dispossession injustice. This chapter has sketched out the human rights and Indigenous rights strategies adopted by distinctly situated Indigenous social actors who relied on their own experiences, oral histories, archives, and intergenerational knowledge to think critically and creatively about means to challenge the border wall while coming together to act collaboratively against the destruction and human rights violations it has caused. Upon consideration of their role at the intersection of Indigenous rights and human rights, resistance activism and law, Indigenous communities found strength in working with "outsiders" and in decolonizing the contested meanings and histories of international law and human rights as part of the process and the means of resisting the border wall and seeking decolonization for themselves, both individually and in collaborative relationships.

Participation in the human rights approach allowed impacted peoples to advance claims for justice and recognition of Indigenous history and analysis by turning them into principles and demands based in international law. Indigenous claims against the border wall were not limited to human rights claims, though, ensuring that the human rights strategy expanded Indigenous resistance rather than absorbing it. In turn, the Working Group on Human Rights and the Border Wall at the University of Texas concluded that human rights could bring unique force to bear against the wall, but only if the approach connected to the efforts of Indigenous and other impacted communities. By emphasizing coordination with affected communities, the Working Group offered a strengthened analysis that reflected the full reality of harm caused by the border wall and also ensured that the strategy remained faithful to the demands of border residents. The human rights approach treated Indigenous claims as central to the analysis but also incorporated the full breadth of human rights law to address violations not directly related to Indigenous rights. The approach thus supported and also augmented the Indigenous rights strategy. The process posed new challenges and opportunities, which could set the stage for crucial next steps at the Inter-American Commission.

At the same time, the Working Group and Indigenous land protectors acknowledged the tensions and weaknesses in the human rights approach. There are ongoing concerns about the disparity in terms of access by Indigenous peoples of the Texas-Mexico border to Indigenous law experts who could bring to bear knowledge and experience from an Indigenous and international law perspective.

Even with these explicit concerns, the combined human rights and Indigenous rights challenges to the border wall, viewed as complementary strategies, led to intercultural and decolonial processes between academics, activists, and community-based Indigenous land protectors and their peoples. While Ndé resistance strategies are complex and varied, they are not perfect in their enactment due to the nature of the Texas-U.S.-Mexico settler-colonial structures and systems and the oppressive resource inequities that affect the strategic objectives of Indigenous women land protectors. Not all collaborations automatically lead to solidarity formations, and many alliances face their own unique sets of challenges. Some alliances hindered the Ndé women's struggle for rights, truth, and justice, while others performed vital roles in shaping the Ndé women's Indigenous feminist theorizing in the flesh, spirit, heart, and land. The commitment and cooperative spirit of interactions worked to make visible the reality of Ndé communities who have deep histories and memories of violence, trauma, and an enduring resistance consciousness. We are faced with significant challenges due to U.S. militarization, displacement, land loss, restricted movement, and limitations imposed on our fundamental civil, constitutional, and international human rights.

The egregious abuses against Indigenous rights seriously impede Ndé women's capacity to challenge the existing power structures. This chapter has sought to initiate a critical reflection on the use of promising strategies taken up by the Ndé women of El Calaboz and across the Texas-Mexico Rio Grande River Indigenous communities, in hopes that our experiences will guide the future development of even more effective means of addressing Ndé peoples' autonomous rights to challenge and confront states on all matters affecting them, specifically issues of Ndé land rights, self-determination, autonomy, human rights, militarization, containment and separation architectures, restricted movement, displacement, land theft and dispossession, national security policy, and Ndé peoples' rights as continuing and remaining geopolitical actors in Texas, the United States, Mexico, this hemisphere, and beyond.

NOTES

1. Eloisa García Taméz is my mother, and I have predominantly chosen to refer to her in this chapter, and elsewhere in the book, by her given name. This is primarily due to the fact that her actions and roles during the period examined in this collection garnered significant attention by the state apparatus. Taméz insisted on protecting a place and community nearly erased by multiple colonizations, and on framing an Indigenous land rights defense in the region and period closely examined in this collection. I resist referring to her as "my mother" because I believe this could flatten her positionality with regard to her resistance of state violence. It could also risk simplistic and distorted misreadings, as her motherhood is not a subject of this chapter or this collection. Primarily, my goal is to convey knowledge regarding her resistance that engages her ethos as an Indigenous social movement figure who confronted, challenged, and resisted colonial and state-sanctioned violence and suppression on her lands.
2. Her cases at that time were still limited to the Organization of American States' Inter-American Commission on Human Rights (2008) and the initial report submitted to the UN Committee on the Elimination of Racism and Discrimination (2007). The "border fence" would later be redefined by me as the "border wall" as part of my advocacy during my doctoral studies at WSU, countering the U.S. Department of Homeland Security's digital disinformation "wars" against her case. Cyberbattles on platforms across the web ensued between the state and me, in which I ultimately learned how to influence and change everyday usage of "border fence" in public discourse to "border wall," over a period of about three months.
3. Margo Tamez, "Place and Perspective in the Shadow of the Wall," in *Autobiography Without Apology: The Personal Essay in Chicanx and Latinx Studies*, ed.

Chon A. Noriega, Wendy Laura Belcher, and Charlene Villaseñor Black (Los Angeles: UCLA Chicano Studies Research Center Press, 2020), 357–84.

4. Denise Gilman, "Calling the United States' Bluff: How Sovereign Immunity Undermines the United States' Claim to an Effective Domestic Human Rights System," *Georgetown Law Journal* 95, no. 3 (March 2007): 596.
5. Gilman, "Calling the United States' Bluff."
6. "Apache" entered into the English language via Spaniards and Spanish colonial experiences prior to the arrival of American settlers. The commonly circulated theory is derived from Frederick Webb Hodge's *Handbook of American Indians North of Mexico*, vol. 1 (Washington, D.C.: Government Printing Office, 1907), 63, in which he claimed the term "Apache" is a Zuni/Uto-Aztekan cultural-linguistic identifier applied to Dene peoples. It is difficult to find primary sources for this claim; nonetheless, it dominates the literature into the twenty-first century. See New World Encyclopedia, s.v. "Apache," https://www.newworldencyclopedia.org/entry/Apache. The Spaniards may have adopted the term as early as 1598. Another etymology of "Apache" could derive from *apa chu* ("big enemy"), a descriptor of Dene peoples by Uto-Aztekan (including the Zuni) peoples whom Spaniards consulted for information about the hunters dominating lands sought for mineral exploration, development, and settlement colonies. By the seventeenth century the term became broadly used by Europeans to refer to many Indigenous peoples/groups in North America who were deemed unconquerable, and thus it took on broad racial, sociological, and psychological meanings. The Dene Ndé in Texas did not commonly refer to or utilize the terms "enemy" or "Apache," ingrained in American militarism, until the early to mid-twentieth century. The social construction of "Apaches," Ndé as enemies in their own lands, is an ideology of myth and exaggeration, implanted in settler-colonial discourses aimed at erasing Ndé history.
7. Norman K. Denzin, Yvonna S. Lincoln, and Linda Tuhiwai Smith, eds., *Handbook of Critical and Indigenous Methodologies* (Thousand Oaks: Sage, 2008), 2, 9, 10.
8. Michelle Guzman and Zachary Hurwitz, "Violations on the Part of the United States Government of Indigenous Rights Held by Members of the Lipan Apache, Kickapoo, and Ysleta del Sur Tigua Tribes of the Texas-Mexico Border" (briefing paper, Working Group on Human Rights and the Border Wall, University of Texas at Austin, June 2008), 8, https://law.utexas.edu/humanrights/borderwall/analysis/briefing-violations-of-indigenous-rights.pdf.
9. See William S. Kiser, "The Business of Killing Indians: Contract Warfare and Genocide in the U.S.-Mexico Borderlands," *Journal of American History* 110, vol. 1 (June 2023): 15–39, https://doi.org/10.1093/jahist/jaad095. See also Jeffrey Ostler, "Genocide and American Indian History," *Oxford Research Encyclopedia of American History*, March 2, 2015, accessed April 23, 2024, https://doi.org/10.1093/acrefore/9780199329175.013.3.

10. On the racialization of Indigenous clothing, visual erasure and Indigenous women, and visual thingification and nonrecognition, see Egla Martínez Salazar, *Global Coloniality of Power in Guatemala: Racism, Genocide, Citizenship* (Lanham, Md.: Lexington Books, 2012); and Margo Tamez, "SOVERYEMPTY: Narrative DeneNdé Poetics in Walled Homelands," in *Indigenous Women and Violence: Feminist Activist Research in Heightened States of Injustice*, ed. Lynn Stephen and Shannon Speed (Tucson: University of Arizona Press, 2021), 209–42.
11. Denzin, Lincoln, and Smith, *Handbook*, 8.
12. *Eloisa García Tamez, Benito J. Garcia, Idalia Benavidez, Jose Benavidez, Eduardo Benavidez v. Michael Chertoff, Secretary, United States Department of Homeland Security; Robert F. Janson, Acting Executive Director, Asset Management of U.S. Customs and Border Protection*, Civil Action No: 08-CV-0555, *First Amended Complaint for Injunctive and Declaratory Relief (Class Action)*, The Texas-Mexico Border Wall (digital archive), The University of Texas at Austin School of Law, https://law.utexas.edu/humanrights/borderwall/law/govt-tamez-Class-First-Amended-Complaint.pdf.
13. Guzman and Hurwitz, "Violations," 9.
14. Gilman quoted from chapter 13 in this volume.
15. Cited in Mary C. Churchill, "'There Ain't No Indians in Texas'—A Red Alert," *Indian Country Today*, October 31, 2001, A4.
16. Eloisa Taméz, interview notes recorded in Margo Tamez's field journal, El Calaboz Ranchería, June 22, 2011. Ellipses represent pauses.
17. Peter H. Russell, *Recognizing Aboriginal Title: The Mabo Case and Indigenous Resistance to English-Settler Colonialism* (Toronto: University of Toronto Press, 2005), 17.
18. Russell, *Recognizing*, 18.
19. Daniel Castro Romero Jr., interview notes from Margo Tamez's field journal, St. Ignacio church, El Ranchito–La Encantada, Tex., June 24, 2011.
20. E. Taméz, interview notes (see note 15 above). The ellipsis represents a pause.
21. On orature and Indigenous oral traditions, see Ngũgĩ wa Thiong'o, "The Language of African Literature," in *The Routledge Language and Cultural Theory Reader*, ed. Lucy Burke, Tony Crowley, and Alan Girvin (London: Routledge, 2000), 434.
22. See Angelique EagleWoman, "The Eagle and the Condor of the Western Hemisphere: Application of International Indigenous Principles to Halt the United States Border Wall," *Idaho Law Review* 45, no. 3 (2008): 1–18; Daniel Ibsen Morales, "In Democracy's Shadow: Fences, Raids, and the Production of Migrant Illegality," *Stanford Journal of Civil Rights and Civil Liberties* 5, no. 23 (2009); Morgan Lewis, "Good Fences Make Good Neighbors, but Do They Make Good Cents: A South-of-the-Border Fence Guide to Theories of Compensation for Property," *Texas Tech Law Review* 41, no. 4 (Summer 2009): 1193; Nicole Miller, "How Property Rights Are Affected by the Texas-Mexico Bor-

der Fence: A Failure Due to Insufficient Procedure," *Texas International Law Journal* 45, no. 3 (Spring 2010): 631; Margaret E. Dorsey and Miguel Díaz-Barriga, "Beyond Surveillance and Moonscapes: An Alternative Imaginary of the US–Mexico Border Wall," *Visual Anthropology Review* 26, no. 2 (2010): 128–35; Terence M. Garrett, "A Critique of the U.S. Department of Homeland Security and the Border Wall in the Rio Grande Valley," in *Continuing Studies in Rio Grande Valley History*, ed. Milo Kearney, Anthony Knopp, and Antonio Zavaleta (Brownsville: Texas Center for Border and Transnational Studies, University of Texas at Brownsville and Texas Southmost College, 2010), 305–24; Gloria Valencia-Weber and Antoinette Sedillo Lopez, "Stories in Mexico and the United States About the Border: The Rhetoric and the Realities," *Intercultural Human Relations Law Review* 5 (2010): 24; Joseph Nevins, "Scenes from an Occupation," *NACLA Report on the Americas* 45, no. 2 (2011): 41–47; Working Group on Human Rights and the Border Wall, "Obstructing Human Rights: The Texas-Mexico Border Wall" (full set of briefing papers, Working Group on Human Rights and the Border Wall, University of Texas, Austin, June 2008), https://law.utexas.edu/humanrights/borderwall/analysis/briefing-FULL-SET-OF-REPORTS.pdf; Chandra Talpade Mohanty, "Imperial Democracies, Militarised Zones, Feminist Engagements," *Economic and Political Weekly* 46, no. 13 (2011): 76–84; Margo Tamez, "Consultation in the Matter of U.S. Condemnation and Possession of Customary Lipan Apache Lands in El Calaboz Ranchería, U.S. v. 26 Acres of Land, and Eloisa G. Támez, et al., 1:08-cv-0351; U.S. v. 41 Acres of Land and Benavides, et al., 1:08-cv-309" (briefing paper submitted to Judge Andrew Hanen, U.S. Court, Southern District of Texas, Brownsville, Tex., April 23, 2009); Margo Tamez, "'Our Way of Life Is Our Resistance': Indigenous Women and Anti-imperialist Challenges to Militarization Along the U.S.-Mexico Border," *Works and Days* 29, no. 57/58 (2011): 281–318; Margo Tamez, "Indigenous Women's Rivered Refusals in El Calaboz," *Diálogo* 19, no. 1 (2016): 7–21.

23. Linda Tuhiwai Smith, *Decolonizing Methodologies: Research and Indigenous Peoples* (London: Zed Books, 1999), 5.
24. Smith, *Decolonizing Methodologies*, 1.
25. Margo Tamez, "NÁDASI'NÉ' NDÉ' ISDZÁNÉ BEGOZ'AAHÍ' SHIMAA SHINÍ'GOKAL GOWĄ GOSHJAA HA'ÁNÁ'IDŁÍ TEXAS-NAKAIYÉ GODESDZOG / Returning Lipan Apache Women's Laws, Lands, and Power in El Calaboz Rancheria, Texas-Mexico Border" (PhD diss., Washington State University, 2010).
26. Patrick Wolfe, "Settler Colonialism and the Elimination of the Native," *Journal of Genocide Research* 8, no. 4 (2006).
27. Enrique Gilbert-Michael Maestas, "Culture and History of Native American Peoples of South Texas" (PhD diss., University of Texas at Austin, 2003).
28. On bodies, sites, texts as archives serving as repositories of memory, knowing, history, and resisting unipolar notions that only settler libraries and museums

are repositories, see Giulia Battaglia, Jennifer Clarke, and Fiona Siegenthaler, "Bodies of Archives / Archival Bodies: An Introduction," *Visual Anthropology Review* 36 (2020): 8–16, https://doi.org/10.1111/var.12203. On "rivered" axiologies and ontologies, see M. Tamez, "Rivered Refusals."

29. M. Tamez, "NÁDASI'NÉ' NDÉ' ISDZÁNÉ."
30. M. Tamez, "NÁDASI'NÉ' NDÉ' ISDZÁNÉ." See also Donald E. Chipman, *Moctezuma's Children: Aztec Royalty Under Spanish Rule, 1520–1700* (Austin: University of Texas Press, 2005).
31. First Foods (also "first foods") refers to foods intimately associated with Indigenous peoples' deep-time (millennia-old) ancestral connection to place. "First Foods" with two capitalized *F*s has become an option to highlight the reverence and respect sought for this concept; it emerged alongside decolonization movements in the academy in response to Indigenous research partners requesting special status for terminology referring to Indigenous food in light of centuries of colonial destruction of Indigenous lifeways and heritage foods. For one of the earliest published uses of "first foods," see Linda Murray Berzok, *American Indian Food* (New York: Bloomsbury, 2005). See also Jamie Donatuto, Larry Campbell, Joyce K. LeCompte, Diana Rohlman, and Sonni Tadlock, "The Story of 13 Moons: Developing an Environmental Health and Sustainability Curriculum Founded on Indigenous First Foods and Technologies," *Sustainability* 12, no. 21 (2020): 8913.
32. Mark Griffiths and Jemima Repo, "Women and Checkpoints in Palestine," *Security Dialogue* 52, no. 3 (2021): 249–65, https://doi.org/10.1177/0967010620918529.
33. Liyana Kayali, "Transformative Incrementalism: Palestinian Women's Strategies of Resistance and Resilience amid Gendered Insecurity and Neoliberal Co-optation," *Security Dialogue*, April 25, 2024, https://doi.org/10.1177/09670106241226653.

BIBLIOGRAPHY

Battaglia, Giulia, Jennifer Clarke, and Fiona Siegenthaler. "Bodies of Archives / Archival Bodies: An Introduction." *Visual Anthropology Review* 36 (2020): 8–16. https://doi.org/10.1111/var.12203.

Berzok, Linda Murray. *American Indian Food*. New York: Bloomsbury, 2005.

Chipman, Donald E. *Moctezuma's Children: Aztec Royalty Under Spanish Rule, 1520–1700*. Austin: University of Texas Press, 2005.

Churchill, Mary C. "'There Ain't No Indians in Texas'—A Red Alert." *Indian Country Today*, October 31, 2001, A4.

Denzin, Norman K., Yvonna S. Lincoln, and Linda Tuhiwai Smith, eds. *Handbook of Critical and Indigenous Methodologies*. Thousand Oaks: Sage, 2008.

Donatuto, Jamie, Larry Campbell, Joyce K. LeCompte, Diana Rohlman, and Sonni Tadlock. "The Story of 13 Moons: Developing an Environmental Health and Sustainability Curriculum Founded on Indigenous First Foods and Technologies." *Sustainability* 12, no. 21 (2020).

Dorsey, Margaret E., and Miguel Díaz-Barriga. "Beyond Surveillance and Moonscapes: An Alternative Imaginary of the US–Mexico Border Wall." *Visual Anthropology Review* 26, no. 2 (2010): 128–35.

EagleWoman, Angelique. "The Eagle and the Condor of the Western Hemisphere: Application of International Indigenous Principles to Halt the United States Border Wall." *Idaho Law Review* 45, no. 3 (2009): 1–18.

Garrett, Terence M. "A Critique of the U.S. Department of Homeland Security and the Border Wall in the Rio Grande Valley." In *Continuing Studies in Rio Grande Valley History*, edited by Milo Kearney, Anthony Knopp, and Antonio Zavaleta, 305–24. Brownsville: Texas Center for Border and Transnational Studies, University of Texas at Brownsville and Texas Southmost College, 2010. https://scholarworks.utrgv.edu/cgi/viewcontent.cgi?params=/context/regionalhist/article/1008/&path_info=Continuing_studies_in_Rio_Grande_Valley_history.pdf.

Gilman, Denise. "Calling the United States' Bluff: How Sovereign Immunity Undermines the United States' Claim to an Effective Domestic Human Rights System." *Georgetown Law Journal* 95, no. 3 (March 2007): 591–652.

Griffiths, Mark, and Jemima Repo. "Women and Checkpoints in Palestine." *Security Dialogue* 52, no. 3 (2021): 249–65. https://doi.org/10.1177/0967010620918529.

Guzman, Michelle, and Zachary Hurwitz. "Violations on the Part of the United States Government of Indigenous Rights Held by Members of the Lipan Apache, Kickapoo, and Ysleta del Sur Tigua Tribes of the Texas-Mexico Border." Briefing paper, Working Group on Human Rights and the Border Wall, University of Texas at Austin, June 2008. https://law.utexas.edu/humanrights/borderwall/analysis/briefing-violations-of-indigenous-rights.pdf.

Hodge, Frederick Webb. *Handbook of American Indians North of Mexico*. Vol. 1. Washington, D.C.: Government Printing Office, 1907.

Kayali, Liyana. "Transformative Incrementalism: Palestinian Women's Strategies of Resistance and Resilience amid Gendered Insecurity and Neoliberal Co-optation." *Security Dialogue*, April 25, 2024. https://doi.org/10.1177/09670106241226653.

Kiser, William S. "The Business of Killing Indians: Contract Warfare and Genocide in the U.S.-Mexico Borderlands." *Journal of American History* 110, no. 1 (June 2023): 15–39. https://doi.org/10.1093/jahist/jaad095.

Lewis, Morgan. "Good Fences Make Good Neighbors, but Do They Make Good Cents: A South-of-the-Border Fence Guide to Theories of Compensation for Property." *Texas Tech Law Review* 41, no. 4 (Summer 2009): 1193–1234.

Maestas, Enrique Gilbert-Michael. "Culture and History of Native American Peoples of South Texas." PhD dissertation, University of Texas at Austin, 2003. Texas ScholarWorks.

Martínez Salazar, Egla. *Global Coloniality of Power in Guatemala: Racism, Genocide, Citizenship*. Lanham, Md.: Lexington Books, 2012.

Miller, Nicole. "How Property Rights Are Affected by the Texas-Mexico Border Fence: A Failure Due to Insufficient Procedure." *Texas International Law Journal* 45, no. 3 (Spring 2010): 631–54.

Mohanty, Chandra Talpade. "Imperial Democracies, Militarised Zones, Feminist Engagements." *Economic and Political Weekly* 46, no. 13 (2011): 76–84.

Morales, Daniel Ibsen. "In Democracy's Shadow: Fences, Raids, and the Production of Migrant Illegality." *Stanford Journal of Civil Rights and Civil Liberties* 5, no. 23 (2009): 23–88.

Nevins, Joseph. "Scenes from an Occupation." *NACLA Report on the Americas* 45, no. 2 (2011): 41–47.

Ngũgĩ wa Thiong'o. "The Language of African Literature." In *The Routledge Language and Cultural Theory Reader*, edited by Lucy Burke, Tony Crowley, and Alan Girvin. London: Routledge, 2000.

Ostler, Jeffrey. "Genocide and American Indian History." *Oxford Research Encyclopedia of American History*, March 2, 2015. Accessed April 23, 2024. https://doi.org/10.1093/acrefore/9780199329175.013.3.

Russell, Peter H. *Recognizing Aboriginal Title: The Mabo Case and Indigenous Resistance to English-Settler Colonialism*. Toronto: University of Toronto Press, 2005.

Smith, Linda Tuhiwai. *Decolonizing Methodologies: Research and Indigenous Peoples*. London: Zed Books, 1999.

Tamez, Margo. "Consultation in the Matter of U.S. Condemnation and Possession of Customary Lipan Apache Lands in El Calaboz Ranchería, U.S. v. 26 Acres of Land, and Eloisa G. Támez, et al., 1:08-cv-0351; U.S. v. 41 Acres of Land and Benavides, et al., 1:08-cv-309." Briefing paper submitted to Judge Andrew Hanen, U.S. Court, Southern District of Texas, Brownsville, Tex., April 23, 2009.

Tamez, Margo. "Indigenous Women's Rivered Refusals in El Calaboz." *Diálogo* 19, no. 1 (2016): 7–21.

Tamez, Margo. "NÁDASI'NÉ' NDÉ' ISDZÁNÉ BEGOZ'AAHÍ' SHIMAA SHINÍ'GOKAL GOWĄ GOSHJAA HA'ÁNÁ'IDŁÍ TEXAS-NAKAIYÉ GODESDZOG / Returning Lipan Apache Women's Laws, Lands, and Power in El Calaboz Rancheria, Texas-Mexico Border." PhD diss., Washington State University, 2010.

Tamez, Margo. "'Our Way of Life Is Our Resistance': Indigenous Women and Anti-imperialist Challenges to Militarization Along the U.S.-Mexico Border." *Works and Days* 29, no. 57/58 (2011): 281–318.

Tamez, Margo. "Place and Perspective in the Shadow of the Wall." In *Autobiography Without Apology: The Personal Essay in Chicanx and Latinx Studies*, edited by Chon A. Noriega, Wendy Laura Belcher, and Charlene Villaseñor Black, 357–84. Los Angeles: UCLA Chicano Studies Research Center Press, 2020.

Tamez, Margo. "SOVERYEMPTY: Narrative DeneNdé Poetics in Walled Homelands." In *Indigenous Women and Violence: Feminist Activist Research in Heightened States of Injustice*, edited by Lynn Stephen and Shannon Speed, 209–42. Tucson: University of Arizona Press, 2021.

Valencia-Weber, Gloria, and Antoinette Sedillo Lopez. "Stories in Mexico and the United States About the Border: The Rhetoric and the Realities." *Intercultural Human Rights Law Review* 5 (2010): 241–312.

Wolfe, Patrick. "Settler Colonialism and the Elimination of the Native." *Journal of Genocide Research* 8, no. 4 (2006): 387–409.

Working Group on Human Rights and the Border Wall. "Obstructing Human Rights: The Texas-Mexico Border Wall." Full set of briefing papers, Working Group on Human Rights and the Border Wall, University of Texas, Austin, June 2008. https://law.utexas.edu/humanrights/borderwall/analysis/briefing-FULL-SET-OF-REPORTS.pdf.

FOUR

Women from the Mountains

Ndé Women's Leadership Since Time Immemorial

HENRIQUE MAESTAS

Walking It In

We come from the mountains. We are Ndé people. I know this, and I know that this is where I belong. I am Dr. Henrique Maestas and I was born in 1969 in Denver, Colorado. I am a designated keeper of the story of 'Isanaklesh, who as First Mother came down from the Blue Mountains and survived the flood because the Giant Clam carried her, pregnant with the Twins. My mother's mothers and my father's mothers come from both sides of Taos Mountain in New Mexico. My mother's name is Vercila Chacon and our Tia Adela and Tia Antonita told us that their Mama Cirila was an Apache woman who came from the Red River above Taos. Our tias told us about my mom's mother, Maria Chacon, and they said that she was Apache. They said she was about four feet nine inches and had a reputation for being tough, even mean. I met her in Denver, but she died when I was very small. In a picture that our tias showed us, my mom's mama and her sisters stand next to the walls of the house that they built. It was well built and is still there.

My grandmothers lived difficult and challenging lives as Apache women caring for their families in rural New Mexico. They imparted traditions and stories that remain with me today, guiding what I do as a scholar, teacher, and Apache man in the twenty-first century. Their stories give us life, and as Dr. Margo Tamez says, their stories give us knowledge, power, and energy to advocate for community and the continuation of our identities. Drawing upon the encouragement of Margo and the inspiration of my Apache grandmothers, this chapter moves between academic analysis and personal reflection to consider the ways in which Ndé women's leadership anchors our collective histories and provides us with guidance for moving through the problems of the modern world. Telling our stories of family reveals how Ndé women's leadership has allowed us to survive Ndé genocide, removal, and multigenerational trauma.

An important part of this work is expressing the "emotional force" of historical processes and events, particularly those filled with trauma.[1] "Emotional force" includes the memories and associations that I feel when I think and write about all of the survivors of, and those who did not survive, violence and marginalization. I associate my own Apache grandmothers coming from the mountains carrying all of our future with great emotional force that is bringing tears from my eyes as I am writing.

This emotional force carries a particular set of analytical questions about my grandmothers. What happened that they had to leave their homes? What did they endure in order to survive so that we could live? Each of these stories carries depths of grief, loss, trauma, and memory. This memory of who we are . . . this is how it feels. This is who I am. I am filled with emotional force when I think about my Apache grandmothers who came to Arroyo Hondo seeking refuge. It fills me with grief that expands in my lived experience, and fills me with outrage because I am one of many Ndé and other Indigenous people who continue to have to seek refuge because of marginalization and persecution today. Addressing these issues of violence and marginalization that cost lives is part of this work so that we can voice these unrecognized dimensions of Native American experience that cannot be seen through the perspective of American Indian federally recognized history. This history of governmental Indians by its very nature denies the fullness of our identity, culture, and history, and in this way violates our human and civil rights as recognized in the United Nations Declaration on the Rights of Indigenous Peoples (UNDRIP).

Dr. Tamez has helped me to see the healing waters of 'Isanaklesh reflected in narratives of survival of our Ndé women ancestors and present-day Ndé women relatives in ways that help me connect to my Ndé heritage and lived experience. Over the course of my life, narratives of survival and transition have helped me to connect myself to key contexts of Ndé women's leadership.

Within the carried story of 'Isanaklesh are reflected the narratives of survival of my Ndé grandmothers. The story takes us through the emotional force of our family memory and history. This chapter has several basic goals:

1. I want to blend academic analysis with personal reflection and traditional Ndé values to talk about my family history and my grandmothers' stories of survival and persistence.
2. I want to connect those stories within the broader context of Ndé women's traditional forms of leadership by highlighting the collaborative work that I completed with the Lipan Apache Elders Council.
3. I want to narrate some of the stories of movement and place-making that have created Ndé territory since time immemorial, established by Ndé women and dogs following Iyanee (buffalo), and recorded in archaeological context and colonial chronicles.
4. I want to share stories of Iyanee (buffalo), food, and medicine that anchor Apache identity in our homelands, such as the oral tradition shared in Ndé women's kitchens.

Taken together, these traditions and values of 'Isanaklesh, Ndé territory, leadership, and medicine demonstrate the importance of women's leadership for my Ndé people.

'Isanaklesh

I received the story of 'Isanaklesh from Meredith Begay, along with a structure of values related to me as taboos—most important of all, to not write or record the story, but to only tell it as Lipan Apache religious tradition. Recently, I have become more familiar with 'Isanaklesh in conversations with Margo Tamez and have seen a source for relating and understanding the lived reality of Ndé women in ways that have persisted since time immemorial. I see profound alignment between the ways that Meredith Begay drew nearly all of our conversations together into a focus on the significance of 'Isanaklesh in everything that we do and the echoes in many conversations that I have had with Margo Tamez. Of incredible importance in all this is Dr. Ines Talamantez, who bridges Meredith, Margo, and myself through decades of attention to studying and writing about 'Isanaklesh, mother, center, and circle which we return to and which is a metaphysical space that we inhabit as Ndé. This section focuses on 'Isanaklesh as the core source and center of Ndé women's knowledge and leadership since time immemorial, not just for Ndé people but also for all of us connected by Dene unity.

Between 2002 and 2004, Dr. Ines Talamantez invited me to work with the Lipan Apache Elders Council on the Mescalero Apache Indian Reservation of New Mexico to write a new entry for the Macmillan Press *Encyclopedia of Religion* on Apache religious tradition, with a focus on Lipan Apache religious traditions, to replace the earlier entry written by Morris Opler decades previous. I made a number of trips to the Mescalero reservation with Daniel Castro Romero Jr. and spent hours each day listening to the Lipan Apache Elders Council and working in collaboration to produce the best Apache religion entry possible. Meredith Begay emphasized many times and in numerous contexts that the Great Apache Homeland ranges from the Pacific Ocean to the Gulf of Mexico and includes parts of Canada, Mexico, and the United States. As I listened, it became clear that the Lipan Apache Elders Council spoke from and to 'Isanaklesh knowledge in almost every interaction and conversation.

'Isanaklesh is the key origin for Lipan Apache people because she is the Mother of the Twins, Killer of Enemies, and Child of Water, and thereby central to Ndé ceremonial life in the Girls' Initiation Fire Ceremony. We are told that as Ndé people we come from 'Isanaklesh, our First Mother, a woman who came down from the tops of the sacred Blue Mountains. Meredith Begay told us that these were the Blue Mountains of Chihuahua, Mexico. Meredith Begay translated 'Isanaklesh as White Face Paint Woman. Stories and ceremonies specify that the white face paint is actually a white clay.[2]

Meredith Begay spoke of the white clay of 'Isanaklesh in a conversation with Dr. Talamantez that turned toward her daughter's study of astrobiology, which theorizes "white clay" to be a key component of cell membranes necessary to organisms on earth. This is an example of Ndé women's leadership highlighting a shared idea of Ndé tradition and Western science, in which "white clay" is a key building block of life. The productivity of this idea in Ndé culture has produced what Meredith called one of the pillars of Apache culture.

Learning about 'Isanaklesh and how she informed women's leadership within the vast Apache homelands helped me prepare for work with Daniel Castro Romero Jr. in the restoration of burial grounds in South Texas between 1999 and 2006. Meredith Begay and Lucy Smith prepared us with songs, stories, and ritual training to restore over four hundred individual burials at five locations. They gave us instructions on the handling of human remains and cultural artifacts from archaeologically disturbed burials with historical and cultural affiliation to Lipan Apache people in South Texas.

There is a set of values that I associate with Dene unity here in which our work with the ancestors prepared us so that we could better take care of the living. This manifested as our burial ground restoration work transitioned into a coalition including the Lipan Apache Band of Texas, the Lipan Apache Elders Council from the Mescalero Apache Indian Reservation of New Mexico, and the Choctaw-Apache Tribe in Zwolle, Louisiana, to produce the study and document titled *The Identification and Reintroduction of the Lipan Apache Foods.*[3] This document includes a study documenting diabetes, obesity, and heart disease in the Lipan Apache Band of Texas and a recipe book emphasizing a return to traditional diet with identification of traditional plants in English, Spanish, Lipan, and Mescalero Apache.

Ndé oral tradition and values guided our work with burials, which represented the end of life; we also learned important information about the ways of peyote, which helps sustain our spiritual and cultural life. During this same time, we worked to preserve parts of the peyote gardens that were destroyed by the construction of U.S. Interstate 69, running along the U.S.-Mexican border.

Lucy Smith, another member of the Lipan Apache Elders Council, told us a story about the emergence of peyote. She said that many Ndé had lived along the Pecos River, and a little boy named Antonio Apache became lost with his mother in the desert. His mother became weak and told him to find help, but he would not leave her. Instead, he wandered around the desert until he heard a little voice telling him to come closer. Once the boy came near he saw a little green spineless cactus, the peyote, and this plant told him that if he and his mother ate it they would find their family. Antonio took the plant to his mother and gave it to her, and it gave her the strength to get up and walk. Antonio and his mother walked over a hill and found their family's camp. After Antonio told the people what had happened, they adopted peyote as sacred medicine for Ndé people.

Lucy Smith is from a clan that has been traditionally responsible for the peyote medicine, and we were given a song and instructions for using the peyote. She said that the peyote has a kind face on top but also has a claw root underneath, and that it can hurt you if you do not respect it and do not treat it right. She said that as far as she knows, the peyote was given to all of the other tribes by her clan and the Lipan, because they are descended from that little boy Antonio who became lost with his mother and found the peyote. She said that today peyote is being overused and abused by all kinds of people. She said that people are using it every weekend, and this is just too much. If you need to eat it all of the time, then you probably need a different medicine. She gave us these clear instructions, telling us that we were to do three things with the peyote as Lipan. We should take peyote and put some back whenever we go, and not just take the peyote out of the places where it grows; we should work to take care of it. We should have ceremony with peyote just on the altar, without eating it. We should just be with it and pray with it. And finally, we should only eat peyote four times a year.

We discussed peyote further with Zelda, Meredith's daughter, who stressed these points. In the story of the peyote, there is also a lost mother, and the peyote calls out inviting them to come in for refuge and safety. This mirrors closely the story of 'Isanaklesh. Margo Tamez has helped me to see that Ndé women have this experience, as each one is an Ndé leader following in the footsteps of 'Isanaklesh, just like in the ceremony when she runs and we all follow.

This section on 'Isanaklesh is meant to provide a window into the reverence and connection that Meredith Begay and Lucy Smith forged for not just Daniel and myself, but the coalition of Ndé people more broadly. This present collection similarly follows the guidance and leadership of our elders Dr. Margo Tamez and Dr. Eloisa Taméz, who have established paths similar to our Ndé women leaders in the past. I am doing my best to follow this path. Central to all of this work is 'Isanaklesh as mother, center, and circle from which we come and to which we are going.

Ndé Women Leading the People Across the Grasslands Following Iyanee (Buffalo)

In this section, I build on previous discussion of 'Isanaklesh and talk about the connection between women and Iyanee (buffalo), which became intricately tied to our identities, culture, and territory.

Since time immemorial Ndé women led our ancestors across the plains following Iyanee, the buffalo, traveling as families with dogs. In my spirit eye—what we sometimes call the original eyes / *ojos originales*—I see women leading the families following Iyanee, our buffalo relatives, across grasslands between the Arkansas and Colorado Rivers and the Rio Grande. The Tamez Clan Mothers, in ways that remind me of Meredith Begay and Lucy Smith, have provided us with a key foundation for institutionalizing this process of reclaiming ourselves guided by the framework of *Gathering Together, We Decide / Íłahałee dáłe' nahk'éé 'át'éh béodaazį́įł.*

An important part of this recovery is telling our Ndé stories, which connect us to who we are and all our relations. Stories that our elders tell us explain our origins and our migrations, as well as our relationship with the Iyanee. Following Iyanee provides a source for healthy lifestyles based on relationships with animals, plants, water, and land, which structured our relationships with relatives and community and extend to Dene/Ndé unity and alliance.

I would like to share a mind's eye or vision perspective of the way that Ndé women led our ancestral families across the plains and *llanos* for at least ten thousand years. Archaeology, anthropology, and history provide traces of cultural data that we as Ndé oral tradition keepers understand in an experiential manner and express through storytelling, ceremony, and traditional practices. Ndé women in this colonial and modern context are not named and are silenced. However, as Ndé storytellers and ceremonial practitioners, there are ways that we can understand this women-centered way of life and provide breath and life to mothers and families through story and spiritual action.

For us as Ndé people, our story is more than just a story of "human beings." For thousands of years Ndé life was grounded in relationship to Iyanee: the buffalo people. Iyanee were the central and true foundation of Ndé culture since time immemorial, before the European invasion beginning in the 1500s. Archaeological evidence reflects Ndé lifestyle following buffalo for thousands of years in North America. Ndé buffalo hunters are the first North American buffalo hunters described in primary sources written by Spanish conquistadors. Today, the Texas Tribal Buffalo Project is a Lipan Apache community effort and one of many Native American initiatives in which bison caretaking is a central part of life. Bison caretaking in 2023 sees the human and buffalo relationship to be key to Ndé survival and resilience in the face of genocidal pressures of Euro-colonial policies and practices in Texas and the Great Apache Homeland.[4]

Early encounters between Spaniards and Ndé peoples confirm the importance of Iyanee (buffalo) to our culture and way of life. Spanish chronicles give a series of descriptions of Querecho, Vaquero, and Apache buffalo hunters in the Texas Panhandle and eastern New Mexico that can be used to detail historical origins for Ndé buffalo hunters. According to Coronado, the first encounter between Spanish and Querecho people took place on May 10, 1541, on the grasslands of the Texas Panhandle. Querecho were described by Coronado as naked buffalo hunters who traveled on foot with dog trains to trade at Cicuye (Pecos), who ranged the Llano Estacado from New Mexico to the Caprock Escarpment canyonlands of Texas. Most historians agree that the Querecho were Apache buffalo hunters, but the Ndé know them as our ancestors.[5]

In 1598 Ndé Vaquero buffalo hunter cultural data was chronicled by Spanish colonial writers in Capitán Zaldívar's party who were guided by Jusepe, a Nahua guide from central Mexico who had lived among the Vaquero Apache and became the main guide and interpreter for all Spanish visits to the buffalo plains at this time. On this expedition, the party came across a large Vaquero Apache trading party returning from Picuris and Taos with ceramics, textiles, and stones that they had just received in trade for buffalo goods:

> [They] came upon a ranchería of fifty tents made of tanned skins which were very bright red and white in color . . . round like pavilions, with flaps and openings, and made as neatly as those from Italy. They are so large

> that in the most common ones there is ample room for four individual mattresses and beds. The tanning is so good that even the heaviest rain will not go through the skin, nor does it become hard. On the contrary, when it dries it becomes as soft and pliable as before.[6]

This next set of descriptions are of particular importance regarding Ndé women's leadership in a time before Ndé buffalo hunters regularly used horses, when they followed Iyanee on foot:

> They used medium-sized shaggy dogs which they harness like mules. They have large droves of them, each girt around the breast and haunches, carrying a load of at least one hundred pounds . . . one after the other dragging the ends of their poles, almost all of them with sores under the harness. When the women load these dogs they hold their heads between their legs, and in this manner they load them or straighten their loads . . . they travel at a pace as if they had been trained with fetters.[7]

This description with its use of the term "fetters" is comparing Ndé women to the porters and their use of livestock in Spanish colonial practice, but we should think of the practice more as harnessing dogs to drag tipi poles to carry family belongings on a structure similar to what would later be known as the travois, used with horses by Plains Indians. Ndé women are reported to have been responsible for training and managing the dogs for smooth travel. This entails teaching women across generations to make and manage this important toolkit for managing a mobile household; this is the way in which Ndé women led Ndé families following Iyanee.

In 1602, Juan de León of the Oñate colony trek provides further details about people whom he calls Vaquero Apache:

> They pack and carry their rancherías on their dogs which have packsores. They follow a traveling order in which one woman led the dog train followed by the other women and children. Men traveled on the sides within sight scouting for game and enemies. They always follow the buffalo.[8]

There appeared to be an observable division of labor, in which Ndé women led dog trains across the buffalo plains along with children and elders, while Ndé men scouted and organized various forms of buffalo kills. The women raised the dogs and were responsible for the belongings of the family, which the dogs carried. The significance of this cannot be overstated.

Ndé families living with Iyanee, following them across a vast buffalo-hunting territory for thousands of years, is what time immemorial means for Ndé people. This is embedded in memory, history, and archaeology, reflecting thousands of years of Iyanee herds followed by Ndé people led by women who kept the families together and cared for the children and the elders. Concretely, women's leadership managed all family possessions and the dogs who carried it all. The men engaged in a form of leadership, dealing with hunting the buffalo and with danger, as well as locating places to camp and processing the buffalo into meat, clothing, and other goods; in addition, Ndé men were also instrumental in trade and alliance relationships.

Ndé people walked in families that made up bands of dozens to hundreds of people. However, gatherings such as trade fairs and shared hunts were common, and these could draw thousands of people including those from other tribes. There were no horses, which would arrive with the Spanish in the 1500s, but they did have dogs. We can imagine Ndé buffalo hunters and the way they walked with their dogs. Women led the families and the communities by raising the dogs and distributing them to other women. Medium-sized shaggy dogs, most likely a type similar to huskies, were each harnessed with a load of at least one hundred pounds set on a travois and dragged the ends of the poles tied to their backs. Women owned the dogs and all of the family's belongings. If we focus on the idea that Ndé women owned everything, we can see cultural values that are still with us in Lipan Apache culture.

Following the traditions outlined above, Meredith Begay similarly talked about the ownership of homes where families lived. This reflects the value that everything begins and ends with 'Isanaklesh and that women should be the center of the Apache world. Meredith explained that women are the only traditional landowners because only women could own things. However, along with ownership, they were responsible for the home and had to stay with the home.

Although many men build tipis and homes today, Meredith reminded me that this was traditionally the work of women. One day she directed

Daniel and me to build a wikiup from branches. She said humorously, "Why are you boys doing this women's work making wikiups and working with animal hides? I don't understand why the girls won't do this. They are the ones who are supposed to be doing this . . . but they just won't do it anymore. So I guess I just have to teach you." A "wikiup," as we were taught, is a shelter made of branches or trees, and a "tipi" is a type of wikiup. However, the wikiup we were making was a dome made of branches. One of the funniest things that I remember she said when we were making the wikiup was: "You know, the dogs shouldn't be in the house, I don't know why some people let the dogs in their houses . . . Come to think of it, people aren't supposed to be in the house either."

I believe that this is a reference to the time immemorial of Ndé buffalo hunting when our ancestors did not live in houses. This was a time when Ndé lived out there on the buffalo plains, walking across the grasslands and prairie, and set up wikiups in temporary camps. Home was walking with Iyanee. Men mostly traveled away from the women and the families, to keep pace with the herds and maintain scouting networks to keep the band integrated and on the same path as Iyanee. The everyday living space was not the house structure, or even the tipi or wikiup. The everyday living space was the walking path that the women led the families and the dog trains along, following Iyanee.

Each day Ndé people traveled, they would come to a place to set up their tipis, buffalo hides set on poles tied together at the top with an eagle feather, as told in Meredith's story about the tipi. Within an hour some fifty tipis painted red and white shone in the afternoon sunlight, soon to become silhouettes against the sunset. In and around the tipis fires burned for family food and Ndé crafts. Although some tipis were small and for only a few people, most were large enough to fit four beds around a fire. Tanned buffalo hides with all of the hair removed were of the highest quality and kept even the heaviest rain from coming through the tipi. Before and after being set up, the tipi buffalo-hide covers were soft and pliable and easily rolled or folded to be transported by dog trains. Ndé women prepared the hides by meticulously cleaning them and chewing them to soften them. Ndé men lived with their wife's family and band, and generations of women nearly always stayed together. Generational Ndé women maintained life and family in an important form of cultural leadership.

Ndé learned and developed a relationship with the Iyanee, making technical improvements with skills, strategies, and technology for a good life. Lands that buffalo herds lived on were shaped by the Iyanee and Ndé, who lived as other large mammals on the plains, part of a humanized landscape that was sustainable for ten thousand years. Ndé lived by walking and stopping in tipi camps and did not cultivate the land. They traded buffalo goods with people who planted and harvested maize and other crops, and the pottery from this trade helps to identify and detail Apache history and prehistory. Ceremonial reverence for Iyanee is the context of Lipan Apache oral tradition.

Today, the Texas Tribal Buffalo Project is a Lipan Apache community, one of many Native American communities recovering bison caretaking as a central part of life. Keeping this personal and grounded, this organization is where my sons live and work with their mother Lucille Rodriguez Contreras. Bison caretaking in 2023 sees the human and buffalo relationship as key to Ndé survival and resilience in the face of genocidal pressures of Euro-colonial policies and practices in Texas and the Great Apache Homeland.

In sum, this is not just an academic exercise. Recovering our connection to Ndé lifeways and values grounded in a relationship with Iyanee in the form of bison caretaking can be an important path to living on the land in a way that focuses on clean air, water, and soil for healthy and stronger people.

Ndé Women, Kitchen Stories, and Food

As the stories above clearly indicate, women were at the center of life, owned most materials in the home, tanned buffalo hides, and fed the family. In this next section, I elaborate upon these stories and connect them with modern-day examples of food production, medicinal practices, and food sovereignty, all of which sustain our Ndé families today. My first story is about Aunt Lolo and Osha root, and how it helped me learn about traditional Ndé women's knowledge of medicine.

My aunt Lolo was the oldest sister in my father's family. In 1992, I visited her after cancer treatment. I came into the house and went straight to the kitchen, where I found her sitting at the table with her head in her hands. I asked how she was, and she said, "Fine," without looking up. She said that it was hard for her to eat and that she felt weak and couldn't get around very well. The good news was that the cancer was in remission. I pulled out a bag of Osha and gave it to her. I told her that it was strong medicine and that she could eat it. She took the bag, opened it up, and put her face in to smell it. She looked up at me and said, "I know this. This is what we used when I was a little girl. In the morning, the men would leave the house with one of these roots in their mouth and the women would stay in the kitchen and drink the tea. This was what we drank in the mornings before we had coffee." She said that she would make tea with it and was happy that I had brought it for her. The oral tradition in our family is that Grandma Simona, my father's mother, lived in Gallinas, north of Las Vegas, New Mexico, and that they had always lived there. The kitchen of her childhood where she would drink Osha tea with her mother was re-created by us in her kitchen in Denver, where she would drink Osha tea again.

This story about Osha root resonated broadly with Ndé people I spoke with later in my life. Between 2002 and 2004, Daniel Castro Romero Jr. and I made trips to Elk, New Mexico, on the Mescalero reservation, for guidance and training from Meredith Begay and the Lipan Apache Elders Council. One of the places where we met was the community center in the town of Mescalero. I brought pecans and pine nuts with me, and as our elders spoke, I shelled nuts and gave them to them to eat. They began telling us what we needed to hear. At one point, we heard Meredith Begay and Lucy Smith speaking Spanish to each other and were surprised. I said that I did not know that they spoke Spanish, and they said that they had always spoken Spanish, but not much anymore. When I asked why not, they told me a story.

Meredith said that when they were young girls in the 1940s there had been a bad drought and they needed Hnishida medicine, which we know as Osha. Because of the drought they could not find it nearby, so they walked south into Mexico to gather the medicine. Once they had it, they started walking on the road returning home and were speaking Spanish, when some White men came up to them, grabbed them, and threw them into the back of a truck. These men said that they were Mexicans and didn't belong there, so they drove them a ways into Mexico and left them there. The girls eventually just followed the mountain paths back home and avoided the roads as much as possible. Meredith said that after that they stopped speaking Spanish and have even made sure to not talk with a Mexican accent.

In sum, Hnishida is Osha, one of our sacred medicines. Oral tradition tells about our relationship to this sacred plant and how we use it to strengthen ourselves and help us with flu-like symptoms and trouble breathing. It is also a stimulant, like coffee, for casual everyday use. Our relationship to this plant goes back to our oral traditions and connects us to our time immemorial. Important in my life, Hnishida is abundant in this Yampa Valley that I live in and is a source of connection to the bears and people who use this medicine in my community.

In April of 2001, I was with my mother and children in my tia Adela's kitchen. We were with her sister, Tia Antonita, and they talked about our Apache heritage from our grandmother's side. We were told that the mothers of both my grandfather and grandmother had come to Arroyo Hondo as Apache women fleeing from something terrible. They found a home in that town, and eventually our grandparents married, had children, and moved to Denver. All these stories were told in their kitchen while we prepared and ate breakfast with eggs, green chile, tortillas, and fry bread. My daughter was also present, so at that moment in their kitchen we had four generations of Ndé women telling us about our Apache heritage. This is the leadership that I am talking about. This is what set me on a path to bring these words out here as part of this chapter. This is how we survive.

A few years later in 2004, I found myself in Meredith Begay's kitchen in Elk, New Mexico. She was sitting across the room and called out to me, "Nephew. Warm up some of the Navajo bread and bring us some deer to eat." The deer was right there still warm, and I asked where the Navajo bread was and she said it was right there in the plastic bag. I found and pulled out some handmade flour tortillas, which I found out was the Navajo bread. I brought the food over for all of us, and we ate and talked about how we were going to do the burial ground work. When I visited Meredith, I often found myself bringing her food or preparing food, like shelling pine nuts and pecans. This was what I did while I listened and learned about what to write and what to do. This is the Ndé women's leadership that I am talking about.

While the kitchen is the source of food, sustenance, cultural persistence, and women's leadership, food sovereignty is the metaphorical kitchen for all Indigenous peoples. Food sovereignty is a way of talking about practical resistance to being subject to the market and related unhealthy food outcomes, and the definition voiced above is a great way of saying it in a global, formal way.[9]

Ndé Food Sovereignty

As discussed above, ancestral Ndé families followed Ndé women following Iyanee to live together on the land. This was the way of life for our ancestors. It was food sovereignty of the highest order. After centuries of settler-colonial oppression, we have nearly lost the ability to feed ourselves in a healthy way. The food sovereignty movement, like the reintroduction of the bison across the Plains, represents our modern strategies. The key difference for me between the turn of the century (1996–2006) and now is that many more of us are directly involved in food sovereignty through bison caretaking and Indigenous gardening. Rey Salazar was our master gardener and taught me most of my foundational knowledge about growing food. We formed relationships with family members and with Lipan and other Indigenous people focused on seeds, sacred offerings, growing food, and holding ceremony.

Today, decades later, I see many Lipan Apache people of all ages identifying as Bison Caretakers and Indigenous gardeners, both of which facilitate food sovereignty. Years ago I moved to the Yampa Valley, which is part of the headwaters of the Colorado River that flows west to the Gulf of California, and here I work in the Ndé Native Food Sovereignty and Indigenous Knowledge Project. Although I learned gardening in Texas, where we could grow almost year-round, I now live in the Rocky Mountains of Colorado and plant a garden at about seven thousand feet, with four to six months of frozen winter, snow measured in feet, and temperatures dropping below twenty-five degrees Fahrenheit. I have blossomed into a naturalist and ethnobotanist, and I have learned about edible foods and medicine in the garden and in the forests around me. For seven years I have worked in this garden that mainly grows quelites, kale, potatoes, peas, and tomatillos. Strong medicines in the garden are yarrow and gumweed. The *quelites chamizales* grow from seeds from Native Seed Search, sourced from Taos Pueblo, near where my mother was born. These are a form of wild spinach or lamb's-quarters that grow up to nine-foot stalks and leaves bigger than your head.

The garden is a place where I learn about how to grow food alongside our relatives in nature without using chemicals, while building soil with only natural ingredients. I feel that over the last four years I have developed a part of food sovereignty, in that if I needed to, I could feed myself and at least a dozen others with the resources nearby. Early in my life this was a goal, and in many ways this is what food sovereignty means to me.

Meanwhile, Lucille Rodriguez Contreras, the mother of three of my children, has the Texas Tribal Buffalo Project in Waelder, Texas, with Enrique Jose Kuautli Maestas and Jesus Tekuani Maestas. They have grown from a ranch established in 2021 with one bull to a growing herd of twenty Iyanee as of the fall of 2023. These developments convince me that the vision of bringing Iyanee to the land and people is coming true. As I understand, the vision includes bringing Iyanee back to the land and to the people and growing the buffalo herds across North America, connecting the Canadian woodland bison herds to the buffalo herds of northern Mexico, as it was since time immemorial.

Conclusion

Ndé women's leadership is the story of Ndé people since time immemorial. We are grounded in 'Isanaklesh, our mother who came from the mountains; Ndé women following Iyanee until the arrival of the Spanish in the 1500s; and elders such as Meredith Begay. Each generation of women passed on our heritage to us. As Ndé people we try to follow the teachings of 'Isanaklesh to nurture our families and our communities. In the process, we have had to change and adapt these traditions to life in the United States of America. We are engaging in bison caretaking and Ndé gardens in the spirit of food sovereignty, and we are sharing our oral traditions more openly than the last few generations. We can see that there was a beautiful Ndé way of life since time immemorial that is a source of Ndé ancestral pride when we compare it to the world we live in today. Our ancestral way of life did not bring the contamination of water, land, air, and life. This is the consequence of European colonialism and Eurocentric enterprise, most recently American business. As is evident, the legacy of colonialism and modern American development has been a complex of environmental disasters, social disintegration, the climate crisis, and mass extinction.

As I see myself, I am Ndé and part of a growing movement: a gathering storm of an Indigenous re-membering of our stories . . . our traditions . . . ourselves, which is still emerging from the deep generational trauma that is demographic and cultural genocide. When we know this, we can recognize that this recovery is not spurious or reactionary; it is a response of survivors long in the making, led by our mothers from the mountains since time immemorial. **'Isanaklesh**.

NOTES

1. Renato Rosaldo, *Culture and Truth: The Remaking of Social Analysis; With a New Introduction* (Boston: Beacon Press, 1993), 1–24.
2. Enrique Maestas, "Apache Religious Traditions," in *Encyclopedia of Religion*, 2nd ed., ed. Lindsay Jones (New York: Macmillan, 2004), 404–7.
3. Enrique Maestas and Lipan Apache Elders Committee, *The Identification and Reintroduction of the Lipan Apache Foods* (Edinburg, Tex.: Lipan Apache Band of Texas, 2007).
4. Texas Tribal Buffalo Project, "Texas Tribal Buffalo Project, Buffalo Ranch Short Film with Lucille Contreras," video, 7:03, YouTube, posted March 21, 2022, by Texas Tribal Buffalo Project, https://www.youtube.com/watch?v=FL_JMK94IvA.
5. George Hammond and Agapito Rey, eds. and trans., *Narratives of the Coronado Expedition, 1540–1542* (Albuquerque: University of New Mexico Press, 1940), 186.
6. George Hammond and Agapito Rey, eds. and trans., *Don Juan de Oñate, Colonizer of New Mexico, 1595–1628* (Albuquerque: University of New Mexico Press, 1953), 400.
7. Hammond and Rey, *Don Juan de Oñate*, 401.
8. Hammond and Rey, *Don Juan de Oñate*.
9. "Food sovereignty is the right of peoples to healthy and culturally appropriate food produced through ecologically sound and sustainable methods, and their right to define their own food and agriculture systems. It puts the aspirations and needs of those who produce, distribute and consume food at the heart of food systems and policies rather than the demands of markets and

corporations." See the first global forum on food sovereignty: "Declaration of Nyéléni," Nyéléni: International Movement for Food Sovereignty, March 27, 2007, https://nyeleni.org/en/declaration-of-nyeleni/.

BIBLIOGRAPHY

"Declaration of Nyéléni." Nyéléni: International Movement for Food Sovereignty, March 27, 2007. https://nyeleni.org/en/declaration-of-nyeleni/.

Hammond, George, and Agapito Rey, eds. and trans. *Don Juan de Oñate, Colonizer of New Mexico, 1595–1628*. Albuquerque: University of New Mexico Press, 1953.

Hammond, George, and Agapito Rey, eds. and trans. *Narratives of the Coronado Expedition, 1540–1542*. Albuquerque: University of New Mexico Press, 1940.

Maestas, Enrique. "Apache Religious Traditions." In *Encyclopedia of Religion*, 2nd ed., edited by Lindsay Jones, 404–7. New York: Macmillan, 2004.

Maestas, Enrique, and Lipan Apache Elders Committee. *The Identification and Reintroduction of the Lipan Apache Foods*. Edinburg, Tex.: Lipan Apache Band of Texas, 2007.

Rosaldo, Renato. *Culture and Truth: The Remaking of Social Analysis; With a New Introduction*. Boston: Beacon Press, 1993.

Texas Tribal Buffalo Project. "Texas Tribal Buffalo Project, Buffalo Ranch Short Film with Lucille Contreras." Video, 7:03. YouTube, posted March 21, 2022, by Texas Tribal Buffalo Project. https://www.youtube.com/watch?v=FL_JMK94IvA.

PART II

The El Calaboz Dispossession Tribunal

Community Testimonies and Witnessing

FIVE

Indigenous in the Shadow of the Wall

A Gathering in El Calaboz

SHANNON SPEED

> *We are here and we have a voice. That's what we are doing—we are telling our truth.*
>
> —Richard Gonzalez, vice-chair, Lipan Apache Band of Texas

It was a warm, sunny afternoon—as they so often are in Central Texas—when I set off from Austin with my friend and colleague, the Mapuche scholar Luis Cárcamo-Huechante, bound for the U.S.-Mexico border town of El Calaboz Ranchería.[1] We had received a remarkable invitation to a human rights event under the border wall *organized by and for Indigenous people.* I had been invited to be a "listener," someone who could record what was said by the participants. Despite being a notoriously bad notetaker (I'm terribly dyslexic), I readily agreed, anxious to have the opportunity to absorb the collective wisdom of this gathering. So, on this sunny day in 2011, we climbed into my Volvo and headed south. It was a five-and-a-half-hour ride into the Lower Rio Grande Valley. As it happened, the eleven-hour round trip would provide ample time for conversation with Luis, then my colleague of only a year or two, and we talked of our lives, cementing a friendship that continues to flourish to this day. If for no other reason than that one, this would have been an extraordinary trip. But that was not the only reason it was extraordinary.

We arrived in El Calaboz in the early afternoon, to the home of Ndé activist, scholar, and professor of nursing Dr. Eloisa Taméz.[2] I had worked tangentially on the complaint Dr. Taméz brought before the Inter-American Commission on Human Rights regarding the border wall, which ran smack through her backyard and, I now saw, towered over her small home like a threatening tsunami. Luis and I were here at the invitation of her daughter, the remarkable Ndé activist, scholar, and poet Dr. Margo Tamez, who had also been a leader in the Inter-American Commission case and had garnered an international movement against the wall through the organization Lipan Apache Women's Defense, which she founded with her mother. Sadly, their lengthy fight was not enough to keep the egregious metal monster off their property, and for the next two days we met in its shadow with the approximately fifty attendees. Many were local Ndé, others from the Ndé diaspora, traditional chiefs, clan heads, and Elders. An inspiring contingent of Tohono O'odham youth had joined us from Arizona. Border activists and scholars Tere Leal, Cynthia Bejarano, and Jeff Shepherd also joined. Luis and I, Mapuche and Chickasaw, were not of this border region, but we came in solidarity as Indigenous scholar-activists. We had all come together at Margo and Eloisa's behest, to speak and to listen, to think together from an Indigenous perspective about Indigenous rights, relations to land, and Indigenous knowledges as articulated in El Calaboz and throughout the Texas-Mexico border region, and to learn from Ndé histories of struggle against settler dispossessions and U.S. violations of their human rights. It was a rare and beautiful gathering.

From my notes: "Rage. About being cut off by wall from lands, sacred sites, and resources (fish, cane, etc.). About what wall represents in terms of current forms of power and oppression."

The border wall's ominous and oppressive presence loomed over the gathering. Many spoke to the violence its imposition represented. A few years earlier, in 2007, a federal judge had ruled that Cameron County property owners had to open their land to government surveyors. Eloisa Taméz refused to grant access to the land, which had been held in her family for 265 years, since the San Pedro de Carricitos Land Grant, established by the Spanish Crown in 1743. She was then sued in 2008 by the Army Corps of Engineers. She fought back with a countersuit against then–U.S. Department of Homeland Security secretary Michael Chertoff, making her one of the first residents to seek to block the dispossession of their lands by the federal government. The U.S. Department of Homeland Security would eventually file 330 lawsuits against scores of landowners along the Rio Grande, in what has been characterized as nothing less than a "land grab."[3] Eloisa Taméz and others would ultimately lose their battle, and the wall was rammed through the area, cutting them off from access to the Rio Grande, and in many cases from significant portions of land between the river and the wall. While it was brutal for all who lost their lands and river access, the brutality was particularly severe for Indigenous peoples like the Ndé, whose lands and peoples traditionally spanned both sides of the settler-imposed U.S.-Mexico border. Margo Tamez characterized the border (and wall) as a "psychic and symbolic scar" that commits "ongoing violence to our identities."

Beyond the particular form of ongoing Indigenous dispossession that the wall represented (represents), the cutting off of access to sacred sites and materials was (is) a further form of violence that was spoken to by a number of participants in the gathering. An activist with the Gila River Alliance for a Clean Environment (GRACE), Lori Thomas Riddle from the Tohono O'odham Nation, spoke to the significance of the river to cross-border nations like her own. Referring to an O'odham children's art project, she commented, "[Even] children who may never have seen the river, may never see it, in every picture there was a river. They know who they are." The centrality of the river in peoples' lives, in their identities as peoples, was palpable in the gathering. Steven Anthony Fernandez (Ndé) of the Apache del Rio Intertribal Association reflected on the spiritual significance of the river and surrounding areas: "The wall affects our sacred places beyond border wall access. [The river] is part of our heritage and we should have access to that. Our spiritual practices are how we recognize ourselves as a nation." Elder Toni Patelo similarly expressed the need to be able "to freely exercise the spiritual practices of our Lipan Apache heritage. [For this we need] access to our sacred sites." Another Lipan participant, whose name was not recorded in my notes, talked about being cut off from extended family burial sites and not being able to carry out traditional responsibilities to the dead. For the late Daniel Castro Romero, chairman of the Lipan Apache Band of Texas, the loss of the special relationship to the land and ability to steward the land, which he called the "social and economic heart of our people," was a tragedy that they were actively working to reverse.

The menacing performance of settler sovereignty that the wall symbolizes is complemented in the Lower Rio Grande Valley by the overwhelming presence of Border Patrol policing, something also keenly felt by the Tohono O'odham at the gathering (and also quite palpably present in the El Calaboz area). A participant from the Tohono O'odham delegation remembered growing up when there was no Border Patrol on their lands. Now the Border Patrol violates their autonomy, patrolling their lands in ATVs and putting up checkpoints all over. He noted that O'odham people are often targeted by Border Patrol as potential immigrants and are surveilled and harassed. He commented on the intrusion and surveillance: "The Border Patrol is just out there sitting on our sacred sites in ATVs watching us." With over twenty thousand agents along the border in 2012, it is not surprising that people felt policed and surveilled, leading Eloisa Taméz to refer to the border area as "an open-air prison."

Participants also lamented the environmental damage wrought by the wall. Naturally, installing an eighteen-foot-high barrier of reinforced steel and concrete, along with the accompanying policing technologies, from drones to ATVs, creates an irreparable impact on the land and its wildlife. Kevin from the Tohono O'odham delegation lamented the "Border Patrol and drones stressing animals and damaging sacred sites" in a way that felt "invasive and forceful." The Real ID Act of 2005 and Secure Fence Act of 2006 allowed the secretary of homeland security to waive all environmental laws in relation to fence construction. DHS exercised this right five times between September 2005 and December 2008, affecting all states along the U.S.-Mexico border.[4] The U.S.-Mexico border is roughly 1,954 miles long and has the highest rate of species endangerment in the United States. More than seven hundred migratory species of birds, mammals, and insects live in the region. The borderlands ecosystems are fragile, and their integrity is vital to the many vulnerable species that inhabit them.[5] The impacts on wildlife from the border wall construction range from increased road mortality to loss of habitat cover and connectivity, from altered wildlife behavior and range due to high-intensity lighting and operational noise to the interruption of mating activities.[6] Multiple reports produced at the time left little doubt that the impacts on wildlife would be significant and irreversible. People at the gathering were intensely aware of what this artificial barrier would mean for beings they consider relatives.

Attendees were also quite conscious of the power play that the wall represents. One Ndé participant, referring to the DHS's proposal to have doors allowing members of cross-border Native nations to move back and forth across the border, commented: "They want to open it for us. But this is about their power and control." As this participant signals, the construction of territorial barriers and the control of territorial access form part of the performance of settler sovereignty. As legal scholar Sherally Munshi framed this:

> The border is itself part of a broader social formation, a racial economy, within which the practices and rationalities that now govern the management of human mobility have been shaped by the imperatives of colonial capitalism and the contradictions of settler nationalism.[7]

Referring to a different settler-imposed wall, sociologist Rachel Busbridge wrote:

> The wall is a colonial production that draws a psychic line between a "civilised in here" and "uncivilised out there," fulfilling the double function of forging a perceived bounded, protective national enclosure at the same time as buttressing the necessity of controlling territory beyond the bounds of that enclosure.[8]

The role of the border and the wall in the ongoing business of managing settler sovereignty and deploying settler power, even in ostensible compromises like the doors, was obvious to all at the gathering. It was this recognition of the power structures at play that led activist Tere Leal, following on the Red de Pueblos Indígenas, to assert the need for Indigenous people to "*volver a ser dueños de la frontera*," by which she meant a return to sovereign control.

This gathering was not simply about lamenting the loss and damage, it was about thinking together about how to resist. Richard Gonzalez, then vice-chair of the Lipan Apache Band of Ndé and president of Native Vets of California, verbalized the urgency of action for today and for the future: "We need to take a stand, not just today but every day. We need to take action to make it right. To defend not just ourselves but our children. We need to act, not just talk. There are many things we can do. Other people can help us." Elder Toni Patelo later shared, "Complaining is not going to get things resolved. It's action that is really going to make things come into focus."

Margo raised the possibility of international forums. Having done significant advocacy at the United Nations (UN) with Lipan Apache Women's Defense, Margo brought knowledge of the UN, particularly through the rights enshrined in the United Nations Declaration on the Rights of Indigenous Peoples (UNDRIP). She shared information about the San Carlos Apache mining issues that were then before the UN Permanent Forum on Indigenous Issues and suggested that forums such as this might be considered. She did observe, however, that she had found the UN to be male-dominated and linear, and noted her frustration that not until Article 22 of the UNDRIP does one find so much as a mention of women and children. She also shared information about her testimony before the Inter-American Commission on Human Rights.[9]

Because many of the wall's impacts are environmental, and taking account of the resource extraction issues, the environmental justice movement also came up. There was some discussion of allyship and the possibilities for building from this movement, but ultimately distrust based on the long-standing ignoring of Indigenous concerns by the movement led people to discount this as a potential approach to struggle. As Margo stated, referencing Native American attorney Lawrence Baca, "Environmental justice—that's about civil rights. That doesn't work well. Civil rights [activists] never come here."

There were also calls for holding the government accountable. Richard Gonzalez spoke as a veteran of the U.S. armed forces: "This is *our* government. We should hold our government responsible for our needs. Vets place their lives on the line for our freedom. Yet where is ours? We need to remind our government of that." In the context of the utter disdain shown by Michael Chertoff and the U.S. Department of Homeland Security for the well-being of the people along the border wall path, calls for government accountability for the damage wrought were certainly not unwarranted. But at the same time, people were calling for self-sufficiency and sustainability as requisites for enacting sovereignty as Native nations. In the words of Richard's nephew, Steven Anthony Fernandez, "We need self-sufficiency. We need to be in a place where we can sustain our own situation." Self-sufficiency and sustainability are crucial components of sovereignty, and the balance between self-sufficiency and government accountability—particularly the trust relationship with the federal government—is a dance that all Native nations are to some extent engaged in. For non–federally recognized nations like the Ndé (where no federal trust relationship exists) that balance tips, perhaps, toward the side of self-sufficiency.

One of the overarching goals of the meeting was to discuss the possibility of creating an Indigenous human rights documentation center in El Calaboz. Margo discussed her efforts to document the struggle waged over the preceding years and made a case for the need for "Indigenous documentation centers to protect our knowledge."[10] The historic resistance of the Indigenous peoples of El Calaboz Ranchería and surrounding areas to the ongoing dispossession of ancestral lands owned communally through Aboriginal and Crown land grant title set in motion significant research by the Tamez family and other Indigenous women "to untangle their community's legal, social, economic and political histories in land-tenure along the Lower Rio Grande Valley."[11] Their research unearthed a long history of legal contestation by Indigenous peoples before succeeding sovereigns, as well as a longer history of state violence and Indigenous dispossession. Margo Tamez documented much of this work in her 2010 doctoral dissertation, drawing on colonial archives, genealogical records, community documents, photographs, government documents, and interviews with community members from the clans of Lipan Apaches.[12] The influence of this work was unmistakable in the gathering, as many Ndé participants reflected on the history and the reconstruction of their knowledge base and claims to sovereignty despite the violence of Spain, Mexico, Texas, and the United States. Tamez referred to this reconstructive work as "both historical and critical memory recovery, which challenge[d] normative conceptions of Native American and Indigenous genocide history."[13]

It would be difficult to find a state with a more genocidal history than Texas (although California, where I now live, might come in a close second). One aspect that characterizes these particularly genocidal states is an extreme lack of documentation of Indigenous peoples and their histories. The erasure from history of entire peoples is a critical component of the settler-colonial project, following on brutal physical elimination. The dedicated work of the Tamez women and other Indigenous women in the El Calaboz area toward "re-learning and re-examining our histories in contemporary contexts of power" was vital liberatory, anticolonial work to recover their past from settler erasure and defend themselves against ongoing violent dispossession.[14] The goal of a documentation center that would capture that research and document that work seemed urgent.

I honestly do not know if this documentation center ever came into being or if the exigencies of struggle, along with the demands of everyday life and the academic-industrial complex, rendered this a distant dream for the future. Regardless, the beauty of this gathering stands. Indigenous peoples—federally recognized, state-recognized, and nonrecognized—came together around a shared fate at the fraught intersection of two settler states and across these states' settler-imposed border. Subject to all the posturing and performances of settler sovereignty, from the policing of territorial boundaries to the rights to surveil and expel, to dispossess and eliminate, these Indigenous peoples remained and continued to struggle against ongoing violence and to exercise their sovereignty as Native nations. They came together to talk about painful histories and multiple and ongoing refusals, and to strategize toward the future. I came away feeling not just hopeful but also empowered. Indigenous peoples, even the most vulnerable to settler violences in the past and in the current moment, were standing strong and united in struggle. At least for that one weekend, under the shadow of the border wall in El Calaboz Ranchería, when people gathered to tell their truth.

NOTES

1. All direct quotes throughout are from my notes.
2. I use the terms "Lipan Apache" and "Ndé" interchangeably in this chapter.
3. Christian Miller, Kiah Collier, and Julian Aguilar, "Texas Land Grab: How the Federal Government Abused Its Power to Seize Property for the Border Fence," *The Texas Tribune*, December 14, 2017, https://www.elpasotimes.com/story/news/2017/12/14/texas-land-grab-how-federal-government-abused-its-power-seize-property-border-fence/952062001/.
4. Marshal Garbus, "Environmental Impact of Border Security Infrastructure: How Department of Homeland Security's Waiver of Environmental Regulations Threatens Environmental Interests Along the U.S.-Mexico Border," *Tulane Environmental Law Journal* 31, no. 2 (2018): 327–44.
5. Garbus, "Environmental Impact."
6. Defenders of Wildlife, "Comments on Draft Environmental Impact Statement for Construction, Maintenance, and Operation of Tactical Infrastructure, Rio Grande Valley Sector, Texas," December 31, 2007; Lindsay Eriksson and Melinda Taylor, "The Environmental Impacts of the Border Wall Between Texas

and Mexico" (briefing paper, Working Group on Human Rights and the Border Wall, University of Texas, Austin, 2008), https://law.utexas.edu/humanrights/borderwall/analysis/briefing-The-Environmental-Impacts-of-the-Border-Wall.pdf.

7. Sherally Munshi, "Unsettling the Border," *UCLA Law Review* 67, no. 6 (2021): 1723.
8. Rachel Busbridge, "Performing Colonial Sovereignty and the Israeli 'Separation' Wall," *Social Identities* 19, no. 5 (2013): 653.
9. See Denise Gilman, "Obstructing Human Rights: The Texas-Mexico Border Wall; Background and Context" (briefing paper, Working Group on Human Rights and the Border Wall, University of Texas, Austin, 2008), https://law.utexas.edu/humanrights/borderwall/analysis/briefing-INTRODUCTION.pdf.
10. See Margo Tamez, "NÁDASI'NÉ' NDÉ' ISDZÁNÉ BEGOZ'AAHÍ' SHIMAA SHINÍ' GOKAL GOWĄ GOSHJAA HA'ÁNÁ'IDŁÍ TEXAS-NAKAIYÉ GODESDZOG / Returning Lipan Apache Women's Laws, Lands, and Power in El Calaboz Ranchería, Texas-Mexico Border" (PhD diss., Washington State University, 2010), ProQuest.
11. Tamez, "NÁDASI'NÉ' NDÉ," viii.
12. Tamez, "NÁDASI'NÉ' NDÉ."
13. Tamez, "NÁDASI'NÉ' NDÉ," viii.
14. Tamez, "NÁDASI'NÉ' NDÉ," 21.

BIBLIOGRAPHY

Busbridge, Rachel. "Performing Colonial Sovereignty and the Israeli 'Separation' Wall." *Social Identities* 19, no. 5 (2013): 653–69.

Defenders of Wildlife. "Comments on Draft Environmental Impact Statement for Construction, Maintenance, and Operation of Tactical Infrastructure, Rio Grande Valley Sector, Texas." December 31, 2007.

Eriksson, Lindsay, and Melinda Taylor. "The Environmental Impacts of the Border Wall Between Texas and Mexico." Briefing paper, Working Group on Human Rights and the Border Wall, University of Texas, Austin, 2008. https://law.utexas.edu/humanrights/borderwall/analysis/briefing-The-Environmental-Impacts-of-the-Border-Wall.pdf.

Garbus, Marshal. "Environmental Impact of Border Security Infrastructure: How Department of Homeland Security's Waiver of Environmental Regulations Threatens Environmental Interests Along the U.S.-Mexico Border." *Tulane Environmental Law Journal* 31, no. 2 (2018): 327–44.

Gilman, Denise. "Obstructing Human Rights: The Texas-Mexico Border Wall; Background and Context." Briefing paper, Working Group on Human Rights and the Border Wall, University of Texas, Austin, 2008. https://law.utexas.edu/humanrights/borderwall/analysis/briefing-INTRODUCTION.pdf.

Miller, Christian, Kiah Collier, and Julian Aguilar. "Texas Land Grab: How the Federal Government Abused Its Power to Seize Property for the Border Fence." *The Texas*

Tribune, December 14, 2017. https://www.elpasotimes.com/story/news/2017/12/14/texas-land-grab-how-federal-government-abused-its-power-seize-property-border-fence/952062001/.

Munshi, Sherally. "Unsettling the Border." *UCLA Law Review* 67, no. 6 (2021): 1720–67.

Tamez, Margo. "NÁDASI'NÉ' NDÉ' ISDZÁNÉ BEGOZ'AAHÍ' SHIMAA SHINÍ' GOKAL GOWĄ GOSHJAA HA'ÁNÁ'IDŁÍ TEXAS-NAKAIYÉ GODESDZOG / Returning Lipan Apache Women's Laws, Lands, and Power in El Calaboz Ranchería, Texas-Mexico Border." PhD dissertation, Washington State University, 2010. ProQuest.

SIX

Testimonial

Enrique Madrid (Jumano Apache)

El Calaboz Gathering, June 24–26, 2011, Listening Session with Appointed Rapporteurs

Testimonial statement submitted to the rapporteurs by Margo Tamez for Mr. Madrid
Recorded by Margo Tamez and Seánna Howard

As Indigenous peoples from the Rio Grande River areas, militarization came in waves to our lands with the Europeans, and this continued for centuries. The American people can never fully conceptualize why their government has repeatedly used armed forces in our communities throughout their border without the American people's full comprehension. Without comprehension, it is impossible to provide informed consent to what the government has done to our communities in their name. On May 20, 1997, an American Joint Task Force Six (JTF-6) operation carried out the murder of Esequiel Hernández. U.S. Marines in camouflage ghillie suits conducting field operations on the Texas border, in the Big Bend, and in a remote Indigenous village adjacent to the Rio Grande River stalked and executed a youth herding his family's goats. To make sense of the prison wall now constructed in El Calaboz, and why Indigenous women created mass resistance to dispossession, the American people have to first decolonize their minds and determine how to discern truth from fictions their government has been dosing them with about "the border" and "border people" since the nineteenth century.

This is something no American mother should ever read. Your headline in your local paper: "Marine Kills a Redford Youth." Why would a U.S. Marine kill an American? Yeah, their whole function is to protect Americans, not kill them. And yet in Redford, Texas, the situation was created where this was possible. Where American soldiers could kill American citizens. Especially youth who are Indigenous to this region.

And so, there's a whole story that is historical here.

Let me just show you [referring to Margo Tamez] what I was telling you in my truck, and you share all this with your mother. This is one book you need on your bibliography for your future research and for the institute you will create for our Indigenous perspectives. This is the congressional investigation into the shooting of Esequiel Hernández, a child of El Polvo village, now referred to as Redford, of the 150th Congress Committee and the Judiciary House of Representatives.

And this has an interesting fact that their investigators dug up. They wanted to know what had happened. And so, they have a little passage on the background. Where did it take place? So it describes Redford. It's a small border town in the Big Bend area of West Texas, about two hundred miles southeast of El Paso. It has just over one hundred inhabitants who live along the northern banks of the Rio Grande, directly across from Mexico. So, there are one hundred inhabitants at this time. And then, it describes where things started to go wrong. The Marines were involved, American soldiers.

The Border Patrol was involved, which was a civilian law enforcement agency. Not military. And then there was a liaison group between the military and the border law enforcement agencies called Joint Task Force Six, headquartered in El Paso. And so, those three organizations were in charge of this mission. They were the ones who ran it. And I'll just read real quickly.

"The Marines' unreadiness for the mission was compounded by the lack of support from three organizations." Let's see. "Of the three organizations responsible for the mission, Joint Task Force Six had the greatest expertise and experience in the military counter-drug operations, but the

Marfa sector, Border Patrol, had the greatest knowledge of law enforcement procedures and local conditions in the Big Bend area."

Those agencies were responsible for providing detailed background information and training to the Marines, but they failed to do so. And this is one of their major failures. Both agencies provided an only fragmentary and sometimes inaccurate picture of local conditions. For example, the Marines were told that Redford was an unfriendly area where 70 to 75 percent of the local population was involved in drug trafficking. This is demonization, so they were criminals, and then they were drug traffickers. And then, at a time when—This is another for your bibliography, and it stops in 1992, so they don't have . . . —he doesn't have the information I have on the use of the propaganda and military rhetoric, and psychological warfare that was used in Redford. We have evidence of how it was used here against Redford, and against the border, but the—let's see. The Immigration Reform and Control Act was passed in 1986 under Reagan. And following the passage of this act, the issue of illegal drug trafficking gained ascendancy, eclipsing undocumented immigration as the most urgent border control matter. The issue of illegal drug trafficking was formally designated as a threat to national security by President Reagan in 1986.

"Drug trafficking" now had suddenly, politically threatened the security of the United States. And then soon after, in Redford, the people, 75 percent, every person over the age of twelve, was a drug trafficker, a criminal, and a threat to the security of the United States. So, now we have an "enemy," and with enemies, you send in Marines, that's the rationale. And this is the definition of militarization, in its broadest sense, refers to the use of military rhetoric, which is propaganda and psychological warfare and ideology, as well as military tactics, strategy, technology, equipment enforcers.

And these are all the tools that the government uses to militarize their region, to militarize the border. But if you add one more tool to this list of tools called violence, then you have not only militarized the region, you have made war on the region. And this is that last tool. They used all of the other tools, and then they added violence, and that makes it a war against the people of the border, and the people of Redford specifically. And then, making a war on your own citizens is tyranny. The use of American troops on Americans. If George the Third sent British soldiers to a British colony called Boston and massacred British citizens, that's tyranny.

If the czar of Russia sends Russian soldiers to Saint Petersburg and massacres Russian peasants, that's tyranny. If President Clinton sends Marines to the border and they kill an American citizen who is Indigenous to the region, that's tyranny. And it has to be stopped, and it has to be nipped in the bud. Because no true society, no true democracy can permit it. It's not allowed. So the United Nations should not permit it either. And ultimately it will get to that point where it will feel strong enough, and at the United Nations, if it follows international law and not politics, but actually the law, it'll be a moral imperative that is strong enough that it can intervene in a nation-state that is tyrannizing its people. So, that's something that needs to be worked for in the United Nations, now and for the entire future.

Now, let me show you how that works. So we are "criminals," "drug traffickers," and "threats" to the United States, all seventy-five of us here in the village. This is coming up. I told you, my mother had won two Presidential Medals from President Bush because she created a library for the local children. They were just poor Indigenous children in the desert. It was a powerful enough act that there was presidential recognition. Okay. And so she became a celebrity and there were reporters from all over the country coming to interview her about two Presidential Medals. Very few Americans win even one.

And she got two. And so, this is an article from the *Denver Post*. They sent a reporter, sent over here about her library. This is 1991, and they asked her, "Well, you have a library?" and he told a story. "Now we know you live on the border and there's a drug problem. Tell us about the problem of drugs." And she said, "I don't know anything about drugs. I'm a librarian. It doesn't occur here. Go talk to the Border Patrol and U.S. Customs. They deal with that." And so they did. The story the reporter put together is this headline: "Library Is Oasis in Drug Capital." This is what U.S. Customs told the reporter about the environment about her library for poor children. And this is what the actual agenda was of the *Denver Post* in reality. The point is, this is an example of the broad propaganda war, and the psychological war in the tool kit that fit the other tool of violence needed to construct the weapon of militarization and murder of an Indigenous youth, an American citizen, and create laws to give themselves impunity, which legitimized it for an American audience that perceives the "border" as separate from the United States, like a perpetual war zone. And to the Indigenous peoples all across the Texas border, it has been. Texas history makes it seem natural. What you're doing against the wall construction is opening up the true history and facts that the Texans and Americans want to stay buried.

Then the preamble, the dateline is Redford, it talks about how in the Mexican desert, all the tons of drugs will soon be coming across the border. Then this is what it says about Redford. "Tons of drugs will soon arrive, lawmen say. 'Redford is the smuggling capital of the Southwest, one of them,' says Michael Lappay of U.S. Customs." Officials don't ever say anything for public consumption unless he's given permission by his superiors.

This is a sentiment that his superior shared, that the U.S. Customs shared, because they used their name. So, Redford, the "smuggling capital" of the Southwest. One of them, at the level of Medellín, Colombia, or the poorest people. Half of them are over fifty. Half of those are women over fifty, they're all old. It's this ludicrous thing, but it is the creation of an enemy. That's what they were trying to do. It turned out that we were made to be the drug traffickers and the criminals. This is October 1991, and in December of 1991, the biggest drug trafficker in this county was caught and he was the Anglo county sheriff.

A billion dollars in cocaine. An Anglo county sheriff, and we're taking the rap for trafficking in drugs.

You may want to investigate this further because the county sheriff was an ex-Marine. When there was this flack with Iran-Contra and Congress, he set up the Oliver North Legal Defense Fund. Another Marine, apparently they were friends in Vietnam or someplace. And what the heck is a county sheriff from Presidio County and the Big Bend financing the defense fund for Oliver North, who was smuggling not only drugs for guns?

Was it going through here? We don't even want to know about that. We have enough problems without getting the CIA involved and Oliver North and President Reagan and the Midland banks. That's another thing that has to be—okay, so we're a cartel. This is one year after Esequiel was killed, a newspaper article. We had a memorial for him. The reporter who didn't come, they don't come, but they write stories about Redford. And so, they ask, who do they ask for information?

Or, "I'm writing a story about Redford." Who do they go to? The Border Patrol and the U.S. Customs. This is the article and the memorial at our church, and all these people came. "The Redford area is one of the farms that utilize a richer soil for growing alfalfa and other crops. There are a few cattle and some people raise goats. The biggest cash crop is the drug business." This is a year after it. Where do we grow marijuana? All our farms, you can see them from the highway. Where are they? Everybody's poor. We can't even afford to buy drugs to use them. [*Laughter.*]

But this is the ambience that they created. This is how propaganda works—on everyone. They made everybody believe everybody here was a criminal involved in drugs to the point that everybody in Redford thought everybody else was dealing in drugs.

I mean, there's still people that think that. And that is what you do. You create this psychology in everybody of suspicion, and it is slander. This is slander and libel because it's written down. So, we can sue them for $75 million for libel for each citizen they said was a drug trafficker and wasn't. It was just a fifty-year-old grandmother. But we don't have the money to sue them for libel. All we want is to get them out of the river, all of their soldiers. That's the very least that they can do.

Let me show you how dirty it got. This is an article. The Texas Rangers came to investigate the local sheriffs. The Marine Corps came to investigate, and the Texas Rangers decided that the Marines had committed murder from the investigation. So they called the grand jury to seek an indictment for murder. And in Texas, if the circumstances warrant, we execute murderers in a state prison. So, for two months, the Marines faced a very high probability of being executed in the state prison for murdering an American citizen and a Texan resident.

And so, the federal government came in and they of course can't allow the execution of Americans by American soldiers. It's one reason they're not supposed to be on American soil, because then they're subject to American laws, including murder. And so, between the time of the fatal shooting and the no bill by the grand jury, the grand jury didn't indict them. After two months, the Department, after the no bill by the grand jury, the Department of Defense reacted strongly. They were upset that their soldiers would be subjected to criminal prosecution for doing their duty. On June 30, the first day of the grand jury, the Department of Defense spokesperson told *USA Today*, "This was not fair to the members of our armed forces."

He went on to say, "It's not fair that American soldiers on a military mission be subjected to the state laws like everybody else." Thus, the American law, laws constructed by European colonizers and immigrants, protects the powerful by providing immunity and no accountability for a U.S. Marine's execution of an Indigenous child herding goats on his family's and community's ancestral lands in El Polvo / Redford. Do you think the people of El Polvo will ever forget? The family and the community constructed a monument to Esequiel which states the true history, and our children learn this history in El Polvo. We won't ever forget. And so, as a result of the community's resistance to the fiction and how we remember this history, the secretary of defense under Clinton, William Cohen, reportedly will ask the border states to sign agreements, to provide immunity to local enforcement officers. In other words, the European mind-set at the root of the American attitude has not learned anything about what it means that Indigenous peoples remember and continue to resist. We resisted here, and now the women of the Lower Rio Grande River resisted less than ten years later. I think it's time for the women to lead our people there and here. That is our true Indigenous government.

SEVEN

Testimonial

April Cotte

El Calaboz Gathering, June 24–26, 2011, Listening Session with Appointed Rapporteurs

Filmed by Mia Boccella

My name is April Cotte, and I have lived for parts of fifteen winters in the small border community of Redford, Texas, which is five hours southeast of El Paso on the Rio Grande.

It's a community that has about—it had about 150 people when I started going there eighteen years ago. And now it has about 100 people living there.

And it's near a community called Presidio, Texas, that has 6,000 people. And along the river on both sides are communities that are all related. And many of the people that you meet in Redford have relatives across the river in Mexico. And when I look around at this community, and especially looking out that way towards the Rio Grande, it could be the same community. Except that that's the desert, it's the Chihuahuan Desert. But it's farms leading all the way down to the river, and I can't see what's on the other side of that here, if there are other towns, but there are farms on this side, on the Texas side, and there are farms on the Mexico side, and everybody is related.

And when I first got there, people would be hunting deer where the deer have always run at the times when they always hunted them, and that would be on both sides of the river. And they would go to get the specific berries, the pitahaya fruits, and specific medicines in the places that they always got them, and they still do that today.

And now it's illegal for them to cross the river to do that. And the people there are Jumano Apache people. Jumanos, Apaches, different—people of different origins, and it's the place that they have always been.

And I just want to speak for a few minutes about some of the things that I've heard from the children there. I've known children there since they were born, and I've seen them growing up. And one of the really tragic things is that those children could be up here talking about the intense militarization on their people. And they talk about things like having guns aimed at them. They talk about things, I had one boy, one ten-year-old, like a five-year-old and a twelve-year-old, said, "Oh yeah, we had to climb over a fence today!"

I said, "Why did you have to climb over a fence today?" They said, "Because *la migra* was chasing us." And I said, "Well what were they doing?" They said, "They were driving really fast toward us, and we were scared."

We had one night where there was a little baby running, or like a two-year-old running across one of the dark roads from one house at a barbeque to another barbeque, and I was on my bike and all of a sudden la migra came speeding around the corner with their lights off. And the father ran out and grabbed the child. And I like fell over to the side of the road, but, in that community the Border Patrol are always stopping people.

One of the Jumano Apache said, "You know it's not about the fence. The fence is something physical you can see. But what we deal with everyday is the virtual fence, the virtual wall." That is constantly—we are constantly monitored. We can't go to visit our friend without being stopped on the way and asked, "Where are you going, what are you doing, who are you—where are you from?" And yes, some of these questions we don't have to answer, but if we choose not to answer the questions, if we choose to not go along with this act of friendliness with the Border Patrol, then we're detained for longer.

Then it can get worse. Then our car needs to be searched. There is a checkpoint in this area where we always have to stop when we go certain places. So that feeling of constantly being under surveillance. We have,

I think, at the time when we were working to stop the border wall, we had, it seemed like we had two FBI agents specifically assigned to just our little area of those two communities. And so, if you think about that, for 6,100 people with two FBI agents, it felt like everything we did was being watched.

But the biggest piece is just that people in Redford's lives every moment of every day they are being watched by Border Patrol agents on hills, on remote back roads, and they come into people's driveways.

And now that the funding has increased for the Border Patrol and all of these agencies, the amounts have increased. We had two agents fifteen years or eighteen years ago when I first went there. There were two agents for this whole region from I think Sierra Blanca all the way to Big Bend. And now, and that's what they said, they said we have two agents on duty at all times. Now there are hundreds of agents. There are huge buildings, bigger than this church, in three of the communities in that area for those agents to organize themselves. When we get stopped if I go the half an hour to Presidio to get something, a grocery that I forgot, I will be stopped by one to six agents, pulling up in front and beside me.

I'm actually really surprised being here that I haven't been stopped yet. I kind of expected it would be the same, and I'm very surprised I haven't even seen them. On the front on the main roads. It's so interesting that they are all out by the wall. I don't know, I'm sure there are some on the main roads too, I'm really curious about that. But for us on all the roads, anywhere we go, we are being stopped.

I'm trying to think of one of the ranchers was arrested on his farm, well, he was arrested a couple times, but one time he was arrested actually in his driveway for allegedly making a threat to a Border Patrol agent. And the threat was that he said, "I'm going to call the Texas Rangers on you!" because the Border Patrol agent has detained him in his driveway for an hour and a half after coming back from his uncle's funeral, with a little baby in the car.

And—that situation, when we debriefed it and talked about it, it was always with this little four-year-old in the room. And I'm bringing this up because this little four-year-old is growing up with this whole dynamic as part of his existence, and he always knows that level of powerlessness that his father had to feel in the face of this immense, intense militarization in his driveway, in his home. And all the children there have seen this and tell stories about when they came in and arrested my parents, and they just, they broke down the door, and they show you these things. And when they killed my uncle. When they killed my uncle, this is how, this is where they did it. This is where, they have all these landmarks that, that they know about. I think that's all I can think of to say.

[*April pauses.*]

Yeah, this is all in a community where again, eighteen years ago, we were—I was part of an organization that led groups on wilderness backpacking trips in both the U.S. and Mexico. And we would call the Border Patrol and say, "Can we cross the river to go to Mexico?" And they would say, "Sure," because it was an informal border crossing. It was a Class B crossing and people crossed back and forth all the time. And it was very common that someone would be bringing milk to Grandma across the river, or bringing medicine. Or the children would come over to school and then go home at night. And this was common up until—2001.

And the day of 9/11—on 9/11, they bulldozed huge cement in front of this part of the river. I mean, imagine the whole river—the whole river is flowing there, and there's this one spot that's an ancient traditional crossing. I think Enrique [Madrid] talks about it being used for twelve thousand years.

There is a little canoe that a man will paddle across the river, a little rowboat. When you go and you pay one dollar and you get taken across, and then when you come back later in the afternoon, he would bring you back across. And at that spot they came and they dumped cement rocks in front of the little road there. Even though there is like little roads all along the river, it's an open border there. And they dumped these rocks and a woman walked out of her house which was fifty feet from where they did this, and she said, "What are you doing?" and they said, "Well, we are protecting you from terrorists. This thing happened in New York and we are protecting you from terrorists now."

We have scholars in these communities that are afraid to study what they know needs to be studied because they're under such surveillance. And everyone—when the U.S. Border Patrol asked for the Marines to come and help survey the border, and Joint Task Force Six was placed in Redford. I think that was 1996. At that time that was an open crossing. That was a crossing that they were allowing us to use. And so, all the people that the Marines were being told were bandits, and smugglers, and drug dealers, and those were our community. They were ranchers, they were people that had family, they were the ones I was saying were bringing milk and medicine.

The people that stood up and spoke against that have experienced harassment. Everyone in the town experiences harassment. There's—yeah, everyone would have just pages of stories of all the times that they have been stopped and harassed. And, the same in Presidio, I don't mean to single out Redford, because the same in Presidio and all these little, there are many communities along the way. So, and people are very scared, because when you are at home with your family at night, in your driveway, and Border Patrol come flying in with their lights off, and start shining lights on the family. They are already too amped up. They are already amped up. And sometimes they'll come out with their guns already out, which is too amped up. The—the people feel very scared to just be staying where they live. And they are still staying there, though, they are very courageous. That's all.

[*April pauses.*]

Yeah, we do have a checkpoint, now an official checkpoint in Presidio [near] Ojinaga, which is a half an hour from Redford . . .

About five years ago we started to travel down to Redford with Apaches from other places that were coming to meet with Jumano Apaches. And, even on those journeys, I remember the first one, we were pulled over at night by six agents. That was the first time I'd been pulled over by six agents. Before that it had always been one agent. And then all of a sudden now, six agents surrounding us, five, or maybe it was four. But one of those times, we went across the river to Mexico to do ceremony, and on our way back from doing the ceremony, the agents—began to—pulled us over to go through the car.

Again, I'd been down there for some ten years before that, or twelve years, and that was the first time, or actually that was the second time that my car had ever gone through [inspection], and it happened twice during those visits.

At that time, they started to go through the car, and one of the people we were with is a medicine man and had his belongings that are protected by federal law and he said, "Do not touch those things in the car, these are my feathers and these are my sacred objects." And that was violated by the Border Patrol agents who proceeded to open it and to ignore what he was saying. And as he was speaking about his legal rights [as a member of a federally recognized tribe to carry eagle feathers], we had six, some, I think it was six more agents approach us, come out of all these rooms, and approach us armed and, standing up, and started to be very amped up in their energy, and coming towards us.

And while the agent was violating his things and touching the feathers and the other objects, they finished and we had to put everything back ourselves.

And—there was one more thing on that—I can't think of it. So, yeah, that was hard, it was a very bad moment.

And then actually, later, a sweat lodge was built down by the river at the traditional crossing. And while we were away from the town, it was dismantled.

And local people are really—like they've been told, no, you can't go to the levee, you can't do all these things they have always done. So the Jumano Apaches are being told they can't go down to the levee to check their water pumps or to—to—go to the river to track to see what's eating their corn—their plants, their sorghum, or alfalfa that they are planting. To try to hunt the wild pigs that are there. But yeah, that's—so the sweat lodge was removed and no one felt like they could say anything or do anything.

Thank you.

EIGHT

Testimonial

Teresa Leal (Ópata-Mayo)

El Calaboz Gathering, June 24–26, 2011, Listening Session with Appointed Rapporteurs

Filmed by Mia Boccella

The wall is a symbol. Here it stands for the same reason as it does in Arizona and Sonora. But it is just walls and barriers. We're here to transform our consciousness about this together.

I came to El Calaboz because I have been walking with Margo's thoughts, spirits, plants, family, and love for many years. The minute she said she was going to do this [gathering] I knew it was a part of me. It's the type of partnership that goes beyond sisterhood. I feel [I am] a part of a diagram she is creating [with the Lipan Apaches], and I want to do some of the same work in my own community. [We can connect the] ongoing situations through satellite education. [We can] make more agile mechanisms to encourage conversations. I came for Margo and the movement, and the least of the reasons is to be here as a "support." [*Background noise interrupts the audio here.*]

I am from the Ópata Nation (Speakers of the River) in the northern part of Sonora. Traveling from up in the mountains, we used to be cohabitating with other nations like the Pima, O'odham, Lipan, etc. We were evasive when the Spanish arrived. Warnings came to us from central Mexico of the trouble the Spanish were causing. Before I begin my talk, I need to say that we are not criminals for voicing our concerns and demands, and we are not victims. Our focus must include bringing back the stories in a way that our youth can understand without instilling hate, though our anger and anguish is justified. We are accused of being "terrorists," and that is shit; that is a psychological war. By gathering together, from across all the Indigenous represented here in the gathering, we can act with a determination, just like people here who invited us to gather, and who are inspiring others not to be silent.

My participation here is to talk about a dynamic that's called circles. The circles are very important because they serve to round things off, to bring things together on different occasions for when we go so far to an extreme, and we go so far around that we end up in the same place as we started, and we close the circle. Circles, as an Indigenous social and political framework, has emerged in Mexico, among Indigenous women of consciousness in social movements.[1] This challenges the Western and colonial control methods to divide and impose competition between Indigenous peoples through the false divisions of us through colonial tribe and nation dictates. The colonial powers have used these to control the resources and manage Indigenous resistances and coalitional identities.

So I will go into this a little more, and speak on autonomy, because the Lipan Apache women who gathered us here are an example of this way which has survived, and we're here to listen and learn from them, and to contribute our observation and understanding, and to respond to them, as they've asked us to gather here to witness their autonomous movement and to respond. They've selected those of us here to consider their continuing independence as Indigenous peoples from lands on both sides of the walled militarized sector, and I'm bringing our framework of circles here, which we find, in this time period, to be necessary to confront current-day systems and structures, and Lipan Apache women in their walled lands are developing something unique that corresponds to our circle model that I will share here in this talk.

The situation in Texas is what I'm here to learn and witness. A key difference, opposite to Arizona, is that the large majority of Indigenous peoples who are Indigenous to these lands, from all of Texas and all the way to the Río Bravo (Rio Grande) river here, are still independent of the federal tribe colonial model, and this is important for social and political theory, for the academics here at this meeting. The governments (Mexico, Texas, United States) were all unsuccessful in gaining any legal control over their root political autonomy and their lands, but they erased the illegal history of this violent transaction and made their ownership mythological. But, as we've learned from the Tamez women's legal cases, these domination myths that have controlled the minds of the masses are, in fact, myths. So, Lipan Apaches and many other Indigenous peoples in Texas are in fact the legal owners, and have been abused and beaten up a long time to keep the truth about the matter all hush-hush.

So the academics here have an important role to play in raising the consciousness of this key difference between Indigenous autonomy in Texas and that in Arizona, and academics gathered here have committed to do this task, in what we are understanding now, so that we and the masses will see more clearly in the future, and be prepared for Lipan Apache women leaders emerging for collective will for self-determination and developing models needed, especially for the youth we see as small children today, and they will be the leaders then, in the future.

So we are learning as well, connected to this, the need to shed colonial propaganda about "nonrecognized," which I'm learning a lot from the Lipan Apache women and traditional leadership and their discussions about how this terminology is a weapon of the colonizers to manage and control the masses and extract Indigenous lands through ignorance. Population mind management control. And, of course, hate, racism, prejudice, greed, and violence that certain groups are using to their advantage to keep Lipan Apaches quiet about their legal land ownership, which Margo discusses in her talk on Aboriginal title in Texas. And this is unique to Texas, and a hidden history.

Just another comment on this, so we can continue creating good relations, in Indigenous Texas, to the Indigenous peoples, the political uses of "nonrecognized" is a genocidal terminology and is purposeful. Those who are using this colonial term are complicit in their genocides here. I know this is a very different framework for Indigenous peoples in Arizona to listen to. And, at the same time, the Indigenous in Sonora would be in alignment with the experiences of the Lipan Apaches in my observation. I want to make a point: this is an important protocol that any persons interacting in these Indigenous territories here should become educated about before causing reckless damage.

As an invited Indigenous rapporteur, I note and absorb this protocol of respect for their *humanidad*-humanity and their true history. I think the circle model we are building in Sonora understands so well these kinds of conflicts and violence between Indigenous peoples with different legal histories across borders. We might think about Texas as a different country, not just another U.S. state, so we can build a circle way of thinking and relating to our relatives here. The circle removes hierarchy. The colonizers imposed hierarchy, superior and inferior, into Indigenous people's minds for a long time. We are creating a model which helps remove this from our consciousness. This means we are still living cultures and we can adapt new ways and identities to gain liberation.

So, in your packages, you will find this diagram. And I'm going to show you the movements that I participate in. We're gonna talk about how we use this dynamic because we've seen that to get a quick education of people, we need to be more visual and lighter.

And people don't read so much. They're not so intense. They don't study so much. And in these times of crisis and rage, we don't have time to pull out so many books and so much information. We need what I call popular education.

For us, it is education in the streets, so we do it very systematically in Sonora (which is the same land as Arizona, but bordered and walled), and in Mexico in the Indigenous communities, especially because we have such a high rate, 75 percent of the Indigenous communities in Latin America, especially in Mexico, are illiterate.

And in the Occidental, the Western idea, they think it means that they don't know anything, but they don't have schooling that can give them that strength, and that's been an element to screw people, to control, to dominate people and inhibit them and bar them from their rights. So when we want to help a community, we have to get over that hurdle that people are considered ignorant and get away from all those letters and documents. People don't read them.

So we don't meet what the government or the academics want, but I think it's very important that we overcome that, especially lately now that we have videos, and we have all the audiovisual, that's all been very important because that eliminates that barrier, and people can understand that because we're using words, spoken words and images, it's visual and personal relationships, personal contact.

So, I like that we're doing this. We were planning for a lot more people, but it's good to start with a small amount of people, so the circles have to be small because, unfortunately, when we have a very big circle, we get lost among so many people. We have too many ideas, too much versatility, and we don't get to the objective that we need, so it's important to recognize and to play with it.

So, I'm going to tell you, I belong to various movements as an Indigenous woman, but one of them is very anthropological, another is very libertarian, another is very grassroots, another is very nationalist, class-based, based on rights for land.

Right now, we're in a movement that's called MORENA. It's MORENA, and it means National Regeneration Movement. And we're working a lot in Mexico to bring together all the frustrations, all the people who are hurt, the victims of the kidnapping, the parents of the disappeared, the parents of the ABC Nursery, the women of Juárez, all the people in our country that is just, you know, it's really giving us a hard time. Well, we use a bad word, but we're not gonna bring that over the TV, right?

So, when we're speaking clearly, the problem is that this volcano, this well of frustration and impunity and desperation of people, which is very well justified, all the justification in the world, but we're gonna have a disastrous movement in Mexico if we don't find a way to go forward. I'm talking about Mexico because the situation and the objectives are very much in common. We have changes in language and color in place, but that's a situation of human beings all over.

So, this concern for me, it obligated me to search for allies. I've always been involved in leftist movements in Mexico. I come from parents and grandparents who were taken to jail because they were leaders of major agrarian and really hardcore movements.

And we were in Obregón. I had a brother of my father. He was hung in front of our house when I was just a really young child, and my mom really got afraid. She came up to Nogales with her children, and we immigrated, and I was brought up here. She was working as a cook, and I was brought up here, but my heart was always down there.

And this is a very typical story. A lot of people are coming out of Mexico now. There is an economic exodus. People are fleeing. Our workers are being hurt, our communities. Our parents, they can't bear to see their children growing up in hunger and fear, and we're seeing so much frustration and people losing faith and this great exodus, we're all seeing it. Nobody's able to get away from it. Nobody can say that it's not gonna touch me. No matter how rich you are, there's no security in the country.

And the number-one concern in the country is whether or not this can be resolved in a peaceful way or if we're gonna have some hope to stand on our feet and fight. And people—there's so many weapons in Mexico. Weapons are all over, but it's in the hands of the cartels and small groups. They're not paramilitaries. It's just people who are so afraid that they need to be armed and to arm ourselves, and the arms are gonna be used eventually against the government.

And in the past twelve years, we have a right-wing—PAN is the name of the party, and they're in the government, and they pay for a lot of policemen, and they have so much national security and spies and militaries. But they don't look for deep, profound changes that will bring peace to people, so that people will feel that here, I'm going to pay my taxes because the government's using it well. And we have so much rampant corruption.

So, we have a movement right now that is being headed up by López Obrador, but it's not his. It's a coalition of all of these groups, like I'm saying. It's like what happened in Uruguay with the broad opposition front, which came a little bit just after the Tupamaros group. They were bombing; they were trying to intimidate the government to have a dictatorship, trying to get them out of power, but the guerrillas couldn't do that, and there was so much frustration.

And a lot of us were agreeing with the Tupamaros, but we had this broad opposition movement. In Mexico, we call it MORENA, and I'm going to read a little bit because it's based on this dynamic of circles.

So, here, when I go to the communities to talk about MORENA, this is MORENA, the one in the middle. So, this is a visual presentation, but so that I won't take up too much time, I'm going to read a little bit about—I changed the format a little bit of MORENA, but it's similar, and I'm going to show you how that would work in a grassroots Indigenous movement. It doesn't matter where you come from, what your ideology is. What you want is to get your autonomy back, your security back, your identity back, respect and be respected.

So, I left that in blank, as if this was—MORENA would be here. You'd have the PRD, half of it, because PRD, which is a political party in Mexico that's divided, and the Convergencia and PT, they're four different parties that are supporting this movement.

And then we have other groups that are very particular that are from civil society that would be—right over here would be the civil society unions, people working with culture, youth, the elderly, and people with disabilities because they're the special people, and so we have civil society in general.

Number five are the autonomous groups who cannot have a party, a political party of their own, Indigenous people, the migrants that are displaced, the immigrants that are transboundary, the faith groups, for example. Here, we could have a lot of people here, but they don't come to get on the train, so to speak, of a political party, but they want to vote for the most honest and best candidate; and then, finally, the NGOs, the nongovernmental organizations, who by law cannot be in a political party.

And then the sixth circle are militant proactive groups, like the settler groups who are there to defend their—they come together, and they want to support anything besides this awful government that's killing us with hunger. And we have peasants and the people in the ejido collective farms, and they also need political support.

And then we have the Greenpeace and other environmental activists. The Children of the Earth is the name of another group. And they're very critical and very hard-line sometimes, but they don't necessarily have to be part of a party to do that.

And then we have those that are looking for gender equity. They're people who have various different relationships, people who have relationships with people of the same sex. There's no need politically to be part of a party, but one has to support the right to abortion, the right not to have discrimination against homosexuals at work, et cetera.

And then, finally, which is something that we need in the left—up to a short time ago, we just started to understand this, that we also need to invite businesspeople, business, companies, formal and informal companies that don't have a permit to set up a shop, but they have one, or people who want to run green companies, for example, but the government puts up many obstacles for them.

And this government especially, for example, it's supporting the multinational companies a lot and the powerful groups, such as Carlos Slim and powerful people. So, we say, no, many businesspeople are not included. They've had to close up. Their resources have run out. They don't have credits, and so they're also part of this movement.

So, as you can see, there are many who are in favor of this movement, but these are just the three who have the right to vote, the electoral rights. The three parties are on the electoral rolls. And so, these circles are going to have to use any of these three parties to use their vote in 2012.

So, why are we talking about elections? Because if we don't have an electoral process, things are going to fall apart totally. So we can't wait until the last moment and start shouting hysterically and being afraid because, instead, it's better to make a cold analysis of how to do this that these groups can choose between these three in order to vote.

And these three groups need these; they need civil society; they need the autonomous group; they need the proactive organizations and movements, so that they can be strong before the opposition, before the enemy, which is the PAN political party or, even a little worse, the PRI political party. And so, this is the dynamic that I use for this.

And so, we'll talk a little bit now about what it would be like for this type of a movement that many of us are convinced that we need to do with regard to the Indigenous question here in the United States. This is starting now with a much greater need, and it's more concrete.

And I see this as something I'm also working on because I'm Ópata, and Ópata people are also from these peoples, and we were given experience to bring something Mexican to the border Indigenous movement because the Indigenous peoples on the borders, we don't see this ridiculous wall as a border, as a barrier that we cannot overcome. It is there for us to overcome.

When we see that wall there, we have to say, "Screw that wall." There's no other way to look at it because I have an uncle over here; I have a daughter over here, my son over here; I have an uncle in Florida; I have a daughter in Mérida. And so, these things, this means nothing to us. It just speaks of a certain arrogance and a blind and stupid pride.

And so, I just wanna say a few more things to stay within my time. Now, for this MORENA exercise, I have an explanation here that explains all of these circles. So, for the movement, when Margo and I were talking about how I could explain the similarities, the movements, I started to make some changes to this MORENA model to see how we could use this model. It's useful to include groups and individuals through their commitment to participate and their approachness, their closeness, to see what the ancestral movement can offer, what the regional and national movement can offer for the good of all. That is basically the preamble.

And so, we're going to talk about—let's say this is the border Indigenous movement, whatever you want to call it. It's not—I think right now, it's just in a formative stage. We're just like a little baby, like Barry [April Cotte's baby] here. It looks really nice, and it's just starting out, but it's going to grow; it's going to get stronger and bigger.

So, the three big groups here, the first would be Indigenous groups and peoples in general, tribes, towns, rancherías, binational people, such as, for example, the Tohono O'odham in Sonora and Arizona, the Apache here, as we were talking about yesterday, the people from the independent ranchería communities, that would be another one, also the binational peoples, because there are binational peoples—for example, the Apaches, the O'odhams, the Ópata also—we live on both sides of the border. And these would be the first of these rings, of these circles.

Number four would be the civil movements. Well, what are the civil movements? Those are the immigrant people, the people who come from Oaxaca, the Mixteco Indigenous, also the O'odham people who live in Arizona or Sonora, and they're coming, going back and forth in that Arizona-Sonora corridor; and also the people who are taking on more specific tasks, doing work such as commerce, the commercial corridors, like the Zapatistas, for example, have a commercial corridor all over the Americas; for example, Just Coffee, fair-trade coffee, green products that we're trying to start common trade activities; also, the immigrants, those who have been expelled, the Aymaras who live here or in Los Angeles or wherever they live, in Bolivia or in Ecuador; they fled from genocide because the people who survived genocides in Guatemala and Chiapas, for example; and the youth groups, the youth groups in the civil movement, in the first one.

The youth have perhaps a very different vision. For example, later on, the Tohono O'odham will come in. The Papago people from Arizona, they've been chaining themselves to the immigration offices. They've been demonstrating in the streets. They've been going out, distributing water in the desert. They've been out following behind the minutemen. They've run them off, throwing stones at them. And these are people, this youth are part of the civil society, but they're a special category.

And, also, the people who are part of the Mother Earth movement, that's another category, the people who are looking to return to our traditions, our love of the earth, our love of Mother Earth, Pachamama, everything to defend the earth because now we're in the sixth sun, and we're really getting screwed if we don't do something now, because those of us who are predators on the earth will all die because we're being poisoned.

And the fifth group are the autonomous groups. Now, the autonomous groups are, for example, the Indigenous; for example, the Tohono O'odham tribal peoples. In the elections, the elected leaders cannot say to the people, "We on our reservation are all Democrats," or, "We're all Republicans," or, "We're all going to require everyone to issue our collective vote to such-and-such candidate." The people themselves are, or have the potential to be or become, consciously and politically autonomous, and to raise consciousness individually and collectively also.

And there are many academics who help a lot, but they cannot say—like, for example, right now in this MORENA movement, we have many thinkers and academics, many, many of them. But they always stop before they say, "I'm from the PRD," or, "I'm with the Workers' Party, the PT."

And so, we're going to bring this to them to see what they can do to help, because this alliance is very important, because the academics have the time and the space and the academic power and the respect from the media and corporations to say, "Okay, look, if that economics professor has said it or this doctor in economics is saying about that, he's bringing us evidence, and so we must believe him; we must do something." Unfortunately, that's how things are.

And next, there are the independent autonomous groups, again immigrants, again those cross-border people again. Immigrants carry a lot in their hearts. They have a lot of stories. That's why they left, escaping. It's a political fleeing. They're victims of harassment, victims of death. There are a lot of stories.

There are many people here in the United States now who are here because they can't be back there. They have declared themselves political and economic refugees, informal, but it doesn't matter. They know, and they are good for expressing this and telling these stories because they've lived through these nightmares.

And once again, the autonomous groups, the NGOs, the militant political parties, the settlements, the environments, the environmentalists, and the gender-equality movements, these are all included in this plan.

So, as we take a step forward, once we've done some reflection on this very visual reflection over these circles, we can talk about what the steps forward are. We can identify who wants to participate.

And in order to say how we're going to participate, we have to come up, fill up with ideas and strategy and decide on these next steps forward to decide how our identity base has basically maybe three concepts: We're multicultural; we are participants and descendants in the history of this country, just as our original ancestors from these lands were.

In order to achieve our autonomy, we must contribute to the good government that we have, to support them, and we must create—for example, there are many representatives or possibly many young people, many militants, who could be empowered through grassroots support to get into the legislature, into the Senate, the Congress, the political representatives of this country.

For example, in Arizona, we have Raúl Grijalva, a congressman. He's very quiet; he's dark-skinned; he's very, very positive, though. And he takes a step forward; he supports us, and we know that even if they shut all the doors on us, we have Raúl Grijalva, who seeks us out. And unfortunately, we didn't elect him. He had to come and convince us that we had to vote for him.

And so, with a stronger movement, we can designate who we will send, who will be the Túpac Amaru who will go out and struggle for us because what has happened in our story, it's revolved around a democratic history, but it's subject to each person who's been in power, who's taken turns taking power, the dictators, the colonizers, and the concept that we must have our own self-government as a goal, as an objective in public life that is guaranteed to have more respect and more democracy, that we can have that idea and we can struggle to create a new nation-state, a post-colonizer.

After everything, all of these things that have happened, this is a great task that's going to require academics, lawyers, and teachers, and agricultural workers and farmers and everything. This is a challenge in and of itself and from the beginning of the dictatorship. And so, this is something that, you know, I could say this better in the gringo language, that we, since colonization and in more recent times with these Mexican and U.S. empires, we have lived, we have survived under many dictatorships, that we must call it what it is.

However, we are still standing, and we have not accepted defeat. We recognize that these governments have stolen our liberty, our will, our lands, and our destiny. The consequences are very clear with the imposition and the construction of these walls, but with our cries and with our life of spiritual resistance, we have not forgotten. Perhaps in silence, perhaps to now, we could say that we have decided that this will not repeat again.

And also, the laws in both nations support the policies that continue to ignore our autonomy, our right to have our lands, to not have these walls. And we must see how we can fight against this because what we have begun is, how is it possible to trust in a justice system that ignores our laws and our human rights, because we continue to be marginalized, and the Indigenous people continue to be ignored?

We cannot be satisfied by offering reconciliation with them, such as maybe a treaty agreement or a contract, because history has shown us that those attempts to try to have equity with the behavior of both governments, they've ignored us completely. We don't even worry about building treaties, about writing treaties. How long has it been since the Tohono O'odham, the Ópata, or the Apache have had a treaty with the Mexican government or the United States? Not anymore. They don't because it doesn't work.

And our experience with politicians says that in current times of this nation, they have been devastating, and we are also the product also of some dictatorships from within our own people, for in both countries, Mexico and United States, there are tribes and elected leaders complicit in exploiting natural resources, for the "economy," for "public safety," for "security," et cetera, though in each case few if any are a long-term solution, seed divisiveness and hierarchy of haves and have-nots, and produce more wealth for the governments and capitalists, in and out of the tribal community, and lead to suppressing dissent, suppressing participation in decisions, and exploiting the people, or providing some of them "jobs" in exchange for their silence and complicity. Meanwhile, the social health declines, human development declines. "Development" to them means militarization and more division and confusion as these systems create or re-create the mind-set of good and bad "Indians," the behaving and the refusing, the ones cooperating and the ones resisting, and those silent in between. And with millions of refugees and millions of displaced from violent displacement of Indigenous peoples dissenting and resisting the violence and displacement, and the making of millions of unemployed, the Mexican government is called the government of "unemployment." Yet this is not Mexico in exclusion of the colonial policies of the U.S. and Canadian extraction capitalists.

And the mestizos and the Indigenous peoples must build our interrelationships, what relationships we must have with each other in order to have exchanges. I've seen that the O'odhams are having more meetings with the Yaquis. The Yaquis are meeting more now with the Mayos, when before they would separate more from each other; they wouldn't see each other. Now they are changing their mind-set and changing their patterns; that is, they are decolonizing their minds and hearts, into a consciousness of the circle, not of colonial domination and superiority to each other, no. They are changing their consciousness about their mutual needs and interests to survive, not in exclusion of each other and of diverse Indigenous and mestizo Indigenous peoples, which in many cases have relational and familial ties to each other that the imposed colonial tribal identity systems disallow them to recognize. These are the peoples thrown away by the colonial systems, the in-betweens. However, they are the human bridges, made invisible and their voices silenced in our actual community history, and we call them *seres puentes*. They are vital humanity, not throwaways, not targets, and they are consciousness and autonomy makers, and helping our circles to remake ourselves whole again. Again, the colonial government systems of identity disallow this autonomy of true community and true power because it means we are in control again. The government plants Indigenous people in our communities to suppress this from happening. The plants use all manner of methods to persuade the masses that some people must be questioned on their Indigenous identity, and kept out, down, and silenced. This shattering of the colonizer in the mind may be a threat to those who have only understood themselves through the colonial identity system, and difficult to de-addict themselves from cooperating with the colonial systems and their control over their existence and mind-set. We work with individuals and groups on this issue of looking deeper and deeper at the colonization in their mind, and to question for themselves why different Indigenous ways of resistance or empowerment seem hostile and threatening to their own existence. Important work.

There was a saying that, as a Mayo person, "If a Yaqui comes up to me, if a Yaqui person comes up to me, why will a Yaqui person come to me, to talk to me? And if I saw them, I would say no way, no." It's like this. It means, like you make a cross symbol, like, "Back up." Why is this? It's because that is how they have divided us, and these divisions only serve a common enemy. They don't serve anyone else.

And so we must recognize that we are part of our society and our families and everything, and that's the personal obligation for us all to reconstruct ourselves, because in fact, these are connected to the en-masse issues we are dealing with as the colonized, such as problems of diabetes and problems of alcohol, and people losing their children. We're losing our children because of problems with domestic violence and abuse and addiction, alcohol abuse, and of course, to the violence our youth are vulnerable to from the larger society and the waves of organized violence against our women and girls, as well as our men and boys, and our gender-diverse people who are targeted for this violence. We must look deep at how we've become forced to devalue certain lives as less than our own, and less valuable because this is part of the equation for Indigenous autonomy struggles.

And so, all of us within our regions must continue to participate in the public issues, special issues that can return that authority to us that we need. And for example, me as an Indigenous person, as a member of an organization, a network, there are many, so many of us Indigenous people on the Sonora-Arizona border.

There are Mazahuas, there are Triqui people, there are Tlaxcalteca people, Yaquis and Mayos and O'odham tribe and many, many, all flavors, and we have formed a network called the People of I'itoi. I'itoi is "god" in the Papago language, the Papago tradition. We are the People of I'itoi.

We have an organization, and this People of I'itoi network has representation. We have representatives on the Binational Health Councils, for example, and we say, "I am an Indigenous person, and you must pay attention to me because I'm the representative of my Indigenous people."

My mother and I go, and we are part of this. When we talk about how much money's available from PAHO, the Pan American Health Organization, or from the EPA or from the SEMARNAT, Mexican environmental agency, and we go and we talk about that.

And for example, now, currently, I'm president of the Binational Health Council. They have a secretary from the Arizona Health Council and a secretary from the Sonora Health Council. They're the ones who have the money; I don't.

But since they continue to fight internally with so much bureaucracy that these binational councils have, we are not just fighting over this for our egos, and they're not paying us to go to these meetings. But we want to see how we can get something for us, get something for health centers in the Indigenous communities, in the Altar Desert, for example, where they're so remotely isolated. If they have a heart attack on the way to Sonoita or Kino or to Sells, the patient's already dying, dead, but they feel ashamed to go to the Mexican rural clinics.

And so, out of that, we formed the Binational Health Council because this is the truth, that we're ashamed of the system. When people say it's all fine, no. Maybe it's fine, but you need a little more work here. So, little by little, we've been adding these ideas, and this is a strategy of infiltration.

And I just—I did this as an exercise to see what something special that I could do for you who see this need to organize. And I think that the most tremendous weapon the enemy has is keeping us isolated and repressed and oppressed, isolated.

For example, as Indigenous people in Mexico, we see the problems with the reservations here in the United States as a method of isolation. But, also, the benefit is that supposedly they're very autonomous, but in reality they're not.

So, basically that is what I wanted to share with you and see if later we can talk a little bit more about this. And just to close now, I would like to read some words from a man, a great thinker in Sonora who's always raising his voice on these issues. And he's always saying that our movement has had it up to here with so many things.

And he says we are all responsible for the collective suicide of this nation, this country headed to the abyss with us, not without us. In addition, today we're wasting our available time to resolve the greatest social ills. Now is the time to apply just as you would to a sick patient, and you would apply this urgent medicine.

Alfonsín in Argentina in 1983 applied a radical theory against the dirty war and the military. Ecuador applied a radical theory against the business class, but now there's a radical theory being applied against the Peruvian oligarchy.

So, think about what is your radical theory to save your house? In Mexico, a radical theory is for those who know that Mexico is suffering and agonizing, and the situation is serious. What is your radical word? What is your radical behavior? What is your radical thinking? What is your decision to save your homeland? You have the word. You have the action to define it, think about it, and decide what you're going to do and claim, speak about your vital needs, protest that your people are not a little girl turning fifteen years old.

You must denounce on the radio all of the daily corruption and business practices and reject your indifference and retake the vital public space that is your reason for being as a person. Let's leave aside this childishness and stupid childish ideas. Amen.

So, that's just what I have to say for us to think about a little bit before—think about with this circle that we're forming. These circles are in Latin America, they're in Taiwan, and they're taking place in many places where we don't want any more walls. This is the best way to defeat these walls, because the walls are, like they say, to isolate and to contain it, as if it's an epidemic.

We are the epidemic, the epidemic of liberation movements, the epidemic of discontent, the protest epidemic that cannot contain us, but it depends on us. It doesn't depend on large amounts of money or large organizations. It's work that we do every day. So, thank you, thank you very much for listening to me.

NOTE

1. *Editors' note*: For further reading on Talking Circles, see Patrisia Gonzales, *Red Medicine: Traditional Indigenous Rites of Birthing and Healing* (Tucson: University of Arizona Press, 2012). In her research with and alongside Indigenous women elders, healers, and ceremonial leaders, Gonzales established several interrelated domains in which Indigenous women enact, create, draw from, and move their knowledge systems and relational practices through circles.

NINE

Testimonials

Hawk Mendoza (Ndé), Milpa Mendoza (Ndé), Maura Tamez (Ndé), Indigenous Ndé Youth (Anonymized)

El Calaboz Gathering, June 24–26, 2011, Listening Session with Appointed Rapporteurs: Indigenous Youth Delegation Testimonials

Interviewed and recorded by Mia Boccella

On the first day of the El Calaboz Gathering, in the late afternoon, the filmmaker and director Mia Boccella, invited by the Tamez family to attend and document the three-day gathering, interviewed Hawk Mendoza, Milpa Mendoza, and Maura Tamez in El Calaboz, in proximity to the separation wall. They spoke to their concerns and hopes for the gathering.

On the second day of the gathering, the Indigenous youth delegation came to the San Ignacio Church community hall in the sister village of La Encantada / El Ranchito, where they presented their collective perspectives and testimonies regarding the historical and current-day violence they have learned as Lipan Apache children, and the cultural knowledge they held that gave them crucial foundations to speak to the impact of intergenerational trauma on them.

On the final day of the gathering, the Indigenous youth delegation presented their collective analysis of the power dynamics in El Calaboz and sister villages. The youth showed the assembly of Indigenous dele-

gations their artwork, maps, and diagrams to illustrate and illuminate their frameworks for collective and relational peace, resistance, justice, and power.

MIA BOCCELLA: Why are you in El Calaboz right now?

HAWK MENDOZA: Besides eating good food, we're here to get information about the wall, to learn about it, to learn about our grandmother's land—the land on the other side of the border, too.

MILPA MENDOZA: Exchange knowledge, and perspectives on the reality that's right in—well, right in back of our grandma's land. I think it's really important that we come together, and bring different perspectives in. The Tohono O'odham . . . that are really important, that are going through similar things, and it's good to share that with each other.

MAURA TAMEZ: Well, I think the problem here is that there's a big wall in the back of my grandma's backyard, and she can't get to it basically. I mean she can't really climb over the wall or anything because that would probably be like a federal offense or whatever. So she has to go around the land, and around the fence to get to the land. So I think this is about trying to get the wall not here so she can access her land, and just for pretty much everybody else, because there are similar problems going on all around here.

MILPA: It's a separation of culture, don't you think?

HAWK: I think that for people who are living in the middle of Nebraska, the best thing to tell them would be, "Come right here to this border wall, and get hassled by the Border Patrol, and witness the BS that's going on here that nobody knows besides the people that are living on this border wall." There's not enough information getting out to the other people about there's a big twenty-foot fence in the middle cutting my grandmother's land in half. This isn't even the border.

The U.S.-Mexico border is on the Rio Grande. The Rio Grande is the border. And they're cutting off a quarter section of her land just to stop "illegal immigrants" [*Hawk gestures with his hands in air quotes*], "aliens," from crossing the border.

MIA: Or, why do you think it's not working?

MAURA: Okay. I don't think the border wall in the backyard of my—in my grandma's backyard is okay, because it's like if I had a border in my backyard, and my little sister and I always like to go play, and a similar thing happened kind of like with the neighbors, like they put up a fence, but we still wanted to play there, so kind of just ask them to take it down. But, obviously in this case if we ask them, they wouldn't take it down. So that's why.

MIA: Who is "they"?

MAURA: Well, I guess the government.

HAWK: I don't think it's all right that there's a big border wall in my grandmother's backyard because it's going against the UN [United Nations], and the UNDRIP, Declaration of the Rights of Indigenous Peoples, it says directly that you can't take away land from Indigenous people, yet that's what they're doing right now. They took away her property, and they were cutting it in half, and that's just the U.S. government that's dealing with this, not doing what the UN is saying. They're going against the rights of Indigenous peoples when they're taking that—when they're putting that fence up right there. So that's why I don't think it's all right. They're violating our rights.

MILPA: People in Nebraska can't even relate. We can tell them what it's about, but they can't put their mind around it because they're not living here with it. And we're not either. We live totally separated from it, but we listen to our mom every day talk on the phone for hours and hours about these struggles, and it affects us too that way.

MIA: How does that make you feel?

MILPA: Well, it makes me feel really defeated, and helpless, because our mom is going on and on and on about all these problems, and we can't do anything about it. We watch her struggle, and strive to be better, and fight this wall, and she can't do anything about it either. And we're really trying, but to see our mom go through that, it's really hard.

MIA: Hawk, how does it make you feel?

HAWK: It saddens me a lot because it's not just the wall is blocking off this part, it's making "illegal aliens" and stuff go around to the dangerous parts. They're going through deserts, through the dangerous parts. And they're dying because it's a difficult journey from these parts. And it's killing people. And the migration paths, the cougar, there's water on the other side. They can't get to it because there's a big border wall here, and it's affecting the natural—

I think when they built this wall, the government, they waived twenty-two natural life policies that protect the land. They just waived them because they wanted to build the wall to "protect us" from "terrorists" when there's no terrorists coming from Mexico. The people who are coming from Mexico are people who are looking for work. They're not going to blow anything up.

Ten years ago there wasn't a fence here, and the day of 9/11 is when they started. They wanted to put a fence up, and because there are "terrorists," and 9/11, the "terrorists" who knocked down those buildings, they came from Canada. So, I don't know why there's a bigger fence on the U.S.-Mexico border than there is in Canada. So, I'm kind of confused as to why that is. And I think probably the main reason is because it's straight-up racism. There are other reasons. Terrorists are not the reason why they put up a big wall. That's just their excuse.

So, it saddens me that they think they can do this, and then it's just like they're putting up a big wall around their land, the U.S., and it's killing people. It's killing animals. It's ruining the circle of life that's going on. The cougars can't get over there. It's not good for the land, not good for the people, not good for the animals, not good for anything. There's not one thing that it's good for except for blocking "terrorists" from entering the U.S.

MIA: And Maura, how do you think of it? Do you have any feelings? I mean, just sad, happy, angry, whatever. It doesn't have to be complicated.

FIGURE 9.1 *From left to right*: Maura Tamez, Hawk Mendoza, and Milpa Mendoza.

MAURA: Like Hawk said, I'm kind of like what Hawk and Milpa said, I'm kind of in between sad, but I'm also kind of disappointed that we can't be here to help this, but the wall is kind of blocking off relatives. Like I was saying, some families, they have, because of this wall, they've been separated literally. A family may be on one side, and the other on this side. Maybe before they used to have barbecues all together, or something, but there's something like that. But now, since the wall is up here, they can't because they're literally on two sides of it. So it makes me feel very sad that people can't see each other, and like Hawk said, it's killing a lot of animal life because migration paths and everything.

HAWK: I would like to comment more. And I think my grandma said that ten years ago, they used to be able to play on the levee, and there were families this border wall cut communities in half. I mean, there are families that were not Mexican. It's not Hispanic. That's not what it is. There's our family over there. Apache. They're on the other side. They're not Mexicans. They're our family, and they're not illegal aliens, either. And they're just generalizing that.

And, ten years ago, my people called up the Border Patrol and were like, "Well, can we go over there, and talk to our grandma to bring some tortillas over to our grandmother?" And it was an informal crossing. I think it was a B border, or B crossing, something B. Whatever. And people could cross whenever they wanted to go see their family on the other side, and that's how it was. But then when 9/11 occurred, they started plans for building this huge wall across this U.S.-Mexico border.

MIA: Anything else you want to say?

[. . .]

HAWK [*later that day, presenting the Indigenous Youth Statement*]: The border wall, what we think about the border wall, what should be done about the border wall, and since we're "the youth," we're not necessarily "working" as hard as the adults, I guess. We're just playing half the time, and working the other half. [*Audience laughter.*] We seem to get distracted by how good the food is most of the time, and here are some of the ideas that we had: The lifestyle of the people on the border wall has been changed by it, obviously, and not in a good way. And the youth are kind of thinking of ways how to maybe unite everybody, and try to figure out a way to, in the future, get it torn down, or taken away.

And, let me see. Some are thinking about it's a big discomfort, isolation, and they're thinking it's a cage, and, "Hey, we want to get out of here." Okay. They're thinking of crazy ideas how to run over the gate, and all sorts. I'm trying to read what you guys are writing. Yeah. You guys wanna talk? [*Gesturing to members of the Indigenous Youth Delegation.*] Here is another youth. [*Hawk passes the microphone.*]

INDIGENOUS YOUTH: Okay. Give me that. Okay, thank you. There are also people thinking about their grandma's land, that's that lady. There's a guy running to, and over the wall. That's that guy. I just want to kill the wall. That was me. You're thinking about [*inaudible*], I'm hungry. That's what I think about the wall. That's him. That's you. That's you. Yes, it is. Yeah.

And, some of us are thinking of a cage, kind of like being in the zoo. You know how lions are in the cage, and people like to look at them? That's kind of what it feels like, right? You're looking down at people, and they're looking at you, poking you with sticks, trying to tease you, giving you fish, and everything. Daily feeding time, you know. That's what happens. That's the part of whenever you think. When you think of the border wall, you think of the zoo. That's what you think we are. That's what they're trying to use us as animals. They try to train us like lion tamers. They try to train us like obedience school. C'mon.

Have you ever heard about back then, 1800s? 1800s up there, whenever they put us in boarding school, and stuck us there, just said, "Hey, you cannot speak this language. You have to speak English." And we're like, "No, I'm not gonna be European. I'm not gonna eat fish, all right? Come on. I already ate fish before you did. I'm not eating any crackers." [*Youth delegates laugh.*] So, that's what happens whenever you think about it. If you think about it now, it's like you're just looking at them. They come to the door. You're like, "What? Don't come to my door. That's my door. Do you have a little sticky note on there that says your name on it? No, that's my door. I bought it first."

That's what you say. If they try to take your door, you have to try to take it back. If you don't take back your door, they'll try to open it for you, but you don't want it to. You have to open your door yourself. And they're trying to do that for you. That's the worst part. The worst part of thinking about the border wall. They're trying to open everything. They don't want you to do it yourself. They want to do it for you, to you. That doesn't mean they think about us. That does not mean they think about us. They think about themselves. They want all the fish for themselves.

They do not want us to have any of our fish. That's our fish, okay. And, so if we think about it, that's our river. That's our fish. They're like, "No. We caught this." And we said, "No, we caught this." And they're like, "This is our land now. We call it the USA." And we said, "I don't like that name. It's a lot of letters. I don't like that name. How many letters are there?" Anybody get that? Nobody gets that. Okay. Okay. [*All the adults in the gathering laugh.*] So, that's what happens when you think about it.

It's not funny. It's not funny when you think about how they treat you. They're like, if you think teenagers, this guy right over here, in school, that's what it's like. You don't fit in. You're like, "What is it with everybody who wants this?" Justin Bieber, that's what he doesn't like. That's kind of what it is. We don't like Justin Bieber. Justin Bieber is European. He took my land. I don't like you, Justin Bieber, okay? That's what happens. And that's what I think, so, eh-ha.

HAWK: There's our youth right there. And there are lots of youths of many and, she pretty much summed it up right there. We don't like the border wall going in. We don't want it there. Did you introduce yourself? You didn't want to say your name.

INDIGENOUS YOUTH: I'm [*anonymized*] and that's my dad back there, the guy in the blue with the glasses on. And I don't know what else that is. Okay. And that's the guy with the alien on his shirt too. That's my brother-in-law.

DANIEL CASTRO ROMERO JR. (CHAIRMAN, LIPAN APACHE BAND OF TEXAS): I would like to ask the youth group some questions. Maybe one, or two. Not really hard. As a leader of one of the [Indigenous] groups in this region, what would you like me to tell the world about how you feel if you could give me more? I heard you make reference to you feel like the fish, but you also feel like they want to open the door for you. But, what one message would you want me to give the president of the United States if I had the opportunity to tell him?

INDIGENOUS YOUTH: We are back, and we are coming after you.

DANIEL: And then the second question is for the statement I think Hawk made, the isolation part. What message would you want me to send the president about your feeling isolated in this region?

HAWK: Well, that wasn't really my statement. It was hers again.

DANIEL: I'm sorry. It was her statement she said.

INDIGENOUS YOUTH: I am going to go out of this cage, and I'm gonna go after that guy. I'm gonna be like, "Hey, you. Give me back my fish. That's what, I'm gonna get you if you don't give me back my fish." That's what I'm gonna say.

DANIEL: And, using one word, what message would you want to send off for the whole world to hear as a group? One word that you can identify how you feel as a group as a youth, what one word would you want to use to get to the world, and I can send that out, and say, "This is what our youth are feeling, and this is what they want. This is what they're expressing. This is what you're saying that you want the world to see." What, using the one word?

HAWK: That's a hard question apparently.

INDIGENOUS YOUTH [*speaking to the youth delegates*]: You don't want to—go back to our group and talk about it and come back and answer that this afternoon? This afternoon when we come back, and talk at the end?

HAWK: She's got it.

[. . .]

HAWK: They say, "Tear it down." That's three words, but that's what they say.

INDIGENOUS YOUTH: That's one word in my language.

HAWK: That's one word in her language. Okay. But, we'll come back later, I think. We're coming back. [*Myst (Aria) Tamez approaches the youth delegation speaking to the rapporteurs.*] Right here we have a drawing, another statement. It's a border wall, and some clouds, and a sun. I don't know if you guys want to look at that. She can't write, but this is her statement. You can submit documents, and anything you want to, you can submit to this panel for them to share.

DANIEL: We have, in our drawing, just to explain, it's a picture of a fence with a sun over it, and clouds. Nothing else. This comes from the mind and the heart of one of our youth. This is how they see the wall. And so you can draw many conclusions from this. What it really comes down to is you're being walled up as a person. That's what I read. But, like I said, everyone can draw their own conclusions. Would you be able to pass this around? Can we pass this around, and let everyone look at it? And, we're gonna pass this around, and just get some thoughts, and what your feelings are.

During the final session, the youth pass the microphone around to each member to state their final recommendations for future work of the El Calaboz Gathering of Indigenous leaders and rapporteurs.

HAWK: . . . to disperse information through comedy. A lot of talkers are comedians out there. They say they make things really funny, and then right away afterward, they say some shocking information, like this border wall, and then they'll be moved through that. So, get peoples' attention through comedy, and stuff like that.

For the comedy, I also think, like, young people are really attracted when something is witty, so I feel like comedians have a gift for that. Just like you said, it catches your attention, and you're like, "Oh, like that's real." And the other thing going with the network, it was establishing a website where information for all groups is accessible, and we can create communication, and maybe that's more so for us who are already in the [El Calaboz Gathering] groups, and we can just easily communicate or be like, "Hey, if you need this information, just email us, and we can create dialogue within other people, and all parts of the nation, and perhaps even the world."

ELIZABETH GARCIA [*addressing the youth's recommendations to the gathering*]: Muy bien, entonces otra vez varias ideas que flotaron en las tres mesas que concuerdan, verdad. Entonces estamos "ad hoc," como dicen en la ciudad de México los chilangos, estamos "ad hoc," que estamos de acuerdo, verdad. Este, entonces es muy interesante ver que aunque estamos diferentes grupos, venimos de diferentes regiones, a veces, eh, concordamos en nuestro pensar y en nuestro saber, que es bien bonito. Okay, muy bien la última, ¿qué tipo de recursos tenemos para lograr esto? Por ejemplo, la ven qué quiere hacer el jefe que dice que ya la tiene Margo y la película que quieren aquí, entonces a la mejor conocemos a alguien con alguna cámara que quiera nos . . .

[Very good, then again several ideas that floated in the three tables that really agree. So we are "ad hoc," as the *chilangos* say in Mexico City, we are "ad hoc," we agree, right. Well, it is very interesting to see that although we are different groups, we come from different regions, sometimes we agree in our thinking and in our knowledge, which is very nice. Okay, very good last one, what kind of resources do we have to achieve this? For example, they see what the boss wants to do who says that Margo already has it and the movie they want here, so maybe we know someone with a camera who wants to let us . . .]

The youth session now presents their art-making process and the creation of their collaborative banner representing their perspectives.

MAURA: I'm not done with this, but I had artwork over there that was really much better than this. I'm not even starting this yet over there on the table. Yeah. On the table I drew a flower, and I kinda picture it as an alien flower because it has a whole bunch of different dimensions that a real flower wouldn't. There are waterfalls coming out of it, or something. It's on the table drying. But, this one I was planning to do a berry bush, but I'm not even finished yet, so, yeah.

DINO: Did you do the drawing on the wall?

MAURA: Yeah, it's in the pile over there. Well, I drew the wall, and I drew birds in it, and nests. So, I was trying to say that birds could still go over it even if it wasn't like humans can really go, or ants can go through. I didn't draw that, but I drew the birds flying over it. Yeah.

DINO: Did you get that information? [*The camera pans their process.*]

FEMALE SPEAKER: Yeah, I got everything.

[*The youth then formally present their work in an outdoor session beneath a shade structure.*]

MAURA: Youth empowerment of 2011, we've watched and been a part of this conference seeing stress, power, dilemmas, and a strong sense of determination, and hope. We think this conference is about bringing together people and their community in order to address the border wall in Eloisa Taméz's backyard. We all think the wall is bad, and we've agreed on that in our youth group. But a better way to extend or elaborate on that statement is to not only say that it's bad, but also to say that we're coming together to exchange ideas, thoughts, and maybe a better way to move forward through this barrier.

MILPA: [*Maura holds up the "El Calaboz Youth Empowerment" banner for all participants to witness.*] Now we're gonna introduce people in our group, and see what they did when we were painting yesterday, as you guys might have seen. So, we all did artwork, and Hawk and I are gonna kind of explain some of the drawings that some of the kids aren't here, so we'll kind of help with that. So Maura is gonna hold the poster, and

FIGURE 9.2 Maura Tamez and Milpa Mendoza at the El Calaboz youth empowerment session.

we're all just gonna talk to you about what we drew, and why we drew that, what we think it symbolizes, and why it's important to this conference. So, who wants to go first? Here, go ahead, Hawk. [*Maura holds up the banner and proceeds to walk around the large circle of gathering participants so each person has the opportunity to view the youths' collective work up close.*]

HAWK: We had a lot of kids yesterday who came to paint, a lot of little, little kids. I was watching a lot of them. And what we told them was, "Try to draw the landscape without the wall." And some of them started drawing that, and then they got distracted. But there's still a lot of important stuff in these paintings that these little kids drew, and, as adults you see a lot of things, and you talked about them, but we miss stuff as the adults. But then the kids come, and they paint something, and you're like, "Blast it out," because that's just amazing what they drew.

They got the message straight, and they drew something amazing, and as adults we see that, and we're like, "Well, we should improve upon that because they had ideas that we didn't." And we're gonna pass these paintings around. [*Milpa begins to pass the youngest children's paintings to the adults assembled in the large circle. The rapporteurs are present in the circle.*] Some of them drew the wall. Some of them, if you really look at them, and try to figure them out, here's some of the youth over here.

Here's the youth that drew them, right over here. Some of the youth. And, if you could just please pass them around, and really look at them, because we have some of the youth who would like to explain what they drew. So, here's [*anonymized*], who wants to explain his paintings.

INDIGENOUS YOUTH (YOUNG CHILD): I drew this flag. I was gonna put two stars on it. But I made this flag because the border splits the state. So, I call it the Double Star State, and I would put the stars side to side in the blue.

MILPA: Can you tell them what color the stars would be?

INDIGENOUS YOUTH: And, the stars, one would be brown, and the other would be white.

HAWK: If you look in that notebook right there, there is some of the beginning ideas of the banner. The notebook is somewhere around, maybe. There's a notebook that we had drawn, and it's just the beginning ideas of it. And, Milpa, would you like to explain the ideas of the poster—the banner?

MILPA: So, we had a lot of ideas, and we were sketching for a long time in our group, and getting distracted talking about food most of the time. But we had this idea, we had an idea, and then we changed it as soon as we got the piece of paper because we had new group members, and they had new ideas. So we kind of had to incorporate that without changing the idea too much. But we wanted to have some part of us on there so that it wasn't just drawings about something that you can't relate to.

So, instead of doing handprints, which was the original idea, like tracing them, and then drawing our names and where we're from inside of them, we did hand foots. So, you put your hand in a piece of paint, and you rub it around, and you put it in a fist so that the bottom part looks like a baby's foot. And, then you dip your finger in the paint, and make toes. And so everyone that was there yesterday before the evening did feet. This is Barry's, April's baby. This is [*anonymized*]'s, mine, April's. I think this is Aria's—that one's Hawk's. Okay.

FEMALE SPEAKER: [*off-camera*] Mine is red.

FEMALE SPEAKER: [*off-camera*] Yours is red. Okay. This is Aria's.

FEMALE SPEAKER: [*off-camera*] The blue one by the yellow one is mine. And then the big one is Hawk's.

MILPA: Okay. That one is Hawk's.

FEMALE SPEAKER: [*off-camera*] Mine has five fingers, five toes.

MILPA: Okay. See, there's the border wall right here, and as soon as it gets to the unity circle, it falls down. So, there's collapsing of the wall, and there's another wall that [*anonymized*] drew, and I want her to explain it more because I'm not sure I could do a good job of that. But it was all of our ideas put together, and that's what was most important. We're not sure if you guys understand it at all, but we drew what we wanted to draw, and that's what we did. So, we just have some statements on there that kind of sum us up.

We are the people. We're the youth, and we come with you guys. So, we represent you in a minor way, I guess. And, we also like burritos. At least the Hernandez family burritos. And, the other one—

FEMALE SPEAKER: [*off-camera*] The ones that you eat, or . . . ?

MILPA: Yeah. The other one is "The people united will never be divided," and last year my mom, and Maura, and Aria, and Hawk, and I, we all went to a protest. What was it about again?

MARGO TAMEZ: It was in Moscow, Idaho, on national protest day across the U.S. and the Americas for the human rights of Indigenous migrants, and we were in Moscow, Idaho. It's the Unitary Movement of the U.S. So, we had a little march there, and Maverick Eagle Woman was from the Dakota Nation, was just bellowing this out the whole march. There's a little one like this, and he was like, "The people united will never be divided." So, the Dakota people were right there with the movement.

MILPA: So, I thought this kind of was representative of us also because we're coming together, and that was a big part of this whole group. We came together from all different places to do something important to help Eloisa Taméz. [*Anonymized*], do you want to explain what you did on this, and why it's important?

INDIGENOUS YOUTH: Well, I made a picture of a cow, and a horse. But, somebody just colored it chocolate-ish, and now it looks like a big thing of chocolate with black around it. Oh, man. Now it's messed up. But anyway, it has a horse, and there's its tail. That's supposed to be the horse, and that's supposed to be the cow. The reason why I put a rabbit there is because I just wanted to. And, this represents us animals. As I said last meeting, we are animals inside a pen, and there's the animals, and they're watching the wall break down. They're so happy. That's why the bunny is there, because it's happy it's going down. That's most all of it.

And, it also has something to say. It says: About this wall is about peoples' hate. People say fight fire with fire. If we always did, the whole world would go up in smoke. Everyone is already in enough chaos already. So, now people think more burdens on others means less on me. No, burdens, like this wall is bothering. Okay. What? Oh, yeah, this guy over here needs to talk, so here you go, guy.

HAWK: So, they covered the banner. A lot of the paintings are missing because a lot of them [children] took them home. But never mind. I was gonna introduce them. The youth is Milpa, my sister, [*anonymized*], Genevieve [our Diné mentor] is the power of the group and the determination of the group, Maura, my other little sister, and if you look over there, I don't know. Can you guys raise your hands when I say your name, please? [*Hawk addresses several young children by first name.*]

MILPA: And then [*anonymized*].

HAWK: And [*anonymized*] weren't here. Are they. And [*anonymized*]. I said [*anonymized*] already. And Aria, my other little sister who is over there. And that's our youth group. And we're the kids that are gonna take this to the next step when we're older. We're gonna be the kids to take this to the next step.

INDIGENOUS YOUTH: It's called the next generation gets after somebody. I'm coming after you next.

At the end of the session, the participants make some final remarks and acknowledgments.

INDIGENOUS YOUTH: I also want to thank a few people. This lady for holding up the banner. That lady for doing a very nice speech. Aria for passing around the pictures, I guess. Hawk for actually keeping the kids in the pen for a while. Manny for doing something at least. My dad, I'll thank him for everything else. My sister, I thank you for doing some stuff. My brother, I just thank you. There you go. All right. So, okay, is it all right if everybody just cheers with me for the people, and everybody else? Is it all right? Is everyone gonna cheer with me? Are you not gonna do it? If you're not gonna do it, you kind of are a little shy, huh? There you go. C'mon! [*Clapping.*] That's good. All right, thank you everybody. Thank you all.

MARGO: Thank you very much, everyone. Thank you for all of your good words, and your spirit. I thank you, and let us, of course, become a circle, and the youth sit with us, and let's make room for the youth to come into the circle because we need your voices, and the next steps, and to hear the impressions that you made upon the [rapporteurs'] listening panel yesterday, and to hear their recommendations, and especially you older ones who are walking in the world of our adult world, right? What that is. So, is there anything else you'd like to say?

MILPA: Earlier in the panel when we were talking to you guys, and Hawk and [*anonymized*] were representing us, you guys asked us a word that we would use to sum up this whole process, and group gathering, and we actually couldn't find one. But we did come up with a lot of words, or at least a couple. Together as a group, we decided, we brainstormed, and came up with hopefulness, perseverance, resistance, and pride, because we're really proud of what everyone is doing here, and everyone is working together really hard, and persevering their hardest, and it really means a lot to us.

We run around, and we are crazy [*smiles and laughter*] most of the time, but we are listening to you guys, and we are around you watching you do your hard talks. So, we really want to thank you, and say that we hope that this has helped you too. So, thank you. [*Applause.*]

PART III

Oral History, Remembering, and Documentation as Resistance

Ndé beenahch'i̲haasdziih, náyéskoináh, yénáałni, hishnił, hwiigo | I speak to you about it, he remembered, she remembered, building, vigorously

TEN

Reflection on the El Calaboz Gathering

APRIL COTTE

When I first saw the border wall tearing through Eloisa Taméz's property, I cried. During fifteen winters in Redford, I saw what current farming, ranching, and daily life looked like in an Indigenous community with thousands of years along both sides of the Rio Grande River. The land along the river in El Calaboz reminded me of that, and I felt so much loss even with my limited view. People could no longer go from their house across their fields to the river to fix their irrigation pumps or ditches, eat from their favorite berry bushes, fish, picnic, or collect ramada materials, firewood, adobe mud, or medicinal plants specific to the river ecology.[1] The flow of thousands of years of human activities was not just altered but blocked, stopped, clogged by this monstrosity.

A sense of power, freedom, and connection flow through the Rio Grande as it journeys down to the sea carrying waters collected by watersheds throughout Apachería, from New Mexico, Texas, and deep in the heart of the Mexican Sierra Tarahumara. Since 9/11, we could not cross the border in Redford,[2] but the river still gives a sense of freedom and abundance.

Seeing the river walled off from the houses in El Calaboz, I felt oppressed, like the U.S. government was standing in my face pushing us away. In Redford, in recent years people have come to fear Border Patrol agents telling them wrongly that they can't walk the levee or go near the river, but our rights to do that have not been blocked by a wall. If I grew up on land by the Rio Grande in El Calaboz and experienced the border wall, I would grieve like I would for a death—that loss of connection to our river, to life-giving water.

I wonder how Dr. Taméz and other residents of El Calaboz live with the wall through their land. How will it affect them over time? Does the wall bother them more, or the harassment? Roberto Lujan, a Jumano Apache in Presidio, said, "We don't have the border wall, but we face a virtual wall every day. They follow everything we do, and every time we leave the border area we have to stop at checkpoints."[3] Enrique Madrid, a Jumano Apache historian in Redford, said recently, "They are using drones in our communities that have the capacity to carry weapons. How do we know that they do not have weapons? We live with that fear." How does living with the virtual wall of militarization on the border also affect Indigenous people every day? People in El Calaboz face both the physical wall and the virtual wall.

I have a clear memory during the gathering in El Calaboz of the long walk to the gate where Eloisa has to go now to cross the border wall to the rest of her property. I felt powerful making this walk with Indigenous people of all ages from all along the border who were putting their lives and livelihoods at risk to protest the injustices of border militarization. I felt sad when two elders returned to the house because the walk was too long. They would have easily made it to the other side if there had been no wall. I felt fear when Border Patrol agents stopped us to question us and two more drove up. In this unconstitutional zone, we could answer something wrong and be detained for hours or days, and my six-month-old nursling was back at the house nearly a mile away. They let us go this time, thank goodness. But then again, why is it a relief to be allowed to carry on visiting the land of our host, Dr. Taméz? Finally we arrived at the vegetation along the river, across from Eloisa's house. I felt comfort and connection as Eloisa talked about the berries, while others shared about the plants and we looked at animal sign. Someone brought my nursling to the wall to see me, now on the other side. Thank goodness he did not want me, as it would have taken thirty minutes to walk back to the gate from the south side of the wall, go through the massive gate, and then walk back down the north side of the wall to get back to him.

During the listening times, it was moving to hear testimony from Tohono O'odham, Ópata-Mayo, Lipan Apache, and other speakers from different Indigenous communities along the border.[4] Many of the stories they shared were so close to experiences I witnessed and heard about from Indigenous people, the Jumanos, Jumano Apaches, and Lipan Apaches, in Redford and Presidio. I realized how important it is for Indigenous people along the border and their allies to have spaces to network, since many are experiencing similar acts of oppression, violations of human and civil rights, and challenges to traditional cultural properties, uses, and ways. The more we understand the breadth of this trauma, and Indigenous people from the border know they are not alone in expressing it, the more powerfully it can be shared with the world.

The modalities used in the conference seemed powerful and effective to me. All attendees affected by border militarization were offered the chance to speak to the human rights listening panel, the special rapporteurs appointed by the Lipan Apache women hosts, and the rest of the group. The simultaneous translation ensured inclusivity. Panelists took notes, organized their observations, and presented back to the gathering, ensuring we were witnessed. Young people documented their experience through creative expressive mediums that were later presented to the panel and all other attendees. The Tamez family could have brought in a listening panel just to hear their story, but I appreciate that they included members of their wider community and accomplished so much more.

I think this type of listening would have felt empowering to people from Redford and Presidio. The inclusion of children, teens, and young adults seemed natural and in line with what I have experienced at gatherings in Presidio and Redford. It was a blessing, as always in my experience, to be in a circle of Indigenous people, especially with my six-month-old son, who received attention, love, and respect from people of all ages.

I have tremendous respect for the Tohono O'odham, Ópata, Mayo, Lipan Apache, and other people who drove in such extreme heat to camp next to the border wall and assemble and share in the deconstitutional zone.[5] It was powerful to hear the different cultural perspectives on the issues of militarization and traditional and current life along the Rio Grande / border.

Teresa Leal (Ópata-Mayo) carries an important perspective that merits its own listening session. She is connected to many different communities of oppressed, poor Indigenous people affected by border militarization in Ambos Nogales on and along the Mexico and Arizona border. Her eyewitness accounts should be shared across the country to shed light on policies that pollute border communities in the deconstitutional zone, send migrants to unfamiliar cities in Mexico without money, and overburden local support programs. She pointed out that the same Indigenous migrants have been following these trails for thousands of years. Coming to El Calaboz in the heat of the summer was challenging for her health and she ended up in the hospital. I am curious how we could support Teresa in getting her messages out with less cost to her well-being. After the El Calaboz Gathering, she said she'd be willing to do a speaking tour in one call I had with her.

It is extremely important to create every space possible for these conversations to take place. Even if the number of people attending seems low, having the spaces sends ripples throughout the communities. Everyone at the church in El Ranchito ranchería, where we met for certain sessions during the El Calaboz Gathering, and all their relatives knew what we were doing whether they were able to come or not. People in the communities that we came from knew about and were thankful for the conversations, the witnessing, the listening, and the documentation activities that were happening.

In the Redford/Presidio area, to claim one's Indigenous heritage could lead to death for many centuries, and still can lead to discrimination. In my experience, it is rare for people to choose to share their Indigenous heritage outwardly, though they have their family's metates and grinding stones or "manos" displayed in their gardens. It seemed to me that the number of locals from El Calaboz participating in the conference was low, and that did not surprise me. Even if locals don't come out, publicizing that Indigenous people on the border are talking about their experiences in local newspapers and radio stations, and even through word of mouth by renting the church hall for these purposes and hiring a local family to cook, may make locals realize they are not alone, enter conversations with one another, and feel empowered to participate in their time and their way.

The risk of having these conversations is greater for people on the border because of the high number of Homeland Security personnel now living in or very near the communities. If El Calaboz is anything like Redford/Presidio, people may have justified fear of losing their jobs, losing elections, discrimination, and worse treatment by the Border Patrol, the FBI, and Customs and Border Protection for their whole families if they speak against the status quo. A meeting like the 2011 El Calaboz Gathering supports locals on the border with regard to their Indigenous heritage and critique of border policies, even if it might be too scary or costly to attend. It also sends a message to local authorities that we are organized and watching them.

Margo and I hosted some conversations on Indigenous people and militarization of the border in 2009 in Presidio. Though only a few people attended our public talks, people asked each other who we were and what we were talking about, which led them to discuss our topics with each other. Radio stations interviewed us. People I met four years later in the area referred to those meetings though they did not attend. Everything we do has impact.

I want funders and supporters to know that in the Presidio/Redford area, and possibly all along the border, for local people to feel safe or willing to risk being involved in a dialogue about the oppressive border structures affecting their lives and their indigeneity, it may take years of building relationships and having simple, open gatherings for people to get to know each other and explore the topics from their points of reference. And people are taking a risk by speaking. It takes a commitment to long-term support of those who speak, in case there is retribution. For many participants, everything will need to be paid, including gas, telephone calls, and printing costs, because they are living in such poverty that they cannot take on any extra expenses.

As an ally to Indigenous people, splitting time between the Presidio/Redford area and the San Francisco Bay Area in California, this gathering increased my feeling of responsibility for educating more people about the issues of border militarization in Indigenous communities. Learning of parallel experiences in Indigenous communities along the border, I further understood the injustices and breadth of ongoing genocide and gained confidence that we, Euro-American settlers, could educate more nonborder residents and people of European heritage about it. I witnessed incredible resilience. As participants returned to the many watersheds of the Rio Grande with renewed strength, hope, and connection, the life-giving river flowed on, despite the border wall, through Apachería to the sea.

NOTES

1. Ramada: an Indigenous shade structure using all-natural, local materials.
2. Redford, Texas, is located on the Rio Grande River and adjacent to Big Bend National Park, located in Jumano Apache and Lipan Apache traditional territory.
3. The "virtual wall" is a direct reference to the U.S. government's utilization of drones, biometric human data collection, autonomous surveillance towers, and sensors on Indigenous communities upon whose lands the U.S.-Mexico border is situated.
4. This refers to the listening sessions held during each day of the El Calaboz Gathering.
5. The lands dispossessed from Indigenous peoples during the border wall Indigenous resistance were identified by constitutional law and human rights experts as a zone in which the United States, over decades, has increasingly and consistently normalized the overt suppression and denial of the constitutional rights and freedoms of non-White U.S. citizens.

ELEVEN

Reflection on the El Calaboz Gathering

"Don't Ever Forget"

LORI RIDDLE

The trip to El Calaboz, Texas, was a unique revelation about the border wall, and I was able to learn about the history of my relatives. When I pulled up to the house of Dr. Eloisa García Taméz, it felt like home; it was inviting and welcoming. It was astonishing seeing the backdrop of the heavily fortified metal wall right in the backyard of Dr. Taméz's home. My tent was yards from the wall. It brought back information and stories about my history, which I lay out below.

When I was young, my grandmother used to tell me, "Don't ever forget you have relatives on the other side of the border." I just dismissed her most of the time until I was a preteen; then I finally decided to ask her, "What do you mean when you're always saying we have relatives on the other side of the border?" She told me, "You know that imaginary line that's between us and Mexico that separated our people? There are villages on the other side, on the Mexico side." I was kind of blown away by that knowledge, but it did make sense. At that time, I thought that I might go see for myself when I was old. At least past the age of fifty years old.

Well, I finally got my chance to go see the O'odham in Mexico. I must have been about thirty-seven years old, and I was mom to an almost adult daughter; I believe she was seventeen around that time. It was a mentor Elder of mine, by the name of Brenda Robertson, who took me to our relatives in Mexico. She asked me to go with a delegation of community members that were going to meet up in Juárez, Chihuahua, Mexico, with the O'odham. There were other tribes too, like the Apache, that were going to meet up with their sister tribes there.

The nations that represented the O'odham tribes from the United States were the Onk Akimal, Akimal, and Tohono O'odham. It was one of the most exciting times of my life, and I remember going through the receiving line and shaking hands with each member from the Mexico side. I stopped and shook the hand of this young girl who must have been about the same age as my daughter at that time. She spoke to me in my language and it was clear as day. She asked if I was her relative, and I spoke to her in our language and said yes, and we both hugged and started crying. During the celebration, I stayed with Miss Robertson while she spoke O'odham with the leader and his partner. It was an awesome time of celebration. I cannot even put into words how that time spent with our relatives made me feel. I guess the closest thing I would liken the experience to is finding out that you have a long-lost relative that you never knew you had—there is that extreme amount of joy.

While I watched and listened to Brenda Robertson talk O'odham with our relatives, it took me back to when my grandfather used to tell me that our language was once so extensive, especially during his grandparents' days. He said his grandfather used to tell him that you could name every animal in the zoo by their O'odham name. We had clear and concise names and labels for everything in the world. I guess since then the Europeans and Spanish conquerors have succeeded in the assimilation process and in taking our language away. The way I look at it, the watered-down language we now use is nothing compared to what our ancestors used back in their day. Not only was our language taken, but also our names were taken. During our first census, it was said, when they attempted to take the names of community members, there was much miscommunication and confusion, so we were given Spanish and Anglo-Saxon names instead of our given names. Names like López, Hernández, Thomas (which is my maiden name), and also names like Brown, White, etc. These names were given as casually as the enrollment numbers assigned to us.

There are pilgrimages, journeys, and other trips between the U.S. and Mexico tribes. Some of them are for religious, traditional, or even personal reasons. A while back, there were discussions between tribes and the government to attempt to streamline trips between the tribes through both countries' security, but those talks fell through quickly because of inadequate documentation on the tribes' part. Most people don't realize that there were quite a few of our elders who never had birth certificates because they were born at home. My grandmother told me she was born at home and those birth certificates were pieced together with incomplete and/or inaccurate information. So the federal government felt that there was insufficient documentation (of a person's birth details, parents' names, tribal community, and lineage) for the special passport issued to Indigenous people displaced from their lands and communities, divided into two different countries, the United States and Mexico. This was going to be one of the options that could be used for O'odham travels back and forth between both countries. In addition, our O'odham religion has never been acknowledged to this day, either in the United States or Mexico. Most religions get acknowledged by the federal government because they are required to file for 501(c)(3) status with the government to be deemed a nonprofit organization.

The militarization of the border wall is, of course, well-documented in the history of Border Patrol checkpoints all along the wall and military encampments such as Fort Huachuca, which are part of the longer history of the militarizing of the borders and boundaries that divided the O'odham. I recall one incident when I was heading out to the Tohono O'odham reservation to help set up a former mother-in-law's computer. It was during the summer and she was a teacher for the San Simon School. The school is roughly a two-hour drive away, and I finished late in the night. I had an old '84 Honda, and I loved driving at night, especially in the hot summers. I was traveling alone, in a car with no AC, with my windows rolled down, and the windows were not tinted, so I was easily visible in the vehicle. I was stopped by three Border Patrol vehicles; two were stopped directly behind me, and the other was kitty-corner in the opposite lane on a two-lane highway. As I turned to look at the vehicle in the opposite lane, I could visibly see a shotgun positioned in the doorway aimed directly at me. I became somewhat panicked and thought to myself, What reason could I have given them to so quickly draw on me in that manner? Before the agent approached me, I quickly grabbed my wallet and started to pull out my driver's license, and decided to also grab my tribal ID, since I was aware that some of these agents were younger and inexperienced with local communities, and could not easily differentiate an Indigenous individual from a Mexican. After a brief exchange, the agent seemed to find my explanation of why I was out and about so late acceptable. I guess the story seemed credible enough to let me go on my way, but the agent still seemed harsh at the beginning of our discussion. After that, I became active in immigrants' rights.

Being part of the gathering in El Calaboz gave me new ways to think about our experiences across the whole length of the border. I came to understand that even though we're thousands of miles apart, we have many common experiences and issues over centuries and into the present. When I visited my O'odham relatives in Mexico, that experience revealed truths and stories about our past that were hidden from us and that aren't being discussed in our community. This history that we are relatives to the O'odham in Mexico is not taught in U.S. or Native American history. Instead, we are taught from an early age to downplay any connection to "Mexico," and that "Mexican" is a negative association. This harms our community's sense of understanding who we were before the border. In my reflection on the visit to El Calaboz, I have come to see the truths expressed by the Indigenous people from there who have been harmed by the separation of their families and communities by the border and the wall. They told their stories exposing the injustices done to them for many generations, and they are fighting for their places, their lives, their voices, and their perspectives. Being there on the land, right there where the wall divides their land in half, with the Border Patrol constantly watching, made me think about why we have never even learned about their history and their continuing existence in either U.S. or Native history. Not from their perspective.

While I was there, I felt at home.

TWELVE

Caging Cultures Along the Texas-Mexico Border to El Calaboz, South Texas

CYNTHIA BEJARANO (CHICANA/MEXICANA/FRONTERIZA) AND JEFFREY P. SHEPHERD (SETTLER; GERMAN, SCOTTISH, AND ITALIAN DESCENT)

On Travel Writing, "the Congo," and "Bearing Witness" Along the Rio Grande

In 2011, we traveled to El Calaboz, in the Lower Rio Grande Valley of South Texas, to participate in the gathering called by the Tamez family to raise awareness about the violations of human rights along the U.S.-Mexico border.[1] As had been widely reported, the Tamez family was engaged in a legal battle with the U.S. Department of Homeland Security (DHS) over the construction of the "border wall" through their ancestral property. Our role in the gathering as "activist-scholars" was to serve as "witness-observers" to the modern assault mounted by the security state upon the land and rights of Indigenous peoples and communities of color along the international boundary.[2] We attended the meeting to lend our voices in opposition to the militarization of the border and to bear witness to the deployment of power against some of the most subjugated landscapes and peoples in North America.

We live and work in the Paso del Norte region (West Texas, southern New Mexico, and northern Chihuahua), and have a personal and professional commitment to the borderlands.[3] Cynthia Bejarano was born and raised in the region and has deep family and friendship roots on both sides of the border. Jeffrey P. Shepherd has lived and taught in the

Southwest for more than twenty-five years and is dedicated to preserving marginalized histories in his classes and research. Starting from our home in Las Cruces, en route to El Calaboz, we traveled along the Texas-Mexico border to observe the construction of surveillance infrastructure associated with the Secure Border Initiative of 2005 and the Secure Fence Act of 2006, and its impact on land, people, and the environment. Our approximately two-week journey enabled us to witness firsthand the buildup of "security" forces along the international border. It also afforded us a glimpse into the political-economic machinery associated with, and the sociocultural impact of, the state-sponsored reign of terror against immigrants, poor communities, and people of color along the Texas-Mexico frontier.

During our trip to El Calaboz, we observed the places, people, and cultures that are characterized so negatively with the hope that we could critique those images with alternate descriptions of state violence and militarization, and of cultural survival and community resistance. Most news stories focused on death and poverty, as if the entire border region was inherently prone to violence and suffering, much like the news stories of war-torn countries around the world. These images typically referenced the "poor Mexican immigrant" and the drug cartel leader against the backdrop of crumbling urban infrastructure and "desert wastelands" patrolled by military vehicles. As we departed, we wondered about the genealogies of these images of the border as a dysfunctional, poor, and "backward" place, and determined that many of these beliefs had not changed much since the nineteenth century.

White Americans' perceptions of the border during the nineteenth century came from a variety of sources, including journalists' accounts during the U.S. invasion of Mexico, military reports and congressional testimony, anthropological studies, and experiences of travel writers and novelists published in magazines and newspapers. Like the narratives of the American West that stoked images of a lawless frontier, accounts of the border helped to construct it in the American imagination as an equally wild and savage region. Of the myriad accounts distributed, one publication about the border had an outsized impact upon its readers.

In 1894, *Scribner's Magazine* published an account from John G. Bourke of his travels along the Rio Grande into South Texas. Bourke was a Civil War veteran, an assistant to General George Crook during the "Indian Wars," and an amateur ethnographer; he thus embodied the soldier–scientist–travel writer of late nineteenth-century American imperialism. The article, "The American Congo," included Bourke's recollection of Mexican communities, their "lifeways," their economic status, and their relationship with the nation-state along the border. Bourke referenced a report that he wrote for the Department of War comparing the Rio Grande to the Nile River in Africa, but in *Scribner's* he compared it to the Congo. In doing so, he noted that the Lower Rio Grande Valley was for most Americans "a sealed book—*terra incognita*," a region trapped in a timeless stasis of old cultures, backward superstitions, grinding poverty, and ignorance.[4]

In its depiction of a "terra incognita" to the Anglo gaze, it is hard not to compare Bourke's narrative of the "American Congo" with Joseph Conrad's well-known tale of Charles Marlow and Kurtz in *Heart of Darkness*. Both exemplify imperial travel writing, which has been analyzed by scholars such as Edward Said and Mary Louise Pratt. Said and Pratt, in *Orientalism* and *Imperial Eyes* respectively, discuss the construction of the non-Western Other in the writings of Europeans. Whereas Said charts the reification of "the Other" in the Western imagination, Pratt considers how "the Other" views the travel writings of the imperial onlooker. Pratt argues that travel writing can "encode and legitimize the aspirations of economic expansion and empire," but it can also serve as a space for "those at the receiving end" to "revise, reject, and transcend" the conditions that those very same narratives purport to describe.[5] When turned upon the imperial nostalgia of the colonizer, travel writing can bear witness to racism, militarism, neoliberalism, and human rights abuses. In short, Bourke's nineteenth-century "American Congo" of South Texas has an anti-imperial analogue in the modern resistance by marginalized communities in the Lower Rio Grande Valley as they push back against the militarization of the border. By narrating our travel into the Lower Rio Grande Valley, we wanted to not only turn the tables on Bourke's "American Congo," but also focus on the inequalities shaping the lives of Indigenous and poor people of the region.

A Counterhegemonic and Anti-imperial Framework

Based upon our trip along the Texas-Mexico border, this essay offers a reconceptualized travel text combined with the human rights framework of the "witness-observer" in an attempt to narrate our bearing of witness to the 2011 gathering in El Calaboz, where Captain John G. Bourke visited in 1894. Although we neither embrace nor adhere to the perspectives of imperial travelogue, through our mode as witness-observers we attempt an undoing of Bourke's 1894 journey down the "American Congo" with an analysis of the militarization of the border. We offer a counterhegemonic account of human rights abuses by reimagining travelogues as a tool to critique abuses against Indigenous and marginalized communities. We view the El Calaboz gathering and its *testimonios* as part of a movement to resist the marginalization of Indigenous peoples in the "borderlands." This marginalization has roots in the presidios, scalp bounties, and hunting expeditions of the Spanish and Mexican eras, and in the military forts and ethnic cleansing campaigns of the U.S. era. Although less sensational than a vigilante posse, Texas Ranger battalions, or U.S. military platoons, large-scale infrastructure projects such as the wall are equally violent and impactful. Indeed, these endeavors reflect the institutionalized and normalized "legitimate" state power over land and peoples through the remaking of space, the transformation of landscapes, and the buttressing effect of rewriting laws, histories, and subjectivities.

Analyzing these developments requires multidisciplinary frameworks that comprehend the ways in which space, place, history, and culture have been subjugated by this project of conquest, cloaked in the rhetoric of "security." We view the militarization of the border through what Timothy Dunn refers to as low-intensity conflict doctrine (LICD). Militarization refers to the use of military rhetoric and ideology, as well as military tactics, technology, equipment, and forces, in spaces not officially understood as war zones. Low-intensity conflict doctrine involves the establishment and maintenance of social control over targeted civilian populations through a broad range of measures via the coordinated and integrated efforts of police, paramilitary, and military forces.[6] As we apply LICD here, individuals in civil society have merged the "fears" of undocumented immigration, illegal drug trafficking, and terrorism into one monolithic threat emanating from poor, disenfranchised communities along both sides of the national border. In effect, poor people of color are defined within the imaginary of a "national security" threat.[7]

We also agree that the post-9/11 security state has created what the ACLU refers to as a "deconstitutionalized zone" where the normal protections of the constitution may disappear.[8] Moreover, the multifaceted apparatus of municipal, county, state, and myriad federal agencies and their tools of surveillance and regulation have resulted in what we call the "*caging of cultures*" as well as the "*cultures of caging*" along the international boundary. By this we mean that the state has sought to "cage" the Indigenous and marginalized cultures of the Lower Rio Grande Valley (LRGV) through the processes of identification, isolation, surveillance, criminalization, and outright incarceration. Peoples and communities are monitored and observed, their every move catalogued and registered in a field of state-sanctioned violence. Additionally, the state has fomented a culture of caging in which incarceration of Indigenous people, Chicanas/os and Latinas/os, and immigrants is commonplace, systematic, and accepted. It has even spawned a multi-billion-dollar industry that provides numerous employment opportunities for people in these underserved regions. In short, the Indigenous and marginalized people of the LRGV—likewise throughout the border region—are rendered expendable, invisible, and "cageable" through a culture of racism and militarization. Our travels along the Texas-Mexico border and our work as scholar-activists and residents of the border area point to the ubiquitous implementation of this "caging" ideology.

Paso Del Norte to El Calaboz: A Drive Along "the Line"

Marfa-Presidio-Ojinaga

We left the Paso del Norte region and traveled eastward along I-10 to our first stop in the Marfa, Presidio, and Ojinaga region. Driving east, we passed military convoys heading to Fort Bliss in El Paso, Texas, or White Sands Missile Range in southern New Mexico, and Border Patrol vehicles throughout the region. Had we left before dawn, we also might have passed the large buses owned by private security corporations contracted by the government to transport migrants along the border to detention facilities or for deportation.[9] Just after leaving El Paso, we had to stop at a Border Patrol checkpoint entering Sierra Blanca, Texas, the first of several checkpoints we encountered. Once we began driving south to Marfa and on to Presidio and Ojinaga, we had to stop at yet another Border Patrol checkpoint situated along the small highway. Agents aggressively asked why our license plates and our driver's licenses did not match. We explained that it was a rental car with California plates and that we lived in New Mexico, but the agent continued to interrogate us about our final destination, our reason for traveling in the remote region during the summer, and why we were carrying food and water with us in an ice chest despite 110 degrees Fahrenheit heat. All of these questions were acceptable within the rights purgatory of the borderlands.

The Alpine-Marfa-Presidio-Ojinaga region is in the northeastern corner of the Chihuahuan Desert where it blends into the southern plains. The vistas of flat land punctuated by jagged ravines and rugged mountains offer an impressive backdrop to the military and telecommunications towers, Air Force Tethered Aerostat Radar System sites, and aircraft surveilling the border.[10] Forty minutes north of Marfa on Highway 90, the U.S. Air Force has installed one of its Tethered Aerostat Radar System (TARS) sites. These are large balloons tied to the ground with tethers up to 15,000 feet long. TARS is used for aerial surveillance of the international boundary and reflects Dunn's low-intensity conflict doctrine. The nearby town of Alpine, Texas, houses the regional Border Patrol sector headquarters. It is also home to Sul Ross State University, named after Sul Ross, a Texas Ranger and one of the editors of the newspaper *The Whiteman*, a platform for racism toward Native and Mexican communities in the mid-1800s.[11]

Marfa and Presidio stand in stark contrast to each other. Marfa, popularly known for the "Marfa lights," is a hipster art colony that serves as a rural getaway for "counterculture" expatriates from Austin, New York, Chicago, and Europe. The Judd and Chinati Foundations accentuate this small town where "alternative" lifestyles and artistic subtleties struggle to coexist with the local Anglo ranching population and Mexican communities. Donald Judd is particularly famous for purchasing decommissioned military barracks and using them for his large permanent art installations.[12]

Presidio, sixty miles to the south, serves as the "business end" of border militarization. It is a working-class town where unemployment is high and people of color are suspect. Median household income is roughly $20,000 (statewide median income is roughly $50,000), and the main industries in town are agriculture, construction, manufacturing, retail, and the Border Patrol.[13] Green-and-white Border Patrol vehicles are ubiquitous and make the town feel like occupied territory. Ironically, according to locals, although the number of agents in Presidio has tripled, most actually live in Marfa.[14] To the east a few miles is the village of Redford, where in 1997 Esequiel Hernández Jr. was shot by a Marine in the 1st Expeditionary Force out of California and under the administration of Operation Alliance, a program associated with Joint Task Force Six.[15]

Presidio to Del Rio

The drive from Presidio to Del Rio involved a significant arc above Big Bend National Park and then southeast toward the border. Del Rio has a population of roughly 36,000 people and sits across the border from Ciudad Acuña, Mexico, which has nearly 140,000 inhabitants. Del Rio is one of five towns in the United States to boast an FBI regional headquarters, and it was nearly the home of the Federal Law Enforcement Training Center for the U.S. Border Patrol and Federal Air Marshal Service now located in the city of Artesia, in southeastern New Mexico. Del Rio is presently home to Laughlin Air Force Base, which played an important role in Cold War surveillance as it housed U-2 spy planes and high-altitude bombers.[16]

The base is the largest employer in the region, followed by the Border Patrol. Most of the employees and active-duty personnel come from working-class backgrounds, recruited perhaps in high school. With very few options, youth from border towns such as Del Rio now enter Customs and Border Protection (CBP) because it is perceived as an easy route into a government job that offers good pay and benefits. Although CBP policy dictates that most agents will not serve in their hometowns, shuffling around the working-class employees from one border town to another does little to increase their opportunities, while it simultaneously perpetuates the tensions between the working-class people of color in the communities where the working-class CBP agents live and work. In short, Mexican American CBP agents from the working class are policing and arresting working-class Mexicans and Mexican Americans all along the border.

One of the most noticeable characteristics of the region is Lake Amistad, a 101-square-mile human-made reservoir created by the construction of Amistad Dam in the 1960s. The dam is roughly 6 miles long and

254 feet high, and is bisected by the international boundary. Originally built for flood control, irrigation, and hydroelectric power, it is managed by the International Boundary and Water Commission and serves as a major recreational attraction. Importantly, it is the largest source of electricity for Laughlin Air Force Base.[17] Although there have not been any shootings like the one that occurred on Falcon Lake, the Border Patrol maintains a marine and aerial presence across the reservoir as a deterrence against drug trafficking and "terrorism."

Del Rio to Eagle Pass

The drive from Del Rio to Eagle Pass is seventy-five miles, and it entailed an increasingly militarized presence, and an especially militarized history. Eagle Pass has roughly 28,000 people, while its Mexican "sister city," Piedras Negras, has approximately 165,000. Eagle Pass claims to be the first "American settlement" on the Rio Grande, established at the onset of the U.S.-Mexico War as a military base known as Camp Eagle Pass. General William L. Cazneau founded the Eagle Pass townsite in the late 1840s, and in 1849 the military established Fort Duncan. After the war, the town and camp sat along a trail for "westward migrants," and the fort served as the launching site for expeditions against Lipan Apaches. In the 1860s it played an important role in crushing the rebellion of Juan Cortina. In both instances, the fort worked alongside Texas Ranger battalions. After decades of deactivation, the fort was reactivated during World War I. Today it serves as a museum and children's library.[18]

Eagle Pass exhibits many of the characteristics of border communities. Maquiladoras constitute a major part of the manufacturing base. The unemployment rate of 12 percent is double the statewide average, and 27 percent of the population lives below the poverty line. Ten percent of Anglos, 88 percent of African Americans, 28 percent of Hispanics, and 29 percent of American Indians live in poverty. Only 10 percent of the population has a college education.[19] The major employers are the public school system, the medical center, Walmart, the grocery chain H-E-B, the Kickapoo Lucky Eagle Casino, the Border Patrol, and a gun and arms manufacturer.[20]

Like the other towns we visited, Eagle Pass has recently seen an influx of Border Patrol agents and apparatus. The Eagle Pass Border Patrol

Station was opened in 1925 and moved in 1985 to its present location on land seized through eminent domain. The Eagle Pass Station of the Border Patrol is responsible for 1,300 square miles, including 56 miles of the border. According to its website, "The frontline agents of the Eagle Pass Station remain ever vigilant in their efforts toward the prevention of terrorists and terrorist weapons from entering the United States and the interdiction of illegal aliens and narcotics smuggling."[21] The post-9/11 rhetoric is omnipresent in justifying the Border Patrol presence, and locals—most of whom were Mexican and Mexican American—were hesitant to discuss terrorism or border security. Of the few that opened up, they said they were mainly concerned about economic sustainability and how the fear of border violence is driving people, mainly tourists, away from the border.

The border wall bisecting the cities is a powerful representation of a police state. The wall construction is more uniform throughout these Texas regions, where it was recently built or reconstructed with evenly spaced towering black bars that are reminiscent of prison wall perimeters. However, the fence stops at several suspect places, such as a golf course. There are also numerous other "holes in the wall."[22] The ease of moving through the municipal golf course, not obstructed by a wall, is evident, yet the abrupt end of the border wall near a neighborhood where it is succeeded by a mangled cattle-wire fence was disturbing.

Eagle Pass to Laredo

The drive from Eagle Pass to Laredo is 150 miles and took us through a Border Patrol checkpoint outside of Eagle Pass. Whereas Eagle Pass was established by the United States during its invasion of Mexico, Laredo was established in 1755 during the Spanish invasion of Ndé lands. It became a Mexican town in 1821, and officially became part of Texas in 1845. During the U.S.-Mexico War, it was home to Fort McIntosh. Throughout the late eighteenth and early nineteenth centuries, Laredo was a hub for the Indian slave trade, serving as a gateway between Ndé and Comanche communities and mines and ranches to the south. After the arrival of the railroads in the 1880s, urban planners employed a grid pattern that mapped together both Laredos, with several ferries and bridges crossing the Rio Grande by the early twentieth century. The

Mexican Revolution, increased Mexican migration into Laredo, and an oil and gas boom characterized the decades before the Great Depression. Ranching and agriculture remained important, but new industries tied to the automobile and transportation economies became dominant and increased the wealth disparities in the region.[23]

The profile of the city echoes that of smaller border towns, only magnified by the scope and impact of cross-border trade. There are hundreds of maquiladoras and related factories along both sides of the border, and they caused a decline in the agriculture, oil, and gas industries until a recent spike in oil-shale exploration ignited an economic boom.[24] According to the Federal Reserve Bank of Dallas, "More than 47 percent of United States international trade headed for Mexico and more than 36 percent of Mexican international trade crosses through the Laredo port of entry."[25] The largest employers are the school districts and the city government, and the Border Patrol is the fourth-largest employer, with 2,000 employees.[26] Laredo has 236,000 people, and Nuevo Laredo has 365,000. Roughly 95 percent of the population is Hispanic, but American Indians constitute 0.4 percent of the population. Approximately 29 percent of the population lives below the poverty line. Laredo has the second-largest pay gap in Texas for women, and it has a 51 percent poverty rate for households headed by single women.[27]

As in many towns we visited, the border surveillance apparatus in Laredo is extensive. The Laredo Sector of the Border Patrol covers 110,000 square miles in more than one hundred counties all the way up to Oklahoma and Arkansas, as well as roughly 170 miles along the Rio Grande. Border Patrol agents work closely with local law enforcement and nearly every branch of the federal government associated with the "wars" on drugs and terrorism. In addition to employing several thousand people, the Border Patrol contributes $80 million to the regional economy.[28]

Looking out of our hotel window in downtown Laredo gave us an unobstructed view of the international bridge and the thousands of cars and people crossing daily into the United States. We watched the customs agents change shifts every day at 8 a.m. and saw dozens of Border Patrol vehicles parked in a lot behind the hotel. Massive floodlights comparable to those used in football fields lined the U.S. side of the river, along with surveillance cameras every hundred yards. The rows of Border Patrol vehicles, SUVs, and even ATVs were visible in the parking lot that abutted the Rio Grande, while the international bridge right above was dotted with lines of people attempting to enter the United States.

Each international crossing point has a customs station where people are inspected and processed. We witnessed, as we do when crossing the section of border in the Paso del Norte region, how people are denied entry and return to Mexico. Those individuals without documentation risk their lives traversing the Rio Grande without a guide, or, even worse, with a dangerous trafficker who opens them to abuse, manipulation, sexual violence, and even death. If apprehended, they fall into immigration detention, or if these holding centers are full, detainees are held in federal or state prison facilities, or private for-profit prisons that contract with the federal government. All of this adds to the "caging cultures" and "culture of caging" arguments that we make in this chapter.

Laredo to El Calaboz

The last part of our trip brought us into the "heart" of the Lower Rio Grande Valley, the area described in detail by John G. Bourke in "American Congo." We drove along Interstate 2 / Highway 83, which parallels the Rio Grande and its winding path southward into the Gulf of Mexico. We drove to Falcon Lake and Reservoir, where in 2010 David Harley was shot by a member of the Zetas Cartel.[29] We passed through a Border Patrol checkpoint in La Grulla and drove by an international bridge in Rio Grande City. We drove through McAllen and into Pharr, and then took a sharp turn onto Highway 281 and tried to go as close as possible to the bridge into Reynosa, Mexico. We turned left and continued along Highway 281 into El Calaboz.[30]

The feel of the region differed from that in other towns, perhaps because of the summer heat and humidity, and the knowledge that the southeastern tip of Texas was a heavily militarized corner of a militarized state. Driving around, we had a sense of being trapped by extensive suburbanization on one side and the expansive surveillance apparatus of the border wall on the other side. As in other towns along the border, the present-day manifestations of surveillance and militarization have deep historical roots. Brownsville, the city closest to El Calaboz, gained prominence when General Zachary Taylor entered the region in 1845 in advance of the invasion of Mexico. Taylor established Fort Texas, later renamed Fort Brown, which played a significant role in the war as a supply depot for U.S. troops.[31] Highway 281 is known as the "Old Military Road" because of its use by the militaries of Spain and Mexico; by the United States to transport troops during the war with Mexico, the Mexican Revolution, and the World Wars; and now by the Border Patrol.[32]

The wall itself is the most noticeable reminder of militarization, but it does not line the entire boundary between the United States and Mexico. The construction of physical barriers against cross-border movement goes back to the nineteenth century, and continued into the 1990s with Operations Hold the Line, Safeguard, and Gatekeeper. These operations involved vehicle and pedestrian barriers that ranged from chain-link fences, steel poles, and "Normandy barriers" to actual sections of wall composed of sheets of corrugated steel. The Secure Fence Act of 2006, however, stipulated that the Department of Homeland Security, through Customs and Border Protection, would build several hundred miles of "wall" along the border. The actual nature of the wall was hotly debated in Congress, and this resulted in a patchwork of materials, structures, and barriers.

Some communities suffered disproportionately from the "wall" while others escaped its excesses. As in other border areas, Brownsville's upper- and middle-class neighborhoods—especially those with country clubs and golf courses along the border—were spared the insult of the steel fences, concrete barriers, and concertina wire that penetrate poor and marginalized communities. The most glaring example of this class-based inequality was at the River Bend Golf Resort in Brownsville. Driving along Highway 281, we saw miles of large steel barriers lining the border, which then abruptly stopped when they reached the resort, and then began again on the other side of the entrance/exit.[33] Class and race privileges of the country-club residents afforded them protection from eminent domain mechanisms used systematically against the poor and disenfranchised communities throughout the borderlands.

El Calaboz and Bearing Witness

The journey along the international boundary contextualized the gathering in El Calaboz, although the testimonios and personal reflections about the human rights abuses and the "caging of cultures" were still shocking. Within this heavily militarized part of the border, we sat to listen and bear witness to the impact not only of post-9/11 militarization, but also of the long history of racism and violence represented by the wall running directly through the Tamez land. Fear, anger, suffering, and anguish were only a few of the emotions voiced as participants worked through the legacies of settler colonialism and persistent trauma.

Simultaneously, participants exhibited an astounding degree of resistance and defiance as they talked about taking back ownership not only of the colonized spaces lacerated by the wall, but of the histories and identities tied to their homelands. Through their testimonios, they "talked back" to the hegemonic, official discourses of conquest and subjugation. Their narratives offered old visions of lands and spaces populated by Indigenous communities moving across the present-day international boundary, living not in "harmony" with the land, but with respect for its significance and reverence for what it could provide. These historical memories provided new and powerful reminders as we listened to accounts of the human rights abuses of the Department of Homeland Security, the U.S. Army Corps of Engineers, the Bureau of Reclamation, and the other agencies dedicated to the ongoing conquest of the region and its people.

We were asked by the Tamez family to serve as human rights observers to chronicle the testimonials that were shared during this gathering. Our role as witness-observers was to document the testimonials shared during the listening panel sessions held at the El Calaboz Community Center. Secondary witnessing entails a communal pledge to tell the stories, in writing or orally, of our own observations and recollections. Just as importantly, we disseminate the testimonios of human rights activists and of victims, whose truths are often overlooked, dismissed, or silenced.[34] It was evident that people's human rights were being violated, yet their testimonials spoke of resistance.

Members of the Tamez family shared their testimonies and their years-long struggle against the Department of Homeland Security to remove the wall from their backyard. Margo Tamez explained that her family submitted a report on May 18, 2011, to the "Special Rapporteur on Indigenous Rights" for the UN addressing human rights and property rights violations on their territory. She discussed the violence occurring in the region, ranging from the wall itself, to interrogations by Customs and Border Protection, to the more deeply rooted violence of negating Indigenous land claims and treaties, criminalizing religious practices, and erasing Native historical presence in South Texas. Racial profiling by agents of the state occurred regularly, as did prohibitions on the gathering of medicinal plants and traditional burial ceremonies. These and other actions violated the U.S. Constitution and the United Nations Declaration on the Rights of Indigenous Peoples. The ultimate significance of these violations was summed up in an observation by Margo Tamez herself: "We are in an open-air prison." This further supports our claim that the state is intensely engaged in the caging of Indigenous, Mexican, and marginalized communities.

Margo Tamez offered trenchant analyses of the border wall, but the voices of youth at the gathering offered particularly profound insights. Youth delegate Hawk Mendoza-Tamez discussed how life for people in the borderlands had changed with increased surveillance and militarization. He noted that even within his lifetime it had become more difficult to cross the border or drive on the U.S. side due to the frequent stops by the Border Patrol. The overall impact of the changes made him feel like people were living "in a cage." An unidentified young woman delegate poignantly echoed Mendoza-Tamez when she observed that the wall, the border checkpoints, and the high-tech surveillance equipment made people feel as though they were living in a cage. She said, "It feels like a zoo, when I think of the border I usually think of the zoo . . . they try to tame us like lions." Perhaps noting the resurgence of opposition to the militarization of the border, she added, "We are back and we are coming after you [the state]." A preteen in the delegation, who was perhaps too young to verbally articulate her feelings on the situation, drew a picture of a wall reaching high up into the clouds.

Delegates from the Tohono O'odham Nation in the Arizona-Sonora borderlands added their perspectives to the discussion. The Tohono O'odham reservation runs along eighty miles of the international boundary and has been at the epicenter of modern immigration and militarization since at least the early 1990s. The passage of the North American Free Trade Agreement (NAFTA) in 1994 led to increased migration into the United States from the interior of Mexico. Operations Hold the Line and Gatekeeper—also in 1994—funneled migrants into the Sonoran

Desert, where they crossed the international boundary and walked right into the Tohono O'odham reservation. The ongoing humanitarian crisis was compounded by post-9/11 policy shifts associated with "the War on Terror." By 2011, the situation on the reservation had worsened as federal agencies intimidated the tribal government, their vehicles destroyed sacred sites, and Immigration and Customs Enforcement and Customs and Border Protection agents harassed citizens of the nation.

Tohono O'odham delegates Amy and Zaid referred to the changes taking place within their community as an "onslaught" of federal agents and anti-immigrant zealots. Of the "heaviness" she noted in El Calaboz, she said it was "the same way at home" on the reservation. "Our freedom is lessening," she said, even though "we're just trying to be, we are just trying to live as O'odham." She said that there were Border Patrol checkpoints at every exit out of the reservation and that the Department of Homeland Security added video surveillance cameras to catalogue the license plate numbers of vehicles passing through the checkpoints. The actual wall consisted of steel columns serving as vehicle barriers, and all of the traditional border-crossing sites had been closed down. These sites had allowed Tohono O'odham on both sides of the border to cross the boundary and visit family and friends. Border Patrol vehicles have damaged the plants and wildlife habitat. Sometimes there are so many vehicles that they look like "flies, they are everywhere," Amy said.

Concluding Thoughts

When we began our journey down the Texas-Mexico border to participate in the El Calaboz Gathering, we were unsure of what we would encounter. The Paso del Norte region, where we live and work, is known around the world as an epicenter of gendered violence, militarization, and migration. Ciudad Juárez, El Paso, and Las Cruces have long been associated with the Border Industrialization Program and the birth of the maquiladora, the implementation of Operation Hold the Line, and the erection of a massive iron-and-steel wall along the international boundary. El Paso houses Joint Task Force Six, the cooperative effort between national and local authorities combating drug trafficking and "terrorism" along the border. The region has been subjected to massive community sweeps and deportation efforts epitomized by Operation Stone Garden. Most recently, the Paso del Norte area has housed refugee children from Central America.

What we learned during our journey and while listening to the testimonios of participants during the gathering is that the entire region sees the caging of cultures as well as the culture of caging. Concepts such as these offer an analytical tool to describe the institutionalized violence that captures, restrains, and oppresses those who live in the borderlands. Focusing specifically on Indigenous, Mexican, and related communities, "caging culture" foregrounds the efforts of the state to limit the voices of people at the margins of society. Capitalist culture complements settler-colonial homogeneity, as nativist and anti-immigrant sentiments undermine cultures of opposition and diversity. Because of steel and concrete walls, ubiquitous Border Patrol vehicles, surveillance cameras, aerial drones, checkpoints, community sweeps, high-technology databases, bio-scanning systems, and cooperation between state, local, and federal authorities, border dwellers feel like they are living in a massive cage or "open-air prison." As one participant noted, living in the borderlands was akin to living in a zoo where the state is the zookeeper.

The "culture of caging" speaks to the ubiquitous and pervasive system of restriction and restraint that undergirds the language, political rhetoric, and public debate associated with the border. Discussions about migration and construction of the wall perpetuate discursive parameters that exclude fundamental debates about, for instance, Indigenous homelands and human rights. Expressions of culture—particularly culture perceived as oppositional—are highly limited. Free speech and criticism against the government are suspect. "Terrorism" is used to scare citizens into forfeiting their rights. The "culture of caging" implores the state, media outlets, and many civic organizations to accept the "inherent limits" of thought about border affairs, particularly about the notion that Indigenous peoples have claims to land bisected by the wall and the international boundary. The "culture of caging" creates and sustains systems and rhetorics that undergird the physical barriers, policies, and surveillance technologies associated with the militarization of the border.

The testimonies that we heard at El Calaboz defined the final leg of our journey along the Texas-Mexico border. The situation in the Lower Rio Grande Valley, where the Tamez family maintains deep roots, reveals the convergence of low-intensity conflict, the "caging of culture," and the "culture of caging." While listening to the testimonies, we were "witness-observers," but we were simultaneously residents of the same borderlands that had been conquered and reconquered by the militarization experienced by the Tamez family. We bore witness to the state-sanctioned violence that appropriated land and resources from the people of El Calaboz. By bearing witness to their testimonies we are able to carry forth their experiences and voices far beyond the specific landscape of the Lower Rio Grande Valley. We heard their stories of victimization and resistance, and their memories of loss and survival. These stories collectively reveal the long-standing injustices that have fallen upon the residents of the borderlands, but they also stand as a testament to their persistence and determination to fight against marginalization, land loss, and criminalization.

NOTES

1. We originally wrote this essay in 2013.
2. "Witness-observers participate in, articulate, and embody the anger, pain, resistance, and consciousness that unify them with . . . others. Serving as a witness-observer represents the synergy between seeing, hearing, feeling and reacting to violence as a secondary witness to an atrocity." Cynthia Bejarano, "Memory of Struggle in Ciudad Juárez: Las Madres' Organic Resistance, Transborder Activism and the Campo Algodonero," *Aztlán: Journal of Chicana/o Studies* 38, no. 1 (2013): 196.
3. Jeff Shepherd is a professor in the Department of History at the University of Texas at El Paso and teaches classes on the histories of Indigenous peoples and the U.S.-Mexico border. Cynthia Bejarano is a professor of gender and sexuality studies at New Mexico State University and teaches classes on border violence, immigration, and human rights. Bejarano is also a longtime activist for the rights of women and children along the border.
4. John G. Bourke, "The American Congo," *Scribner's Magazine*, May 1894.
5. Mary Louise Pratt, *Imperial Eyes: Travel Writing and Transculturation*, 2nd ed. (London: Routledge, 2007), 4.
6. Timothy Dunn, *The Militarization of the U.S.-Mexico Border, 1978–1992: Low-Intensity Conflict Doctrine Comes Home* (Austin: Center for Mexican American Studies, University of Texas at Austin, 1996).
7. Dunn, *Militarization of the U.S.-Mexico Border*, 5.
8. "Are You Living in a Constitution Free Zone?," American Civil Liberties Union, December 15, 2006, https://www.aclu.org/national-security_technology-and-liberty/are-you-living-constitution-free-zone.

9. Wackenhut buses used to transport migrants all along the border.
10. "Tethered Aerostat Radar System," Factsheets, Official Website of the U.S. Air Force, March 29, 2010, accessed through Archive.today, http://archive.today/20120719065800/http://www.af.mil/information/factsheets/factsheet.asp?id=3507.
11. Gary Clayton Anderson, *The Conquest of Texas: Ethnic Cleansing in the Promised Land, 1820–1875* (Norman: University of Oklahoma Press, 2005).
12. The Judd Foundation was established by artist Donald Judd to manage his private living space and art studios. See "Marfa," Judd Foundation, accessed March 5, 2024, http://www.juddfoundation.org/marfa. The Chinati Foundation was established in 1979, also by Judd, on the grounds of a decommissioned military base, Fort D. A. Russell, to house large art installations and exhibits. See the Chinati Foundation website, https://www.chinati.org/ (accessed March 5, 2024).
13. "Presidio, Texas," City-Data.com, Advameg, Inc., accessed March 5, 2024, http://www.city-data.com/city/Presidio-Texas.html.
14. Brandi Grissom, "Isolation, Poverty Keep Tiny Towns Safe—for Now," *Texas Tribune*, July 16, 2010. See also Alberto Thomas Halpern, "Border Patrol Plans New Presidio Station," *The Big Bend Sentinel*, February 23, 2012.
15. Monte Paulson, "Fatal Error: The Pentagon's War on Drugs Takes a Toll on the Innocent," *Austin Chronicle*, December 25, 1998.
16. "Del Rio Sector Texas," U.S. Customs and Border Protection, U.S. Department of Homeland Security, accessed March 5, 2024, http://www.cbp.gov/border-security/along-us-borders/border-patrol-sectors/del-rio-sector-texas.
17. "Amistad Reservoir," *Handbook of Texas Online*, Texas State History Association, last modified February 25, 2021, http://www.tshaonline.org/handbook/online/articles/roa10.
18. Ben E. Pingenot, "Eagle Pass, TX," *Handbook of Texas Online*, Texas State Historical Association, last modified September 21, 2023, http://www.tshaonline.org/handbook/online/articles/hee01.
19. "Eagle Pass, Texas," City-Data.com, Advameg, Inc., accessed March 5, 2024, http://www.city-data.com/city/Eagle-Pass-Texas.html.
20. Eagle Pass Chamber of Commerce (website), accessed March 5, 2024, http://www.eaglepasstexas.com/.
21. "Eagle Pass Station," U.S. Customs and Border Protection, U.S. Department of Homeland Security, last modified October 13, 2016, accessed March 5, 2024, http://www.cbp.gov/border-security/along-us-borders/border-patrol-sectors/del-rio-sector-texas/eagle-pass-station.
22. Melissa del Bosque, "Holes in the Wall," *Texas Observer*, February 22, 2008.
23. City of Laredo (website), accessed March 6, 2024, http://www.ci.laredo.tx.us/.
24. "Laredo, Texas," City-Data.com, Advameg, Inc., accessed March 6, 2024, http://www.city-data.com/city/Laredo-Texas.html.
25. "The Southwest Economy, First Quarter 2011," Federal Reserve Bank of Dallas, accessed July 8, 2014, http://www.dallasfed.org/index.cfm.

26. Texas A&M University Texas Real Estate Research Center, *Market Report 2011: Laredo*, accessed July 8, 2014, http://recenter.tamu.edu/mreports/2011/Laredo.pdf.
27. Aldo Amato, "Gender: Pay Gap Called Large," *Laredo Morning Times*, April 1, 2014, p. 1.
28. "Laredo Sector Texas," U.S. Customs and Border Protection, U.S. Department of Homeland Security, accessed March 6, 2024, http://www.cbp.gov/border-security/along-us-borders/border-patrol-sectors/laredo-sector-texas.
29. Jason Buch, "Reputed Cartel Member Gangster Arrested in Falcon Lake Death," *Houston Chronicle*, October 8, 2012.
30. Time constraints kept us from crossing into any part of Mexico.
31. Alicia A. Garza and Christopher Long, "Brownsville, Texas," *Handbook of Texas Online*, Texas State Historical Association, last modified September 20, 2023, http://www.tshaonline.org/handbook/online/articles/hdb04.
32. Dixie L. Jones, "Old Military Road," *Handbook of Texas Online*, Texas State Historical Association, June 15, 2010, accessed through the Wayback Machine, May 10, 2025, https://web.archive.org/web/20120422000416/http://www.tshaonline.org/handbook/online/articles/exo02.
33. For a discussion of the construction of the wall, see Denise Gilman, "Seeking Breaches in the Wall: An International Human Rights Law Challenge to the Texas-Mexico Border Wall," *Texas International Law Journal* 46, no. 2 (Spring 2011): 257–93.
34. Bejarano, "Memory of Struggle," 196.

BIBLIOGRAPHY

Amato, Aldo. "Gender: Pay Gap Called Large." *Laredo Morning Times*, April 1, 2014, p. 1.

American Civil Liberties Union. "Are You Living in a Constitution Free Zone?" December 15, 2006. https://www.aclu.org/national-security_technology-and-liberty/are-you-living-constitution-free-zone.

Anderson, Gary Clayton. *The Conquest of Texas: Ethnic Cleansing in the Promised Land, 1820–1875*. Norman: University of Oklahoma Press, 2005.

Bejarano, Cynthia. "Memory of Struggle in Ciudad Juárez: Las Madres' Organic Resistance, Transborder Activism and the Campo Algodonero." *Aztlán: Journal of Chicana/o Studies* 38, no. 1 (2013): 189–204.

Bosque, Melissa del. "Holes in the Wall." *Texas Observer*, February 22, 2008.

Bourke, John G. "The American Congo." *Scribner's Magazine*, May 1894.

Buch, Jason. "Reputed Cartel Member Gangster Arrested in Falcon Lake Death." *Houston Chronicle*, October 8, 2012.

Chinati Foundation (website). Accessed March 5, 2024. https://www.chinati.org/.

City-Data. "Eagle Pass, Texas." City-Data.com, Advameg, Inc. Accessed March 5, 2024. http://www.city-data.com/city/Eagle-Pass-Texas.html.

City-Data. "Laredo, Texas." City-Data.com, Advameg, Inc. Accessed March 6, 2024. http://www.city-data.com/city/Laredo-Texas.html.

City-Data. "Presidio, Texas." City-Data.com, Advameg, Inc. Accessed March 5, 2024. http://www.city-data.com/city/Presidio-Texas.html.

City of Laredo (website). Accessed March 6, 2024. http://www.ci.laredo.tx.us/.

Dunn, Timothy. *The Militarization of the U.S.-Mexico Border, 1978–1992: Low-Intensity Conflict Doctrine Comes Home*. Austin: Center for Mexican American Studies, University of Texas at Austin, 1996.

Eagle Pass Chamber of Commerce (website). Accessed March 5, 2024. http://www.eaglepasstexas.com/.

Federal Reserve Bank of Dallas. "The Southwest Economy, First Quarter 2011." Accessed July 8, 2014. http://www.dallasfed.org/index.cfm.

Garza, Alicia A., and Christopher Long. "Brownsville, Texas." *Handbook of Texas Online*, Texas State Historical Association. Last modified September 20, 2023. http://www.tshaonline.org/handbook/online/articles/hdb04.

Gilman, Denise. "Seeking Breaches in the Wall: An International Human Rights Law Challenge to the Texas-Mexico Border Wall." *Texas International Law Journal* 46, no. 2 (Spring 2011): 257–93.

Grissom, Brandi. "Isolation, Poverty Keep Tiny Towns Safe—for Now." *Texas Tribune*, July 16, 2010.

Halpern, Alberto Thomas. "Border Patrol Plans New Presidio Station." *The Big Bend Sentinel*, February 23, 2012.

Jones, Dixie L. "Old Military Road." *Handbook of Texas Online*, Texas State Historical Association, June 15, 2010. Accessed through the Wayback Machine, May 10, 2025. https://web.archive.org/web/20120422000416/http://www.tshaonline.org/handbook/online/articles/exo02.

Judd Foundation. "Marfa." Accessed March 5, 2024. http://www.juddfoundation.org/marfa.

Paulson, Monte. "Fatal Error: The Pentagon's War on Drugs Takes a Toll on the Innocent." *Austin Chronicle*, December 25, 1998.

Pingenot, Ben E. "Eagle Pass, TX." *Handbook of Texas Online*, Texas State Historical Association. Last modified September 21, 2023. http://www.tshaonline.org/handbook/online/articles/hee01.

Pratt, Mary Louise. *Imperial Eyes: Travel Writing and Transculturation*. 2nd ed. London: Routledge, 2007.

Texas A&M University Texas Real Estate Research Center. *Market Report 2011: Laredo*. Accessed July 8, 2014. http://recenter.tamu.edu/mreports/2011/Laredo.pdf.

Texas State Historical Association. "Amistad Reservoir." *Handbook of Texas Online*. Last modified February 25, 2021. http://www.tshaonline.org/handbook/online/articles/roa10.

U.S. Air Force. "Tethered Aerostat Radar System." Factsheets, Official Web Site of the U.S. Air Force, March 29, 2010. Accessed through Archive.today. http://archive.today/20120719065800/http://www.af.mil/information/factsheets/factsheet.asp?id=3507.

U.S. Customs and Border Protection. "Del Rio Sector Texas." U.S. Department of Homeland Security. Accessed March 5, 2024. http://www.cbp.gov/border-security/along-us-borders/border-patrol-sectors/del-rio-sector-texas.

U.S. Customs and Border Protection. "Eagle Pass Station." U.S. Department of Homeland Security. Accessed March 5, 2024. http://www.cbp.gov/border-security/along-us-borders/border-patrol-sectors/del-rio-sector-texas/eagle-pass-station.

U.S. Customs and Border Protection. "Laredo Sector Texas." U.S. Department of Homeland Security. Accessed March 6, 2024. http://www.cbp.gov/border-security/along-us-borders/border-patrol-sectors/laredo-sector-texas.

THIRTEEN

Brick by Brick

Using Human Rights and Critical Perspectives on Indigenous Peoples' Social Movements to Build Momentum Against the Texas-Mexico Border Wall

DENISE GILMAN

The U.S. government has built a towering wall along hundreds of miles of border between the United States and Mexico.[1] Over the last decade, as intense debate took place over immigration reform and counterterrorism in the United States, the government faced increasing political pressure to do "something" to control U.S. borders. With more meaningful reforms stymied by political disagreements, the U.S. Congress offered a physical wall as the most tangible and immediate response it could deliver.

Wall construction resulted in harsh impacts for Indigenous and other communities along the border. At the same time, it presented a unique opportunity to build new coalitions and approaches to challenge government actions that arrogantly harmed human dignity without attempt at redress. The gravity and complexity of the problem led diverse advocates to join together in seeking out all potential means for addressing the border wall. As part of this process, I and other social actors deployed international human rights law and Indigenous claims as tools to build momentum against the wall—brick by brick.

This chapter explores the interconnected human rights and Indigenous claims brought forward to challenge the government's actions in constructing a border wall between Texas and Mexico. In doing so, it also offers a tentative assessment of the role and value of human rights–based claims addressing abuses in the United States, and specifically in Texas. This chapter offers my professional and personal analysis as a lawyer and member of the Working Group on Human Rights and the Border Wall at the University of Texas at Austin, on the effort to bring international human rights law to bear on the border wall problem.

Part One: The Human Rights Challenge to the Border Wall

The Secure Fence Act, adopted in January 2006 and subsequently amended by the 2008 Consolidated Appropriations Act, mandated the construction of "reinforced fencing" along 670 miles of the country's southern border. Pursuant to this legislation, the U.S. government built stretches of eighteen-foot wall along more than 250 miles of the U.S.-Mexico border and installed hundreds of additional miles of vehicle barriers.[2] More than 100 miles of intermittent wall segments were installed on the Texas-Mexico border alone in 2008 and 2009.[3]

The construction of the wall destroyed important environmental resources, involved extensive taking of private lands owned by small property owners living in its path, and dramatically impacted the means of subsistence and way of life of persons living in border communities, including the members of several Indigenous groups. These impacts generated widespread opposition to the border wall, particularly in Texas.

Approach of the University of Texas at Austin Working Group on Human Rights and the Border Wall

In response to the looming threat of construction in Texas, a collective of faculty and students at the University of Texas at Austin (UTA) formed at the beginning of 2008 to analyze the human rights implications of the construction of a wall on the Texas-Mexico border under international law. The collective at UTA called itself the Working Group on Human Rights and the Border Wall (the "Working Group").

The Working Group initiated its efforts to engage human rights to address the border wall as a result of conversations with advocates and residents from the Texas-Mexico border region. Individuals and communities impacted by the wall expressed deep concern about the unavailability of meaningful avenues for achieving redress for the government's actions. Nonlegal strategies, such as marches, rallies, and public statements against the wall by important figures—including Dr. Juliet García, president of the University of Texas at Brownsville (UTB), as well as the mayor of Eagle Pass, Texas—played an important role in making the harms caused by the border wall visible. However, these strategies were not on their own making any meaningful impact on the progress of wall construction. Litigation in U.S. courts proved no more successful in changing the course of the wall construction project. Numerous actors filed litigation to challenge the wall, including the Tigua (Ysleta del Sur) tribe, a coalition of border mayors, environmental groups, affected landowners, and the Cities of El Paso and Eagle Pass, Texas. A large number of property owners also vigorously defended against suits filed by the federal government to condemn their property for wall construction. However, legislative action and restrictive court interpretations of constitutional rights had already weakened U.S. law to such a degree that it could not serve as an effective mechanism for protecting rights against government intrusion and discrimination. In the end, the courts ruled in favor of the wall.

The Working Group turned to human rights law as an additional means of confronting the harm caused by the border wall. International human rights norms provided a set of legal standards for assessing the impacts of the border wall and identifying specific violations of rights. The Working Group targeted the Inter-American Commission on Human Rights of the Organization of American States (hereafter called the "Inter-American Commission") as the principle forum for its international human rights law analysis because of the commission's character as a regional human rights body for the Americas. The Working Group concluded that the commission's focus on the United States and Latin America would allow it to delve into this particular problem in greater depth than other international bodies. The Inter-American Commission also plays a crucial human rights role vis-à-vis the United States. The commission applies the American Declaration of the Rights and Duties of Man to the actions of the United States as a source of international legal obligation as a result of U.S. membership in the Organization of American States. The Inter-American Commission is also the only international entity with jurisdiction to accept and decide individual human rights complaints against the United States. Although the Working Group decided not to initiate an individual case regarding the border wall, the ability of the Inter-American Commission eventually to entertain a petition against the United States provided additional weight to the body's consideration of the issue.

From the beginning, the Working Group focused on wall construction along the Texas-Mexico border, although the wall project spanned the entire southern border of the United States. The particular configuration of harms caused by the wall in Texas was uniquely invidious. In response, advocates and residents of Texas aggressively sought to develop multidimensioned tools and strategies for addressing the problem. The U.S. government planned to construct a wall through land that Margo Tamez's family had owned along the Rio Grande River for centuries, and which still served as home to her mother, Dr. Eloisa Taméz. Dr. Margo Tamez reacted immediately to the threat of the wall and, working with her mother, developed multiple communications, legal, and organizing strategies to challenge the wall. In the fall of 2007, she contacted UTA faculty to urge engagement with the border wall, resulting in the formation of the Working Group.

Since the Working Group became involved as a result of the particular Texas dynamic of activism against the wall, the collective wished to remain responsive to that activism. The members of the Working Group, who live and work in Texas while frequently engaging in international human rights research and advocacy elsewhere in the world, also felt a special obligation to address the human rights violations they saw taking place in Texas in their own backyard.

At the same time, the Working Group recognized that the construction of stretches of border wall in Texas, while they had severe negative local impacts, did not constitute only a local problem. The border wall issue intertwines with immigration and other national debates as well as international treaty and diplomatic relations concerns. By maintaining its center of gravity in Texas while adopting an international human rights approach, the Working Group intended to utilize a strategy that fit with the scale of this local/national/international problem.

The Working Group collaborated closely with residents along the Texas-Mexico border in developing the human rights approach to the border wall. Those living along the border served as vital sources of knowledge of the wall's impacts, which had not been tapped or even acknowledged by decision-makers in the U.S. government. Border communities also had unique means and methods of exposing the extent of the human rights harms caused by the wall that simultaneously complemented and were supported by the efforts of the Working Group.

The Working Group thus joined with affected individual property owners, Indigenous communities, lawyers, and activists along the border both to document and to denounce the impacts of the wall. The Working Group coordinated particularly closely with the Tamez family to ensure that its work complemented other challenges to the border wall. Collaboration with Environmental Sciences faculty at the University of Texas at Brownsville (UTB), located in the heart of the Rio Grande Valley along the Texas-Mexico border, also proved crucial to the Working Group's analysis. The faculty at UTB engaged in complex statistical analysis to provide revealing conclusions about the disparate negative impacts of the wall on particular communities. They fortified their statistical analysis by checking their conclusions against the reality of wall construction unfolding along the river before their eyes.

While human rights *law* served as an important measuring point, the Working Group nonetheless adopted an explicitly multidisciplinary approach to its human rights analysis. The collective included faculty and students at the University of Texas at Austin from the Geography Department, the Anthropology Department, the LBJ School of Public Affairs, the Teresa Lozano Long Institute of Latin American Studies, and the Immigration Clinic, Environmental Clinic, and Rapoport Center for Human Rights and Justice at the Law School. Construction of the border wall called for an analysis that incorporated mapping and statistical measures, an understanding of Indigenous and other communities located along the border, knowledge of natural resources and environmental harms caused by the wall, and other expertise. The combination of the international human rights law analysis with the work of non-law disciplines made it possible to develop a much more comprehensive picture of the border wall.

The Working Group did not represent the university in its efforts, providing adequate independence to its members to write and speak about the wall's impact. The group's efforts did enjoy institutional backing from components of the university, which allowed the Working Group to carry out its work more effectively and also added weight to the conclusions offered by the collective. The Rapoport Center for Human Rights and Justice at UT Law School served as an institutional home for the project, and the UT Office of Thematic Initiatives and Community Engagement (later the UT Community Engagement Center) also provided support.

The Working Group's Conclusions Regarding Human Rights Violations

Once it had decided on a strategy, the Working Group conducted extensive research and interviews and filed requests with the U.S. government under the Freedom of Information Act (FOIA) to obtain additional information. Members of the Working Group also visited areas of the border affected by construction. The Working Group then applied the international human rights law norms found in the American Declaration of the Rights and Duties of Man (also known as the Bogotá Declaration, henceforth called the "American Declaration" here), as interpreted in the light of the American Convention on Human Rights and other international instruments, to assess the actions of the U.S. government in constructing the border wall. The Working Group concluded that the wall along the Texas-Mexico border violated international human rights law in numerous and serious ways described below.[4]

The Rights to Property and Equal Protection

Article II of the American Declaration guarantees equality before the law. Article XXIII guarantees the right to private property.

To build the wall, the United States took property that had been held by families for generations, in some cases dating back to land grants from the Spanish Crown issued in the 1700s and 1800s. In addition, although human rights law provides Indigenous communities with heightened property rights, given the impact of property loss on Indigenous peoplehood, culture, and survival, the U.S. government seized property from families with Native American heritages and identities, such as the Tamez family. The taking of land and fence construction also resulted in the inability of some property owners to reach large portions of their property that abut the river and are used to graze and water livestock, to irrigate crops, and to fulfill other economic purposes. These property takings thus have the potential to destroy their livelihood.

The United States also treated property owners on the border unequally. The wall crossed numerous small plots of land owned by members of ethnic and racial minority groups,[5] resulting in takings of property from these landowners. Meanwhile, more lucrative developed properties and resorts eluded the wall's path. The wall had a particularly negative impact on Native American communities. The U.S. government's wall construction affected the traditional lands of the Lipan Apache, Kickapoo, and Ysleta del Sur and impacted their ability to observe traditions they have celebrated along the Rio Grande River for generations, leading to harms against these communities not experienced by other groups.

According to the jurisprudence of the Inter-American Court of Human Rights, government actions that intrude on the rights to property and equal protection constitute violations of human rights unless they are necessary for the achievement of a legitimate and lawful governmental goal and are proportional to that goal.[6] The Secure Fence Act sets out that the goal of the border wall is to protect and control the border by preventing unlawful entries by intended immigrants, terrorists, or drug traffickers.

Because terrorists do not seek to enter the United States through the Texas-Mexico border, the construction of a wall along that border is not effective in preventing terrorism. Nor has the construction of a wall along the Texas-Mexico border been shown to serve as an effective means of preventing or controlling unauthorized immigration.[7] Official reports of the U.S. government demonstrate that intermittent physical barriers do not deter migration but simply redirect border crossings into more dangerous terrain. The stop-and-start border wall built along the Texas-Mexico border thus has little impact on unauthorized entries into the United States but does have a deadly effect on immigrants. In any case, levels of unauthorized immigration depend most heavily on the national economy and on policy decisions made in the interior of the United States regarding immigration flows.[8] The physical barrier at the border misses the target in terms of addressing unauthorized immigration issues.

While the goals of impeding unlawful immigration and protecting national security are presumably legitimate as a matter of international human rights law, the construction of the border wall cannot be considered effective, much less proportional, in achieving these objectives. The United States should have considered and adopted other means of effectuating its objectives that would not have resulted in grave harm to human rights, but it failed to do so.

The Right to Freedom of Investigation and Expression

Article IV of the American Declaration guarantees the right to "freedom of investigation, opinion, expression and dissemination." The United States has violated this provision by failing to act with transparency regarding wall construction. For example, the United States has never provided specific information regarding the exact mileage and placement of the wall. The United States government also failed to reply in a full and timely manner to the Working Group's FOIA requests, although those requests sought highly relevant information; for example, about the factors used to determine placement of the wall and consultations with Indigenous communities.

The government violated the right to freedom of investigation, dissemination, and expression as it made it excessively difficult to obtain and make known information about the wall. The lack of information also impinged on the human right guaranteed to impacted individuals, particularly Indigenous communities, to be meaningfully consulted about a major government project such as the border wall.

The Rights to Culture and Family Life

Articles V and XIII of the American Declaration provide for the right to "family life" and culture respectively. The wall has irreparably damaged a centuries-old culture in which communities along the Texas-Mexico border have viewed themselves as cross-border in nature and families have lived and worked on both sides of the river. These families and communities see the Rio Grande River "as a meeting point rather than a dividing line" and the wall as an affront to their culture and way of life.[9]

In addition, the wall negatively impacts Indigenous culture. The Lipan Apache, Kickapoo, and Ysleta del Sur all live and travel along both sides of the Rio Grande River and use the land along the border for religious and ceremonial rites. The wall impinges upon these cultural traditions.

Finally, the wall has caused severe harm to the environment, to wildlife, and to nature preserves along the border. The residents of the Texas-Mexico border area, including Indigenous communities, have traditionally held an important connection to the natural resources along the Rio Grande River and to the river itself. For example, Dr. Eloisa Taméz has described the river itself as "spiritual" and has identified specific use she makes of plants native to the area. Environmental degradation caused by the wall undercuts the culture of residents of the Texas-Mexico border area in violation of their human rights.

The Right to Judicial Protection

Article XVIII of the American Declaration guarantees the right to judicial protection. The U.S. courts give the government broad discretion to take land, particularly in the name of national security, and have not been amenable to constitutional or statutory claims involving border wall construction. The legal provisions, which normally require the government to follow careful processes to avoid harm when undertaking a huge infrastructure project like the border wall, have been stripped away. Congress passed federal legislation that gave DHS the authority to overlook a long list of federal laws that would normally apply to protect Indigenous rights and the environment, and DHS's use of that authority survived all legal challenges in the United States. Legal recourse and judicial protection have thus not been available.

Actions Taken by the Working Group

The Working Group presented these findings in a set of briefing papers submitted to the Inter-American Commission in June 2008. The Working Group then requested and obtained a general hearing on the border fence issue during the 133rd period of sessions of the commission, which took place in Washington, D.C., in October of 2008.

After presenting its briefing papers and conducting the hearing before the Inter-American Commission, the Working Group sustained the human rights challenge to the U.S. government's actions through other efforts. The Working Group made its research and findings known to the public and to policymakers by continuing to communicate with the media, making presentations, and developing a website.[10] In addition, almost a year after filing its original FOIA requests, in March 2009 the Working Group filed litigation in federal court to demand that the government provide documents responsive to the requests. The U.S. government finally produced some records, although the Working Group has continued to push to obtain critical information.

The Working Group also pursued further efforts to involve the Inter-American Commission. In April 2009, a federal judge in South Texas issued an order allowing the U.S. government to take possession of a portion of the property owned by the Tamez family. Within days, an eighteen-foot-high wall stretched across the property. The Working Group alerted the Inter-American Commission to this turning point in the efforts to resist border wall construction. Then, at the end of 2009, the U.S. government began to seek condemnation of additional land along the newly installed border fence, including more of the Tamez family property. In response, the Working Group successfully petitioned the Inter-American Commission to demand an explanation from the U.S. government regarding the continued construction of the border fence and the efforts to take additional land.

Reflecting on the Strengths and Weaknesses of the Human Rights Strategy

The human rights challenge to the border wall before the Inter-American Commission on Human Rights led to international attention and even official condemnation. The hearing before the commission attracted U.S. and international media.[11] After the hearing, at the end of its period of sessions, the commission expressed concern about the "troubling information" it had received about the human rights impact of the Texas-

Mexico border wall. The commission decried the wall's disproportionate impact on "people who are poor, with a low level of education, and generally of Mexican descent, as well as Indigenous communities on both sides of the border."[12] The commission more recently demanded an explanation from the U.S. government regarding continued construction of the wall.

The validation by an intergovernmental human rights body of the legitimacy of claims of human rights violations perpetrated by the U.S. government cannot be dismissed. The attention and new supranational focus generated by the presentations before the Inter-American Commission also certainly helped to shift the paradigm according to which the wall project had been viewed. The human rights strategy did not, of course, succeed in halting the taking of property or the construction of hundreds of miles of fence. However, the use of human rights tools to challenge the border wall had subtler but important results.

Use of international human rights law allowed the harms caused by the border wall to be described as rights violations where they were experienced that way but were invisible in the U.S. legal regime. International human rights law norms provide more expansive understandings of rights than U.S. law. For example, the government must engage in intentional discrimination to violate equal protection under U.S. constitutional standards, but an equal protection violation takes place under international human rights law when a government's actions have a disparate impact or effect.[13] These more expansive international human rights norms applicable to the United States enjoy credibility as a codification of the expectations of the international legal order regarding human rights.

Similarly, the use of international human rights law placed the focus on harms that went to the core of the border wall's impact but did not otherwise receive significant attention. The impact of the border wall on Indigenous communities took on a central role in the human rights analysis because of the expansive protections guaranteed to these communities under international human rights law. Similarly, the right to culture protected in international human rights law presented the perfect platform for profiling the environmental damage caused by the wall as well as the wall's impact on the cross-border culture existing along the Rio Grande River.

The human rights challenge had a difficult-to-measure effect, along with other factors, on the handling of the border wall issue by the United

States. The Department of Homeland Security has made more maps and information available and has provided responses to FOIA requests regarding the border wall. Any future proposals to extend the wall will be introduced into a context in which the border wall has already been framed as a human rights concern, and they may falter more quickly.

It is nonetheless valuable to assess the value of the human rights approach to allow critical decision-making in the future about whether, when, and where to deploy human rights law in the United States. Two inquiries take on central importance. First, is human rights law an effective tool to address government-inflicted harm in the United States? Second, is human rights *law*, or *any* law-based approach, effective at addressing structural harms, such as the border wall, which may have nonlegal as well as legal causes and effects?

Some have argued that the human rights law approach to the border wall was undesirable, because human rights law is ineffective in achieving change in the United States. The Working Group regularly faced skepticism from the press and other academics and advocates about the decision to use international human rights law and to go before the Inter-American Commission. This critique focuses on the unenforceability in the United States of international human rights law and the rulings of human rights bodies.

The United States regularly treats human rights norms as lacking mandatory effect, at least without legislative implementation.[14] The United States has explicitly taken the position that the decisions of the Inter-American Commission are advisory rather than binding.[15] This reality meant that the Working Group never expected that the Commission would order the U.S. government to stop border wall construction and that the United States would deem such a decision binding and follow it. The goal was always one of naming the harms as human rights violations and obtaining official international approval of such naming for the purpose of exerting pressure for change.

Critics of the human rights approach nonetheless juxtapose the lack of enforceability of international law with the immediate and almost certain execution of U.S. court decisions as a means of questioning the use of international law. This comparison fails to see the limitations that also exist in relation to litigation in the U.S. courts.

The success rates in litigation of civil rights and constitutional claims—which would be the U.S. vehicles for human rights claims—are notably low.[16] This reality played out in the case of the border wall. U.S. litigation was unsuccessful in halting wall construction, because U.S. courts ruled unfavorably. Without a favorable decision, enforceability is irrelevant. Even a "win" through litigation in U.S. courts often does not result in a dramatic result in terms of policy changes in favor of rights protection. Increasingly conservative U.S. courts have steadily cut back on meaningful remedies, such as broad injunctive relief, that would mandate government reform.[17]

U.S. litigation thus does not provide a direct avenue to a decision that will lead to positive change, regardless of the presumptive enforceability of U.S. court decisions. As a result, U.S. litigation is increasingly viewed as a means of creating pressure for reform, by generating media and public interest and destabilizing the status quo.[18] As with the human rights approach, then, U.S. litigation should be seen as one tool among many, each with unique strengths and limitations, which may be utilized to press for a rights-protective outcome.

Advocates must assess the utility of deploying litigation in U.S. courts, international human rights law, or other approaches, alone or in combination, to address any particular problem, and must determine the proper place of each strategy in the overall effort. As to the border wall, it was desirable to deploy human rights, along with other tools, to build up resistance to the wall—brick by brick.

The existence of similar limitations on U.S. and international human rights law approaches raises the next question, though, of whether *any* legal strategy can function effectively against a problem like the border wall. The border wall resulted from complicated political and social forces, and it largely functions symbolically rather than in pursuit of a rational, legally bound objective.[19] The harms caused by the wall also evade treatment as cognizable harms, as they transcend legal categories of economic or even emotional damages. As a result, the argument goes, the law has little to say about the border wall.

However, as just noted, advocates against the border wall did not use the law in isolation, but rather as a complement to other efforts to force government change. Law certainly must have *some* role to play when used this way, although certainly not an exclusive or dispositive role. After all, the United States used the law to obtain its objectives of imposing the border wall and, in so doing, contorted the law into new forms that facilitate rather than limit government abuse. Legal strategies must therefore be incorporated into the broader strategy to counteract these effects.

Nor can a rigid distinction be maintained between the law on the one hand and social, political, or even performance roles on the other hand. Politics and social dynamics shape the law and litigation. In turn, the law fulfills an important expressive role in society beyond the purely legal sphere.[20] For example, an adjudicatory decision can serve an important shaming function or can reestablish a proper sense of right and wrong. Even the threat of litigation, without any actual application of the law, may generate public attention and even lead political actors to change positions.

The human rights strategy deployed against the border wall served important performance functions. The United States had blithely proceeded forward with the border wall project, appearing full of confidence that it could act with impunity. The human rights challenge forced the United States to respond formally to charges that the wall violated rights before an international body that refused to accept U.S. imperviousness. The United States saw itself obliged to send high-level government representatives to a hearing at the Inter-American Commission, which was held largely in Spanish, and to respond to the conclusions of the Working Group and the testimony of Dr. Margo Tamez. After the hearing, at the commission's command, the United States filed a written response to the concerns set out at the hearing. The U.S. government has been required to respond to the commission subsequently as well.

The United States government was called to task by an international body in proceedings that it barely knew how to manage. The result was the creation of a crack of fallibility in the U.S. government's stance and a perception of gravity in the accusations levied against the border wall. While the specific impact is difficult to identify, this legal process undeniably functioned to change the social and political status quo around the border wall. The resulting shift in government attitude, however subtle, created space for a corresponding adjustment in policy.

The critique of the use of law also insists, however, that legal challenges fail to force the systemic change necessary to address structural problems. As the argument goes, litigants only reify existing power structures by agreeing to the rules of legal claims and litigation. For example, legal scholar Daniel Morales argues that litigation around the border wall "only reinforces the existing power relationships that lead to . . . problem[s] in the first instance."[21] Timothy Dunn similarly asserts that litigation on border issues reinforces the marginalization of immigrants and Mexican Americans while human rights law inadequately addresses "bureaucratic power structures."[22]

A legal approach does require certain concessions to the basic legal order, whether international or domestic. Thus, for example, the human rights analysis of the border wall did not question in any profound way the legitimacy of governmental goals related to controlling migration and protecting national security. As commentators have suggested, the analysis also accepted basic principles relating to nation-state boundaries and possibly even countenanced the labeling of some individuals as outsiders who must be excluded and the labeling of others with similar characteristics (such as Mexican roots) as insiders entitled to protection based on U.S. residence.[23]

However, the use of the law did not in fact preclude a human rights challenge to the structural racializing and exclusionary aspects of border wall construction. While the human rights analysis focused on border residents rather than migrants, residents along the Texas-Mexico border are treated much like outsider migrants. They are marginalized, because they are identified and viewed as minorities connected to Mexico and Latin America by blood and culture, and because they live in a region closely associated with Mexico. A vision of border residents as undeserving of the full panoply of rights provided to "true" Americans allowed for construction of the border wall in the first place. It is difficult to imagine that harms of the magnitude created by the border wall could be visited upon the White citizenry on the East Coast without outrage and a political retreat.

The Working Group's human rights law challenge demanded that attention be paid to this reality of marginalization of residents along the border. The human rights claims that asserted violations of the legal rights of border residents to equal protection and respect for their unique culture and connection to their property constituted a direct challenge to the racial and exclusionary policies implicated in the border wall.

More importantly, though, the critique of legal strategies as insufficiently radical must be weighed against the desires of individuals suffering from human rights violations. It seems fundamentally unfair and profoundly disempowering to ask victims of abusive government actions to abstain from taking action available to them on the argument that they should wait for a more transformative long-term solution. Impacted individuals may make a rational decision to use all possible mechanisms, including human rights and other legal strategies, in an effort to ameliorate the harm they face. In the case of the border wall, individuals and communities along the border sought out human rights law as a strategy.[24] They deserve respect for their exercise of autonomy in making that decision.

NOTES

1. This chapter was originally an unpublished working paper completed in 2011.
2. U.S. Government Accountability Office, "Secure Border Initiative: Technology Deployment Delays Persist and the Impact of Border Fencing Has Not Been Assessed," September 2009, p. 21, https://www.gao.gov/products/gao-09-1013t.
3. It was extremely difficult to obtain exact information from the government about the locations of fence and the full mileage constructed. The mileage estimate for the Texas-Mexico border is obtained by extrapolating from governmental and nongovernmental sources, including reports by the Government Accountability Office and the website of the Department of Homeland Security as well as articles in *Time*, the *Austin American Statesman*, and other periodicals.
4. These conclusions are laid out in the reports prepared by the Working Group. University of Texas Working Group on Human Rights and the Border Wall, "Obstructing Human Rights: The Texas/Mexico Border Wall" (full set of briefing papers submitted to the Inter-American Commission on Human Rights, June 2008), https://law.utexas.edu/humanrights/borderwall/analysis/briefing-FULL-SET-OF-REPORTS.pdf.
5. While these landowners might generally be referred to as Latino, I do not use this term here as it masks the complexities of the situation. Affected individuals often have intertwined Mexican / Latin American, Indigenous, and Anglo lineages and may be connected with families who recently migrated to the United States or who date their residence in the Texas-Mexico border area to a time that precedes incorporation of this area into the United States and even the creation of the modern nation-state.
6. I/A Ct. H.R., Saramaka People v. Suriname 2007: para 127; I/A Ct. H.R., Advisory Opinion OC-18/03 2003: paras. 84–86.

7. Blas Nuñez-Neto and Yule Kim, *Border Security: Barriers Along the U.S. International Border* (report, Congressional Research Service, May 13, 2008), https://law.utexas.edu/humanrights/borderwall/maps/barriers-may-2008.pdf, 32; U.S. Government Accountability Office, "Secure Border Initiative."
8. See Michael Hoefer, Nancy Rytina, and Bryan C. Baker, "Estimates of the Unauthorized Immigrant Population Residing in the United States," Office of Immigration Statistics, Department of Homeland Security, January 2010, https://www.dhs.gov/xlibrary/assets/statistics/publications/ois_ill_pe_2010.pdf.
9. Arian Campo-Flores and Andrew Murr, "Brownsville's Bad Lie," *Newsweek*, May 5, 2008.
10. Members of the Working Group presented in fora ranging from the Western Social Science Association to the National Farmworker Conference. In 2010, the Rapoport Center for Human Rights organized a conference dedicated to analyzing walls, including the Texas-Mexico border wall, from an international perspective. A number of ideas presented in this chapter were originally developed in a paper presented by the author at that conference: Denise Gilman, "Seeking Breaches in the Wall: An International Human Rights Law Challenge to the Texas-Mexico Border Wall," *Texas International Law Review* 46, no. 2 (2010): 257–94. The address of the website developed by the Working Group is: https://law.utexas.edu/humanrights/borderwall/.
11. Articles about the hearing appeared in the *New York Daily News*, the *Houston Chronicle*, *El Universal*, and *EFE*, among others.
12. Inter-American Commission on Human Rights, "IACHR Concludes Its 133rd Period of Sessions," press release no. 46/08, October 31, 2008, https://www.cidh.org/Comunicados/English/2008/46.08eng.htm.
13. I/A Ct. H.R., Advisory Opinion OC-18/03, Juridical Condition and Rights of the Undocumented Migrants 2003: para. 103; U.N. Hum. Rts. Comm., General Comment No. 18: Non-discrimination 1989: para. 6.
14. Restatement (Third) of the Foreign Relations Law of the United States 1987:§111.
15. Louis Henkin et al., *Human Rights*, 2nd ed. (New York: Foundation Press, 2009), 617–20.
16. Theodore Eisenberg, "Litigation Models and Trial Outcomes in Civil Rights and Prisoner Cases," *Georgetown Law Journal* 77 (1989): 1578, 1600.
17. Myriam Gilles, "An Autopsy of the Structural Reform Injunction: Oops . . . It's Still Moving!," *University of Miami Law Review* 58 (2003): 161–62.
18. Charles F. Sabel and William H. Simon, "Destabilization Rights: How Public Law Litigation Succeeds," *Harvard Law Review* 117 (2004): 1015.
19. Wendy Brown, "Walls—What They Make and What They Break" (keynote lecture, Rapoport Center for Human Rights Spring 2010 Conference, University of Texas School of Law, Austin, February 2010).
20. Elizabeth S. Anderson and Richard H. Pildes, "Expressive Theories of Law: A General Restatement," *University of Pennsylvania Law Review* 148, no. 5 (2000): 1529–37.

21. Daniel I. Morales, "In Democracy's Shadow: Fences, Raids and the Production of Migrant Illegality," *Stanford Journal of Civil Rights and Civil Liberties* 5 (2009): 51–53.
22. Timothy J. Dunn, *Blockading the Border and Human Rights* (Austin: University of Texas Press, 2009), 10, 49–50.
23. Morales, "In Democracy's Shadow," 53–55.
24. Eloisa Taméz, "Eloisa Tamez Post-hearing Comments," interview outside Brownsville Federal Courthouse, February 7, 2008, video, 6:57, posted on February 8, 2008, by borderwall, http://www.youtube.com/watch?v=SQ1OZMUWGwM.

BIBLIOGRAPHY

Anderson, Elizabeth S., and Richard H. Pildes. "Expressive Theories of Law: A General Restatement." *University of Pennsylvania Law Review* 148, no. 5 (2000): 1503–75.

Brown, Wendy. "Walls—What They Make and What They Break." Keynote lecture, Rapoport Center for Human Rights Spring 2010 Conference, University of Texas School of Law, Austin, February 2010.

Campo-Flores, Arian, and Andrew Murr. "Brownsville's Bad Lie." *Newsweek*, May 5, 2008.

Dunn, Timothy J. *Blockading the Border and Human Rights*. Austin: University of Texas Press, 2009.

Eisenberg, Theodore. "Litigation Models and Trial Outcomes in Civil Rights and Prisoner Cases." *Georgetown Law Journal* 77 (1989): 1567–1602.

Gilles, Myriam. "An Autopsy of the Structural Reform Injunction: Oops . . . It's Still Moving!" *University of Miami Law Review* 58 (2003): 143–71.

Gilman, Denise. "Seeking Breaches in the Wall: An International Human Rights Law Challenge to the Texas-Mexico Border Wall." *Texas International Law Journal* 46, no. 2 (2011): 257–94.

Henkin, Louis, et al. *Human Rights*. 2nd ed. New York: Foundation Press, 2009.

Hoefer, Michael, Nancy Rytina, and Bryan C. Baker. "Estimates of the Unauthorized Immigrant Population Residing in the United States." Office of Immigration Statistics, Department of Homeland Security, January 2010. https://www.dhs.gov/xlibrary/assets/statistics/publications/ois_ill_pe_2010.pdf.

Inter-American Commission on Human Rights. "IACHR Concludes Its 133rd Period of Sessions." Press release no. 46/08, October 31, 2008. https://www.cidh.org/Comunicados/English/2008/46.08eng.htm.

Morales, Daniel I. "In Democracy's Shadow: Fences, Raids and the Production of Migrant Illegality." *Stanford Journal of Civil Rights and Civil Liberties* 5 (2009): 23–88.

Nuñez-Neto, Blas, and Yule Kim. *Border Security: Barriers Along the U.S. International Border*. Report, Congressional Research Service, May 13, 2008. https://law.utexas.edu/humanrights/borderwall/maps/barriers-may-2008.pdf.

Sabel, Charles F., and William H. Simon. "Destabilization Rights: How Public Law Litigation Succeeds." *Harvard Law Review* 117 (2004): 1016–1101.

Taméz, Eloisa. "Eloisa Tamez Post-hearing Comments." Interview outside Brownsville Federal Courthouse, February 7, 2008. YouTube video, 6:57, posted on February 8, 2008, by borderwall. http://www.youtube.com/watch?v=SQ1OZMUWGwM.

University of Texas Working Group on Human Rights and the Border Wall. "Obstructing Human Rights: The Texas/Mexico Border Wall." Full set of briefing papers submitted to the Inter-American Commission on Human Rights, June 2008. https://law.utexas.edu/humanrights/borderwall/analysis/briefing-FULL-SET-OF-REPORTS.pdf.

U.S. Government Accountability Office. "Secure Border Initiative: Technology Deployment Delays Persist and the Impact of Border Fencing Has Not Been Assessed." September 2009. https://www.gao.gov/products/gao-09-1013t.

FOURTEEN

A Community-Based Lawyer's Perspective

On Being, Belonging, and Lipan Apache Women's Spiritual Resistance to the Wall

AURORA VASQUEZ

I am the daughter of Mexican immigrants who spent their entire working careers in this country laboring as migrant farmworkers. I was born in Northern California, and the upside of having immigrant parents with a deep connection to their native country was their insistence on passing that connection on to their kids. That explains why, well into my early teens, they would take my sisters and me into Mexico as often as they could. The trips were great, but not without confusion for me, because my family "on the other side" was not unlike my family in the United States; they looked similar, spoke the same language, cooked the same dishes, shared some of the same childhood memories, and also spoke fondly of the United States of America.

The primary source of my confusion, however, was that militarized place we had to pass through: the U.S.-Mexico border, or "la frontera," as it was often referred to. Looking back, I understand that what I was struggling with was the fact that as we traveled between the two countries, the earth beneath my feet was continuous but our life as a people was not.

Fast-forward, and in 2008 I was sitting in my office in Washington, D.C., some nine years into my career as a community-based lawyer. I moved to D.C. in 2002 in the very real and salient shadow of the shocking tragedy of September 11, 2001. The nation was still deeply saddened; many were angry, others suspicious, and the politicos were busy planning next steps (mostly behind closed doors). In the process, immigrants—and those of us presumed to be immigrants because of our names and physical appearance—were being rapidly othered. For many Latinos the writing on the wall was both clear and familiar. After all, during a prior crisis, although an economic one, the U.S. government had no hesitation making Brown people out to be the problem.[1] In so doing, they militarized Brown existence in what turned out to be a national hunting of Mexicans for the purpose of loading them onto buses and trains—without regard for their U.S. citizenship status—in a forced "repatriation" to Mexico.[2]

What was coming down the pike became alarmingly evident with the passage of sweeping federal legislation including the Patriot Act of 2001 and, later, the Secure Fence Act of 2006.[3] A further foreshadowing of the extent to which Brown existence was to be militarized yet again was the fact that in 2006 we also began seeing a reemergence of efforts to give local law enforcement the power to enforce federal immigration laws. Not long after, we saw that combination evolve into a tool that provided cover for anti-immigrant hatred similar to that seen during the Great Depression. The thread that wove everything together this time around, however, was not economic depression. Rather, it was "national security," a phrase that seeded the deeply unsettled feeling that took root in the pit of my stomach.

I am still not entirely clear what, in 2008, led me to undertake a casual review of the Secure Fence Act. But I do recall that at that moment, the kid who had struggled to understand why it is okay to separate families with a line designated in a given location was about to resurface. Very quickly it became clear that the new law was not at all about building fences on the actual border. That is, the Bush administration's goal of gaining "operational control" over the border did not mean there would be tall wooden fences, picket fences, barbed wire fences, or any of those long, pretty, rolling fences you might see lining the outermost edge of a horse ranch. I may not have known precisely what a fence on the southern border would look like, but I understood that it would be more akin to a wall, and that it would be a significant undertaking. After all, the Secure Fence Act not only contemplated the role of the Border Patrol, it also brought in the Department of Homeland Security. With anti-immigrant and anti–people of color sentiment rapidly picking up steam around the country in the long shadow of September 11, my attention turned to other matters. But in the back of my mind a thought lingered: exactly *where* would the wall be built, and what might it mean for the people who live on bordered lands? The following year, the answer to that question found me.

It came in the form of a woman named Margo Tamez who reached out in 2008 because, as she explained, a sacred female figure had visited her in a dream and called upon her to gather the people in opposition to the border wall. Not at all sure how I—sitting in D.C. while they sat in Texas—could possibly be one of "the people" who ought to be gathered, I listened. Margo explained that her mother, Eloisa Taméz, held title to a Spanish Crown land grant now called El Calaboz, negotiated and secured by her Indigenous ancestors in 1736–47. This ranchería, it turned out, had long been part of the Lipan Apache community. It ran along the edge of the Rio Grande (i.e., the U.S.-Mexico international border), where it stood as testament and witness to the international border's bifurcation of the Lipan Apache peoples' negotiated and granted lands. In its present form, El Calaboz and neighboring lands also included a large levee (built by the United States government) that bifurcated the land even further.[4] That is, the massive levee physically separated their lands, leaving portions to the north and south of it.

In reality, the structure was more than a levee; it was another physical divide between the Indigenous peoples north of the border and those to the south. Plus, the U.S. Border Patrol had taken to regularly driving on the levee, bringing into the community a level of permanent militarization that in prior times they had resisted. To be clear, the families living around the area of El Calaboz were not the wealthy White ranchers or the Canadian snowbirds who came to the banks of the Rio Grande for the picturesque view, the considerably lower cost of food, the lower housing costs, the affordable medical care, and the warm Texas sun. Rather, much like my own parents, these families were people of scant economic means and, therefore, little ability to hire high-powered lawyers to help them stave off the most recent efforts to take their lands.

An effort to take their lands was fully underway by the time Margo reached out. That is, the U.S. government had returned to El Calaboz and neighboring lands with the not-so-subtle message that the new border "fence" would be going through their property with or without their approval. One of the most astounding parts of the story was that there were blueprints of sorts, plans that showed where the wall would be built. These plans clearly demonstrated that, like the levee, the wall would be cutting through significant portions of the border people's lands. What was different, however, was that the proposed placement of the wall included some residents' backyards and living rooms while altogether skipping over the river-facing properties of wealthy White landowners and Canadian "winter Texans." In short, it was clear the U.S. government intended to leave the land belonging to certain United States citizens—including portions of El Calaboz—south of the wall.

All of these facts were critical to what happened next. That is, the lawyer in me was very interested in how the U.S. government would justify the building of a border wall that far inland. I was also interested to understand how they planned to obtain the land they intended to build upon. However, it was the daughter of immigrant parents, the one who struggled to wrap her mind around why it was okay to separate an entire people—who quite literally occupied the same stretch of land—with a thing called a border, that took me to El Calaboz.

On that first visit I saw spent rifle cartridges visibly dotting Eloisa's property. These cartridges were oddly out of place, but they made their presence very known, as though someone had set them down intentionally. I walked along the levee with Margo and Eloisa under the warm Texas sun and the watchful binoculars of U.S. Border Patrol agents and members of the U.S. Army Corps of Engineers in the distance. Margo was a fountain of information, seemingly bottomless in her depth of knowledge and humanity. Her mother had the presence of a person whose wisdom comes from having seen and lived things likely beyond my understanding. I remember standing on the levee with these two women and thinking, as I looked toward the waters, how lucky I was to have been called. I also remember feeling that I was, as of that moment, not quite the person I had been when I stepped off the plane.

Something was different, but I could not put my finger on it. Instead, the logical lawyer part of me rapidly turned to what I suspected—from a legal perspective—would come next: eminent domain. "Takings," my mind told me, would be the sword to strike the final blow against any effort to challenge the wall.

The likelihood of that happening did not stop anyone. The wall was challenged, but more importantly, so too was my lens on how I occupied the spaces and places I traveled through as an attorney and a human being. Simultaneously, a body of people—marked by friendship, kinship, spirit, and concern over the emerging wall—rose from seemingly nowhere. Phone calls from people I had never met but who wanted to know how they could help began rolling in. I even got phone calls from people I had only read about in books, such as Armando Rendón and Nephtalí De León. The White Painted Woman—the ancient, ancestral, sacred, and spiritual matriarch of the Apaches, the one who predated the Catholicism of Apaches during colonial occupation—seemed to be calling the people together. An Indigenous pride—such as I had never experienced firsthand—seemed to be swelling like a new spring in Texas. That moment also brought other deeply grounded people into my orbit—such as Arnoldo García, April Cotte, and Michael Paul Hill. It also included the opportunity to attend a sacred Lipan Apache coming-of-age ceremony for Margo's eldest daughter, Milpa, in August of 2008.

I recall not knowing many details about the event even when it came time to board my flight to Texas. I trusted that Margo, who had extended the invitation, would see me through it. What I did know is that I would travel to somewhere in South Texas for a ceremony that few had witnessed, and that I would be there for the weekend. The attendees would sleep outdoors and there would be tradition to participate in, all before the ceremony itself took place. I remember feeling honored and humbled at once to be not only present, but part of those traditions in that moment in time. I helped make tortillas, helped serve food, observed Milpa's tent off in a special place away from the rest of us, and had countless conversations about the Indigenous lens on life. I was also given the responsibility of stitching together a small garment that would be worn during the ceremony. In that open space everything and everyone around me felt old and new at once, and it was as if a piece of me that I had not fully realized was missing was suddenly settling into place. The ceremony itself was a wonder that really went beyond words, or was perhaps too sacred to be captured by words. Suffice it to say that the handful of young girls who participated seemed to be a part of the very air and the sun all at once, and when they ran, it was as though all things past, present, and future existed at once. I left that ceremony with the understanding that in my role as a community-based lawyer I in fact had an inherited responsibility to the past, present, and future.

In the end, we did not stop the wall. We did, however, help raise a reemergence of sorts. That is, in 2008 we called up, from its dormant state, a resistance that had long been in that exact place along the Texas border. And with the help of Margo and Eloisa, the doors were thrown wide open. A part of me still wonders if there was more I could have done. As a community-based lawyer, could I have done more than examine documents, records, and portions of dense law to identify where the attempt to snatch up privately owned lands had gone awry? Could I have done more than help locate small landowners and subsequently persuade them that it was worthwhile to speak up against the U.S. government? Could I have done more than merely helping to interview plaintiffs and take down their statements for the emerging lawsuit?

Yet I would be remiss if I did not also acknowledge that during this time I learned many things that were less about lawyering and more about being; things which have, in fact, made me a better attorney, a more effective strategist, and a more diplomatic human being. Perhaps that was the ultimate point of this particular journey; perhaps that is why when the White Painted Woman called, Margo somehow heard her whisper my name. And if there remains work to be done to reconnect those dispossessed of their peoplehood and their land, I can only hope that the next time the Holy Mother—White Painted Woman—speaks, I will be close enough to hear the call.

NOTES

1. Abraham Hoffman, in *Unwanted Mexican Americans in the Great Depression: Repatriation Pressures, 1929–1939* (Tucson: University of Arizona Press, 1974), examines collaborative efforts between local law enforcement, local agency heads, and Secretary of Labor William Doak to use aggressive deportation methods that failed to distinguish between undocumented Mexicans, Mexicans with permanent residency, and U.S.-born Mexicans, with the goal of driving large numbers of people out of the country to free up jobs for those deemed to be "real Americans."
2. Released during the Great Depression, a 1931 report by the U.S. National Commission on Law Observance and Enforcement—a section of the Bureau of Immigration, which was found to be employing constitutionally questionable processes—indicates that anti-immigrant sentiment heightens during times of

economic hardship. The report says: "The deportation laws of the United States are administratively enforced and the agents of the Bureau of Immigration of the Department of Labor, operating in the interior of the United States, each have the whole duty of enforcing these laws in their districts. This makes of such an agent a detective, a prosecutor, and a judge—three functions which we have found it safe, in no other phase of life, to intrust to any one individual." U.S. National Commission on Law Observance and Enforcement, *Report on the Enforcement of the Deportation Laws of the United States* (Washington, D.C.: Government Printing Office, 1931), 5.

3. "Fact Sheet: The Secure Fence Act of 2006," The White House: President George W. Bush, October 26, 2006, https://georgewbush-whitehouse.archives.gov/news/releases/2006/10/20061026-1.html.
4. Between 1929 and 1944, the U.S. Section of the International Boundary and Water Commission (IBWC) constructed "Canalization, American Dam, Rectification, Boundary Markers, Fences, Lower Rio Grande Flood Control Projects, etc." in the Lower Rio Grande Valley. The IBWC did not enact consultation with Indigenous peoples with traditional, customary, and legal mechanisms that predated the nation-states of the United States and Mexico, nor did it provide access to juridical systems of legal complaint, redress, and compensation for forcibly dispossessed lands. See "Historical Timeline," International Boundary and Water Commission, United States and Mexico, U.S. Section, accessed April 5, 2024, https://www.ibwc.gov/about-us/historical-timeline/.

BIBLIOGRAPHY

Hoffman, Abraham. *Unwanted Mexican Americans in the Great Depression: Repatriation Pressures, 1929–1939*. Tucson: University of Arizona Press, 1974.

International Boundary and Water Commission (IBWC). "Historical Timeline." International Boundary and Water Commission (IBWC), United States and Mexico, U.S. Section. Accessed April 5, 2024. https://www.ibwc.gov/about-us/historical-timeline/.

U.S. National Commission on Law Observance and Enforcement. *Report on the Enforcement of the Deportation Laws of the United States*. Washington, D.C.: Government Printing Office, 1931.

White House. "Fact Sheet: The Secure Fence Act of 2006." The White House: President George W. Bush. October 26, 2006. https://georgewbush-whitehouse.archives.gov/news/releases/2006/10/20061026-1.html.

FIFTEEN

Decolonizing the Archive

Reflections from the Border of an Identity

ROSALVA RESENDIZ

I grew up in the Texas-Mexico borderlands, the native lands of a diverse group of seminomadic peoples living along the northwestern coastal plains of the Gulf of Mexico, from the Galveston area to San Antonio, and southward to the Pánuco River in Tamaulipas. They ranged from South Texas to northeastern Mexico, across the Rio Grande River, to the states of Tamaulipas, Coahuila, and Nuevo León. Before the Rio Grande River / Río Bravo was a boundary, it was the lifeline for many tribes and bands with many languages and dialects. By some estimates there were over six hundred tribal names recorded. Those that spoke Coahuiltecan called the river Ganapetuan; in the language of the Carrizos/Comecrudos it was Atmau Pakmau; and for the Cotonames the river was Ax Katam. To these groups, the river wasn't a boundary or a border: it was a lifeline.

Centuries' worth of colonization displaced many tribes, and some joined the Coahuiltecans. One of those peoples was the Guachichiles of Uto-Aztekan linguistic roots, and more came later from the north, such as the Lipan Apache and the Comanches. I am a descendant of the Huichol/Wixarika, who are kin/descendants of the Guachichil/Cuauchichil of the Gran Chichimeca, in the present-day Mexican states of Aguascalientes, Jalisco, Nayarit, Guanajuato, and Zacatecas.

I grew up at the edge of the borderlands in a small two-bedroom wooden-frame home. I had coyotes in my backyard, howling from the top of the levee. In that same space, Border Patrol agents parked their vehicles as they stood watch, waiting to catch human-smuggling *coyotes* taking people across the river into the United States. In this space, I found myself at the intersection of intergenerational traumas and had to confront and unearth my indigeneity. As I tried to understand our subjugation, oppression, and erasure, I found myself learning the master's tools to find the archives that would deconstruct the myths of the "cosmic race" of mestizos/as. Through a postcolonial and decolonial lens, I came to find my voice by writing against the myths and narratives of our subjugation. As a graduate student, I was introduced to W. E. B. Du Bois, Dorothy Smith, Linda Tuhiwai Smith, Kimberly Crenshaw, Patricia Hill Collins, Gloria Anzaldúa, and Cherríe Moraga, which resulted in the acquisition of a theoretical arsenal to be used to deconstruct and decolonize.

For my doctoral dissertation, I turned to postmodern critical-race feminism and the situated subject position, to explore, analyze, deconstruct, and resist the narratives and lenses of White patriarchy.[1] This took me to my childhood memories and stories of the female soldiers/*soldaderas* of the Mexican Revolution fighting for their rights to their ancestral lands, living both in subjection and with agency.[2] Through the archives of oral history, I began to examine the representations of Indigenous mestiza women in corridos/ballads and (auto)biographies, including my own.[3]

Many years later, my nephew Ramón introduced me to Margo Tamez's dissertation. Through her work, I found myself at the intersections of her family's struggle, resistance, and trauma. And, hence, this is where this story begins, which led to the making of a documentary through a decolonizing lens.[4] In the process of decolonizing, we embarked on a truth-telling mission, but we also embarked on a healing journey. I write my *testimonio* to archive our resistance to colonialism, imperialism, and settler colonialism, as well as to share the intergenerational trauma that cuts and intersects across time and space. I grew up in these borderlands confused about my identity as an Indigenous person living with subjugation/oppression/erasure. And as I searched, I found myself at the intersections of colonial intergenerational trauma.

Theory of the Flesh: Deconstructing the Landscapes

The concepts of postcoloniality and decoloniality can be romantic notions for those who live on the U.S.-Mexico border, where militarization and colonialism are everyday social facts.[5] The border is a place where colonization is not a distant memory but continues as an ongoing historical process. Those on the border have continued to suffer the effects of colonization, which has attempted to subjugate the Indigenous, the Spanish, the Mexican, the Chicanx, and the "undocumented." Gloria Anzaldúa's *borderlands* have been romanticized as a place where the roots of consciousness grow.[6] But for the Chicanxs/Indigenous/mestizos/as that live on the border, we struggle to plant and grow the seeds, as military checkpoints constrict our movement.

For those of us that live on the border between identities, understanding ourselves becomes a nightmare of contradictions and conflict, yet when we immerse ourselves in how our brown bodies navigate the landscapes of White supremacy and Indigenous erasure, our flesh situates us in a position to create theory. Moraga's "realist" theory of Chicanx identity focuses on the "theory of the flesh," accounting for the social and physical locations of our brown bodies, and as such, it provides a framework through which we can explore the process of decolonization within militarized zones and colonialist spaces.[7] Moraga acknowledges the need to take into consideration our social and physical locations, the epistemic value of experiential knowledge, and the oppositional struggle against dominant ideologies and institutions. Moraga's theoretical framework of "Chicana realism" is a tool that helps those of us living in militarized zones understand the multiple struggles we face in deconstructing settler colonialism. The border is not a place where Chicanx consciousness thrives; it is a place where Chicanx consciousness survives. The border is a place where Chicanx-identifying people face opposition from Mexican Americans and Hispanics, who fight for acceptance from so-called real Americans, the Anglos or gringos. The reality of living under militarization forces the Chicanx Indigenous mestizo/a to struggle with decolonization on a daily basis. For those of us who live under these conditions, we fight every day to retain a Chicanx Indigenous consciousness.

The process of decolonization has always existed alongside colonization, as elements of our indigeneity remain in our language and culture. We refuse to forget. Living on the Texas-Mexico border has helped us maintain ties to family, customs, and language, but mostly to settler colonialism, which continues to reproduce racist hierarchies. Many living on the border choose to forget their past, embrace the colony, and become enforcers of the militarized zone, craving acceptance from an imperialist country to the point of becoming both enemies of their own people and "pacifiers"/gatekeepers or participants in the criminal justice–industrial complex.[8] "The authority of coloniality has consistently required visuality to supplement its deployment of force," and on the border this remains an everyday fact.[9] We learn to accept hierarchies of oppression and subjugation: White over Brown, Brown over Black, mestizo/a over Indian, English over Spanish, citizen over undocumented, male over female, rich over poor. We understand all these prejudices are part of us, but instead of rejecting them, we reproduce them in the "post"-colony, desperately searching for validation of our belonging here in this country, although we have always been here.

My theory of the flesh began before I was even born. I was born on the border of Texas/Mexico, a brown-colored Indigenous mestiza navigating landscapes dominated by colonialism, imperialism, White supremacy, and patriarchy. My reality was crossed by physical, ideological, and metaphysical borders/narratives, creating contradictions and confusion as I navigated a colonial and imperialist identity of oppression. But at the intersections of our border narratives, our Indigenous spirit managed to survive/resist/live. At these borderlands, I was able to find my Chicanx Indigenous mestiza consciousness. It is from these margins that I came to respect and honor the Indigenous warriors who fought valiantly for their native lands, in particular the Indigenous/mestiza female warriors of the Mexican Revolution of 1910, as subjects and agents.[10]

Fifteen years after my PhD graduation, Ramón (my nephew) did his graduate studies at the University of Washington's Native Voices Program. It reaffirmed our Indigenous roots. We didn't have a "blue card," we were just marked by our brown skin and the oral history of our family.[11] It became painfully obvious that the United States had erased our claims to the Americas and made us immigrants when we were Indigenous to these lands. We were robbed of our claim to our identity because we were conquered people, subject to the myths and racial geographies of the colonizer and settler colonialism.[12] When he invited me to be part of his documentary project, I was elated to be part of a decolonial effort focusing on Indigenous resistance on the border. We have resisted in so many ways, and to have the opportunity to talk/write/shoot back against colonialism and imperialism was monumental for me as a Chicanx Indigenous mestiza scholar. I had studied border history for years, finding our roots, understanding the complexities of identity for Mexican American Indigenous mestizas/os, erased by the colonial archive. I didn't hesitate to accept Ramón's invitation to co-produce and co-direct *El Muro | The Wall* (2017). The purpose of the documentary was to *document* and *archive* the struggle and resistance of the first U.S. citizen to sue the Department of Homeland Security, Dr. Eloisa Taméz, when it attempted to seize her ancestral land under the pretext of "national security."[13]

As noted elsewhere throughout this collection, Dr. Eloisa Taméz's story of resistance is one of the many stories of Indigenous resilience and survival that the colonized have lived in the flesh. Her story is also the story of all of us who have had to survive a legacy of trauma created by colonial and imperialist structures of White supremacy and land theft.

A Journey of Decolonial Collaboration to Recover Histories and Memories

In November 2015, I had the honor of meeting Dr. Eloisa Taméz. She seemed regal to me and reminded me of my childhood heroines, the soldaderas of the Mexican Revolution, memorialized in our oral tradition of corridos/ballads. The soldaderas of the Mexican Revolution were strong, brave Indigenous and mestiza women who fought alongside their partners for the rights to their lands.[14] Professor Taméz was accompanied by her daughter Dr. Margo Tamez. I had read Dr. Margo Tamez's work "Space, Position and Imperialism in South Texas," as well as her dissertation.[15] Along with her mother, Margo fought for what remained of the San Pedro de Carricitos Land Grant of 1761 in El Calaboz Ranchería. Professor Taméz's land was by the Rio Grande River, next to Highway 281, also known locally as the Military Highway because it had originally served as the Spanish colonial–era *camino militar*.[16]

After our initial introduction, we began filming in 2016. The project would take us from the Texas-Mexico border at the mouth of the Rio Grande (el Río Bravo del Norte) to the mountains of Big Bend, and to the Canada-U.S. border. As we started the interviewing process, the stories told by Eloisa echoed memories of my childhood, intersected by the history of these lands. For me, *el bordo* was a boundary before the real boundary, but for Professor Taméz's mother, the levee had dispossessed her of part of her land in the 1930s. That same levee had cut across the land where I grew up, which was at some point part of the Espíritu Santo Land Grant. Today, part of this area has been encased behind the U.S. border fence, standing behind my childhood home.[17]

I grew up in the remnants of that land grant, in a home owned by a man surnamed Pizaña, who also owned a ranch. We wondered if he was a descendant of Aniceto Pizaña, one of the leaders of El Plan de San Diego of 1915. Aniceto Pizaña, along with Luis de la Rosa, led an uprising in South Texas, calling for sedition and the union of Mexican mestizos/as and Indigenous, Asian, and Black peoples. Their uprising ended in a reign of terror by the Texas Rangers.[18]

In 1915, the Texas Rangers lynched and murdered mestizos/as and Indigenous people by labeling them Mexican bandits.[19] In South Texas, the legacy of the Texas Rangers was one of fear, a fear that Eloisa Taméz recounted in stories of her childhood. We also grew up with that fear. We knew that the Texas Rangers had been tools of the state that had dispossessed many of the land grant owners of their property and cattle.[20] I grew up with corridos/ballads that told the tales of violence against Brown people by the Rinches / Texas Rangers, also known as *los diablos tejanos.*

Our family stories were reflected in the film, as we heard Eloisa express the same fears and obstacles that Indigenous people and mestizos have faced as they have resisted erasure by colonialism and imperialism. Those intersections made us more consciously aware that we had to honor our representation of Indigenous resistance, to provide the Other's perspective. In doing so, we were extremely careful to hear each of the stories told by our participants and their perception of facts from the standpoint of the conquered. This deliberately entailed creating a space that decentered Anglo-imperial settler narratives of the nation-state.

A Bordered Reflection: *Al borde del bordo*

As far as I can remember, the search for my identity and place has been ongoing. I grew up on the border of *el bordo.* El bordo was the levee that had been built near the river and stood next to my childhood home. At the top of the levee, *la migra* / Border Patrol agents stationed themselves on the dirt road to oversee the space in between el bordo and the Rio

Grande River. Beyond el bordo there were markers of a previous culture, with cemeteries holding the bodies of settlers, mestizos/as, and Indians. I grew up in a colonized space, militarized by the United States, with symbols of war scattered across the city. We grew up knowing that we were conquered people, with relics of cannons of the Mexican-American War sitting quietly on Paredes Line, in a city named after Major Jacob Brown, who died in that same war and whose fort stands by the international bridge, still making the claim of an imaginary Texas boundary.

A Preface on the Border of an Identity

In 1519, the governor of Jamaica sent out an expedition led by Alonso Álvarez de Pineda to map what we now refer to as the Gulf Coast. He named our river el Río de las Palmas (the River of Palms), for the numerous palm trees found in the region. The area remained an Indigenous stronghold for more than two hundred years until José de Escandón established the Spanish colony of Nuevo Santander, which also included the area known as "El Seno Mexicano" in today's Mexican state of Tamaulipas and the Rio Grande Valley / South Texas. In late 1748, he led a caravan of 750 soldiers and over 2,500 Spanish settlers and Christianized Indians from the El Seno frontier. The caravan marched through areas such as San Luis Potosí, and as it proceeded, more settlers joined.[21]

My father's family was from both the borderlands of Mexico and the United States. My grandmother was a U.S. citizen, and my grandfather was supposedly an immigrant, whose family had lived in Texas and Mexico before the Treaty of Guadalupe Hidalgo. We also knew that many of our family members had been deported in the 1930s, although they were U.S. citizens.[22] Our family stretched from the mountainous regions of San Luis Potosí to the Texas-Mexico border, to San Antonio, to Dallas, to California, and to Chicago. We seemed to have always traversed the river from many parts of the Americas. When we met Dr. Margo Tamez, she told us that she held the family archive and our surnames were in her family records. She confirmed what we already knew.

My U.S. relatives spoke little of our Indigenous mestizo/a roots, trying to distance themselves from the Mexican and Indian, yet it was well known that my father's paternal grandmother, Perfecta González, was a

Huichol Indian, a descendant of the survivors of the Chichimeca Wars. The Chichimecas were never defeated, but they never won either.[23] They "blended" into and were erased in the mestizo culture of Mexico, settling (or rather, being settled by colonization) into the nationalist myth of the cosmic race, very much like the Lipan Apache after the Remolino Massacre of 1875.

I never knew much about my grandmother, except that her blood colored my skin and shaped my features. She wore the traditional dress of the Huichol Indians and had married Candelario Reséndiz, a light-skinned, blue-eyed Mexican who owned a ranch in San Luis Potosí. My father carried a book about Huicholes that he always held dearly. I learned about their vision quests and the sacred peyote. He seemed to be in search of his people and his Indigenous roots. For my father, his paternal ancestry was more important than his maternal ancestry, since he had suffered abuse from his maternal grandfather, Carmen Reyes.

Not much is known about Carmen Reyes. In the 1920s he was married to my great-grandmother and lived in North Texas. He worked on the levees in the 1930s, and after they were completed, he was deported. It is believed that he was a U.S. citizen and was one of the many Mexicans who were dispossessed of their homeland. He settled along the Texas-Mexico border in Valle Hermoso, Tamaulipas. My father used to say that he was cruel and abusive. When he died, my father rejoiced in his death with a joyous drunken celebration at the age of fifteen. These stories left a long-standing picture of the cruel practices reproduced by the descendants of the Spanish in my imagination—intergenerational trauma. The Reséndiz family was noble and the Reyes family was cruel; those were our family myths.

As a little girl, I was aware that I had been created by a dark-skinned Spanish-speaking Indigenous mestizo father and a light-skinned Spanish-speaking Indigenous mestiza mother, indoctrinated into Catholicism, alienated from the Indian, and negotiating the Spanish and English languages. We grew up within a racist culture, but it wasn't the White U.S. Americans who first taught me about White supremacy; it was my mother's Mexican family, pointing out my brown skin tone next to their "Spanish" lightness. We were raised knowing that brown meant Indian, and there was shame. The elite classes were White, and therefore I could never aspire beyond my lower-class Indigenous mestiza brownness. At the age of nine, I was reminded by one of my mother's sisters that although I was intelligent, her white-skinned child would always be superior.

Like most dispossessed Mexican Indians and mestizos/as, we were poor. My father was a naturalized U.S. citizen, his mother a Texan and his father from Mexico. My mother was a permanent resident with a green card. I was a Mexican American, and that was very clear to me as a child. We had family on both sides of the border; some were U.S.-born, while others were from different areas of Mexico.

My mother was the daughter of Ciro R. González Cano, a descendant of Mexican landowners from an hacienda in San Pedro, General Terán, Nuevo León, Mexico. He was considered White, with a European background that was Spanish, Italian, French, and English—a criollo—yet he was Indigenous mestizo. He was the youngest child of his father's first marriage, born in 1901, losing his mother at an early age and then raised by a stepmother. This story would be repeated with my own mother, who was kidnapped by her father and raised by a stepmother. She was a bastard child until her father claimed her and took her away from her godmother. She never saw her biological mother again, but she remained grateful to have been recognized by her father.

When I was a young child we traveled to Matamoros every weekend to see my godparents. I felt so much more at home in Mexico, and it was with great sadness that I would return to the United States. I remember sticking my head out the window while we crossed the bridge. The breeze made me feel the difference between one country and the other as we passed the plaque in the middle of the bridge signifying the boundary, above the Rio Grande River. In Mexico, the river was el Río Bravo, because of its historic flooding and its dangerous undercurrents, which at times would eat up the migrants trying to cross to Brownsville. Living alongside el bordo, we saw many undocumented people cross through our home. My father and mother always helped the newcomers and warned them about the difficulties they would face in this country.

When we were children crossing the border there was always a certain amount of fear and trauma. We would go to Mexico frequently to visit the doctor and buy medicine, since we had no health care. And upon our return, we had to make sure we didn't act suspicious, because our medicine was "illegal." So my mother would hide the medicine and we would practice what we had to say. We also practiced our citizenship line, "We are American citizens" (as if America was only the United States). We were prepared to respectfully respond to the customs agents, and there was always the fear that they might not let us in. My father would show his citizenship documents, which he had blown up to 8½ by 11 inches to make sure that there were no misunderstandings. He remained fearful throughout his life. Dr. Tamez spoke of this fear as well. When she was a child, her teacher would taunt her with threats of deportation, even though these were her ancestral lands.

When I started school, I began to learn English, the language of the Anglo settler, and slowly forgot the Spanish tongue. I spoke in English and Spanish, back and forth, from one language to another, learning to speak in *anglicismos*. So, when I crossed over to Mexico to see my godparents, I became a *pocha*, a hybrid speaker, performing what is now recognized as "code-switching."[24] But it also meant that we were hybrids, and therefore abnormal but enviable because of our citizenship status. But when we crossed back to the United States, we were still second-class citizens living on the margins of the colony.

At the age of five, my paternal grandmother passed away and my maternal step-grandmother arrived in my life. My mother's family disapproved of my father, a poor, dark-skinned, working-class man, and my mother was disowned by her family for the first five years of my life. They were elitist and valued Whiteness over the Indigenous. My mother's light-skinned daughter arrived looking for her. I had never wondered about them. I had a loving paternal grandmother and godparents. With the arrival of my mother's family came the abuse and intergenerational trauma brought forth by Hispanic Whiteness. For them, the Indian was a savage, a *naco*, low-class, inferior, and undesirable. And therefore, my father was inferior, and his children were degraded according to the level of their darkness. My brother wasn't called by his name; instead he was called *el prieto* (the dark one), reminiscent of what Anzaldúa describes in her work. I was considered ugly because my features were Indigenous, more than my sisters' were. My father's name was too Indigenous, so they kept changing his name. My father was very patient with them, and they never seemed to bother him. He gave me strength and pride in my indigeneity. But I learned about the caste system that the Spaniards brought to the Americas, which supposedly created a new race, as it/

they tried to erase our claim to our lands and the violence through which we were dispossessed—including through "miscegenation" and rape. This caste system continues to be part of Mexican culture and society. I constantly hear people trying to distance themselves from the Indian by recalling that their grandmothers or grandfathers were from Spain, situating themselves higher in the racial hierarchy. Yet most Mexicans have European last names, a reminder that we are all the descendants of violent colonization, an attempted Indigenous genocide.

The trauma of colonization, imperialism, patriarchy, and White supremacy has been with me since the age of five. My home at the edge of the militarized borderlands has haunted me in my dreams, a reminder of the pain my heart feels and the inability to express the intersecting traumas. From that center, I saw settler colonialism in praxis. I remember seeing the Border Patrol parked on el bordo, watching for "*mojados*/wetbacks," as they were and are commonly called. On the other side of the levee there stood a farmhouse. There were plots of sorghum that looked like tall golden-orange grass. There were rows of grapefruits which we would pick from the trees to take home to my mother. There were unpaved roads, *caminitos* that we would walk with our father and where we picked wild berries. There was a cemetery in between the river and el bordo. Walking through this in-between space, it felt as if it hid secrets. It felt magical because it felt as if you were nowhere, and it felt mysterious because of the history buried in that cemetery. The cemetery sat quietly, with tombstones over one hundred years old that were part of the legacy of the land grants and signified the presence of a previous colonial empire. My dad would take us on walks behind el bordo and tell us stories about its past. They used to say that there was a ranch with a dungeon that had held slaves. We never saw the ranch, but we came to find the ranchería El Calaboz—that is, the *dungeon*.

Behind our home, there was more farmland. I never knew who it belonged to. We used to watch the planes spraying pesticide over the land. From our backyard we could see a man inside the little yellow plane, and when I was a child it seemed so exciting. We didn't know to practice caution as we ran outside to see them fly over us. I remember the smell of the spray to this day, and to this day I suffer from asthma. They didn't care who got hurt. We were at the margins of the city, those dispossessed by el bordo.

The Archive, Power, and Coloniality

Arriving to a Chicanx Indigenous mestiza/o consciousness is a painful process, which the colonial archive has at times seemingly made impossible to embrace. Our identities are found at the intersections of the archives and our collective memories. Our identity is a result of settler-colonial violence, which subjugated our people into racist caste hierarchies. I use the term "Indigenous mestiza/o" purposefully, to acknowledge the multiple borders we have negotiated to maintain our roots in these lands.

Our work is more than theoretical. It intersects with our lived experiences of intergenerational trauma as we find our Indigenous roots and voices. Decolonial methods help us reframe systemic narratives to bring discomfiting histories of violent erasure to the fore and expose the injustices against Indigenous people. In co-creating the documentary *El Muro | The Wall* with the Tamez family, we have amplified the voices struggling against the erasure of indigeneity. And in recognizing their struggle, we have also recognized the struggle of all Indigenous people, as well as unearthed memories and trauma that intersect with our lived experiences and oral history. Decolonizing methodologies allows us to contest/resist the masters' narratives by situating ourselves as producers of our own knowledge and histories of subjugation and resistance.

In telling my story, I have added to the collective memory of our peoples. Decolonizing the archives requires that we excavate the ideal types created by the nation-state and the coloniality of power created by the White supremacy of settler colonialism, which obfuscate our own ability to reconcile with our indigeneity. Although the master's tools will reify epistemic Whiteness, through a decolonial lens we can begin to dismantle/resist the colonial narratives of inferiority and subjugation to empower Indigenous people as a whole.

NOTES

1. See Patricia Hill Collins, *Black Feminist Thought: Knowledge, Consciousness, and the Politics of Empowerment*, 30th anniversary ed. (New York: Routledge, 2022); Linda Tuhiwai Smith, *Decolonizing Methodologies: Research and Indigenous Peoples* (London: Zed Books, 1999).
2. Judith Butler, *The Psychic Life of Power: Theories in Subjugation* (Redwood City: Stanford University Press, 1997); Rosalva Resendiz, "Female Subjectivity and

Agency in Popular Mexican Corridos (Ballads): An Examination of Images and Representations of Soldaderas (Female Soldiers) in the Mexican Revolution 1910–1920" (PhD diss., Texas Woman's University, 2001); Jeanette Rodríguez, *Our Lady of Guadalupe: Faith and Empowerment Among Mexican-American Women* (Austin: University of Texas Press, 1994).

3. Rosalva Resendiz, "Female Subjectivity."
4. Ramón Resendiz, Rosalva Resendiz, and Irene Klaver, "Colonialism and Imperialism: Indigenous Resistance on the US/Mexico Border," *Perspectives on Global Development and Technology* 16 (2017): 15–33.
5. Wendy Brown, *Walled States, Waning Sovereignty* (New York: Zone Books, 2010).
6. Gloria Anzaldúa, *Borderlands / La Frontera: The New Mestiza* (San Francisco: Aunt Lute Books, 1987).
7. Paula M. L. Moya, "Postmodernism, 'Realism,' and the Politics of Identity: Cherríe Moraga and Chicana Feminism," in *Feminist Genealogies, Colonial Legacies, Democratic Futures*, ed. Chandra Talpade Mohanty and M. Jacqui Alexander (New York: Routledge, 1997).
8. Timothy J. Dunn, *The Militarization of the U.S.-Mexico Border, 1978–1992: Low-Intensity Conflict Doctrine Comes Home* (Austin: Center for Mexican American Studies, University of Texas Press, 1996); Ramon Gutierrez, "Internal Colonialism: An American Theory of Race," *Du Bois Review* 1, no. 2 (2004): 281–95; Richard Quinney, "Class, State and Crime," in *Classics of Criminology*, 4th ed., ed. Joseph E. Jacoby, Theresa A. Severance, and Alan S. Bruce (Long Grove: Waveland Press, 2012), 173–82.
9. Nicholas Mirzoeff, *The Right to Look: A Counterhistory of Visuality* (Durham, N.C.: Duke University Press, 2011), 6.
10. Rosalva Resendiz, "Female Subjectivity."
11. A "blue card" is a colloquial reference to a Certificate of Degree of Indian Blood, which confirms enrollment in a federally recognized American Indian nation.
12. María Josefina Saldaña-Portillo, *Indian Given: Racial Geographies Across Mexico and the United States* (Durham, N.C.: Duke University Press, 2016).
13. Ramón Resendiz, Rosalva Resendiz, and Klaver, "Colonialism and Imperialism"; Margo Tamez, "Space, Position and Imperialism in South Texas (Dr. Eloisa Garcia Tamez v. U.S. Secretary Michael Chertoff, U.S. Department of Homeland Security, U.S. Border Patrol, U.S. Army Corps of Engineers)," *Chicana/Latina Studies* 7, no. 2 (2008): 112–21.
14. The Mexican Revolution remains an important national consciousness-making moment regarding land, decolonization, and Indigenous armed struggles against landowning criollos (mainly European-descended) in Mexico, who continued to benefit from the colonial legacies of the Spanish Empire, which deeded them the hacienda and encomienda systems. The revolution was itself an armed struggle by poor Indigenous and mestizo peasants against *terratenientes* (the national bourgeoisie) that resulted in the repartitioning of lands into the modern/present-day ejido systems, which were "ethnically identified,

clan-based indigenous groups who could establish they had historically formed a community by proving their status as townships dating back to the colonial period." María Josefina Saldaña-Portillo, *The Revolutionary Imagination in the Americas and the Age of Development* (Durham, N.C.: Duke University Press, 2003), 221.

15. Tamez, "Space, Position and Imperialism"; Margo Tamez, "Returning Lipan Apache Women's Laws, Lands and Power in El Calaboz Rancheria, Texas-Mexico Border" (PhD diss., Washington State University, 2010).
16. Hubert J. Miller, *José de Escandón: Colonizer of Nuevo Santander* (Edinburg, Tex.: The Santander Press, 1980); Tamez, "Space, Position and Imperialism."
17. Milo Kearney and Anthony Knopp, *Border Cuates: A History of the U.S.-Mexican Twin Cities* (Austin: Eakin Press, 1995); Miller, *José de Escandón*.
18. Alfredo Mirande, *Gringo Justice* (Notre Dame, Ind.: University of Notre Dame Press, 1987); Américo Paredes, *A Texas-Mexican Cancionero: Folksongs of the Lower Border* (Austin: University of Texas Press, 1976).
19. Mirande, *Gringo Justice*; Paredes, *Texas-Mexican Cancionero*.
20. Monica Muñoz Martinez, *The Injustice Never Leaves You: Anti-Mexican Violence in Texas* (Cambridge, Mass.: Harvard University Press, 2018); Mirande, *Gringo Justice*; David Montejano, *Anglos y mexicanos en la formación de Texas, 1836–1986* (Mexico City: Alianza Editorial, 1991); Nicholas Villanueva, *The Lynching of Mexicans in the Texas Borderlands* (Albuquerque: University of New Mexico Press, 2017).
21. Miller, *José de Escandón*; Martin Salinas, *Indians of the Rio Grande Delta: Their Role in the History of Southern Texas and Northeastern Mexico* (Austin: University of Texas Press, 1990).
22. Francisco E. Balderrama and Raymond Rodriguez, *Decade of Betrayal: Mexican Repatriation in the 1930s* (Albuquerque: University of New Mexico Press, 1995).
23. Martha Menchaca, *Recovering History, Constructing Race: The Indian, Black, and White Roots of Mexican Americans* (Austin: University of Texas Press, 2001).
24. Anzaldúa, *Borderlands*.

BIBLIOGRAPHY

Anzaldúa, Gloria. *Borderlands / La Frontera: The New Mestiza*. San Francisco: Aunt Lute Books, 1987.

Balderrama, Francisco E., and Raymond Rodriguez. *Decade of Betrayal: Mexican Repatriation in the 1930s*. Albuquerque: University of New Mexico Press, 1995.

Brown, Wendy. *Walled States, Waning Sovereignty*. New York: Zone Books, 2010.

Butler, Judith. *The Psychic Life of Power: Theories in Subjugation*. Redwood City: Stanford University Press, 1997.

Collins, Patricia Hill. *Black Feminist Thought: Knowledge, Consciousness, and the Politics of Empowerment*. 30th anniversary ed. New York: Routledge, 2022.

Dunn, Timothy J. *The Militarization of the U.S.-Mexico Border, 1978–1992: Low-Intensity Conflict Doctrine Comes Home*. Austin: Center for Mexican American Studies, University of Texas at Austin, 1996.

Gutierrez, Ramon. "Internal Colonialism: An American Theory of Race." *Du Bois Review* 1, no. 2 (2004): 281–95.

Kearney, Milo, and Anthony Knopp. *Border Cuates: A History of the U.S.-Mexican Twin Cities*. Austin: Eakin Press, 1995.

Martinez, Monica Muñoz. *The Injustice Never Leaves You: Anti-Mexican Violence in Texas*. Cambridge, Mass.: Harvard University Press, 2018.

Menchaca, Martha. *Recovering History, Constructing Race: The Indian, Black, and White Roots of Mexican Americans*. Austin: University of Texas Press, 2001.

Miller, Hubert J. *José de Escandón: Colonizer of Nuevo Santander*. Edinburg, Tex.: New Santander Press, 1980.

Mirande, Alfredo. *Gringo Justice*. Notre Dame, Ind.: University of Notre Dame Press, 1987.

Mirzoeff, Nicholas. *The Right to Look: A Counterhistory of Visuality*. Durham, N.C.: Duke University Press, 2011.

Montejano, David. *Anglos y mexicanos en la formación de Texas, 1836–1986*. Mexico City: Alianza Editorial, 1991.

Moya, Paula M. L. "Postmodernism, 'Realism,' and the Politics of Identity: Cherríe Moraga and Chicana Feminism." In *Feminist Genealogies, Colonial Legacies, Democratic Futures*, edited by Chandra Talpade Mohanty and M. Jacqui Alexander, 125–50. New York: Routledge, 1997.

Paredes, Américo. *A Texas-Mexican Cancionero: Folksongs of the Lower Border*. Austin: University of Texas Press, 1976.

Quinney, Richard. "Class, State and Crime." In *Classics of Criminology*, 4th ed., edited by Joseph E. Jacoby, Theresa A. Severance, and Alan S. Bruce, 173–82. Long Grove: Waveland Press, 2012.

Resendiz, Ramón, Rosalva Resendiz, and Irene Klaver. "Colonialism and Imperialism: Indigenous Resistance on the US/Mexico Border." *Perspectives on Global Development and Technology* 16 (2017): 15–33.

Resendiz, Rosalva. "Female Subjectivity and Agency in Popular Mexican Corridos (Ballads): An Examination of Images and Representations of Soldaderas (Female Soldiers) in the Mexican Revolution 1910–1920." PhD dissertation, Texas Woman's University, 2001.

Rodríguez, Jeanette. *Our Lady of Guadalupe: Faith and Empowerment Among Mexican-American Women*. Austin: University of Texas Press, 1994.

Saldaña-Portillo, María Josefina. *Indian Given: Racial Geographies Across Mexico and the United States*. Durham, N.C.: Duke University Press, 2016.

Saldaña-Portillo, María Josefina. *The Revolutionary Imagination in the Americas and the Age of Development*. Durham, N.C.: Duke University Press, 2003.

Salinas, Martin. *Indians of the Rio Grande Delta: Their Role in the History of Southern Texas and Northeastern Mexico*. Austin: University of Texas Press, 1990.

Smith, Linda Tuhiwai. *Decolonizing Methodologies: Research and Indigenous Peoples*. London: Zed Books, 1999.

Tamez, Margo. "Returning Lipan Apache Women's Laws, Lands and Power in El Calaboz Rancheria, Texas-Mexico Border." PhD dissertation, Washington State University, 2010.

Tamez, Margo. "Space, Position and Imperialism in South Texas (Dr. Eloisa Garcia Tamez v. U.S. Secretary Michael Chertoff, U.S. Department of Homeland Security, U.S. Border Patrol, U.S. Army Corps of Engineers)." *Chicana/Latina Studies* 7, no. 2 (2008): 112–21.

Villanueva, Nicholas. *The Lynching of Mexicans in the Texas Borderlands*. Albuquerque: University of New Mexico Press, 2017.

SIXTEEN

El Muro

An Early Case Study on Archival Resistance Beyond Borders, Walls, and Settler-Colonial Visuality

RAMÓN RESENDIZ

In this chapter, I present a critical ethnographic reflection on the material and visual settler-colonial condition of the Texas/U.S.-Mexico borderlands. I foreground the potential to enact transnational Indigenous resistance to, refusals of, and solidarities against settler-colonial occupation, erasure, and militarization across the Americas. I draw on the Chicana feminist *testimonio* tradition to articulate my thoughts and standpoint as a Chicanx documentary media producer, discussing the conception of *El Muro* | *The Wall* (2017) and the broader hemispheric effects of U.S. imperialism, visually rendered through the militarization of the U.S.-Mexico borderlands. I situate the production of *El Muro* as an aesthetic and archival intervention within the history of U.S. settler colonization and western expansion, an exercise of what I term *archival resistance*: an act of deliberate resistance against the violence and hegemony of colonial archives.[1]

Introduction to the Land of the Ocelot

In 2017, I began my doctoral coursework at NYU in the Department of Media, Culture, and Communication, following the completion of *El Muro* | *The Wall* (2017). *El Muro* was my master's thesis at the University of Washington's Native Voices Indigenous Media Program, and it was a documentary film project made with the collaboration of Dr. Eloisa G. Taméz and Dr. Margo Tamez, directed and co-produced by me and my aunt, Dr. Rosalva Resendiz. The film documented the Tamez family's fight against the U.S. Department of Homeland Security's use of eminent domain to condemn their ancestral Lipan Apache land for the purposes of building the U.S. "border wall" under the Bush administration following the passing of the Secure Fence Act of 2006. The production of this documentary took place at the intersections of archival research, storytelling, activist media, and community action research, which Linda Smith has termed "writing back."[2] It was a case study of what I have come to understand as a form of *archival resistance* to colonial archival violence: a deliberate act of contesting and documenting hegemonic historical mischaracterizations, making visible the violence mediated and obfuscated by colonial archives, and thereby resisting settler historical discourses. Archival resistance must be done in the present: bridging the imaginative and material by actively rectifying the erased and invisible histories of oppression against subaltern peoples. This form of resistance is enacted through cultural productions interrogating the essentialisms created by state hegemony, erasures, and the colonial archive as a site of knowledge production.[3]

El Muro was also an exercise in trust and decolonial practices. This entailed doing justice to the trust given to us by the Drs. Tamez and the Lipan Apache Band of Texas Tribal Board, who, through their review process, permitted us to work with their Elders, storytellers, and cultural knowledge keepers. It is critical to note that the Lipan Apache / Ndé have been persecuted on their traditional lands by the Crown of Castile, Mexico, the Republic of Texas, the Confederate States of America, and the United States. This historic persecution has made them the targets of multiple attempted genocides, most notably the 1873 Remolino Massacre by U.S. Army colonel Ranald Slidell Mackenzie, in which the United States illegally crossed into Coahuila, Mexico, to perpetrate an "assault upon 180 [Lipan and Kickapoo] traditional lodges."[4] However, the reports only note that "nineteen Indians [were] killed . . . and forty women and children [were] taken prisoner," a number disputed by Lipan Apache peoples as grossly underestimated.[5] This violent chapter of the persecution of Indigenous peoples from the South Texas borderlands had dire consequences for the descendants of those who survived, many of whom were forced to hide as detribalized "assimilated Mexicans."[6]

However, being Mexican in Texas after 1848 came with its own set of race-based violence from Anglo settlers, because Mexicans were treated as second-class citizens, ethnically persecuted, and lynched.[7] The fact that several Indigenous groups were forced to hide their indigeneity as a survival strategy warrants further scrutiny, as it echoed what Brian DeLay has termed the construction of the Texas creation myth.[8] This myth held that Texas has no federal Native American reservations, because Indigenous people were all either exterminated by the Texas Rangers or simply died off after the U.S. Indian Wars. DeLay asserts that this erroneous historiography was conducted by White supremacist historians such as Walter Prescott Webb in *The Great Plains* (1931), *The Texas Rangers* (1935), and *The Great Frontier* (1952), and was subsequently visually reproduced in the film genre of the "Western."[9] These historic imaginaries and omissions were reflected in institutional archives throughout the state, and as such were critical flashpoints of contestation when we started the production of the film.

Documenting the Colonias of the Settler "Post"-Colony

My earliest engagements with the concepts of colonization, postcolonization, and settler colonization began in South Texas. I grew up in the colonia of Cameron Park, an unincorporated slum-like neighborhood in Cameron County adjacent to the border town of Brownsville, Texas, which is the sister city to the Mexican city of Matamoros, Tamaulipas. I did not know the subaltern marker that being from Cameron Park carried, nor the fact that the border was replete with colonias (Spanish for "colonies"), emblems of the territorialization of the Third World within the geographic demarcations of the First World. Acclaimed Chicana feminists Gloria Anzaldúa and Cherríe Moraga offered an understanding of this in their book *This Bridge Called My Back: Writings by Radical Women of Color* (1983) and in Anzaldúa's *Borderlands / La Frontera: The New Mestiza* (1987).[10] They made visible the material ways marginality compounded on Brown, Black, and queer racialized bodies on the margins of society and on the margins of the United States. In 2001, shots of

Cameron Park itself featured in Hector Galán's documentary film about the South Texas colonias, *The Forgotten Americans: Poverty on the Texas Border*.[11]

Like many in the region, I grew up in a nonnormative family, raised by an extended network of grandparents, aunts, and "ex-cons," a result of the war on drugs as well as the lasting traumas of violence perpetrated by the colonial regimes that shaped the way histories have been memorialized, documented, repressed, and understood. It took many years for me to understand that I hadn't just grown up in the Texas borderlands as the transnational descendant of Indigenous and mestizo ancestors in the settler colony of Texas, but that I had become a refugee on the unceded lands of the Lipan Apache / Ndé, and that it would be through their decolonial struggles that I would more intimately come to understand the depth of the colonial wounds caused by New Spain (the Spanish Empire) and the formation of the modern nation-states of Mexico, Texas, and the United States.

When I was a child, my father was a student at the school formerly known as UTB-TSC (University of Texas at Brownsville–Texas Southmost College), located on the remnants of the then-decommissioned Fort Brown. The place bore the name of Jacob Brown, a U.S. Army major who died from his wounds during the U.S.-Mexico War, the conflict by which the United States acquired Texas and the Southwest, giving rise to the modern borderlands. UTB-TSC disbanded into Texas Southmost College and the University of Texas–Pan American (UTPA), where Gloria Anzaldúa received her BA in English in 1968, before UTPA became the current University of Texas Rio Grande Valley (UTRGV) in 2015. Knowing and materially traversing these spaces has lingered in my mind throughout my academic career and continues to shape my identity as a Chicano Tejano feminist.

My experiences growing up in Cameron Park, in Cameron County, Texas—named after Ewen Cameron, an officer in the Republic of Texas Army—inform much of my understanding of the continued realities of colonization. That Cameron Park was a colonized space, a shantytown shaped by the actions of multiple prior colonial regimes, demarcated as *outside* of the city of Brownsville, was a stark material reality. Ironically, Paredes Line Road, the main thoroughfare that today serves as the boundary line of this material and imaginative bordering, is named after Dr. Américo Paredes, whose book *"With His Pistol in His Hand": A Border Ballad and Its Hero* (1958) was instrumental in breaking down the racist constructions of Mexicans by White supremacist scholars.[12] Journalists and historians such as Walter Prescott Webb wrote profusely about the racial inferiority of Mexicans to legitimate the use of violence for land theft and the ethnic cleansing of Mexicans and "Indians" following the 1848 Mexican cession.[13] These racist writings described Mexicans as a degraded race due to the racial mixing between European colonists and Mesoamerican Indigenous peoples. This differed from the nationalist mythical construction of *mestizaje*—a central component of Mexican national identity in the nineteenth and twentieth centuries, which culturally held more "positive" views regarding "racial mixing" in "postcolonial" Mexico.[14] In the United States, these racist beliefs furthered the idea of a Mexican pathology that was used to explain a perceived inability to develop and secure the land from First Nations in Texas and the Southwest, due to Mexican laziness, cowardice, or lack of conviction in achieving development.[15] Mexicans were vilified as treacherous, synonymous with Indians (hierarchically inferior to Native Americans from the Great Plains) and *banditos*—in short, they were ignoble savages to be cleansed from the land.[16]

As I have grown older, I have been made keenly aware of how the limits, barriers, and violence in the demarcations of modern state borders help define citizenship, race, class, and liberal notions of rights. I have pondered how these concepts are tested in places where the state border intersects racialized noncitizen subjects to determine their right to exist as people across settler-occupied geographies in which they are biopolitically rendered *ethnographic others*.[17] Thus, it is on the edge of the nation-state that federal border policy becomes visible over the bordered landscape, and over the hyperracialized immigrant. This is where the epistemic violence of settler-colonial borders is made material and felt in the flesh of the undocumented border crosser.[18] This is also where the violence of U.S. exceptionalism is made most visibly evident over the body of the asylum seeker, immigrant, and non-White citizen. These power dynamics crystallized in the material construction of the U.S. border wall, as well as in the rhetoric that supported this military infrastructure at the expense of Indigenous, Latinx, and Chicanx communities on the border.

"(Un)seen" Violence of/on the Mexico-U.S. Border

Reflecting on my now thirty-year-long relationship with the Mexico-U.S. border, one of my clearest observations is that the border is a nexus of visualizing regimes in which *the ethnographic subject* is rendered most visible, yet is also most unseen. "Seen" here refers to how the violence of borders is inscribed over subaltern and Indigenous bodies when they encounter the material boundaries of the United States. This encounter with the United States as the dominant colonial power in the hemisphere recalls Aníbal Quijano's observations about how colonial legacies remain entrenched within sociopolitical power structures in Latin America—that is, the "coloniality of power."[19] Thus, the U.S.-Mexico border materially catalyzes and racializes the asylum seeker into a member of "non-white," "other" populations, rendering their presence and their right to live and exist as "illegal" and criminal based on how they are literally *seen* by settler state authorities.

The presence of the racialized asylum seeker or undocumented immigrant on the border stems from an array of mass global processes brought about by the violence of racial capitalism, Euro-American imperialism, and extractivism, which have destabilized and created the current subaltern world as mediated, imagined, and materially extracted.[20] Extraction is performed not only upon the land but also upon the racialized body in forms of *unseen labor* in the agricultural fields, sex work, domestic work, caretaking work, service industry work, and construction work, and in the monetization of the U.S. immigration detention system of undocumented people.[21] The latter circulates prominently across news media in stories about so-called caravans from Central America—mass influxes of unaccompanied minors seeking asylum, and the routinized detention of families, most of whom are destined to be separated, detained, and deported at the border.

The borderlands form a complex of visual regimes genealogically constructed by the legacies of various colonial and settler-colonial visualizing state entities spanning roughly the last five hundred years. These state entities constitute a distinct convergence of visualities that inform historical imaginings of race, memory, White possessive settler-colonial settlement, and Indigenous dispossession and erasures throughout North America. Here, settler-colonial visuality follows what Patrick Wolfe has called the "logic of elimination"; Wolfe reminds us that "settler colonialism does not simply replace native society tout court. Rather, the process of replacement maintains the refractory imprint of the native counterclaim. This phenomenon is not confined to the realm of symbolism."[22] In "Invention, Memory, and Place," Edward Said discusses how museums and monuments are a curatorial exercise of imaginings and visualizations of history and the nation.[23] Benedict Anderson similarly notes this relationship in the final section of *Imagined Communities*, "Census, Map, Museum," where he makes the connection between the museum, history, and the state clear.[24] Said's and Anderson's insights underscore the fact that these processes and observations are not new, and they outline the mediating relationship at work in the ways monuments, museums, imaginations of history, ideas of citizenship, state-sponsored violence, and the making of the nation are intrinsically related. This is especially the case regarding decommissioned military institutions turned museums such as Fort Brown, in Brownsville, Texas, and the Alamo in San Antonio, Texas, both of which have received national landmark status from the National Park Service, constituting an official avowal of the historic framings mediated by these institutions. Drawing on these insights into the relationship between visuality and state/systemic violence, *El Muro* applied a critical lens to the ways visuality works on the Mexico-Texas/U.S. borderlands.

The Border Since 2017

The year 2017 was a significant one for the borderlands and the communities from which *El Muro* came because of the rhetoric of a border fence / "border wall" used by the Trump administration as a stand-in for a new era of xenophobic and nativist policy at the U.S. Department of Homeland Security (DHS). Emblematic of these shifts were the Migrant Protection Protocols, popularly termed the "remain in Mexico law," as well as the use of Title 42 of the U.S. Code to legitimize the expulsion of and forceful denial of entry to asylum seekers from Central America. That year saw a newfound convergence of the inhumane deterrence policies enacted by the DHS as part of the administration's "zero-tolerance approach." These hardline immigration policies included the forced separation of 5,500 children who were "detained" by the U.S. government away from their parents—with internal records attesting to the deliberate cruel intent of administration officials to use these separations as a means of deterrence for asylum seekers. According to the Southern Poverty Law Center's 2022 article "Family Separation—A Timeline," as of November 29, 2021, 1,703 children remained separated from their families under the Biden administration, putting the lives of these people in limbo and leaving them without restitution.[25] Additionally, since 2015, thousands of ICE detainees, adults and minors alike, have come forward to report cases of sexual assault while in U.S. custody.[26] At least fifty-seven immigrant women detainees were subjected to nonconsensual gynecological procedures including forced sterilization while under ICE custody at a for-profit detention center in Irwin County, Georgia.[27] These are a fraction of the U.S. "immigration news" headlines that have struck me since 2017. All of them raise grave concerns about the subhuman mistreatment by the U.S. federal government faced by undocumented immigrants and asylum seekers; all of them took place on a material border and upon racially "bordered" subjects. Unsurprisingly, none of these "news stories" have held either federal perpetrators or the political actors who orchestrated said human rights violations accountable.

The national political changes that impacted and became visible on the border were some of the same factors that had previously gone into the theoretical conception of *El Muro*, centering on the denial of human rights to Indigenous peoples in the borderlands, and the ways in which the state and archival institutions obfuscate and normalize the regulating of Indigenous people's bodies and lands through settler-colonial policies, practices, and epistemologies. The U.S. immigration system designates many Central and Latin American undocumented immigrants as Latino/a or Hispanic, biopolitically racializing and normalizing these "ideal" types. This process reproduces colonial racial geographies and logics over the bodies of Indigenous people, Indigenous-descended people, and people of color whose indigeneity has been erased, obfuscating transnational notions of indigeneity that transcend the limiting borders of the modern nation-state.[28] Such erasures normalize the effects of five hundred years of colonial occupation, "miscegenation," rape, and the dispossession of subaltern Indigenous populations in the Americas. Indigeneity, in this respect, is constructed, policed, obfuscated, constrained, and/or erased by the geographic and temporal boundaries of the modern nation-state and its monopoly on violence.

However, indigeneity, when approached beyond the bounds of the United States' nativist normalization of the European immigrant and "expatriate" naturalization discourse in the Americas, reminds us that the United States *is* a settler-colonial nation-state. Its foundations rest upon the occupation of Indigenous lands and the normalization of White possessive rights to "own" and occupy said lands.[29] This is made particularly clear in the borderlands of the United States, where the effects of U.S. immigration and foreign policy from the Monroe Doctrine (1823) to the Cold War–era creation of the School of the Americas (1963) are made domestically visible—as this is where the subaltern, displaced, and dispossessed racialized immigrant, upon materially crossing into the United States, embodies the repercussions of U.S. hemispheric political and military interventions since 1823.[30] Thus, whereas the United States' history of conquest, violence, and war against Native Americans remains an undeniable fact everywhere within the boundaries of the United States, the United States' international imperial violence most clearly materializes at its borders and within its immigration system.

Working to See Beyond Border and Immigration News

The questions that guided my work in 2014, when I began the preproduction of the project that eventually became *El Muro*, were: How does the U.S. legitimize its sovereignty over Indigenous lands, and how is this history normalized and reflected in the North American landscape? What are the processes by which the nation-state built its borders, and why does that now include the building of a wall? What is the role of the settler-colonial state in determining notions of indigeneity to the land, and how is this done? Further, what would this imply in a transnational and decolonial framework? What are the stakes in the building of walls, and the historicizing and legitimating of settler racial and legal logics, and to whom do they matter? I note some aspects of the political situation of the borderlands in 2017 to address how the Mexico-Texas/U.S. borderlands were being discussed and operated on in the national imaginary by the state, as well as the ways these landscapes were being framed across mainstream news media.

Entering the Archive: From a Documentary to a Broader Study of Visuality

By the time we had entered principal production for *El Muro* (which at the time was titled *Operación Ocelotl*)[31] in the spring of 2016, a decade had passed since Congress had enacted the Secure Fence Act of 2006. Signed into law by George W. Bush, the law funded and instituted the building of the U.S. border wall.[32] Dr. Eloisa Taméz had gained local and national notoriety for her resistance to the building of the wall across her ancestral lands; she was a retired Army Nurse Corps colonel, a professor with a PhD in health education, and a Lipan Apache / Ndé tribal Elder.[33] Eloisa worked together with her daughter Dr. Margo Tamez, the Lipan Apache Band of Texas, human rights reporters, lawyers, and legal scholars to fight against the construction of the border wall. Dr. Margo Tamez's dissertation had amassed a legal archive attesting to their Indigenous land claims and legacy of survival against the violence brought about by multiple colonial incursions into their lands. They had taken their fight to the U.S. federal courts, the United Nations Committee on the Elimination of Racial Discrimination (UNCERD), and the Inter-American Commission on Human Rights (IACHR), part of the Organization of American States.

Unfortunately, as *El Muro* attested, federal courts decided that the U.S. government had the legal authority to use eminent domain to build the wall. This was despite international legal outcry from the UNCERD and the IACHR regarding the human rights violations and cultural violence this structure entailed against Indigenous peoples in the process. The Drs. Tamez and the Lipan Apache Band of Texas nevertheless fought against the encroachment on their ancestral lands and have continued to raise awareness about how these settler militaristic infrastructure projects impact people. This was the story *El Muro* sought to document and further expose.

El Muro provides some of the background necessary to contextualize a practical application of what I have since termed *archival resistance*.[34]

It critically engages with questions about the role of archival documents in the processes of legitimating and contesting settler walls and laws, and the construction of Eurocentric racial and ethnic taxonomic regimes reified by the colonial archive.[35] As a documentary, *El Muro* was produced with the specific intent of being a decolonial didactic tool that visually exposed the complexities of settler-colonial erasures and methods in the making of the modern U.S.-Mexico border, while foregrounding archival histories of Indigenous resistance to colonization and militarization on their lands.[36] Some of the key themes and concepts addressed throughout the film regarding historiography, notions of the archive, settler colonization, coloniality, and decoloniality have greatly influenced the overall theoretical framework that informs my understanding of archival resistance to erasures, settler visualities, invisibilizing, and the obfuscation of visual registers of violence on the border of Mexico and the United States.

Reflections on the Borderlandscape

As I traveled throughout Texas, I saw a visibly militarized and extracted landscape. From South Texas, the U.S. border wall built under the Bush and Obama administrations remains visible. The ecotone at the mouth of the Rio Grande River, where it flows into the Gulf of Mexico, is now permanently occupied by SpaceX's rocket launching site. The South and Central Texas landscape is filled with petroleum extraction infrastructures that have made the land black through hydraulic fracturing, oil rigs, and petrochemical plants. Day and night, gas flares paint portions of the sky, signifying the burning of methane and the release of other hydrocarbons into the environment. The effects of these extractive practices are visible on and near the Gulf Coast in the form of oil rigs, and in West Texas near the Big Bend National Park region in the form of oil pipeline infrastructures such as the Trans-Pecos Pipeline. Though my research specifically homes in on settler archives and visuality in Texas, failing to note these characteristic elements of northern Mexico and the southern U.S. border would omit how neoliberal extraction and the effects of NAFTA have transformed the ecology of this landscape in deep ways.[37]

I note the contemporary Texas landscape because the deep entwinement between visual culture and systemic violence is co-constitutive of *visuality*, which "supplement[s] the violence of authority and its separations, forming a complex that [comes] to seem natural by virtue of its investment in 'history.'"[38] *Visuality* is produced by and produces historic processes invested in the production of subaltern mass compliance, normalizing acts and visualizations of material violence as the "natural" order of things. Authority and violence here must be understood in relation to the construction(s) of the modern nation-state, and through the varied bureaucratic and ideological state apparatuses through which it exercises and enacts governance and manufactures ideological consent.[39] This process of producing mass compliance is vested in rendering "the systemic/system" as natural, and thereby imperceptible to the singular individual—a literal obfuscation of and alienation from an existence beyond the manufactured visualizations of the modern nation-state.

These transnational extractive capitalist industries play a crucial role in shaping the landscape of the U.S.-Texas borderlands, and in multiple third spaces throughout the Americas where the borders of the nation-state are micro-logically re-created within the subaltern racialized subject. Much like the Texas historical institutions that present archival visualizations of history, these extractive capitalist infrastructures constitute what Macarena Gómez-Barris has rightfully termed an *extractive view*, which normalizes capitalist extraction in the natural landscape while reproducing imaginings of terra nullius, "nobody's land" devoid of people, culture, and life prior to the arrival of Europeans—re-creating and normalizing the racialized ideal types of the modern nation.[40]

These extractive infrastructures provide a contemporary layer that helps in understanding the way capitalism creates a settler-colonial visuality that erases Indigenous existence, resistance, and ancestral land claims. Akin to military infrastructures, they reinforce modern national borders—in this case, the U.S. border with Mexico, which the state of Texas works to memorialize and actively produce through inhumane immigration policies. These infrastructures are archivally and institutionally grounded through the violence by which Anglo settlers colonized the land since the Texas revolution/insurrection against the Republic of Mexico (1835–46). Though a thorough analysis of extractive industries in Texas is outside the scope of this reflection, I note their presence, because they continue to actively shape the landscape.

Centering Transnational Indigeneity and Archival Resistance

I elucidate the relationship between these contemporary extractive enterprises and the archive because all extractive practices on which settler capitalist exploitation takes place are historically entwined. The U.S. border wall was made in the same ways that settler governments now defend capitalist extraction: by erasing how these lands were acquired. This connection is rendered visible through the *archival exposure* of land tenure in Texas, Faye Ginsburg's concept for how images from official and/or state sources are reclaimed and "exposed" by the subjects of these images, peoples and populations whose humanity has been degraded by states, ideologies, institutions, and image-making regimes.[41] As Monica Muñoz Martinez demonstrates in *The Injustice Never Leaves You: Anti-Mexican Violence in Texas*, this land was taken through violence directed at the Mexican and Indigenous communities who have been largely left out of this narrative.[42]

A more nuanced understanding of the U.S. border wall continues to be warranted, as this contemporary site of military infrastructure reflects the colonial processes initiated by the various colonial regimes that have occupied North America—the "colonial complexes of visuality," according to Nicholas Mirzoeff.[43] These entities include the lasting legacies of the kingdom of Castile, criollo elites (ethnic Spaniards born in the Americas), Texan-Anglo settlers in the Republic of Texas, the Confederate States of America, and, most recently, the United States. As settler, colonial, and imperial institutions, these regimes have continuously worked to eliminate Indigenous peoples from the land and from memory, imagining them as relics of a distant past (*taxidermied* and understood as static specimens), or as altogether nonexistent and wholly erased.[44]

Here archival resistance problematizes and decenters the legitimation of geographic bordering practices produced by the United States at the intersections of visual culture, cultural production, (un)documentation, and ethnographic documentary media. Approaching documentary media through such a framework entails asking: What is the role of settler archival institutions in making history visible, and what histories do they make seen? How does the violence of settler colonialism remain unseen, and how is this mediated and rendered (in)visible? How is this violence materially and visually mediated, and where and how is this encountered? How can documentary filmmakers breach the obfuscation of systemic (post)colonial violence and produce documentary media that imagines an existence for Indigenous peoples as a potential site of justice to contest settler-colonial visualities? Can visual documentary media rupture White supremacist myths of White replacement? And, can we make the effects of U.S. capitalist interventionism, foreign policy, and extractivism in Latin America visible as a cause of mass migrations from Latin America in the first place?[45]

From *El Muro* to a Future of Archival Resistance

Given the immensity of the archive and the discomfiting narratives created by settler accounts of history that dominate museums, monuments, and mainstream cinema, I posit that visual documentary media occupy a critical role in making the violence of White supremacist settler myths, erasures, and state-sponsored systemic violence visible. Such documentary media create a space of resistance to the hegemony of the settler-colonial archive, making their production critical toward fomenting decolonial visions and imaginaries. As I conclude my thoughts on what has been my role in attempting to "make seen" the transnational violence of settler colonization, racial capitalism, and patriarchy through the production of *El Muro*, I reflect upon one of the key theoretical interventions that has arisen from this work: the notion of *archival resistance*, which the film achieved through a mixed-method practice of visually documenting the stories and lives of persecuted peoples and their ancestors.

As an action, *archival resistance* encompasses the production of digital and material documentary media that create a space of imagination to disrupt the violence of colonial thinking, historic erasures, and ethnonationalism. As an aesthetic practice, it is composed from a multitude of visual frameworks that include decolonial, postcolonial, Indigenous feminist, ethnographic, and institutional and noninstitutional perspectives that expose the relationship between violence and the archive.[46] By reclaiming and reexposing the images and documents of the archive to resist the dominant dehumanizing narratives imposed upon marginalized peoples, the practice engages in Ginsburg's notion of *archival exposure*.[47] Through this exposure, the archive of the colonial encounter may be rendered visible and thus countervisual.[48]

Critical archival documentary media can produce theoretical interventions at the intersections of the post-, neo-, and settler-colonial temporal regimes that have shaped the material landscapes in the U.S.-Mexico borderlands, and can force us to inquire further into the creation of decolonial practice, action, memory, and storytelling, and the imagining of decolonial visions in response to systemic violence. As such, I consider *El Muro | The Wall* and the collaborative solidarities we engaged in through its production to be an exercise in archival resistance, as this work made visible the internal fissures of contestation through the archive in a concerted effort to contextualize the violence of settler-colonial visuality. I am eternally grateful to all the participants who joined this work with me and my kin.[49]

NOTES

1. Ramón Resendiz, "Landscapes of Violence: Documentary Media, Countervisualities, and Archival Resistance on the Mexico-U.S. Borderlands" (PhD diss., New York University, 2023).
2. Linda Tuhiwai Smith, *Decolonizing Methodologies: Research and Indigenous Peoples* (London: Zed Books, 1999).
3. Leela Gandhi, *Postcolonial Theory: A Critical Introduction*, 2nd ed. (New York: Columbia University Press, 2019); Resendiz, "Landscapes."
4. Margo Tamez, "Returning Lipan Apache Women's Laws, Lands, and Power in El Calaboz Ranchería, Texas-Mexico Border" (PhD diss., Washington State University, 2010), 281–82.
5. Tamez further notes that tribal Elders and Indigenous historians speculate this is an underreported number and that the numbers were much higher, both of people who were killed during the attack and of women and children who were captured. See Tamez, "Returning," 281–82.
6. This history is covered at length in Margo Tamez's dissertation and is the focus of Susan D. Rose and Manuel Saralegui's oral history documentary *The Lost Ones: The Long Journey Home; A Documentary Film* (Carlisle, Penn.: Dickinson College Community Studies Center, 2009). This history is also touched upon in *El Muro | The Wall* (dir. Ramón Resendiz and Rosalva Resendiz, 2017). See Ramón Resendiz and Rosalva Resendiz, "Towards a Decolonial Archive: A Reflection on the Operational Inaction Process of Critical Trans-border Documentary Production Practice," in *Challenging Borders: Contingencies and*

Consequences, ed. Sheila McManus, Julie Young, and Paul McKenzie-Jones (Alberta: Athabasca University Press, forthcoming); and Tamez, "Returning."

7. David Montejano, *Anglos y mexicanos en la formación de Texas, 1836–1986* (Mexico City: Alianza Editorial, 1987); Monica Muñoz Martinez, *The Injustice Never Leaves You: Anti-Mexican Violence in Texas* (Cambridge, Mass.: Harvard University Press, 2018); Américo Paredes, *"With His Pistol in His Hand": A Border Ballad and Its Hero* (Austin: University of Texas Press, 1958).
8. Brian DeLay, "Independent Indians and the U.S.-Mexican War," *American Historical Review* 112, no. 1 (2008).
9. See Walter Prescott Webb, *The Great Plains* (Boston: Ginn and Company, 1931); and Walter Prescott Webb, *The Texas Rangers: A Century of Frontier Defense* (Boston: Houghton Mifflin, 1935). On the Western, see André Bazin, *What Is Cinema?*, ed. and trans. Hugh Gray (Berkeley: University of California Press, 2004).
10. Cherríe Moraga and Gloria Anzaldúa, eds., *This Bridge Called My Back: Writings by Radical Women of Color* (New York: Kitchen Table: Women of Color Press, 1983); Gloria Anzaldúa, *Borderlands / La Frontera: The New Mestiza*, 1st ed. (San Francisco: Aunt Lute, 1987).
11. Hector Galán, dir., *The Forgotten Americans: Poverty on the Texas Border* (Galán Incorporated, 2001).
12. Jovita Idar's work predated Paredes. Her journalism and folklore work during the 1920s was crucial toward breaking down the misrepresentation of Mexicans in Texas as well. See Gabriela González, *Redeeming La Raza: Transborder Modernity, Race, Respectability, and Rights* (New York: Oxford University Press, 2018); and Paredes, *With His Pistol.*
13. DeLay, "Independent Indians," 35; Martinez, *Injustice*; Paredes, *With His Pistol.*
14. Throughout this chapter I will refer to "racial mixing" and "miscegenation" in quotes to remind us that very few of these interactions were consensual. See Enrique Krauze, *Mexico, Biography of Power: A History of Modern Mexico, 1810–1996* (New York: Harper Collins, 1997); Montejano, *Anglos y mexicanos*; Emma Pérez, *The Decolonial Imaginary: Writing Chicanas into History* (Bloomington: Indiana University Press, 1999); María J. Saldaña-Portillo, *Indian Given: Racial Geographies Across Mexico and the United States* (Durham, N.C.: Duke University Press, 2016).
15. DeLay, "Independent Indians."
16. Paredes, *With His Pistol.*
17. Fatimah T. Rony, *The Third Eye: Race, Cinema, and Ethnographic Spectacle* (Durham, N.C.: Duke University Press, 1996); Edward Said, *Orientalism* (New York: Vintage Books, 1979).
18. Moraga and Anzaldúa, *This Bridge.*
19. Aníbal Quijano, "Coloniality of Power, Eurocentrism, and Latin America," *Nepantla: Views from South* 1, no. 3 (2000): 533.
20. Macarena Gómez-Barris, *The Extractive Zone: Social Ecologies and Decolonial Perspectives* (Durham, N.C.: Duke University Press, 2017).

21. Moraga and Anzaldúa, *This Bridge*; Robert T. Chase, ed., *Caging Borders and Carceral States: Incarcerations, Immigration Detentions, and Resistance* (Chapel Hill: University of North Carolina Press, 2019).
22. Patrick Wolfe, "Settler Colonialism and the Elimination of the Native," *Journal of Genocide Research* 8, no. 4 (2006): 389.
23. Edward Said, "Invention, Memory, Place," in *Landscape and Power*, ed. W. T. J. Mitchell (Chicago: University of Chicago Press, 2002).
24. Benedict Anderson, *Imagined Communities: Reflections on the Origin and Spread of Nationalism*, 2nd ed. (New York: Verso Books, 1991), 163.
25. "Family Separation—A Timeline," Southern Poverty Law Center, accessed January 27, 2024, https://www.splcenter.org/our-issues/immigrant-justice/family-separation.
26. Richard Gonzales, "Sexual Assault of Detained Migrant Children Reported in the Thousands Since 2015," NPR, February 26, 2019, https://www.npr.org/2019/02/26/698397631/sexual-assault-of-detained-migrant-children-reported-in-the-thousands-since-2015; Lomi Kriel, "ICE Guards 'Systematically' Sexually Assault Detainees in an El Paso Detention Center, Lawyers Say," *ProPublica*, August 14, 2020, https://www.propublica.org/article/ice-guards-systematically-sexually-assault-detainees-in-an-el-paso-detention-center-lawyers-say.
27. This case is still pending litigation, and the Irwin County Detention Center, where these women had been detained, has as of May 2021 lost its contract with ICE because of ongoing federal investigations into these human rights abuses. See Jose Olivares and John Washington, "ICE Detention Center Shuttered Following Repeated Allegations of Medical Misconduct," *The Intercept*, May 20, 2021, https://theintercept.com/2021/05/20/ice-irwin-hysterectomies-medical/.
28. María J. Saldaña-Portillo and María Cotera, "Indigenous but Not Indian? Chicana/os and the Politics of Indigeneity," in *The World of Indigenous North America*, ed. Robert Warrior (London: Taylor & Francis Group, 2014); Saldaña-Portillo, *Indian Given*.
29. Aileen Moreton-Robinson, *The White Possessive: Property, Power, and Indigenous Sovereignty* (Minneapolis: University of Minnesota Press, 2015); Pérez, *Decolonial Imaginary*; Saldaña-Portillo, *Indian Given*.
30. The School of the Americas was renamed the Western Hemispheric Institute for Security Cooperation by the U.S. Department of Defense in 2001; it was preceded by various U.S. paramilitary training centers for Latin American countries beginning in 1946 with the Latin American Training Center-Ground Division. Lesley Gill, *The School of the Americas: Military Training and Political Violence in the Americas* (Durham, N.C.: Duke University Press, 2004).
31. The working title *Operación Ocelotl* was a reference to the fact that South Texas marks the northernmost natural habitat of the ocelot (*Leopardus pardalis*), which is indigenous to the Americas. This feline was one of several indigenous species whose habitats were threatened by the construction of the U.S. bor-

der wall and continue to be threatened by the development of transnational extractive infrastructures in the Rio Grande watershed. These developments include the SpaceX rocket launching site on Boca Chica Beach, which is less than a mile away from the mouth of the Rio Grande.

32. Ramón Resendiz, Rosalva Resendiz, and Irene J. Klaver, "Colonialism and Imperialism: Indigenous Resistance on the US/Mexico Border," *Perspectives on Global Development and Technology* 16 (2017): 15–33.
33. In 2019, she received a Frederick Douglass 200 award, given by the Frederick Douglass Family Initiatives and the Antiracist Research and Policy Center at American University in Washington, D.C., for her Indigenous land rights activism.
34. Resendiz, "Landscapes."
35. Wendy Brown, *Walled States, Waning Sovereignty* (New York: Zone Books, 2010); Gandhi, *Postcolonial Theory*; Smith, *Decolonizing Methodologies.*
36. Resendiz, Resendiz, and Klaver, "Colonialism and Imperialism"; Resendiz and Resendiz, "Towards a Decolonial Archive"; Tamez, "Returning."
37. The results have been discussed in Devon Peña's *The Terror and the Machine: Technology, Work, Gender, and Ecology on the U.S.-Mexico Border* (Austin: University of Texas Press, 1997); Rosa-Linda Fregoso's *meXicana Encounters: The Making of Social Identities on the Borderlands* (Berkeley: University of California Press, 2003); David Bacon's *The Children of NAFTA: Labor Wars on the U.S./Mexico Border* (Berkeley: University of California Press, 2004); and Alyshia Gálvez's *Eating NAFTA: Trade, Food Policies and the Destruction of Mexico* (Oakland: University of California Press, 2018).
38. Nicholas Mirzoeff, *The Right to Look: A Counterhistory of Visuality* (Durham, N.C.: Duke University Press, 2011), 3.
39. Anderson, *Imagined Communities*; Antonio Gramsci, *Prison Letters* (London: Pluto Press, 1996).
40. Gómez-Barris, *Extractive Zone.*
41. Faye Ginsburg, "Archival Exposure: Disability, Documentary, and the Making of Counternarratives," in *Documenting the World*, ed. Gregg Mitman and Kelley Wilder (Chicago: University of Chicago Press, 2016).
42. Martinez, *Injustice.*
43. Mirzoeff, *Right to Look.*
44. Rony, *Third Eye.*
45. Gill, *School of the Americas*; Gómez-Barris, *Extractive Zone*; Peña, *Terror of the Machine.*
46. On decolonization: Frantz Fanon, *The Wretched of the Earth* (New York: Grove Press, 1961); Pérez, *Decolonial Imaginary*; Smith, *Decolonizing Methodologies.* On the postcolonial: Gandhi, *Postcolonial Theory*; Said, *Orientalism.* On Indigenous feminism: Anzaldúa, *Borderlands*; Philip J. Deloria, *Indians in Unexpected Places* (Lawrence: University Press of Kansas, 2004); Michelle Raheja, *Reservation Reelism: Redfacing, Visual Sovereignty, and Representations of Na-*

tive Americans in Film (Lincoln: University of Nebraska Press, 2010). On ethnography: Rony, *Third Eye*. On institutional and noninstitutional frameworks: Pierre Bourdieu, "The Field of Cultural Production," in *The Field of Cultural Production: Essays on Art and Literature*, by Pierre Bourdieu, ed. Randal Johnson (New York: Columbia University Press, 1993); Paul DiMaggio and Walter Powell, *The New Institutionalism in Organizational Analysis* (Chicago: University of Chicago Press, 1991).

47. Ginsburg, "Archival Exposure."
48. Gandhi, *Postcolonial Theory*; Mirzoeff, *Right to Look*.
49. To watch *El Muro | The Wall* (2017), please visit: http://elmurothewall.documentaryworlds.com/.

BIBLIOGRAPHY

Anderson, Benedict. *Imagined Communities: Reflections on the Origin and Spread of Nationalism*. 2nd ed. New York: Verso Books, 1991.

Anzaldúa, Gloria. *Borderlands / La Frontera: The New Mestiza*. 1st ed. San Francisco: Aunt Lute, 1987.

Bacon, David. *The Children of NAFTA: Labor Wars on the U.S./Mexico Border*. Berkeley: University of California Press, 2004.

Bazin, André. *What Is Cinema?* Edited and translated by Hugh Gray. Berkeley: University of California Press, 2004.

Bourdieu, Pierre. "The Field of Cultural Production." In *The Field of Cultural Production: Essays on Art and Literature*, by Pierre Bourdieu, edited by Randal Johnson, 29–73. New York: Columbia University Press, 1993.

Brown, Wendy. *Walled States, Waning Sovereignty*. New York: Zone Books, 2010.

Chase, Robert T., ed. *Caging Borders and Carceral States: Incarcerations, Immigration Detentions, and Resistance*. Chapel Hill: University of North Carolina Press, 2019.

DeLay, Brian. "Independent Indians and the U.S.-Mexican War." *American Historical Review* 112, no. 1 (2008): 35–68.

Deloria, Philip J. *Indians in Unexpected Places*. Lawrence: University Press of Kansas, 2004.

DiMaggio, Paul, and Walter Powell. *The New Institutionalism in Organizational Analysis*. Chicago: University of Chicago Press, 1991.

Fanon, Frantz. *The Wretched of the Earth*. New York: Grove Press, 1961.

Fregoso, Rosa-Linda. *MeXicana Encounters: The Making of Social Identities on the Borderlands*. Berkeley: University of California Press, 2003.

Galán, Hector, dir. *The Forgotten Americans: Poverty on the Texas Border*. Galán Incorporated, 2001.

Gálvez, Alyshia. *Eating NAFTA: Trade, Food Policies and the Destruction of Mexico*. Oakland: University of California Press, 2018.

Gandhi, Leela. *Postcolonial Theory: A Critical Introduction*. 2nd ed. New York: Columbia University Press, 2019.

Gill, Lesley. *The School of the Americas: Military Training and Political Violence in the Americas*. Durham, N.C.: Duke University Press, 2004.

Ginsburg, Faye. "Archival Exposure: Disability, Documentary, and the Making of Counternarratives." In *Documenting the World*, edited by Gregg Mitman and Kelley Wilder, 150–65. Chicago: University of Chicago Press, 2016.

Gómez-Barris, Macarena. *The Extractive Zone: Social Ecologies and Decolonial Perspectives*. Durham, N.C.: Duke University Press, 2017.

Gonzales, Richard. "Sexual Assault of Detained Migrant Children Reported in the Thousands Since 2015." NPR, February 26, 2019. https://www.npr.org/2019/02/26/698397631/sexual-assault-of-detained-migrant-children-reported-in-the-thousands-since-2015.

González, Gabriela. *Redeeming La Raza: Transborder Modernity, Race, Respectability, and Rights*. New York: Oxford University Press, 2018.

Gramsci, Antonio. *Prison Letters*. London: Pluto Press, 1996.

Krauze, Enrique. *Mexico, Biography of Power: A History of Modern Mexico, 1810–1996*. New York: Harper Collins, 1997.

Kriel, Lomi. "ICE Guards 'Systematically' Sexually Assault Detainees in an El Paso Detention Center, Lawyers Say." *ProPublica*, August 14, 2020. https://www.propublica.org/article/ice-guards-systematically-sexually-assault-detainees-in-an-el-paso-detention-center-lawyers-say.

Martinez, Monica Muñoz. *The Injustice Never Leaves You: Anti-Mexican Violence in Texas*. Cambridge, Mass.: Harvard University Press, 2018.

Mirzoeff, Nicholas. *The Right to Look: A Counterhistory of Visuality*. Durham, N.C.: Duke University Press, 2011.

Montejano, David. *Anglos y mexicanos en la formación de Texas, 1836–1986*. Mexico City: Alianza Editorial, 1987.

Moraga, Cherríe, and Gloria Anzaldúa, eds. *This Bridge Called My Back: Writings by Radical Women of Color*. New York: Kitchen Table: Women of Color Press, 1983.

Moreton-Robinson, Aileen. *The White Possessive: Property, Power, and Indigenous Sovereignty*. Minneapolis: University of Minnesota Press, 2015.

Olivares, Jose, and John Washington. "ICE Detention Center Shuttered Following Repeated Allegations of Medical Misconduct." *The Intercept*, May 20, 2021. https://theintercept.com/2021/05/20/ice-irwin-hysterectomies-medical/.

Paredes, Américo. *"With His Pistol in His Hand": A Border Ballad and Its Hero*. Austin: University of Texas Press, 1958.

Peña, Devon G. *The Terror of the Machine: Technology, Work, Gender, and Ecology on the U.S.-Mexico Border*. Austin: University of Texas Press, 1997.

Pérez, Emma. *The Decolonial Imaginary: Writing Chicanas into History*. Bloomington: Indiana University Press, 1999.

Quijano, Aníbal. "Coloniality of Power, Eurocentrism, and Latin America." *Nepantla: Views from South* 1, no. 3 (2000): 533–80.

Raheja, Michelle. *Reservation Reelism: Redfacing, Visual Sovereignty, and Representations of Native Americans in Film*. Lincoln: University of Nebraska Press, 2010.

Resendiz, Ramón. "Landscapes of Violence: Documentary Media, Countervisualities, and Archival Resistance on the Mexico-U.S. Borderlands." PhD dissertation, New York University, 2023.

Resendiz, Ramón, and Rosalva Resendiz. "Towards a Decolonial Archive: A Reflection on the Operational Inaction Process of Critical Trans-border Documentary Production Practice." In *Challenging Borders: Contingencies and Consequences*, edited by Sheila McManus, Julie Young, and Paul McKenzie-Jones. Alberta: Athabasca University Press, forthcoming.

Resendiz, Ramón, Rosalva Resendiz, and Irene J. Klaver. "Colonialism and Imperialism: Indigenous Resistance on the US/Mexico Border." *Perspectives on Global Development and Technology* 16 (2017): 15–33.

Rony, Fatimah T. *The Third Eye: Race, Cinema, and Ethnographic Spectacle*. Durham, N.C.: Duke University Press, 1996.

Said, Edward. "Invention, Memory, Place." In *Landscape and Power*, edited by W. T. J. Mitchell, 242–61. Chicago: University of Chicago Press, 2002.

Said, Edward. *Orientalism*. New York: Vintage Books, 1979.

Saldaña-Portillo, María J. *Indian Given: Racial Geographies Across Mexico and the United States*. Durham, N.C.: Duke University Press, 2016.

Saldaña-Portillo, María J., and María Cotera. "Indigenous but Not Indian? Chicana/os and the Politics of Indigeneity." In *The World of Indigenous North America*, edited by Robert Warrior. London: Taylor & Francis Group, 2014.

Smith, Linda Tuhiwai. *Decolonizing Methodologies: Research and Indigenous Peoples*. London: Zed Books, 1999.

Southern Poverty Law Center. "Family Separation—A Timeline." SPLC, accessed January 27, 2024. https://www.splcenter.org/our-issues/immigrant-justice/family-separation.

Tamez, Margo. "Returning Lipan Apache Women's Laws, Lands, and Power in El Calaboz Ranchería, Texas-Mexico Border." PhD dissertation, Washington State University, 2010.

Webb, Walter Prescott. *The Great Plains*. Boston: Ginn and Company, 1931.

Webb, Walter Prescott. *The Texas Rangers: A Century of Frontier Defense*. Boston: Houghton Mifflin, 1935.

Wolfe, Patrick. "Settler Colonialism and the Elimination of the Native." *Journal of Genocide Research* 8, no. 4 (2006): 387–409.

SEVENTEEN

Decolonize the Erasure of Texas Indigenous History at UTSA's Institute of Texan Cultures

A Call for Indigenous-Centered Storytelling Practices

ANNETTE PORTILLO

As others have related in this anthology, the collective witnessing of dispossessed lands, the silencing of oral histories, and misrepresentations of Indigenous people are traumas many of us have endured and actively resist; we have all survived to tell our stories of survivance.[1] Like others in this collection, my personal story growing up in the borderlands is essential to understanding how I relate to the present-day militarized U.S.-Mexico borderlands. As a Chicana who grew up between San Diego, California, and Baja California, Mexico, and is now a resident of San Antonio, Texas, I embody the pervasive and systemic trauma that borderlands residents internalize. The Border Patrol's green vans regularly terrorized Mexican American, Chicanx, and Indigenous people in our San Diego barrios, and the border wall was an ever-present reality for all of us. Despite the creative and unique blending of cultures, languages, and identities on the borderlands, the racist national imagery of our communities in books, television, movies, and museums portrayed us as ignorant, indolent, and violent. Thus, as a result of my personal experiences, it became my life's work as an educator and activist to counter these egregious stereotypes through teaching and writing—that is, truth-telling.

My critical analysis and case study of the Institute of Texan Cultures at the University of Texas at San Antonio as it relates to Texas Indigenous history and culture is grounded in my material lived experiences and my positionality as an Indigenous studies scholar. The Institute curates history and culture, but it is also influenced by contemporary political extremism, like the acts of violence termed "light up the border" campaigns, orchestrated by White vigilante groups who have participated in tandem with the much larger effort of the Department of Homeland Security to "militarize" the border through state-sanctioned terrorism. These actions—that is, the terrorism of vigilante groups and the institutional violence of border maintenance—target people of color, but they prove particularly harmful to Indigenous people. In my childhood home along the U.S.-Mexico borderlands of San Diego, the Kumeyaay were literally bifurcated by a border and witnessed not only the separation of tribal communities, but also the desecration of sacred lands and spaces.[2] Thus, these multiple forms of violence shape historical representations of Indigenous people while also threatening Indigenous people's existence in the contemporary political, social, and cultural landscape of the borderlands.

This past lived experience is similar to my current witnessing of the borderlands region in South Texas, where settler colonialism and militarized nation-states have caused some of the most fractured Indigenous identities and communities in Texas. In addition, the borderland of South Texas encompasses multilayered histories of genocide committed against Indigenous and Mexican American people. This chapter seeks to demonstrate some of the ways in which the nation-state has erased Indigenous Texas history from the landscape through cultural appropriation and misrepresentations, as seen in public spaces such as a popular and significant museum in San Antonio, Texas. This erasure is embodied at the Institute of Texan Cultures (ITC), a Smithsonian affiliate managed by the University of Texas at San Antonio. For decades, the ITC has actively promoted a sanitized and romanticized historical narrative about Texas Indigenous people that ironically excludes the voices of multiple Indigenous communities. These erasures and silences have made it difficult for Indigenous people in the present to have their voices heard on important issues such as environmental degradation, police violence, structural racism, cultural sovereignty, and, of course, their rights to land taken during the construction of the border wall.

As several contributors to this collection have noted, the lawsuit filed by Dr. Eloisa G. Taméz against then-secretary of the Department of Homeland Security Michael Chertoff raised critical questions about indigeneity in Texas. Not only were the lawsuit and the larger campaign of resistance to militarization a profound stance against state power, they were a pivotal act of historical reclamation. As Eloisa, her daughter Dr. Margo Tamez, and their allies protested federal impunity, they also taught Texans about the deep historical ties of the Lipan Apache people to the land now called Texas. Their numerous public statements, interviews, and editorials deconstructed deeply held historical myths about the state and revealed the violence and racism experienced by Indigenous peoples. Their narratives contradicted many of the popular tropes that characterize textbooks used across the state, and they implicitly critiqued representations of Indigenous peoples in many museums. Thus, this chapter seeks to unpack the dominant historical narratives that clouded the ability of Texas to understand how a Lipan Apache professor could sue the Department of Homeland Security to defend her ancestral lands along the Rio Grande; these are the same narratives that guide museums such as the Institute of Texan Cultures. As such, my chapter contributes to the larger project of decolonization embraced in the Tamez case, the meeting in El Calaboz, and this pathbreaking collection.

Despite positive developments over the past few decades with regard to including Indigenous voices and perspectives in many museums, persistent Eurocentric representations of Indigenous peoples' history and culture continue to distort their experiences with the surrounding settler-colonial population.[3] This chapter focuses on the Institute of Texan Cultures to explore larger questions associated with the perpetuation of stereotypes and dissemination of misinformation, which erase and silence the multilayered histories of Indigenous people in Texas. As part of an ongoing effort to "revamp" and "restructure" the entire museum space of the ITC, I was asked by Lupita Barrera (director of research and education) and Bryan Howard (director of exhibits and collections) in the summer of 2011 to provide a critical analysis of the "Indian Section," which was clearly outdated, and to participate as a consultant in a long-term project to restructure it.[4] Since the objective of the initial report was to provide not only constructive criticism of the "Indian Section" but also suggestions for improvement, I took into consideration the ITC's affiliation with the Smithsonian Institution and the possibility of utilizing this prominent national resource as a means for engaging in substantial restructuring. In addition, given the ITC's affiliation with the Smithsonian, I found it fitting to include suggestions that speak to the National Museum of the American Indian (NMAI), as these critiques offer a foundation from which to begin assessing the space and long-term planning in order for the suggested changes to be accomplished.[5]

Although initial critiques and suggestions for restructuring were not as expansive as the plans to design and construct an entire museum such as the NMAI, this long-term project called for similar attention to detail and sustained consultation with Texas Indigenous communities. Thus, I began this report by centering the following questions: Whose voices are present in this space? What silences exist and why? And how can we reimagine a space that not only educates visitors but also contributes to the cultural sovereignty of Indigenous peoples? In part this chapter discusses an overview and analysis of the "Indian Section" at the Institute of Texan Cultures; it provides suggestions for how these displays/exhibits can be restructured; and then it discusses the future of the ITC as a result of new initiatives by UTSA administrators.[6]

Overview and Suggestions for Restructuring the "Indian Section" of the ITC

As one enters the Institute of Texan Cultures, one is immediately immersed in a space that is constructed through Western-centered museology.[7] In fact, the first part directly to the left of the entrance is called the "Indian Section" and has not changed since it was first constructed in the late 1960s.[8] The erasure of particular communities such as Lipan Apache (Ndé Dene) people is jarring, particularly considering the prominent role they played in Texas history. Some of the Indigenous communities "mentioned" in narratives and exhibits at the ITC are the Tiguas from Ysleta del Sur Pueblo, the Comanche, the Coushatta, and the Caddo. As visitors walk through the multiple displays, they can see a timeline of "Indians in Texas" that charts out a linear and chronological development of Indigenous people, thereby showing their "evolution."

Upon walking through this space, visitors are drawn to several large murals that depict romanticized images of Indigenous people. Several directors and docents indicated that the large mural depicting Native Americans from the Southwest, including a young woman carrying an olla on her head, is what attracts most visitors. In fact, the docents mentioned that the "Indian Section" has also been reported as a "favorite among the kids," who, most likely, are visiting the ITC on school field trips.[9]

According to the docents, another favorite exhibit in this space is the large tepee standing in front of a large mural. Both the mural and the tepee perpetuate the legacy of colonization, which rests on a myth of Indigenous persons as only existing in the past, with no real contextualization. Moreover, the tepee and the mural offer a generic and stereotypical portrayal of a nameless group from the southern Great Plains. While there were such groups in Texas, namely the Lipan and the Comanche, the mural offers a homogeneous and incomplete representation of Indigenous groups, because it says nothing about the more sedentary peoples living along the Rio Grande, the Gulf Coast, or northeastern Texas, for instance. Moreover, the imagery of highly mobile Plains Indians perpetuates the notion that Indigenous people moved around frequently and did not lay "claim" to specific territories. This assertion has been used by settler colonialists to justify wholesale theft of lands and the implementation of the regimes of private property and capitalist exploitation.

During an initial tour of the space, I noticed a few items, referred to as artifacts, which seemed out of place in this particular exhibit. The most notable were two twigs placed together to form an X. This X-shaped artifact gently leans in the doorway of the tepee. I was informed that this had been placed at the entrance because numerous times children have crawled into the tepee during their visits. Thus, the X was to prevent them from entering. But many Indigenous people did not use such an item to prevent entrance into a tepee. In contrast, most Indigenous families welcomed visitors. Several other exhibits provide similarly inaccurate depictions, as visitors are given the ability to observe "Indigenous life" from a safe and objectified distance.

For example, one of the largest exhibits in this space is the "Creation and Cosmos Cave," which is meant to reflect the religious beliefs, practices, and cosmology of Native people. But the cave, with dark winding pathways and small display cases dispersed throughout, has no real relevance to the history or spirituality of Indigenous peoples in Texas. It says nothing about emergence or origin stories, nothing about Indigenous astronomy and mapping, and nothing about the deep relationships between Native people and the land. It should be noted that this "cave" happens to be one of largest exhibits in this area and perhaps one of the most popular attractions for young children.

After assessing this exhibit among others it became clear that ITC was following a Western-centered epistemology. This approach is not unlike that of other museums that attempt to (re)present Indigenous peoples' history and culture. For example, in her article "The National Museum of the American Indian as Cultural Sovereignty," Amanda Cobb contextualizes the relationship between museums and Indigenous communities and provides a useful model for rethinking how we might reenvision this section of the ITC. Cobb notes that museums have always been "institutional tools of culture" and "instruments of colonization and dispossession."[10] That is, "museological practices are underpinned by Western epistemologies, systems of classification, and ideological assumptions that, when applied to Native Americans, have functioned in exploitative, objectifying, and demeaning ways."[11] According to Cobb, historically, Indigenous people have been (re)presented and displayed in museums through the following common exhibit styles: (1) geographical displays, where objects are grouped by region or cultural affiliation and visitors are given the opportunity to interact with the objects as "tourists"; (2) historical period displays, where objects are categorized chronologically in a linear style and Indigenous peoples are shown "progressing" toward a Western idea of civilization; (3) habitat displays, made of dioramas that allow visitors a "glimpse" into a particular moment/time; and (4) open-storage displays, where objects are shown regardless of their region or age.[12] Similar to Cobb's analysis, it was clear that the "Indian Section" of the ITC represents Indigenous people through a Western epistemological framework, which erases the complex and multifaceted Indigenous cultures, worldviews, and traditions. After critical observation, I noted that the "Indian Section" of the ITC, as it currently exists, includes a majority of the display types Cobb describes.

One of the most notable examples of these biases is the "history period display" that "records," through illustrations and a timeline, the so-called development of Indigenous people in Texas. This chronological timeline provides visitors with only one way of experiencing the complexity of Indigenous peoples' histories. In fact, this linear timeline does not offer any oral stories told from the first-person point of view or even Indigenous communities' representation of themselves and their connection to ancestral homelands. Instead, the timeline, painted with red and white lines on 3-D boards, depicts an archaeologically centered understanding of Texas's first inhabitants by showing dated arrowheads from various periods spanning 12,000 years. That is, the display itself is akin to a Eurocentric evidence-based "scientific" poster presentation of the kind typically used to "prove" empirical data via carbon dating and classification. As a scholar of autobiography studies and oral storytelling practices, I am critical of this methodology. This alleged evidence and the findings of scientists are the *only* evidence provided to tell the history of Texas Indigenous people at the ITC, thereby silencing Indigenous voices and traditions of history-telling. Given that the ITC has not revised this section for over sixty years, it is understandable why the archaeological perspective remains central to these exhibits, and why the museum is so problematic for Indigenous people.

Another "historical period display" exhibit seeks to explain the origins of humans in Texas and North America generally. It consists of a flat poster presentation that includes brief narratives and photographs as well as hand-painted illustrations. The first panel asks: "Who was first?" which is, perhaps ironically, depending on your perspective, a direct challenge to the Doctrine of Discovery and simultaneously an upholding of the myth of "Discovery." It also implies that whoever was "here first" is entitled to the land and supports the concept of "ownership," which is diametrically opposed to Indigenous concepts of communalism.[13] Thus, the underlying message continues to validate and privilege "scientific evidence" over Indigenous creation stories. A decolonial method for re-thinking this exhibit would be to instead display multiple creation stories, passed down from one generation to the next, consisting of a collective memory of people who have inhabited this land since time immemorial. An approach that was less concerned with "who arrived first" would also open conceptual space for groups that migrated to Texas or were deported here without casting moral judgments on them.

In contrast, the current exhibit systematically silences the voices and stories of Indigenous people via archaeological digs that seek to "prove" answers to the question "Who was first?" Thus, although the panels suggest that, based on "recent" archaeological digs and findings, there could have been persons inhabiting the land before the "Clovis," this narrative is still strongly based within the field of archaeology, with little to no consideration of Indigenous-centered oral stories of creation.[14] In essence, through Western-centered epistemological practices, the historical period display continues to explain or *justify* who occupied Texas first. In addition, this "history" display board presumes that the ancestral homelands of Indigenous people have always been in Texas. Thus, my final report proposed that the restructuring and revision of these narratives was crucial and critical, since this display is at the beginning of the ITC's "Indian Section" and is one of the first visual representations that museum visitors experience.

In the final assessment, my report proposed to the ITC that if the title panel "Who was first?" were to remain, it could instead be utilized to provide a more comprehensive teaching moment than what currently exists. In fact, the panel narratives might better interrogate the debates surrounding the Bering Strait land bridge theory, which is widely accepted by many archaeologists, but not by Indigenous peoples. Many Indigenous communities are often asked to "prove" their ancestral ties to homelands in North America in order to be federally or culturally recognized. But these same communities actively resist the Bering Strait land bridge theory through Indigenous-centered epistemologies. And although the information and exhibit are outdated and perpetuate a homogenized ideology of indigeneity, the report proposed that this section should foreground Indigenous voices as well as critique the theories that have been posited by scientists.

More importantly, as an R1 university, UTSA should consult and collaborate with Indigenous people in order to better incorporate Indigenous-centered perspectives on Texas Indigenous history within the "museum" space at the ITC. In fact, restructuring might include collaborating with Indigenous peoples to write a land acknowledgment, which could then be centered on a panel at the beginning of the exhibit.[15]

The Future of ITC: Suggestions for Decolonizing the "Indian Section"

As mentioned earlier in this chapter, in order to decolonize the ITC and remedy the clear erasure of Indigenous presence and voices, I argue that this space should be critically restructured in order to adhere to UTSA's primary mission and goals as an R1 university. More importantly, as part of the University of Texas system and under the sponsorship of the Smithsonian Institution, the ITC is responsible for accurately disseminating Texas Indigenous history to the community. Thus, the most significant recommendation of my report in terms of revisions and expansions of the existing exhibit would be to first collectively collaborate with local Indigenous communities in an oral history project. The only way this museum space can be decolonized is to center Indigenous expertise and participation in the telling and dissemination of any histories that claim to be about Indigenous people from and in Texas. This can take the form of creating specific Indigenous-centered initiatives that give communities full and complete access to the current holdings of the ITC and provide them the resources to better engage with the existing material items, cultural artifacts, documents, and recordings that the ITC houses.[16]

If the ITC were to begin its reenvisioning process through oral histories, this would allow community members to be more directly involved with the ways in which their history is disseminated. That is, this space lends itself to allowing Indigenous communities to take an active and empowering role in self-representation as collaborators rather than simply informants.

As an Indigenous scholar, my initial suggestion for restructuring this space was to eliminate the section that greets visitors with the display that asks, "Who was first?" I argue that upon entering this space it would be more appropriate to center the collective voices, stories, and histories of Texas Indigenous people, and to completely eliminate the archaeological and ethnographic othering that currently exists within the narratives and dated images. Since the ITC is located in one of the most visible tourist areas in downtown San Antonio and children frequently visit it for field trips, it is imperative that accurate information on Texas cultural history be disseminated in this space. It should be noted that the ITC is currently open and continues to host "field trips" for school-aged children and tours by docents who are nonexperts. As an educator and mother, I strongly believe that museum spaces, although problematic, have the potential, especially in South Texas, to contribute to a more accurate history about Indigenous peoples for school-aged youth.

Another aspect of the "Indian Section" that should be reconceptualized is the glass cases that visitors see throughout the exhibit. Currently, the display cases house random artifacts and descriptions of particular objects that are seemingly out of context. And the cases take up much-needed space that could be better utilized to enhance other aspects of history-telling. In order to truly decolonize this space, my report recommended that these displays be replaced with more contemporary forms of history and storytelling that counter the current Western-centered methods, which greet visitors with overly romanticized and sanitized tellings of Indigenous history in Texas. In addition, I suggested that two murals could actually be used as teaching tools if they chose not to remove them. For example, by including a see-through screen or a drop screen from the ceiling that would partially cover the current murals, the ITC could utilize a traditional museum display in combination with contemporary technology. Therefore, the docents' lecture on the historical message of the murals would not be disrupted, but one component would be followed by an alternative narrative that discusses current events and incorporates the multilayered complexity of Indigenous history in Texas.

Another example of how the existing exhibit might be updated would be to include a section that speaks directly to the transnational borderlands region of South Texas, especially the bifurcation of Indigenous people by two nation-states, the United States and Mexico. Given the ongoing issues and current events occurring in the borderlands related to *immigration*, one exhibit could center a discussion around the United States' insistence on building a border wall in South Texas, which has displaced Indigenous and Mexican communities in the border regions. The museum could explain how Indigenous peoples in Texas have ties to cultures and communities in Mexico, and that indigeneity in Texas requires an awareness of history below the international border. Moreover, one exhibit could discuss the case *Eloisa Garcia Tamez, et al. v. Michael Chertoff*, in which Taméz resisted the Department of Homeland Security, struggling against the construction of the border wall on her homelands.[17] This exhibit would allow visitors a more comprehensive and complex understanding of how the border wall displaced and continues to displace Indigenous communities living in the borderlands region and forcibly prohibits Indigenous Latin American communities from crossing in order to access humanitarian assistance. This type of exhibit would allow a more nuanced and complex discussion about transnational Indigenous people across, between, and within the U.S.-Mexico borderlands region.

As stated previously, since the ITC was established in 1968, it is clear that the existing silos and exhibits originally intended to show the everyday life of Indigenous people can now be interpreted as stereotypical misrepresentations. Thus, the decolonizing process should include, at the very least, an introduction to more current research and stories told by Indigenous communities that counter these dated histories. The museum should also include representations of contemporary Indigenous communities in Texas: of families living in urban cities, in rural spaces, or on one of the three reservations in the state. Important elements of modern culture could include any of the powwows held across the state, the Texas Tribal Buffalo Project, youth skateboarding, Indigenous hip-hop, and the struggles that Indigenous students face in the universities.

Historically, oral tradition was a significant aspect of every Indigenous community, and storytelling was and continues to be important for Indigenous peoples. Thus, another suggestion for highlighting traditional storytelling practices could be to utilize contemporary technologies. My initial report suggested that the ITC place a video screen in the exhibit where visitors can actually see and hear stories told by members of Indigenous Texan communities. In fact, this method (videos) is already used in other ITC exhibits, and there are similar examples at the NMAI that utilize this type of technology, where recurring documentary videos are looped in order for visitors to experience listening to stories. In order to more accurately portray Indigenous people in the twenty-first century, it is important to include these types of exhibits that seek to more accurately (re)present communities.

Cultural Sovereignty: Countering Stereotypes and Misrepresentations

After reviewing the multiple exhibits in the ITC's "Indian Section," it is clear that what is missing are the very voices that this section proposes to be (re)presenting. For Indigenous people, the museum space is one of contention and trauma, and for many individuals, these spaces are painful reminders of the continuing legacies of colonization and genocide. Thus, it is important to acknowledge the trauma associated with such spaces, because it is only with truth-telling that Indigenous people can heal. In her article "Acknowledging the Truth of History: Missed Opportunities at the National Museum of the American Indian," Amy Lonetree states:

> The only way for Native people to heal from the historical trauma that we have experienced—genocidal warfare, land theft, ethnic cleansing, disease, the attempted destruction of our religious and ceremonial life at the hands of the government and Christian churches—is for us to speak the truth about what has happened, document the suffering and name perpetrators of the violence in our history.[18]

In other words, the suffering of Indigenous peoples as a result of colonization and missionization should be central to the history-telling in these exhibits. More importantly, since this exhibit is part of the University of Texas system, teaching students and the public about Indigenous life is significant. Allowing Indigenous people to take control of their own histories and stories at ITC will be an empowering experience, as it will provide Indigenous communities cultural sovereignty.

Although discussion of these histories might be difficult, it is the responsibility of the ITC and those involved in the project to confront stories about colonization. By not acknowledging these histories we are in essence silencing Indigenous peoples' voices and committing cultural genocide. It is especially imperative that, as an institution of higher learning, the University of Texas at San Antonio provide an accurate history that affirms Indigenous perspectives and presence. Indigenous stories of survivance are much more than stories of survival or endurance. According to Gerald Vizenor, "The nature of survivance creates a sense of narrative resistance to absence, . . . nihility, and victimry. Native survivance is an active sense of presence over historical absence."[19] Thus, the stories told about historical trauma—such as massacres, missionization, and genocide—are a direct acknowledgment of the struggles that will then provide a context for the various methods of resistance and survival.

This *presence* would ensure that UTSA recognizes its responsibility to its audience at the ITC, which encompasses local residents of San Antonio and tourists from outside the state. More importantly, it is imperative that Indigenous communities who visit the ITC, especially youth, not be confronted with gross misconceptions about themselves. Since the institute is a public space and reaches a wide audience, it is critical that it acknowledge the reception of all audiences who bring with them differing experiences and worldviews. In addition, the audience should not simply be passive recipients of knowledge in the form of history displays, artifacts, photographs, and brief written narratives, but rather this space should be interactive, with audiences participating in the history-telling through a communal storytelling and listening process.

NAGPRA: The Responsibility of the Institute in Documenting and Repatriation

During interviews with several representatives from the ITC, I learned that the institute is currently following the guidelines of the Native American Graves Protection and Repatriation Act (NAGPRA).[20] This was not always the case, since the law was passed in 1990. Thus, for the purposes of my initial report I included an appendix that detailed the NAGPRA policy. It is imperative that UTSA and the ITC be attentive to NAGPRA, especially during the restructuring process. That is, the ITC should do everything it can to (re)document and take inventory of all objects, artifacts, remains, intellectual property, photographs, and recordings owned by UTSA, the ITC, and the Center for Archaeological Research (CAR), as well as the Anthropology Department. For example, the "artifacts" that are displayed and have been recovered through archaeological excavations should not simply be treated as "evidence" that proves particular historical "facts"; rather, they need to be treated with "traditional care." According to Cobb, tribal museums and consequently NMAI took into consideration that "many cultural objects are alive rather than inanimate and often require curators to allow them to 'breathe' rather than suffocate in sealed plastic containers."[21]

This last point brings up another critique of the exhibit space, which displays artifacts in glass cases. Although the concern is obviously with those objects that visitors have been exposed to at the ITC, it is important that all artifacts and remains in the possession of UTSA/ITC be documented and if necessary repatriated. One way to engage NAGPRA might be to have an actual exhibit that displays brief portions of the policy goals and the most recent amendments and ongoing struggles associated with repatriation and intellectual property. The mission of the ITC states:

> The museum is a component of The University of Texas at San Antonio. It plays a role in the university's community engagement initiatives by developing quality, accessible resources for educators and lifelong learners on topics of cultural heritage. It strives to develop a rich and vibrant culture in the arts and humanities that will expand the community's awareness and appreciation of Texas through an engaging series of exhibits, programs, and special events.[22]

In addition, members of the ITC recently acknowledged that it seeks to involve more faculty and students in its endeavors. Thus, this would provide a great opportunity for students from UTSA in the interdisciplinary fields of history, anthropology, English, American studies, museum studies, and archaeology to come together in a collaborative effort that would allow them to "research" the existing archives at the institute as well as the special collections on campus. This could take the form of a course or even a summer workshop that highlights NAGPRA.

One example of a "course" that could be taught as part of the curriculum at UTSA would be cross-listed between English, anthropology, American studies/history, and museum studies, and would utilize NAGPRA as the basis for the readings and subsequent trips to the archives and exhibits at ITC.[23] According to ITC oral historian Rhett Rushing, there are not enough staff members to document or digitize every recording and/or photograph, and therefore a course on "museum studies" that incorporates a hands-on component requiring students to actively engage with the material housed at the institute would serve multiple purposes.[24] In the spirit of collaboration, this course could also be team-taught and include lectures from several experts in the field of Indigenous studies across different disciplines. What better way to engage students than through interdisciplinary studies where they can interact with faculty with different expertise and methodological approaches? In addition, members of Texas Indigenous communities can be invited to participate and provide Indigenous-centered perspectives regarding the future plans for the ITC as it relates to the "Indian Section."

Conclusion

Indigenous peoples throughout Texas are at a turning point in their history: racism, disproportional incarceration, and militarization continue to marginalize our communities on the one hand, but on the other, we are reemerging and revitalizing our communities in unprecedented ways. We are developing our economies, graduating from high school, entering college, and speaking back against institutional barriers to our self-determination. And yet dominant discourses about our histories and cultures continue to pose barriers to accurate self-representation. Reactions to the Tamez family and their refusal to forfeit their land to the federal government revealed ongoing racism against Indigenous peoples in the Texas-Mexico borderlands.

The misrepresentations and erasures of Indigenous peoples at the ITC are part of these larger, systemic problems facing Indigenous communities in Texas. My initial report and this essay are intended to illustrate how the "Indian Section" can better represent particular communities through a reenvisioning process that is inclusive. It is imperative that UTSA follow protocols to collectively engage with Indigenous communities across Texas as they become agents of their stories, rather than mere objects to be gazed at in display cases. In fact, one of the discussions can even be to complicate and reject the dichotomy of "federally recognized" and "non–federally recognized." These oral stories would provide a more comprehensive history that decolonizes the existing dominant Western museological approach to (re)presenting Indigenous peoples at the ITC.

Lastly, it should be noted that this chapter has been a work in progress for a decade and began as the report I was asked to conduct in 2011. The initial report was submitted to the ITC, but I never received a response or follow-up. I concluded that either my recommendations and criticisms were something the administrators were unwilling to take into consideration or they simply thought a nonresponse would be sufficient to maintain the status quo at the ITC. In fact, at the time there were two board members at the ITC who were both anthropologists invested in the Eurocentric museology that the report critiqued. In one conversation, one individual stated that he strongly believed colonization was "good for Indian people." I was summarily silenced in the most egregious ways regarding my recommendations by those who were in charge of the ITC, and had minimal contact with anyone after my report was originally written.

Since then, there have been major changes at the ITC, and new administrators and curators have been hired as a result of a long-term strategic plan called "ITC Centennial 2068," which proposes to reimagine the future of the museum. This plan began several years ago and engaged support from stakeholders in the community who see it as a way in which to continue restructuring the nearby Hemisfair Park. It is my hope that, whoever the new leaders are in these roles as curators and directors, the future of ITC includes the myriad voices, histories, and stories, and that these stories are told from the perspective of communities rather than by docents and nonexperts through a skewed historical lens. It is ironic that after I circulated this essay to several members of this new "reenvisioning" board, soon to be decision-makers in the future of the ITC, I now see the language and ideas from my report/essay being used on the most recent websites advertising the plans for the ITC. For example, on one website there are now plans, albeit minimal, to expand the "American Indian exhibit."[25] The narrative on this site notes that this section will "offer museum visitors a more comprehensive look at Texas Indigenous peoples." In addition, there are plans to expand the gallery space and include more tribal communities such as the Mission Indians as well as a new look at the "Urban Indian" living in today's Texas. The ITC director, Veronica Rodriguez, has built bridges with members of the American Indians in Texas at the Spanish Colonial Missions (AIT-SCM) to provide more local voices for the exhibit. She states that the ITC eliminated the section that housed the pottery in an effort to modernize the museum.

I am hopeful that my report and the most recent one that circulated among current board members had some effect on these new changes that are now taking place in this reenvisioning process. After all, all the current proposed changes to this section are what I outlined in my report. I know that "private" collections have been returned, hence the expansion, so it is imperative that UTSA/ITC continue to abide by the federal law NAGPRA as they restructure and document their current inventory.

NOTES

1. I am grateful for the collective constructive criticism from Drs. Margo Tamez, Jeffrey Shepherd, and Cynthia Bejarano. Their insightful comments were invaluable as I edited this essay for final publication, and the way in which all the editors participated in weaving together stories to truth-tell is an example of Indigenous communal storytelling practices.
2. For further background, see my article: Annette Portillo, "Performing a Strategic Transborder Citizenship: Delfina Cuero Remaps Kumeyaay Presence Through Storytelling and Place Naming," *Western American Literature* 50, no. 3 (Fall 2015): 187–207.
3. For example, the establishment of the Smithsonian National Museum of the American Indian, the passage of the Indian Arts and Crafts Act, and the passage of the Native American Graves Protection and Repatriation Act all occurred between 1989 and 1990.
4. A decade later there was never any attempt to move forward with suggestions proposed in the initial report.
5. According to NMAI's website, it cares for one of the world's most expansive collections of Native artifacts, including objects, photographs, archives, and media covering the entire Western Hemisphere, from the Arctic Circle to Tierra del Fuego.
6. In fall 2020, the new directors indicated that they may be willing to reread this case study and rethink the ways in which Indigenous peoples are "represented" at the ITC.
7. The complexity of Indigenous identity and "naming" is beyond the scope of this case study, but I have chosen to use the following terms interchangeably in an attempt to avoid rigidly defined categories that homogenize diverse communities: *Indigenous, American Indian,* and *Native American.*
8. The ITC was created by the Texas Legislature in 1965 and originally served as the Texas Pavilion at HemisFair in 1968. The University of Texas system took control of the ITC museum in 1973. According to their web page, the ITC was created and continues to serve as a space where the experiences of people from across the globe who now call Texas home can be given a voice.
9. It is understood that most local schools bring their students to ITC because Texas history books make a brief mention of Native Americans and Texas Indigenous groups. I was informed that children between the ages of seven and eleven find the "Texas Indian Section" most appealing.
10. Amanda J. Cobb, "The National Museum of the American Indian as Cultural Sovereignty," *American Quarterly* 57, no. 2 (June 2005): 486.
11. Cobb, "National Museum," 488.

12. Cobb, "National Museum," 495.
13. It should be noted that the idea of having to "claim" land or "prove" one's origins is a result of colonialism.
14. In *Red Earth, White Lies*, Vine Deloria Jr. argues that "tribal elders did not worry if their version of creation was entirely different from the scenario held by a neighboring tribe. People believed that each tribe had its own special relationship with the superior spiritual forces that governed the universe. . . . Tribal knowledge was not fragmented data arranged according to rational speculation. It was simply the distilled memory of the People describing the events they experienced and the lands they had lived in." See Vine Deloria Jr., *Red Earth, White Lies: Native Americans and the Myth of Scientific Fact* (Golden, Colo.: Fulcrum, 1997), 36.
15. It was announced by UTSA's provost in 2021 that the university would begin a major reenvisioning process for the ITC. This fifty-year plan proposes to ensure that the reenvisioning process is informed by community voices from across San Antonio by way of task forces and steering committees.
16. As I walked through ITC's "Indian Section," one of the questions I could not ignore and asked several curators was how UTSA/ITC was adhering to the federal law NAGPRA and if they had disclosed all their holdings, artifacts, recordings, etc., which might allow for community members to repatriate items if necessary or gain better access through digitization and other forms of dissemination.
17. For more information on this lawsuit, see "Lawsuits Filed Challenging the Government's Actions," Working Group on Human Rights and the Border Wall, University of Texas at Austin School of Law, accessed February 12, 2024, https://law.utexas.edu/humanrights/borderwall/law/lawsuits-government.html.
18. Amy Lonetree, "Acknowledging the Truth of History: Missed Opportunities at the National Museum of the American Indian," in *The National Museum of the American Indian: Critical Conversations*, ed. Amy Lonetree and Amanda Cobb (Lincoln: University of Nebraska Press, 2008), 321.
19. Gerald Vizenor, *Native Liberty: Natural Reason and Cultural Survivance* (Lincoln: University of Nebraska Press, 2009), 1.
20. The Native American Graves Protection and Repatriation Act (NAGPRA) requires federal agencies and institutions that receive federal funds (including museums, universities, state agencies, and local governments) to repatriate or transfer Native American human remains and other cultural items to the appropriate parties by: (a) consulting with lineal descendants, Indian Tribes, and Native Hawaiian organizations on Native American human remains and other cultural items; (b) protecting and planning for Native American human remains and other cultural items that may be removed from federal or tribal lands; (c) identifying and reporting all Native American human remains and other cultural items in inventories and summaries of holdings or collections; (d) giving notice prior to repatriating or transferring human remains and other cultural items. See "Native American Graves Protection and Repatriation Act,"

National Park Service, U.S. Department of the Interior, accessed February 12, 2024, https://www.nps.gov/subjects/nagpra/index.htm.

21. Cobb, "National Museum," 493–94.
22. "About: A Component of the University of Texas at San Antonio," UTSA Institute of Texan Cultures, accessed February 12, 2024, https://texancultures.utsa.edu/about/.
23. In 2015 UTSA's College of Liberal and Fine Arts instituted a new minor called "museum studies," and this would provide the perfect opportunity for us along with other faculty to collaborate on several new courses dedicated to museology as it relates to Indigenous peoples.
24. Since my initial report of the ITC, there have been some proposed changes that include a major reenvisioning initiative for ITC in its entirety. In addition, I was invited to be a team member on a library grant proposal, "Faces and Places of Texas: Preserving and Digitizing the Institute of Texan Cultures' Audiovisual Collections." This federal grant has since been awarded (2022) from the Institute of Museum and Library Services and will be used to digitize and catalogue audiovisual items that were produced by the Institute of Texan Cultures for over fifty years. It will include cataloguing and rehousing more than three thousand multimedia items and digitizing two hundred of the most at-risk formats within the collection.
25. It was always my intention to ask that the ITC "rename" the space, since "Indian Section" is problematic. This website refers to the section using the terms "American Indian," which is also problematic as it is primarily used in academia. I would suggest that "Indigenous" be used instead. See "Expanding American Indian Exhibit at ITC," UTSA Institute of Texan Cultures, last modified March 25, 2022, https://texancultures.utsa.edu/itc-news/expanding-american-indian-exhibit-at-itc/.

BIBLIOGRAPHY

Cobb, Amanda J. "The National Museum of the American Indian as Cultural Sovereignty." *American Quarterly* 57, no. 2 (June 2005): 485–506.

Deloria Jr., Vine. *Red Earth, White Lies: Native Americans and the Myth of Scientific Fact*. Golden, Colo.: Fulcrum, 1997.

Lonetree, Amy. "Acknowledging the Truth of History: Missed Opportunities at the National Museum of the American Indian." In *The National Museum of the American Indian: Critical Conversations*, edited by Amy Lonetree and Amanda Cobb, 305–27. Lincoln: University of Nebraska Press, 2008.

National Park Service. "Native American Graves Protection and Repatriation Act." National Park Service, U.S. Department of the Interior. Accessed February 12, 2024. https://www.nps.gov/subjects/nagpra/index.htm.

Portillo, Annette. "Performing a Strategic Transborder Citizenship: Delfina Cuero Remaps Kumeyaay Presence Through Storytelling and Place Naming." *Western American Literature* 50, no. 3 (Fall 2015): 187–207.

UTSA Institute of Texan Cultures. "About: A Component of the University of Texas at San Antonio." Accessed February 12, 2024. https://texancultures.utsa.edu/about/.

UTSA Institute of Texan Cultures. "Expanding American Indian Exhibit at ITC." Last modified March 25, 2022. https://texancultures.utsa.edu/itc-news/expanding-american-indian-exhibit-at-itc/.

Vizenor, Gerald. *Native Liberty: Natural Reason and Cultural Survivance.* Lincoln: University of Nebraska Press, 2009.

Working Group on Human Rights and the Border Wall. "Lawsuits Filed Challenging the Government's Actions." Working Group on Human Rights and the Border Wall, University of Texas at Austin School of Law. Accessed February 12, 2024, https://law.utexas.edu/humanrights/borderwall/law/lawsuits-government.html.

EIGHTEEN

"despite this intolerable and ridiculous wallness, a humanness prevails"

[email, post-gathering reflection]

TERESA LEAL

The email response by Teresa Leal to the initial call for post-gathering reflections calls our attention to the embodied experiences of knowing walled and militarized places, and the ways in which these spaces detain and restrain us and take time from us. Teresa's extensive digital activist work enacted unity through relationality, reciprocity, solidarity, empowerment, and self-determination. She worked ardently alongside Indigenous migrants in Sonora to develop mutual aid networks to confront Indigenous peoples' forced economic and physical displacement from the land and the predatory labor systems that violate their human rights in Mexico and the United States. For those of us whose lives she touched, her influence as an Elder organizer focused us on illuminating the wall's connection to privatized prison detention, corruption, and the regimatic status quo of police brutality in the walled regions. Teresa taught thousands of human beings how to deconstruct racist and sexist legal systems and demonstrated in everyday life the beauty and vitality of a lifetime of active civil disobedience.

From: Teresa Leal
To: MARGO

Hola Comadre, no life goes on in the same way, but my laptop died and I have not been able to get another. And going to an internet cafe is unaffordable sometimes so I just stick to the immediate needs in order to cut down on time. Tonight we are both lucky because I just got to Tucson to visit my daughters for one day and am using their desktop computer . . . So I can get this to you if it's not too late.

Since I returned from the gathering, I have had problems with my breathing also, so I try to focus on the immediate local emergency issues as much as possible too, but once I get some relief, I cannot—and must not—desist from the permanent struggles.

ABOUT THE WALL I will just provide a description of things in general because [. . .] of this time crunch.

The material wall continues to grow more solid and psychotic as time goes on and yet people are quietly bowing down to longer lines and waiting. Most of us who have to cross every day are finding that we need to begin much earlier than two years ago—about 2 hours earlier—in order to meet our scheduled times and tasks. As I get up every morning I listen to the national news while I prepare for my personal not-so-new news about how much time it will take me to travel 4 blocks north to the dividing wall. Wait in line and then walk 2 blocks to get to work at the museum. My average is about a 1.5-hour wait, lots of conversations with people in line while I listen to my radio walkman so that I can finish the newscasts that I used to listen to at home. I am now bringing hot tea and even a book to read as I wait. Also got a little cart—like those that carry your suitcase—because it's too much wasted energy to be standing in the hot sun for so long with this dead weight. Being creative or stubborn as I am, I am now able to detect people that have been recently deported—usually young Mexican Indians—and shamelessly offer them my U.S. cell phone in order for them to reconnect with the life they suddenly left behind in the States when they got picked up by ICE. I have learned to detect those that are looking lost or standing close to the shitty wall as if to be able to reach over it to the life they miss.

As a result of standing and feeling their frustration and terrible impotence, I have now added another move to my getting up every morning . . . I charge both my cellphones—Mexican and U.S.—so that in case I detect this desolation in their eyes, I can at least break that disconnect by offering my cellphones. THANK GOD FOR CRICKET UNLIMITED CALLS AND TEXT MESSAGES. I am also able to monitor the context of their conversations which are another way to peek into the social and political devastation that governments ignore completely. These young people talking to their spouse or children and offering nothing more than complaints or questions about what will happen or is happening to them. But no real plan or hope in their voices . . . because they have none because in the walled zones making plans is interrupted by making time to wait and be processed in hopes that they can do the basics.

As I stand in line I also see the Wackenhut corporation [G4S Secure Solutions] buses arrive by the fence and more deported people deboarding. Many limping because they are recovering from many days of walking in the hot desert sun with no food or water until they realize that all they want to do is get caught by the Migra and avoid dying like others they have had to leave behind in their death marches that initially began as a path to a new beginning or at least an end to poverty and slavery. I watch these young people walk in a single line through a fenced-in path that begins in the U.S. Migra border center at the wall and leads them to a Mexican Migra processing office a few yards into Nogales, Sonora. I watch their sad faces as they get off the bus, pick up their belongings bunched up in a plastic bag with their name on a tag. But the irony is that as soon as they cross the line and are back in Mexico, their faces relax and their walk gets lighter . . . even if they are limping or in a wheelchair—that is taken away from them as soon as they are about to set foot back home. I heard one young man call his wife on my cell: "Don't worry, mijita, you may not have as many material problems as I do here, back in Ohio, but at least I am free and can be my Mexican self again without fear of being picked up by the Migra or ICE."

This long-line patience is also instilling in us something that scares the shit out of anarchists like me . . . It's making people more and more submissive. I have always considered that poor people and women are "better candidates" for subjugation. But now, walking in line for at least 1.5 hours every day is now making a broader public more submissive than ever. I now see rich people, educated people, macho men and elegant ladies suddenly bow down to the migra inspector. Their alert and proud faces are immediately transformed into dapper and stupid, obscure-looking victims of these agents that bark at them as they stand at the inspection site flanked by two armed feds with high-powered rifles ready to shoot at the least sight of resistance. And these sudden victims become quiet dummies who would beg or admit to anything the inspector says as long as their passport is not taken away from them. And even I feel ashamed to watch them because I cannot call out to them and coach them into demanding their rights. I have watched a pretty young woman wet her pants and stand in a puddle of her urine while the inspector asks her why she looks so nervous.

The physical wall is now also creating economic devastating walls. As I speak every other business in town is now closing or fighting desperately not to. Every other business is now a pawn shop or a sparsely supplied store that tries to sell whatever they have as fast and as cheaply as they can because the flow of Mexican consumers on the U.S. side and the U.S. tourists in Mexico are less and less able to buy the goods they used to buy.

Another wall is the wall of fear . . . fear of ICE on this side and the Cartels on the Mexican side. Both are not as different as they are portrayed because they both share a stupidity and corruption that make them one and the same. The material wall is actually becoming a containment wall. A way to retain and not let in any measure of governmental or official, effective relief or solution to get in. So, those that are kept in or out find that there is no other recourse but to find a safe place to hide and wait it out. But wait for what?

And yet, *despite this intolerable and ridiculous wallness, a humanness prevails* and hits this shit like a lightning bolt. They come in tiny sparks of interactions that allow for a young mother picked up by Arpaio in Phoenix and forced to sign her voluntary deportation under the promise that she would get reunited with her two babies . . . to recover her children through the constant moves of reporters, pastors, and activists. To watch Juanita break into teary smiles, while they hug each other on the Mexican side . . . watch her glare at the damned wall that almost divided them.

I watch and listen to my 85-year-old mother beg around her neighborhood and church every morning in order to gather ingredients to make hundreds of sandwiches a month to feed those deported young people that wore out their 5-day stay at the migrant services centers. I watch her cry when she relays the stories they tell because she is the grandmother who prays for them while she also scolds them for jumping the wall and risking their lives in a country that doesn't want them. "Ay Mihijito, go back to your tierra and familia because there you are loved and missed," she tells them while she helps them cover their blisters with nice clean cotton socks. But then I want to cry, when she comes home to confide in me that she fears for these young people who will return home and find hunger, injustice and no jobs. "Ay Mihijita I know that is a recipe for becoming a peon for the cartels . . . but what can they do? What can we do? Only God knows." And I, her only daughter, can only console her and tell her she is doing the best that she can and the rest is up to her God or to my god knows what . . . Yet certainly not to a Pinchi government!!!!!!!

As a conclusion to this catharsis, I can only say that my final report on the wall is that in a constant and vulgar way, it has temporarily effectively stopped people's dreams, pride and de facto right of way through this life. But it has not stopped people's resolve to neutralize its intent for annihilation of their right to prevail. That it has not stopped our Indian spirit to ignore those dark intentions and continue with our red road of resistance. It has not stopped our right to topple those walls and turn them into bridges. It has not stopped our right to wishful thinking that will someday give me the funds to create a multipurpose migrant clearinghouse to intervene effectively and autonomously on behalf of People who walk this earth for whatever reason they choose.

Paz mujer
teresa leal

Nogales, FRONTERA
"La Madre Tierra MORENA no se vende . . .
se AMA y se Defiende."
NO MÁS SANGRE / NO MÁS HAMBRE

RESISTANCE ARTWORK

didíigo biłgoshni hwiigo | witness tell stories powerfully (strongly, vigorously)

Storying Visual Witnessing

Melanie Cervantes

Artist's Statement

The artworks included in this collection were commissioned by Margo Tamez at the height of the Tamez women's resistance to the U.S. construction of the border wall through the middle of their ancestral lands in El Calaboz Ranchería.

I (Xicanx) have never lived far from the California coast. Born in Harbor City, California, and raised in a small city in the South Bay of Los Angeles, I now make my home in the San Francisco Bay Area. Here, I create visual art that is inspired by the people around me and my communities' desire for radical social transformation. My intention is to create a visual lexicon of resistance to multiple oppressions that will raise consciousness, inspire curiosity, and inspire solidarities among communities of struggle.

In 2007, I co-founded Dignidad Rebelde, a graphic arts collaboration that produces screen prints, political posters, and multimedia projects grounded in Third World and Indigenous movements that build people's power to transform the conditions of fragmentation, displacement, and loss of culture that result from histories of colonialism, patriarchy, genocide, and exploitation. Dignidad Rebelde's purpose is to illustrate stories

"Not One More Inch" by Melanie Cervantes.

of struggle, resistance, and triumph in artwork that can be put back into the hands of the communities who inspire it.

I have exhibited extensively across the country, including at the Yerba Buena Center for the Arts and the San Francisco Museum of Modern Art (San Francisco), the National Museum of Mexican Art (Chicago), and the Museum of Modern Art (New York), and internationally at the Musée d'Aquitaine (Bordeaux, France), Galerija Alkatraz (Ljubljana, Slovenia),

"Ni Una Pulgada Más" by Melanie Cervantes.

and the Museo Franz Mayer (Mexico City, Mexico). My work is in the permanent collections of the Center for the Study of Political Graphics, the Latin American Collection of the Green Library at Stanford, the Rauner Special Collections Library at Dartmouth College, and the Library of Congress, as well as various other public and private collections throughout the United States.

I am the inaugural recipient of the two-year Art in Resistance Fellowship (2019–20), as well as being recognized, as Dignidad Rebelde, with the Piri Thomas & Suzie Dodd Cultural Activist Award from Communities United for Restorative Youth Justice (2016), the Community Award, National Association of Chicana/Chicano Studies (2015), an award from the NALAC Fund for the Arts (2012), and the Exemplary Leadership award from San Francisco State University (2010).

I hold a BA in ethnic studies from the University of California, Berkeley.

Monica Villarreal

Artist's Statement

THE WALL, metal sculpture, 2015, 21 ft × 10 ft.

This sculpture was one of seven pieces that were part of the *Migration Is?* installation during Round 41 at Project Row Houses. It is a twenty-one-foot-high metal sculpture that mimics the U.S.-Mexico border wall. The sculpture is the same size and made out of the same material as the actual border wall that sits along Texas. This simple but beautiful wall takes over land and creates a border between the audience and the house, giving the viewer a skewed view of the home. It was created with the purpose of giving the viewer the same sense of incarceration and militarization that is felt by inhabitants on both sides of the U.S.-Mexico border wall.

MADE IN AMERICA, stencil on paper, 2014, 5 ft × 180 ft.

This installation was exhibited at the Voices Breaking Boundaries, Borderline Production—Livingroom Art series in 2013. It was inspired after a visit to Margo Tamez in El Calaboz, Texas, where we witnessed how part of her land was occupied by the wall. I was inspired to create art that spoke of the highly militarized environment that is being generated by

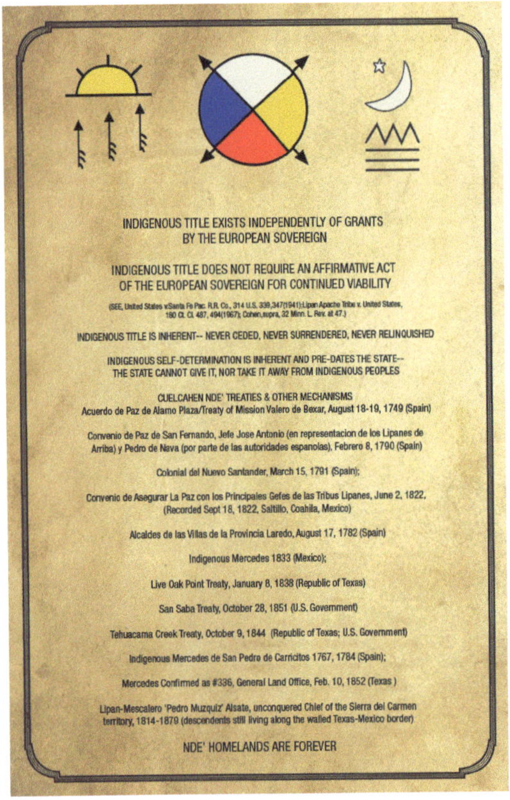

"Honor Ndé Treaties" by Monica Villarreal.

"History Lesson" by Monica Villarreal.

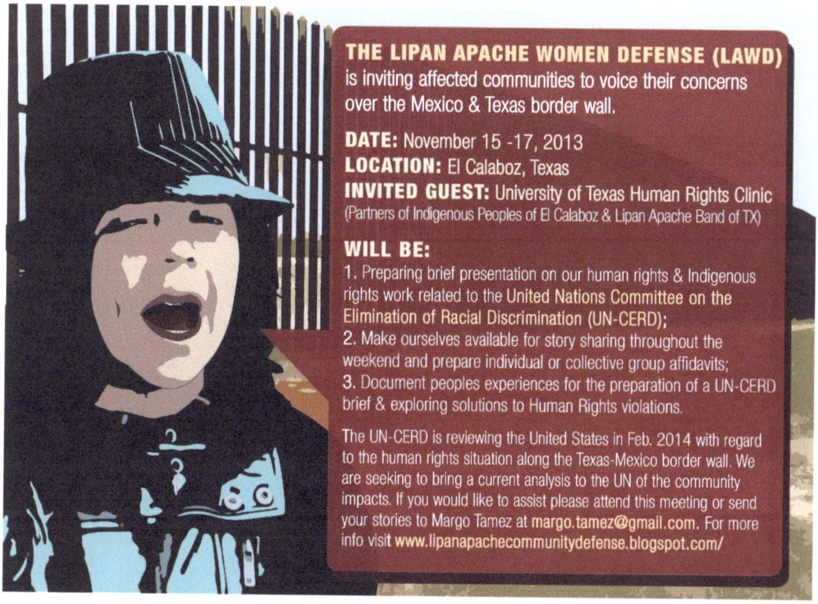

"Follow-Up Gathering in El Calaboz: Lipan Apache Women Defense (English)" by Monica Villarreal.

"Reunión Seguimiento en El Calaboz: La Defensa Femenil Lipan Apache (Español)" by Monica Villarreal.

Image of the artist with wall constructed in front of her house, in Houston, Texas.

the presence of the border wall and U.S. Border Patrol. The intent of the M16 stencil along the fence surrounding the whole house was to create a striking image large enough to make people stop and read the message. It also gave the viewer the same sense of intrusiveness and aggression that is felt along the actual border.

“Made in America” by Monica Villarreal.

Madeline Ríos

They Inspired Indigenous Peoples to Action: A Reflection as a Language Translator on Understanding Key Actors in Movements

I first met Margo Tamez at an immigrant rights event where she shared her family's experience in a court battle against the U.S. government to prevent a segment of the border fence from being built on their lands. As she described the ensuing court battle, based on a steadfast assertion of the rights of Indigenous peoples to their lands, her solidarity with the undocumented clearly shone through as an integral complement to that struggle. Years later, when the border fence went up despite their heroic resistance, I was invited to the gathering at El Calaboz. The trip allowed me to witness and learn about the devastating effects of militarization on Indigenous border communities, while also gifting me with a short but treasured glimpse into Indigenous Łibayé Ndé ways. I often write poetry, and two of my poems relate directly to that experience. The first is dedicated to Margo, whose intellectual honesty, dedication, and identity persevered even in the most trying moments and led to the poem "My Hero." The second, "The Wall," was written several years later. Despite the years and miles that separated me from El Calaboz, the ugliness of the border fence still evoked a certain traumatic effect within me as I stared at a wall of apathy at a poetry reading in the form of an audience unmoved by the stories of resistance of our peoples.

My Hero

My hero was exhausted when I met her
From years of research and writing
Lawsuits and speaking tours, caring for family, keeping up with school
And watching the bulldozers come
As she knew they would
When her family decided
To fight the Wall

Frustrations and defeats
Moments of confusion, thoughts of disillusion
Were clearly present
As we visited the town where her nephew
Was killed by the Marines,
As we watched it slowly die
Under the suffocation
Of closed schools surrounded by barbed wire fences
Badly dredged canals
The border patrol
And identity denied.

We shared our worlds, the pollen and the corn
Jacob and Jesus
Eloisa, touched by lightning
The history of law and wars
The bustling river where feasts were held, turned into a no-man's land
The reason why it feels so different when you live in
Texas.

My hero leads a room full of children as they learn the intricacies of beading a sacred pouch

Where colors contrast and align to form the image neither could portray alone
My hero does not deny any branches of her roots
Her Apache blood is intertwined with Basque
She knows she carries colliding worlds within her way of being
My hero doesn't simplify
The illuminating contradictions
Of truth.
With passionate yet tempered courage
She follows through on the endless task of pursuing justice to conclusion
Even on days without glory.
Like the trees that give the breath of life
Cycling through fresh green shoots and fallen leaves
But always rooted and solid
My hero gives me strength, because my hero is real.

The Wall

So there I was, pouring my heart and art
Into the beauty of my people's struggle
And all they wanted to hear about
Was Cinco de Drinko
And my menstrual cycle

Staring through a wall
As tall and rusty as the border fence
Like a deer in shock
Seeing its path to the river blocked
by a force beyond its understanding,
All I could do was turn my back
And walk the other way.

Arnoldo García (Purépecha)

Prisoner

(preface to the abolition of my family)

I have
no country
no passport
no birth certificate
no maps
no language
no mother
no father
no brother
no sister
no grandfather
no grandmother
no roots
no shadows
no suns
no land
no house

no breath
no lungs
no mind
no body
no spirits
no people
to claim me

Nowhere to plant and unearth the placentas of my explosive fists
Nowhere, no land, no horizon, no dreams
to call my ancestors from

My ancestors are lost
in the dusty winds
in the turmoil of the ocean waves
in the graffiti of prison cells
in the nameless songs I howl in the bed of my nights
in the walls that split the atom of my existence
in the shot up body of my other selves
in the unmarked graves of seas, plains, mountains, deserts, fields and cities
in the nazca lines of my palms
in the fossil fueled bones of migrant campesino indios
in the liver of my anguish
in the salmons belly up in the drought-filled rivers
in the burial grounds under the parking lots of malls
in the ruins everywhere wrought by red and black serpent clouds
in the evanescent rings of trees crackling in the firestorms of capitalism
in the muted cries of the last matriarch dying of cancer
in the terror of drowning in a hospital bed

I know
the smooth barrels of guns
the certainty of my rage
the feverish high of neutron drugs
the other bodies that ignite my own
the wounds, the wounds, the wounds that serrate my skin
the clandestine tears

the grunting police
the razor wires
the crazed inmates
who gives death and metes out precarious existences
who forgets me
who remembers me
who cuts me up
who erases me
words that have no pages to call their own
I know
I know
I know
my body
that belongs to the wardens and the landlords
that has been crushed under by tanks
that has been foreclosed in the womb
that can be handcuffed
on any corner of any day
that can be indicted
by any shade of white
by any tone of white
by any discomfort of white

I am
all the colors
I am
the rainbow machete
harvesting the rains
I am
scapegoat and virus of love
I am
no one more important than a landless indio
I am
the promise of a storm, a hurricane,
the tenderness of the longest day of labor
I am
the unread the unwritten the underground story

toppling our own frustrations and outrage
I am
turning into the calm before
the clenched fist and the quilt of my embrace
I am
nomadic homeland
horizon maker
carrying my dead and my living
from grave to grave
from sunrise to sunset
from laughter to rage
from gasps of grayness
to the carmine flows of the unending kiss
I am
an abandoned sun . . .

Before your name becomes a wound

Before your name becomes

a wound on my tongue

a scar on my heart

a drowning in my lungs

Before your name becomes

revenge for a past that was never yours

fists that crush the face of your lover the sky

a crumpled man, a prisoner of oblivion

I will hold on to you

I will become your second shadow

I will burst the pus of the sun

To shallow the pain

of these neighborhoods

that push us into the grave

of their pigment.

Your name is a wound

that bleeds from the constellations

that opens into a canyon

where the wild river of your rage

roars into the border and the oceans

Time goes backward

The glaciers are melting

The clouds are engorged

with the moans

of my dying grandfather

of my serene grandmother

who push you back across space

so you can finish living

so you can settle down between horizons

free of walls and ghosts

Your name is a wound

The wound will stop time

Your name will become a cloud with roots

shade from the maddening threat of prisons

an opening to free yourself from yourself

Defying all bullets that you have fired

and have been fired at you.

A wound against all wounds

A silence against all cries

A man against himself

that saves yourself

You must first touch your own wound

pronounce it liberation

a compact to end all wounds

You will never forget who you are

until you forget who you've been

A wound that walks around

slashing the land with rage

A wound that screams blaming the sky

for the blue of your weariness

A wound of quicksand and freezing solitary

You were hungry

And you refused my prayers

You were angry

And you ignored the sage

You were a child

And you got your way. . . .

The B word

Freedom does not ask for a visa.
Justice doesn't need a passport.
Human rights are our only borders, our only country, our only security, our only nationality.

Human rights is the color of our skin,
the pleasure of our bodies,
the place where class does not matter,
where class begins and begins to end,
where clean air, water and soil conspire with us,
where the natural world takes over
and we take our place in the web of life called
time, space, cosmos, universe, the Milky Way, *la Vía Láctea*.

In community and through communities,
can our words and actions for a different, more just, fair world not only make sense but also stand up and start walking?

Everyone is
a border brother,
a border sister;
you carry the border wherever you go.
The border follows us wherever we go:

There's the 1492 border, the mother of all borders that we know.

Racial slavery began in 1492, when a small group of white men thought they could own the world and whoever lived there by declaring it so, by declaring it theirs.

There's the landing of the Plymouth Rock border.
Malcolm X was right: "We didn't land on Plymouth Rock; Plymouth Rock landed on us."

There's the 1776 border; the 1848 border; the 1865 border; the 1880 Chinese Exclusion border; the 1890 Wounded Knee border; the 1905 White Gentleman's Agreement border to keep Japanese and Asians out.

The 1905, 1910, 1917 revolutionary borders when czars everywhere were overthrown and Bolsheviks, Zapatistas and Villistas called for new human borders everywhere

The 1492 border showed up again as World War I.
The 1929 crash border that brought us World War II crushed humanity with hunger and desperation of their borders;
The 1936 Spanish Civil War border that called for internationalists to cross and double-cross all borders.
The 1939 border of running over everyone and everything with tanks, storm troopers, blitzkriegs and concentration camps for our border brothers and sisters.

The Soviet Union and the U.S.A. had their own brand of forced laborers,
braceros are braceros regardless of who's in charge of the border.

The Nazi-Fascist borders paled in comparison with the Nagasaki-Hiroshima
atomic bomb borders.

Capitalism's 1492 borders made full circle when they ended World War II.

The Jim Crow borders,
the maquiladora borders,
the bracero borders,
the military-industrial complexion borders.

The military industrial complexion? Whiteness.
For those who think that race, color without class analysis is poor,
they have yet to learn that if you aren't color-conscious your class consciousness will be white, Eurocentric, ignoring more than 95% of world history and the movements for liberation, land, justice and humanity.

Because when I say border, I am saying Europe, I am uttering Christopher Columbus, I am raising fists against colonialism, neocolonialism, imperialism, empires, I am speaking in silenced languages, disappeared peoples, destroyed natural worlds,

Color is class
the darker colors the darker and lower you find yourself in the working classes,
the poorest are darkest,
Indigenous peoples, Africans, mestizos, Asians, Arabs, Muslims, Mexicans, Salvadorans, Mayan, Lakota, Tohono O'odham, Yaqui . . .

When you see us
you see the landless,
the perennially sub and unemployed,
the homeless (but not without a homeland, even if it is the perennially imaginary Aztlán),

we who have no representative in Congress, have never had one in the
White House.
We who have been thrown off their lands,
treated as strangers,
as minors incapable of determining their own dreams,
experimented on with small gifts of smallpox,
poisoned with diseases,
cast off,
put in reservations,
ghettos
and migrant labor camps

In Mexico, Meso-America, Canada, France, England, Spain, Nicaragua, Cuba, and elsewhere, the history of the struggles for freedom is inscribed, tattooed, branded, insinuated, instructed, breathing through our pores, in our pigmentation.

This is the pigment of our imagination.

For poor and working class whites, their whiteness is aspiration to and sentinel of power and powerlessness to keep the darker brothers and sisters down.

Every border since 1492 has been imposed to quash the natural world and our place in her.

Every border has been used to impose a redefinition, a refinement of whiteness.

Tonight I take back their words and erase their presence,
erase their violent system of conquest, occupation and spiritual deceit;

Resurrect the Taínos, the Caribes, the Haitís, the guajiros, they who welcomed lost strangers, fed them, gave them fresh water, nourished them back to health—and lost everything for it.

Tonight let our borders sleep together, gestate, dream, make love together.

My border is
my skin
my ancestral skeleton
walking across fields
and waiting on street corners for work

Let the cosmos with its biggest bang pull apart the 1492 borders,
until they burst in the sixth sun,
scattered without redemption or hope.

Leave us behind in the MesoCosmos of our borders,
our lives to till the stars

and regain our place in the natural world . . .

Diana Lucas-Joe

Testimonio

I'm P'urhépecha married Navajo digital poetic dissent online from el valle with
Yaqui-Tarascan of my mother and father, and Diné kinship through marriage.
I was moved to tears as I read carefully the report. I can say only in a humble way that it is quite clear, and very professional indeed!
I want to help so very badly with testimonial. I have the testimony that speaks on behalf of my mother, a traditional one-of-her-kind partera.
Mother is quickly advancing in her years and I am her only port for voice. I am deeply saddened since all these laws and policies have passed on us, all of us.
Mother is from Brownsville, she is from Tarasca, P'urhépecha people. A woman of very little formal education, yet a woman of great gifted way!
I am constantly networking online—primarily if not solely in the area of Indigenous peoples' rights and protection of our natural corridors and surroundings from the center above, and the center beneath!
I am a grassroots consultant, out here on the Navajo reservation.

I am not very savvy about a whole lot of a whole lot, but I am willing to stay whole.
Stay blessed, Cihuatl Yolotl

>><<

"No Bueno: Indigenous protocols if you're not Indigenous to here"

When I asked my elderly
Momma in 2007, what she thought about our homelands getting fenced in,
she said "No bueno, let's go march against that, mija!"

I am married to a Navajo.
I have raised our children here and now our grandchildren~
Little ol' small fry like me . . . from Brownsville originals!
hehe

Mi hogan es tu hogan
come visit!

I'll take ya off the beaten trail!
Love and harmonizin'

I was born on the banks of the sacred Rio Grande
my umbilicus ceremony is always in place there.

DO NOT:
wall it up, wall it over, or wall across it!

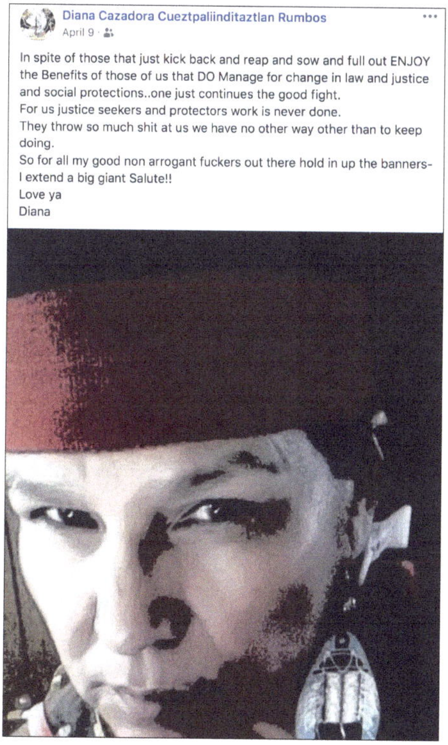

"The good fight is never done" by Lucas Joe.

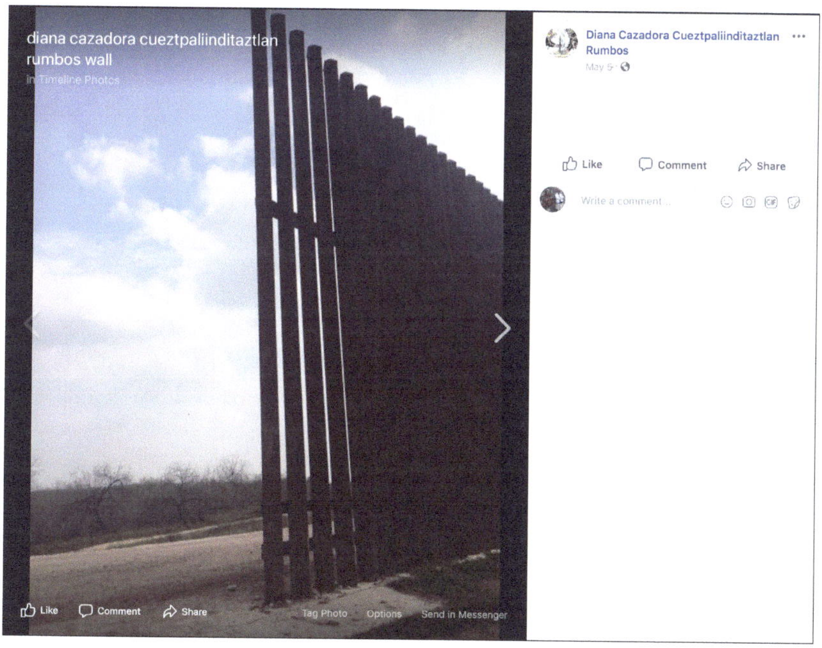

"Documenting the cage construction" by Lucas Joe.

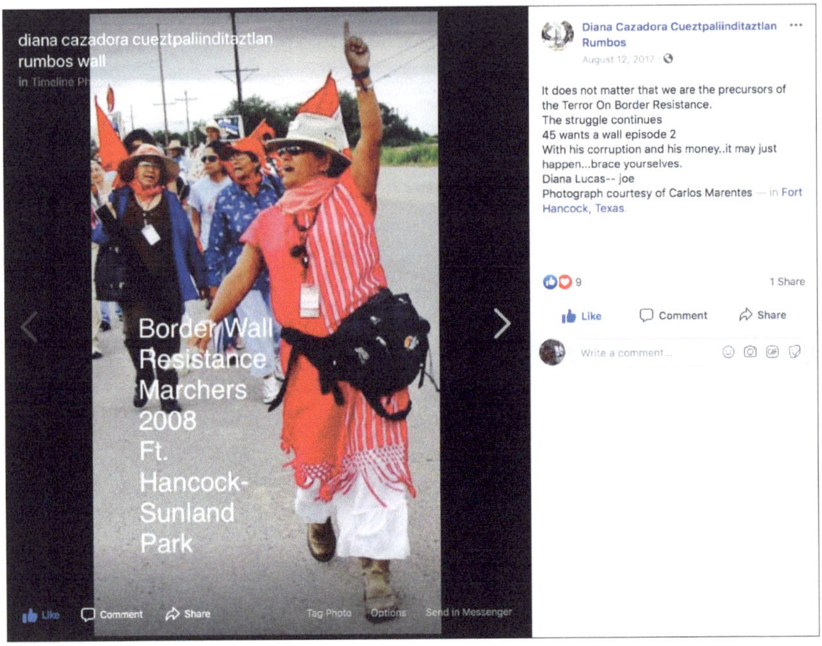

"It does not matter that we are the prisoners of terror on border resistance" by Lucas Joe.

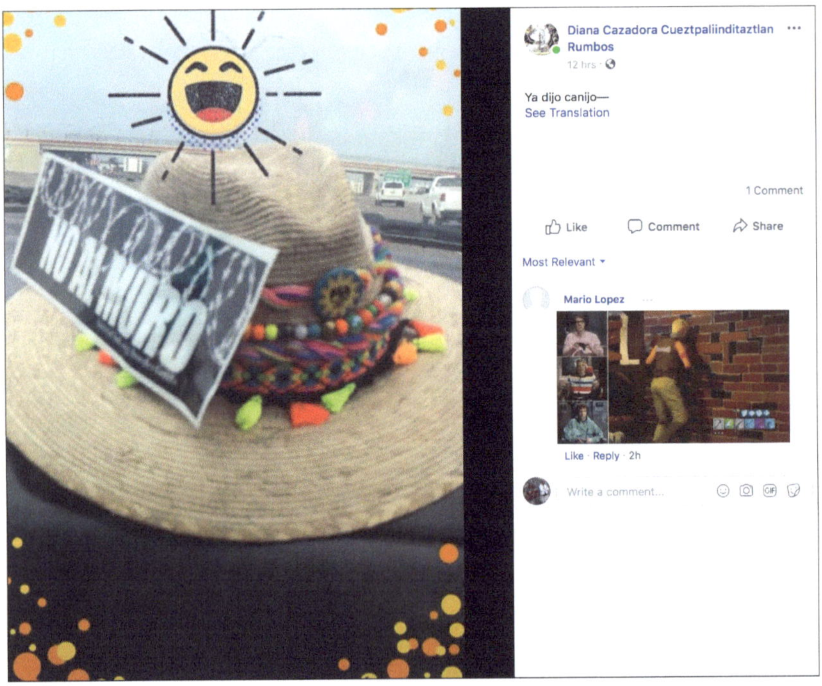

"No al muro" by Lucas Joe.

Government Watch List
DOJ
CIA
FBI
DEA
and possibly others- lol

lol
Me la Pelan-
As if I don't know on my
own....
Any person that's woke hahaha is on watch
The minute you quit drinking the koolaid...bet your silly tits u gonnna get watched haha

*This certain site makes it all look all fancy info gatherers..just so in the end u bust out the plastic and pay up!
lol
I was like, if ppl want to know about me-I'll fawking tell truth mutha fawkers.
All these hide and seek fools
haha
Not I, said the dog!
What you see is what I made for myself..lol-

Not ashamed
Not:
Embarrassed ever never!

Not on a pedophile watch roll!

Not on a hurting babies and or defenseless
Ppl list.
Not a keeper of animals or strange things just to fill a void-
He he
Not a hoarder of food or materials
Not greedy
Not money hungry
Not
Not
So yea
Somehow I was redirected to some truth finder site which made it look like I was top notch raise brow specimen-haha sooooo glad I am not all secrets!

"Government Watch List" by Lucas Joe.

"This border wall makes me sick" by Lucas Joe.

"Out of office reply: I will be protesting detained/separated children today" by Lucas Joe.

"When I asked my elderly Momma what she thought about our homelands" by Lucas Joe.

PART IV

Bénáońzi̱i̱ní | Embodying Indigenous Recognition

Embodied Belonging and Re-creating Kinship Beyond Walls

NINETEEN

Healing Savage Souls, Re-creating, and Belonging

Indigenous Tattoo Revival as a Contemporary Form of Indigenous Embodied Biography of Continuing Independence and Resistance

DION KASZAS

Introduction and Creating Connections

My name is Dion Kaszas. I am a Hungarian, Métis, and Nlaka'pamux cultural tattoo practitioner, scholar, and visual artist embedded in the revival of Indigenous cultural and ancestral tattooing in Canada. More specifically, my genealogy makes me a Bill C-31 member of the Lower Nicola Indian Band on my mother's side.[1] On my father's side, my paternal Hungarian great-grandparents landed in Halifax, Nova Scotia, in April of 1924. My maternal fourth great-grandfather on my dad's side died at the age of ninety-three in Batoche, Saskatchewan, on May 12, 1885, fighting in the Métis resistance. My genealogy is filled with my ancestors' resilience and resistance; they used every weapon at their disposal against colonial attempts to wipe them out of existence. This resilience and resistance is imprinted in my DNA, and it is marked in my skin. I've been directly affected by settler-colonial erasures, and by steadfast Indigenous women confronting the colonial laws intentionally written to strip us of our identity, place, belonging, and rights. In *McIvor v. Canada* (1989), my aunt Sharon McIvor sued the federal government, arguing that the Indian Act discriminated against Indigenous women by denying them legal status and social, economic, cultural, and political rights, and that it denied their lineal descendants legal recognition of their identity, thus violating the Canadian Charter of Rights and Freedoms. My aunt's case, resolved in 2009 in her favor, busted through the wall of Canada's settler-colonial legal system deployed to erase Indigenous rights. Her case opened paths for Indigenous women and their descendants facing walls of injustice. Through my aunt's twenty-year battle to stand her ground for justice for the multitudes affected, I recognize the significance of the Tamez women's legal and political demands. My aunt's long struggle influenced my understanding of the long road of justice, and of my generation's responsibility to participate in the resistance against erasure. These women single-handedly confronted two powerful settler-colonial nations, leaving a legal archive for current generations to know who we are, be proud of our identity, and know where we are from so we will not surrender to dehumanizations intended to deny our existence.

In my art, my hands create earthlines of expression and understanding using the simplest tools: fingers, a pencil, and a paintbrush. When a perceived mistake, line, or impression is out of place, I use an eraser to try to correct it. My everyday use of an eraser has become a useful thought experiment for analyzing a complex historical reality. For millennia, humans left impressions of their cultures on the landscape. Stories, languages, and worldviews developed in relationship with land and animal relatives, creating expressions of humanity. Many of these culture and identity expressions included marking the human body with various images, using varieties of tools and ink.

Following these millennia-old traditions, I engaged in a revival of Indigenous tattooing as a form of personal exploration and healing, and as a defiant act of resistance to settler colonialism. Throughout this essay, I will be weaving my personal story, which includes my work in the revival of Nlaka'pamux and Indigenous tattooing, with the work I continue doing with Margo Tamez. Although it may seem like the tattooing practices of a First Nations artist have little connection to the 2007 Tamez court case and the 2011 Gathering in El Calaboz, they are in fact woven together, representing twin strands of border making, boundary creation, and the long tradition of Indigenous resistance to imperialist violence and identity erasure. Building on my MA thesis grounded in the Nlaka'pamux weaving methodology, I weave my personal narrative in this chapter to discuss several important issues.[2] First, I explain where tattooing is situated within the contestation between settler colonialism in Canada, as the nation-state sought to erase First Nations cultural identity, and the resistance strategies embedded in tattoo revitalization. Second, I discuss how my personal journey with tattooing helped me heal myself and others from multiple kinds of trauma. Third, I discuss the global revitalization of tattooing, particularly among Indigenous youth as they offer the promise of a new generation of decolonization. Finally, I make connections between the Tamez family's resistance against border militarization and the challenges confronted by First Nations people regarding self-representation via personal tattooing and cultural revitalization.

Discovering Nlaka'pamux Tattooing

I had no idea my culture and my ancestors practiced tattooing until I found *Tattooing and Face and Body Painting of the Thompson Indians* by the anthropologist James Teit while sitting at a tattoo shop waiting to get tattooed. The seed for the revival of Nlaka'pamux tattooing was planted that day in 2006, though it lay dormant for many years. Teit outlined five reasons for tattooing among my ancestors: The first was connected to adornment or ornamentation among young people in order to make themselves more pleasing to potential partners. The second was that tattoos could show fidelity and love, and make marriage enduring. Third, our tattooing was associated with puberty and acquisition of guardians; this included tattoos that ensured success, health, or protection, served as a record or offering, recorded an ordeal to show courage, or were a preventative against weakness and premature old age. Fourth, we practiced tattooing in connection with dreaming and guardian spirits, to ward off death and cure sickness. Finally, tattoos were used for identification.[3]

Teit was not the only ethnographer interested in the history of tattooing. In the article "The World's Oldest Tattoos," the authors comment, "The practice may have originated at least as early as the Upper Paleolithic" (about 40,000 years ago).[4] Several instruments used for tattooing dating between 10,000 BC and 38,000 BC have been located in Europe.[5] Archaeological evidence of tattooing in North America is extensive; one example is the 3,500-year-old Dorset ivory maskette representing a woman with tattooed marks on her face.[6] The recent identification of a tattooing tool found in Utah dating back 2,000 years reveals the practice of tattooing in North American Indigenous realities long before arrivals of colonialist conquerors.[7] Aaron Deter-Wolf and colleagues posit that "Indigenous cultures from every continent except Antarctica included tattooing as an essential element of their cultural fabric."[8]

I recount this history to contextualize that Indigenous peoples inherited ancestral, cultural tattooing traditions. Too often, scholars, academics, tattoo artists, and journalists recount the tale of Captain James Cook and his sailors bringing tattooing from Polynesia to the West. When I see popular culture and academic articles misrepresenting tattooing in the West, void of Indigenous peoples' deep-time and historical context, it reminds me of the intentional attempts to erase us, our bodies, and our tattoos from the colonial landscape. Al Schwartz suggests, "The whole point was to do away with identity. As long as people have identity, they have a sense of place."[9] Our identity erasure has everything to do with thefts of land and destruction of our worldview and lifeways.

Remembering Responsibilities and Meeting Mentors

In 2008, I entered the University of British Columbia Okanagan with a double major in Indigenous studies and philosophy. That year, I walked into a class and was introduced to Syilx (Okanagan) thought through the teaching of one of my mentors, Dr. Jeannette Armstrong. In this class, I became acquainted with the Okanagan story "How Food Was Given." This story showed me how I am part of many communities, and at various levels interconnected to my family, to the larger community, to the environment, and finally to all that is. It has shown me that my contribution and my voice may be the most meaningful songs that will help to regenerate the life of another being.

At a time before humans lived on this earth, the animal people were told by the Creator to figure out how the people-to-be would survive, considering they did not have fur, claws, or a way of gathering nutrients from the earth. With this central question, they convened to discuss this matter. The four chiefs included Black Bear, who represented all the animals that walk on land; Saskatoon Berry, who represented all the fruit-bearing plants; Bitterroot, who represented all the roots; and Salmon, who represented all the creatures in the water. These chiefs sat in a circle facing each other, trying to figure out how these humans would survive. After a long time with no solutions, Saskatoon Berry, Bitterroot, and Salmon all looked to Bear, commenting, "You are the oldest and wisest among us. You tell us what you are going to do." With that, Bear announced that he would give himself and the animals he represented as food for the people. All the other chiefs followed Bear's example.[10]

With that settled, Bear laid down his life to make these things happen. After Bear's gift of his life, all the animal people gathered to sing songs to bring Bear back to life. All the animals sang their songs, and Bear did not come back to life. At various times Fly would buzz by and ask if he could sing his song, but he was shooed away. After everyone had sung their songs, finally, with nothing left to lose, Fly was allowed to sing. He sang, "You laid your life down, you laid your body down."[11] Fly's song was powerful, and Bear came back to life.

At the beginning of the 2009 academic year, I ruptured my spleen, which poisoned my blood and resulted in the deterioration of my aortic valve to the point that I needed replacement surgery. I was forced to withdraw from my classes for the 2009 academic year. During this year recuperating, I applied and was accepted as a tattoo apprentice. I finished my apprenticeship a year later and have been working as a professional tattoo artist since then. As the next academic year approached, I decided I needed to go back and finish my bachelor's degree.

As I reentered academia, I dropped the philosophy major and continued as an Indigenous studies major. In the second semester of 2010–11, I entered the class Indigenous Historical Perspectives. The instructor was Margo Tamez, an invaluable mentor who has become a dear friend and colleague. In this class, the dormant seed that was planted in 2006 began to be nurtured and watered through the reflective reading assignments and keyword lens work. In this course, I produced the final paper "Excavating Cultural Treasure: Indigenous Tattooing in the Northwest of North America," which situated my inquiry into Indigenous tattooing as a process steeped in the Indigenous human rights articulated in the United Nations Declaration on the Rights of Indigenous Peoples (UNDRIP). Specifically, Article 11, Section 1, addresses the rights of Indigenous peoples to develop our cultures.

Throughout my undergraduate and graduate work, I continued to look at the revival of Indigenous tattooing and what it was doing around the world. Fuel for the fire: bringing traditional tattooing back to Indigenous people started with my desire to do something that would help to support youth in their culture. I became curious about theories of modern Western tattooing as a form of identity construction and resistance. Jill Fisher asserts, "Tattooing for Indigenous peoples as well as non-Indigenous can be a means to reappropriate the physical body from the socially diseased body, as a means to resist the cultural forces that have commodified the body and continue to do so"[12] The Māori's revival of Moko (Māori tattooing) as a resistance against "dominant ethnic identity" was further fuel for the revival of Nlaka'pamux tattooing in the light of Article 11, Section 1, of the UNDRIP. The fire in my soul began to roar, and I outlined the beginnings of a tattooing revival movement.

The Papal Ghosts That Haunt the Americas

While much of what I discuss is situated in Canada, there is applicability to the United States. Every ship that left European shores did so with the Doctrine of Discovery propelling expectations to find lands full of resources and populated by exotic, disposable savages. In her research on the Texas-Mexico militarized and walled region, Margo Tamez points to the necessity of examining colonial laws, myth, and propaganda: "To engage and challenge the nineteenth-century Texas creation myth within larger contextual debates on settler colonialism in North America is useful, as such work creates a shared analysis of indigenous cartographic erasures and decolonizes the Texas creation myth and claim to sovereignty premised upon the genealogy of European legal discourses."[13] Certain discourses that Tamez encounters in the United States, Mexico, and Texas archives, such as "'empty/bare/waste lands' and 'terrenos baldios' . . . *terra nullius* and the Doctrine of Discovery," are encountered in the Canadian context.[14] The legal justification at the heart of the Spanish invasion into Indigenous people's lives after 1493 deployed an unthinkable level of violence in the Caribbean, in Mexico, and throughout what would become the United States.

The United States' treaty negotiations with Mexico reveal the continued fruits of the seed of superiority that was previously planted in Europe. When the United States took half of Mexico's territory, it "framed this violent taking as 'an event foreordained by providence, fulfilling the Manifest Destiny of the United States to spread the benefits of democracy to the lesser peoples of the continent.'"[15] However, imperialist propaganda erased the horrific violence borne by Indigenous peoples. Tamez stresses that the legal, political, and policy frameworks used to subjugate Indigenous peoples in the settler bordering of the Americas "were always intertwined in sexual, spiritual, cognitive and material domination."[16] Tamez argues that colonial justifications for the "dehumanization, sexual violence, domination and theft of resources were predicated upon deep indoctrination of Ndé inferiority, barbarism, and violability."[17] The indoctrinating cognitive weapon of *the savage needing saving via civilization* was spread across the Americas through violence. European occupiers spread false representations of Indigenous peoples that served to justify violent suppression of Indigenous uprisings and armed resistances. In sum, a close reading of Tamez's analysis of the uses of colonial propaganda shows that it worked to cast Indigenous peoples as monolithic, animalistic, and disposable monsters, not human beings.

In *Indigenous Identity and Resistance: Researching the Diversity of Knowledge*, Chris Andersen argues that Canada uses considerable resources to maintain control over "the production of symbolic violence," and the deployment of state power creates the illusion that this is "just the way things are." Borrowing from Pierre Bourdieu, Andersen elaborates on how we, as "beings born of a social world," accept a wide range of alleged realities and unquestionable situations.[18] Socially violent worlds are hidden in plain sight; colonization conditioned us to bury our analysis of our oppression and to accept things as they are. Tamez argues that these socially conditioned acts of violence became racist "stock narratives" which settler societies inscribed into the environment, saturating mass consciousness. She states that these discourses, "also known as pioneer myth, lore, and creed, . . . are powerful narratives underpinning the modern nation-state which perpetuate settler-colonialist ideologies [normalizing] colonization, conquest, and manifest destiny."[19]

In bringing civilization, Britain deployed stock narratives using the civilization/savages dichotomy, outlined in the Royal Proclamation of 1763.[20] The Dominion of Canada entrenched the notion of savages in the Indian Act of 1876, articulating apartheid "reserves" and "Indians" into existence.[21] The Indian Act, like its precedents, functions to eradicate Indigenous peoples as autonomous nations with rights to Indigenous lands and territories. The Doctrine of Discovery seeded the 1876 Indian Act's Section 12, whereby the definition of a person is "an individual other than an Indian."[22] In the Indian Act, Canada reveals its moral void, defining who is and isn't Indian, ultimately meaning who is and isn't human.[23] The papal ghosts haunt every treaty, piece of legislation, and decision made by a so-called supreme court, perpetuating the idea that our identity is uncivil or savage.

The attempted erasure and eradication of the Indigenous peoples of the Americas was like a frenzied sprint across the world's oceans by European nations to acquire land and wealth, and certain cognitive tools were used to accomplish the objective of acquiring Indigenous lands. First and foremost, the imperative of superiority informed every enterprise. Superiority created a legal justification for the destruction of peoples for the purpose of land exploitation. Indigenous resistance was the first and continuing hurdle that the imperial and colonial nations had to navigate. The Doctrine of Discovery, which erased Indigenous peoples' humanity, leaving our land metaphorically empty, was a globalized weapon. The myth of the savage was tooled to erase our rights, and used as a justification for our imprisonment and the destruction of our bodies, cultures, and histories.[24]

Mentorship, Mentoring, and Building Community

Throughout my education at the University of British Columbia Okanagan, Margo Tamez was pivotal in my development as an Indigenous scholar and activist. Her mentorship helped to bring out the talents the Creator gifted me with. One of the teachings she shared with me was the importance of including and building community in Indigenous research. Enacting this, Margo included me in her family and community, sharing time in her home with fellow students, visiting with her family as we explored whatever academic issue was on the table, or exploring the lands important to our everyday lived experiences.

In 2012, Margo acted as my supervisor for an Undergraduate Research Award project, which allowed me to conduct research into Nlaka'pamux visual culture. Part of this research was taking a thirty-kilometer hike into the Stein River Valley, at the heart of Nlaka'pamux spiritual life. This valley contains over three hundred pictographs located at over seven or eight sites. At the end of this project, Margo, her family, and I drove three and a half hours to the Stein and I shared with them the beauty of this valley and some of its cultural treasures. We shared food and good conversation during this trip that bonded us. It also emboldened me in my commitment to community engagement and my responsibility to do good in the world.

Adding to that thread, my work as an Nlaka'pamux scholar has been rooted in the Creator's question, "What will you do for the people to be?" ever since I encountered it in 2008 through the Syilx story "How Food Was Given." Although Margo does not phrase the work she does as a scholar, academic, professor, and teacher in this way, the connection is evident. I was introduced to the realities of my relatives who live in the militarized Texas-Mexico border region through Margo and her family's work. Margo provided me with multitudes of examples of what an engaged, ethical Indigenous scholar looks like. The way she weaves her experience as an Ndé (Lipan Apache) woman, activist, mother, scholar, and community member into everything she does has been an invaluable lesson. I was honored when she approached me to work as a research assistant for her SSHRC-funded project Indigenous Women's Refusals to Leave Indigenous Homelands and as an editor and creative consultant for a feature-length documentary film, an ongoing collaboration.

Erasing Tattoos: Erasing the Land from Us

As I honed my skills as a tattoo artist, I continued thinking about the parallels between tattooing and resistance on one hand, and tattoo and cultural erasures on the other. In "Indigenous (Re)inscription: Transmission of Cultural Knowledge(s) Through Tattoos as Resistance," Pauline Alvarez recounts numerous examples of the surgical removal of

Indigenous people's tattoos. She references the notebook of Albert L. Green, an Indian agent who worked in Nebraska from 1869 to 1872, where he outlined his disapproval of an Otoe ceremony. Once the ceremony was banned by the Northern Superintendency, Green recounts, the "greatly prized 'KRAKA' (tattooed) mark" was discredited and "after years was in many cases removed by a surge[o]n, leaving a deep scar."[25] Many examples exist of the forced removal of tattoos from Indigenous people, but some of the most brutal were those enacted by Edward C. Hinkley and the dermatologist Dr. Kenneth Baker. In a presentation to the "Co-Ordinating Council for Research in Indian Education annual conference held in Arizona in 1962," Hinkley described two ways he promoted the removal of tattoos from Tohono O'odham students.[26] He recounted using trichloroacetic acid and a scalpel, saying that "if you go deep enough to get rid of the ink . . . for obvious reasons you will come up with depigmented areas."[27] These mutilations, committed throughout the history of superiority violence in the Americas, highlight the brutalities of attempted erasures of Indigenous peoples' embodied knowledge systems.

As I think through the many ways erasing has been used against us as Indigenous peoples, it becomes challenging to witness the realizations that emerge. Erasing or erasure as a methodology can be expressed in a variety of ways, and examining it exposes realities including the justifications for Indigenous dispossession, denial, loss, seizure, deprivation, destitution, removal, and nonrecognition. Weaponizing law to uphold a racist superiority complex has justified erasures of our rights and lands. Settler laws, deployed through residential school, adoption, and education, erase our self-worth, language, and cultural practices. I have argued that "if my people and I disappear into the multicultural melting pot of the nation state of Canada, and if the only difference that remains is that we have a slightly darker skin tone, then this genocidal history also disappears."[28] If genocide history is whitewashed by policies and legislation, then the nation-state is absolved of its criminal history of child abuse, murder, and land theft. Indigenous decolonizing tattoo practices resist this way of thinking found across settler-colonial systems through embodied articulations of how we are claiming and returning our land, how we are stating the genuine recognition of our rights to self-determination, and how we are embodying the inherent right to be human.

Pauline Alvarez confirms my standpoint when she asserts that settler colonialism physically and metaphysically eliminates Indigenous people so we can no longer contest our dispossession, and that settler-colonial projects necessitate the ongoing erasure and elimination of Indigenous peoples to legitimate settler claims to land.[29] The erasure of my value and my ancestors' value—as human beings with hopes, dreams, relationships, loved ones, emotions, and the ability to feel pain—was and is the cost of settler identity. The land, which my ancestors entrusted me with the responsibility to be a steward of, has become commodified, and I dehumanized. Alvarez reminds us "that the maintenance of Indigenous dispossession demands the disappearance and erasure of Indigenous bodies."[30] Confrontations against violent erasure sustained by *McIvor v. Canada* and *Eloisa Garcia Tamez v. Michael Chertoff et al.* awakened collective embodied belonging and reclamations.

To Keep Our Youth Here One More Day

We emerged into existence through the prayers, ceremonies, and tears that our ancestors offered to the Creator, and, because of this, I understand we have responsibilities. Before, our ancestors could read our lineage, our skills, our dreams, our story, our hopes, and our status etched in our skin. When trained to read our youth's markings, we understand that these are voicing their unique responsibilities and their ancestors' resilience, and that resistance will continue. Today, as before, our tattoos do the healing work and signal our pride and honor at belonging to our ancestral communities and cultures. We are using our tattoos as an avenue to define the reality imposed upon us and to endure.

The year 2010 was pivotal in the development of my future work as a cultural tattoo practitioner because it gave me purpose and motivated me to find a way to help anchor young Indigenous people in their culture. In this year, I was reminded of my own struggle and the struggle that many Indigenous youth have with identity. The Creator asked the animal people, "What will you do for the people to be?" Who we are is related to the question of what we are called to do. From this place, I get my sense of responsibility, and this is the reason I do what I do. If that one mark, that one tattooed line, is enough to keep one of our young people here for one more day, then it is valuable. My responsibility comes from my heart, a heart that wishes my young friends could see the value they have.

Tattoo Revivals with Indigenous Youth from El Calaboz, the Walled Region in the Shadow of the Truth and Reconciliation Commission, British Columbia

The impact and value of interactions we have, for people we visit and interact with, is sometimes overlooked in this fast-paced world. This was definitely true for me when it came to the conversations and interactions I had with Margo's children. The value and impact of our interactions didn't become evident until each one of them reached out to me to collaborate with them on the manifestation of their embodied Ndé tattoo projects. With Milpa and Maura, we collaborated on designing and envisioning what the tattoos would look like, and then I tattooed them, or one of my tattoo students tattooed them. With Hawk, I always enjoyed getting a message or email with questions about what I thought about a design or tattoo idea he had. With each, I could see the movement of these strong youth reclaiming themselves in their indigeneity through their embodied Ndé tattoo projects.

It has been a very special experience for me to see each of Margo's children grow into powerful youth ready to confront the challenges and injustices of this world from an Ndé standpoint. Year after year, I knew they were listening as Margo and I met and talked about my research and her family's struggle in the walled region. Occasionally we would get a chance to chat about the tattoos they might wish to embody and discuss the importance of getting markings that connect us to our ancestors. Each of them has chosen markings that speak to the intergenerational strength and resilience of their ancestors and the violence their immediate family reframed as the good struggle. The experience of working with and alongside Margo, Milpa, Maura, and Hawk confirms my initial hunch that the revival of Indigenous tattooing is connected to healing, affirming, and reaffirming our indigeneity, and can be used as a tool of resistance for their generation.

FIGURE 19.1 "Ripples Across the Generations," by Dion Kaszas. 36" × 48", 2024. A portrait of Margo Tamez: the base red/orange layer is a photograph of an oil painting, and the blue layer is digital overlay.

"Using Something Old to Fix a New Problem"

As a diasporic Nlaka'pamux person, for me the process of reviving our tattooing practices has been one of remembering. When I first stitched my own leg, I began to remember who I was at the deepest core of my being. I began to remember the intergenerational beauty and resilience that is stitched into my genes. I started to remember how I was connected to my ancestors, and not only my Nlaka'pamux ones, but all I am connected to as far back as I can trace and farther. My blood was calling out for me to remember what my responsibilities are. I began to remember the power of the mark. To remember the power of an Indigenous identity.

When I began this work, I had a sense that tattoo reclamation could act as a vehicle for our peoples' healing and grounding in their "true selves."[31] My initial hunch came from my research into historic Nlaka'pamux tattoo practices, and the assertion by James Teit that our "tattooing also served preventive or curative purposes."[32] My comprehension expanded when I read Lars Krutak's "The Power to Cure," which connected the past to the ongoing present, stating that for over "five millennia tattooing has been a permanent part of medicinal culture the world over."[33] Investigating Indigenous trauma and justice, I knew there was a connection between Indigenous truths and tattoo healing methodologies. Krutak further states that "tattooing worked to help negotiate humanity's relationship with the body as it continually struggled with those physiological and spiritual processes that threatened to injure and destroy it."[34] Indigenous youth's experiences navigating colonial borders, familial trauma, and societal numbness are a dire issue. Krutak also states, "Among ancient and more recent cultures, therapeutic tattooing was employed for a variety of ailments to induce physical, psychological, and spiritual healing and well-being."[35] The traditional use of tattooing by Indigenous peoples can be understood to be "a medical epistemology."[36] For Nlaka'pamux and Ndé, the women gave us models for engaging new forms of interlinked spatial resistance beyond borders.

At the Traditional Tattoo Festival held in Kohala, Hawai'i, Julia Mage'au Gray, who is a self-described Papua New Guinean skin marker, gave an inspiring presentation. She posed the question:

> What does it mean versus what does it mean to wear it? Because that's actually the question people should be asking, not what does it mean? Oh it's the centipede. I am strong. It's what does it mean to wear it? It means that I'm connected to my people, my old people's thinking. It means that I am the new old. It means that I am the ancestor. It means that when you look at me you see everybody that came before me, and I know who I am.[37]

We inherited a beautiful, powerful healing technology from our ancestors. As we continue to reinvigorate the medical epistemology of skin marking in our communities, its power will continue to be revealed.

At the core of our beings, many of us feel the effects of centuries of genocidal treatment of our ancestors.[38] In an interview for the exhibition *Body Language*, Corey Bulpitt, a Haida cultural tattoo practitioner, said, "We are using something very old to fix a new problem." My friend and colleague Nahaan, a Tlingit cultural tattoo practitioner, says: "Sometimes clients will have cut marks on their wrists. Some people are cutters and sometimes they don't want to show it anymore, they don't want to see that every day. And so, when I do cover up some of those scars, it is firsthand showing me that they're putting their culture on top of the pain, on top of the traumatic experiences that they've endured."[39] Whether we have physical marks that show the pain that we have endured or not, we can still use our tattoos to cover our minds, hearts, and souls with our culture.

After extensive research into the revival efforts of Indigenous peoples, my original theory that anchoring identity under the skin through the embedding of culture can be a suicide prevention strategy has become a living practice of revitalizing well-being through cultural revitalization. Our use of ancestral tattooing is a reinvigoration of medical epistemologies of our ancestors, and it makes these visible to our youth for cultural continuity.[40]

#TattooMedicine

The tattoos that currently living Indigenous peoples embody assert that the colonial and imperial attempts to erase us are unsuccessful. As I have said elsewhere, "Tattooing for many Indigenous folks today is medicine reconnecting us to our communities, traditions, and the core of our beings. It is medicine that begins the process of healing from generation after generation of trauma."[41] In "Expression of Identity: Māori Ta Moko and the Utilization of the Internet," Lingeia D. Gorre notes, "After more than 130 years of being kept in a state of limited power, the indigenous peoples of Aotearoa/New Zealand conceived the Maori Renaissance as a form of resistance and reclamation of identity as power."[42] Indigenous peoples are investing themselves in knowing that our identity is our power. Our personal identification, as Nlaka'pamux, Maori, Samoan, Cree, or Métis, is the foundation from which our souls and our nations will rise. I see the revitalization of Nlaka'pamux tattooing as reclaiming our culture, identity, and ways of living and being in this world. It is taking back our bodies and reconnecting us to our communities and relationships and our ancestors and heritage. "When we embody our traditional markings, we are resisting colonialism and affirming who we are, making us visible as Indigenous people to ourselves and to the world."[43]

Many of the folks I tattooed were tattooed with their ancestral marks. This is a way of asserting the resilience and autonomy of their nations, communities, and peoples. These tattoos are communicative tools speaking to diverse audiences, and a continuation of one of the traditional functions of our tattoos. Our tattoos speak to those in our communities in many similar ways to the ways they did in our ancestral communities. Today, our tattoos also speak to a different, broader audience—the colonial structures that have perpetrated genocidal violence against our land and peoples in the past, in the present, and into the future.

In the story of the four chiefs, humanity's place in the circle was a topic of important debate, and they convened to discuss it. Gathering together, they decided that all life is inextricably connected. The song of the humble fly, symbolizing those deemed less important by the dominant, tellingly embodies truth to power. When our warriors, wearing our tattoos, stand against destructive oil extraction, mining, walls, and political violence, they assert our continued unsurrendered rights to be stewards of our lands. Today our tattoos speak in different ways than our ancestors' tattoos did because of the contexts we find ourselves in as Indigenous peoples confronting colonial regimes. Our tattoos speak to and honor those who ensured we are still here today. My Nlaka'pamux tattoos are prayers for my nephews, my nieces, and the people to be. Our tattoos stand as a testament to our brilliance, our resilience, and our continuing struggle, as we keep gathering together to make this world better for the coming generations.

NOTES

1. Bill C-31, An Act to Amend the Indian Act (33rd Parliament, 1st Session, 1985).
2. Dion Kaszas, "Embodying the Past in the Present for the Future: Practicing, Supporting, and Highlighting Indigenous Tattoo Revivals Through Indigenous and Creative Research Methodologies" (MA thesis, University of British Columbia, 2018), 13.
3. James Teit, *Tattooing and Face and Body Painting of the Thompson Indians of British Columbia*, ed. Franz Boas (Washington, D.C.: Government Printing Office, 1930; repr., Salinas, Calif.: Coyote Press), 406.
4. Aaron Deter-Wolf et al., "The World's Oldest Tattoos," *Journal of Archaeological Science* 5 (2016): 2, http://dx.doi.org/10.1016/j.jasrep.2015.11.007.
5. Steve Gilbert, *Tattoo History: A Source Book* (New York: Juno Books, 2000), 11.
6. Lars Krutak, *The Tattooing Arts of Tribal Women* (London: Bennett & Bloom; Desert Hearts, 2007), 146.
7. Andrew Gillreath-Brown et al., "Redefining the Age of Tattooing in Western North America: A 2000-Year-Old Artifact from Utah," *Journal of Archaeological Science: Reports* 24 (2019): 1064–75.

8. Deter-Wolf et al., "World's Oldest Tattoos," 1.
9. Rachel Uranga, "Marks Across Time: For Some California Indians, Facial Tattoos Make a Bold Connection to a Fading Tradition," *The Sacramento Bee*, August 31, 2001.
10. Sources for the story: Okanagan Tribal Council, *Kou-skelowh / We Are the People: A Trilogy of Okanagan Legends* (Penticton, B.C.: Theytus Books Ltd., 2004) (quote at 13); Okanagan Nation Alliance, "Four Food Chiefs Sculpture," Okanagan College (website), accessed April 13, 2025, https://www.okanagan.bc.ca/indigenization/four-food-chiefs, under the section "How food was given captikʷł."
11. Okanagan Tribal Council, *Kou-skelowh*, 25.
12. Jill Fisher, "Tattooing the Body, Marking Culture," *Body and Society* 8, no. 4 (2002): 104, https://doi.org/10.1177/1357034X02008004005.
13. Margo Tamez, "dáanzho ha'shi' 'dał'k'ida', 'áá'áná', 'doo maanaashni': Welcoming 'Long Ago', 'Way Back' and 'Remember'—as an Ndé Decolonization and Land Recovery Process," *Intensions* 6 (Fall/Winter 2012): 4.
14. Tamez, "dáanzho ha'shi," 4.
15. Tamez, "dáanzho ha'shi," 5, citing Richard Griswold del Castillo, *The Treaty of Guadalupe Hidalgo* (Norman: University of Oklahoma Press, 1990), xii.
16. Margo Tamez, "Indigenous Women's Rivered Refusals in El Calaboz," *Diálogo* 19, no. 1 (2016): 15, https://doi.org/10.1353/dlg.2016.0030.
17. Tamez, "Rivered Refusals," 15.
18. Chris Andersen, "Mixed Ancestry or Métis?," in *Indigenous Identity and Resistance: Researching the Diversity of Knowledge*, ed. Brendan Hokowhitu et al. (Dunedin: Otago University Press, 2010), 29.
19. Tamez, "Rivered Refusals," 7.
20. Gerald Hallowell, ed., *The Oxford Companion to Canadian History* (Oxford: Oxford University Press, 2004), s.v., "Royal Proclamation of 1763," https://doi.org/10.1093/acref/9780195415599.001.0001.
21. An Act to Amend and Consolidate the Laws Respecting Indians, S.C. 1876, c. 18 (Can.).
22. Tracey Lindberg, "The Doctrine of Discovery in Canada," in *Discovering Indigenous Lands: The Doctrine of Discovery in the English Colonies*, ed. Robert Miller (Oxford: Oxford University Press, 2010), 117.
23. Tracey Lindberg, "Contemporary Canadian Resonance of an Imperial Doctrine," in Miller, *Discovering Indigenous Lands*, 140.
24. Tamez, "Rivered Refusals," 8.
25. Richard E. Jensen, ed., "Agent to the Oto: The Recollections of Albert Lambron Green," *Nebraska History* 69 (Winter 1988): 179–80.
26. Pauline Alvarez, "Indigenous (Re)inscription: Transmission of Cultural Knowledge(s) Through Tattoos as Resistance," in *Tattoo Histories: Transcultural Perspectives on the Narratives, Practices, and Representations of Tattooing*, ed. Sinah Theres Kloss (New York: Routledge, 2019), 7.

27. Quoted in Alvarez, "Indigenous (Re)inscription," 7.
28. Kaszas, "Embodying the Past," 51.
29. Alvarez, "Indigenous (Re)inscription," 2.
30. Alvarez, "Indigenous (Re)inscription," 7, 8, paraphrasing Leanne B. Simpson.
31. Kaszas, "Embodying the Past," 124.
32. Teit, *Tattooing*, 407.
33. Lars Krutak, "The Power to Cure: A Brief History of Therapeutic Tattooing," in *Tattoos and Body Modifications in Antiquity: Proceedings of the Sessions at the EAA Annual Meetings in The Hague and Oslo, 2010–11*, ed. Philippe Della Casa and Constanze Witt (The Hague: Chronos, 2013), 33.
34. Krutak, "Power to Cure," 33.
35. Lars Krutak, "Therapeutic Tattooing in the Arctic: Ethnographic, Archaeological, and Ontological Frameworks of Analysis," *International Journal of Paleopathology* 25 (June 2019): 100, https://doi.org/10.1016/j.ijpp.2018.05.003.
36. Krutak, "Therapeutic Tattooing in the Arctic," 9.
37. Julia Mage'au Gray, presentation at Traditional Tattoo Festival, Kohala, Hawai'i, October 27, 2019.
38. Dion Kaszas, "Echoes of the Ancestors: Inherited Knowledge and Responsibilities," in *Body Language: Reawakening Cultural Tattooing of the Northwest*, ed. Beth Carter and Dion Kaszas (Vancouver: Bill Reid Gallery of Northwest Coast Art, 2018), 13.
39. Nahaan, presentation at Earthline Tattoo Training Residency, University of British Columbia Okanagan, Kelowna, B.C., July 25, 2016.
40. Dion Kaszas, "Ep 001 Introduction to the Transformative Marks Podcast with Indigenous Tattoo Artist Dion Kaszas," video, 38:27, YouTube, posted on January 9, 2024, by Dion Kaszas, https://youtu.be/OkcK0HEmJqQ.
41. Kaszas, "Echoes of the Ancestors," 14.
42. Lingereia D. Gorre, "Expression of Identity: Maori Ta Moko and the Utilization of the Internet" (MFA thesis, University of Southern California, 2007), 21, ProQuest.
43. Kaszas, "Echoes of the Ancestors," 12.

BIBLIOGRAPHY

Alvarez, Pauline. "Indigenous (Re)inscription: Transmission of Cultural Knowledge(s) Through Tattoos as Resistance." In *Tattoo Histories: Transcultural Perspectives on the Narratives, Practices, and Representations of Tattooing*, edited by Sinah Theres Kloss, 157–75. New York: Routledge, 2019.

Andersen, Chris. "Mixed Ancestry or Métis?" In *Indigenous Identity and Resistance: Researching the Diversity of Knowledge*, edited by Brendan Hokowhitu et al. Dunedin: Otago University Press, 2010.

Deter-Wolf, Aaron, Benoît Robitaille, Lars Krutak, and Sébastien Galliot. "The World's Oldest Tattoos." *Journal of Archaeological Science* 5 (2016): 19–24. http://dx.doi.org/10.1016/j.jasrep.2015.11.007.

Fisher, Jill. "Tattooing the Body, Marking Culture." *Body and Society* 8, no. 4 (2002): 99–107. https://doi.org/10.1177/1357034X02008004005.

Gilbert, Steve. *Tattoo History: A Source Book*. New York: Juno Books, 2000.

Gillreath-Brown, Andrew, Aaron Deter-Wolf, Karen R. Adams, Valerie Lynch-Holm, Samantha Fulgham, Shannon Tushingham, William D. Lipe, and R. G. Matson. "Redefining the Age of Tattooing in Western North America: A 2000-Year-Old Artifact from Utah." *Journal of Archaeological Science: Reports* 24 (2019): 1064–75.

Gorre, Lingereia D. "Expression of Identity: Maori Ta Moko and the Utilization of the Internet." MFA thesis, University of Southern California, 2007. ProQuest.

Gray, Julia Mage'au. Presentation at Traditional Tattoo Festival, Kohala, Hawai'i, October 27, 2019.

Hallowell, Gerald, ed. *The Oxford Companion to Canadian History*. Oxford: Oxford University Press, 2004. https://doi.org/10.1093/acref/9780195415599.001.0001.

Jensen, Richard E., ed. "Agent to the Oto: The Recollections of Albert Lambron Green." *Nebraska History* 69 (Winter 1988): 169–81.

Kaszas, Dion. "Echoes of the Ancestors: Inherited Knowledge and Responsibilities." In *Body Language: Reawakening Cultural Tattooing of the Northwest*, edited by Beth Carter and Dion Kaszas, 6–25. Vancouver: Bill Reid Gallery of Northwest Coast Art, 2018.

Kaszas, Dion. "Embodying the Past in the Present for the Future: Practicing, Supporting, and Highlighting Indigenous Tattoo Revivals Through Indigenous and Creative Research Methodologies." MA thesis, University of British Columbia, 2018.

Kaszas, Dion. "Ep 001 Introduction to the Transformative Marks Podcast with Indigenous Tattoo Artist Dion Kaszas." Video, 38:27. YouTube, posted on January 9, 2024, by Dion Kaszas. https://youtu.be/OkcK0HEmJqQ.

Krutak, Lars. "The Power to Cure: A Brief History of Therapeutic Tattooing." In *Tattoos and Body Modifications in Antiquity: Proceedings of the Sessions at the EAA Annual Meetings in The Hague and Oslo, 2010–11*, edited by Philippe Della Casa and Constanze Witt, 27–34. The Hague: Chronos, 2013.

Krutak, Lars. *The Tattooing Arts of Tribal Women*. London: Bennett & Bloom; Desert Hearts, 2007.

Krutak, Lars. "Therapeutic Tattooing in the Arctic: Ethnographic, Archaeological, and Ontological Frameworks of Analysis." *International Journal of Paleopathology* 25 (June 2019): 99–109. https://doi.org/10.1016/j.ijpp.2018.05.003.

Lindberg, Tracey. "Contemporary Canadian Resonance of an Imperial Doctrine." In *Discovering Indigenous Lands: The Doctrine of Discovery in the English Colonies*, edited by Robert Miller, 126–70. Oxford: Oxford University Press, 2010.

Lindberg, Tracey. "The Doctrine of Discovery in Canada." In *Discovering Indigenous Lands: The Doctrine of Discovery in the English Colonies*, edited by Robert Miller, 89–125. Oxford: Oxford University Press, 2010.

Nahaan. Presentation at Earthline Tattoo Training Residency, University of British Columbia Okanagan, Kelowna, B.C., July 25, 2016.

Okanagan Nation Alliance. "Four Food Chiefs Sculpture." Okanagan College (website). Accessed April 13, 2025. https://www.okanagan.bc.ca/indigenization/four-food-chiefs.

Okanagan Tribal Council. *Kou-skelowh / We Are the People: A Trilogy of Okanagan Legends*. Penticton, B.C.: Theytus Books Ltd., 2004.

Tamez, Margo. "dáanzho ha'shi' 'dał'f'ida', 'áá'áná', 'doo maanaashni': Welcoming 'Long Ago', 'Way Back' and 'Remember'—as an Ndé Decolonization and Land Recovery Process." *Intensions* 6 (Fall/Winter 2012): 1–23.

Tamez, Margo. "Indigenous Women's Rivered Refusals in El Calaboz." *Diálogo* 19, no. 1 (2016): 7–21. https://doi.org/10.1353/dlg.2016.0030.

Teit, James. *Tattooing and Face and Body Painting of the Thompson Indians of British Columbia*. Edited by Franz Boas. Repr., Salinas, Calif.: Coyote Press. First published 1930 by the Government Printing Office (Washington, D.C.).

Uranga, Rachel. "Marks Across Time: For Some California Indians, Facial Tattoos Make a Bold Connection to a Fading Tradition." *The Sacramento Bee*, August 31, 2001.

TWENTY

Máashdlógee | Butterfly

MILPA MENDOZA

Tattoo by Amberley John
Photography by Pierre Richard

Amberley John tattooed me in September of 2018. My tattoo is of a butterfly, in black ink on the side of my neck. It's detailed with an intricate pattern. I decided to ask Amberley to tattoo me because a huge part of me wanted a big change. At the time, I was questioning my identity and unsure of whether or not I was even happy. The butterfly was kind of like a promise of change. I wanted to be brave and to face the world, and for that reason I chose a butterfly to be tattooed on my neck.

FIGURE 20.1 Portrait of Milpa Mendoza and her butterfly tattoo. Tattoo by Amberley John. Photograph by Pierre Richard, 2018.

The tattoo was empowering. Suddenly I felt so edgy [*laughs in cringe*], and it felt like a redo. Like in movies when the main character makes a mistake and there's a montage that depicts all the ways they become a better person. I think I had to make mistakes in order to understand my own bad habits and hold myself accountable. My butterfly from Amberley serves as a reminder of good memories, and bad ones too. Somehow I can't remember what it was like to not have this tattoo because it was very instrumental in the development of myself over the past five or six years of my life. I think we develop our true selves over time, and artistic expression can represent a time in our lives that ultimately gives us a meaningful perspective.

TWENTY-ONE

Hadndín | Pollen

MAURA TAMEZ

Tattoo by Amberley John
Photograph by Ashleigh Galaxie

The first tattoo I got was a sketch of cattails I drew on the back of a receipt a couple summers after my coming-of-age ceremony. Amberley John did the tattoo in the backyard where my mother lives on the OKIB reserve (Okanagan Indian Band No. 1). Cattails as my first tattoo were significant for me as they are an important medicine in my life. I am honored to have Amberley as the artist, and it felt special knowing how tattooing has impacted her as an artist.

FIGURE 21.1 Maura Tamez's forearm with tattoo. Tattoo by Amberley John, 2018. Photograph by Ashleigh Galaxie, 2024.

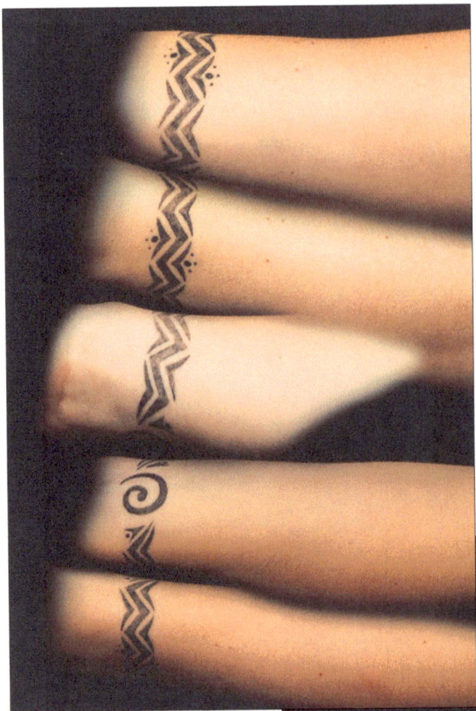

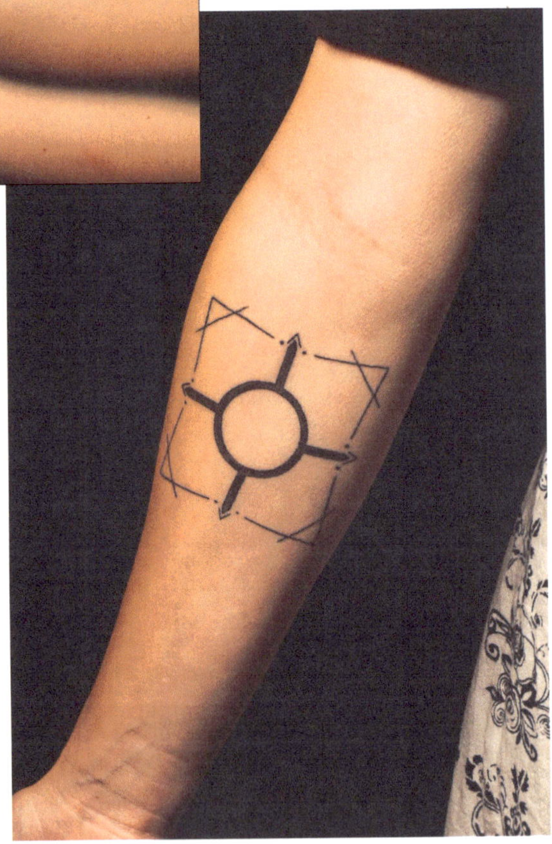

FIGURES 22.1 AND 22.2 Myst Tamez-Hrabovsky's forearms and tattoos. Tattoos designed by Myst Tamez-Hrabovsky, 2019. Photography by Pierre Richard, 2019.

TWENTY-TWO

Shits'ís | I Am

MYST TAMEZ-HRABOVSKY

Designed by Myst Tamez-Hrabovsky
Photography by Pierre Richard
[Concept: Among the first Indigenous generation born in the first decade of the twenty-first century, Indigenous youth exist and claim existence differently than what is imagined by society, community, and family. Being raised in Indigenous community at this time, during Earth-wide shifts, has impacted everything.]

I was seventeen or so (late 2019) when I got my tattoos. These are my own art designs that I got tattooed. Honestly, this was a way for me to stop harming myself. I struggled a lot with my mental stability when I was younger, a lot more than I do now. I needed some type of reminder for when I wasn't in control of my body, to not harm it. So I put my art on the parts of my body I harmed the most. It worked, and now I want more tattoos, not for the same reasons, but just to feel more love for my own body. I see tattoos as a way to help my mental health connect to my physical body in a good way that makes me happy to admire my body as my own, not something separate from me.

TWENTY-THREE

Shash hant'á | Bear Chief

HAWK MENDOZA

Photography by Michelle Alvarez
[Concept: Recovering and reclaiming the reawakening of Bear clan within Lower Rio Grande River peoples' manhood and matriarchal kinship, through revitalizing Ndé storytelling, healing, addressing trauma and body memory, oral tradition, and Indigenous male self-care and healing.]

I'm an Ndé storyteller and performer. Forgiveness (of myself and others) has been one of the hardest journeys. I am recognizing that I can overcome traumas through a deeper commitment to my personal healing. The challenges of racism and oppression, violence against women, the police state, bail bond oppression, capitalism, genocide, destruction of

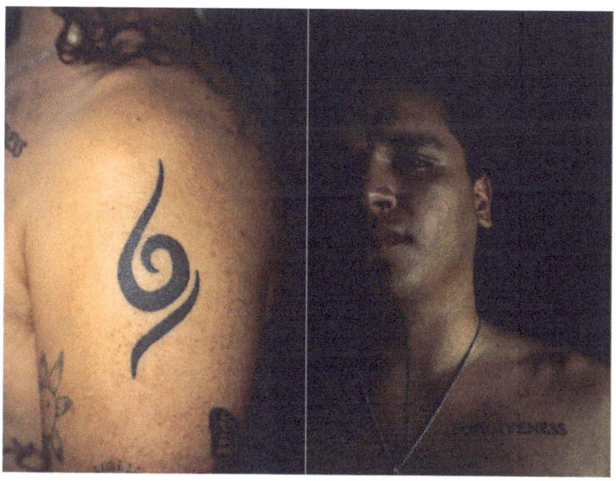

FIGURE 23.1 Portraits of Hawk Mendoza and tattoos. Photography by Michelle Alvarez.

Mother Earth, inflation, housing and food insecurity, and fascism are very real and painful day-to-day realities. I dream of reclaiming and re-awakening Ndé healing arts, bringing back Ndé storytelling, and living humbly in balance. I enjoy traveling to our healing places in the mountains across our territory, and want to do this more so that we will be healing, addressing trauma and body memory, awakening the oral tradition, and living more healthily together.

PART V

Epistemological and Methodological Interventions for Decolonized Futures

iłeg͟ozhiish, yiskao, aandahyé | through time, tomorrow, farther (movement into future)

TWENTY-FOUR

The *Wame* Still There

KOYANA FLOTTE

The *wame* or creosote bush (*Larrea tridentata*) is revered as a symbol of transition, encountered as a blessing to those journeying from life to death. When a United States Marine shot Esequiel Hernández in 1997, the wame and Esequiel's goats stood as the last witnesses to his murder. Esequiel's death pierced across the U.S.-Mexico borderscape, leaving many of us scarred for life. At the time, I was just a second grader, living in Ojinaga, Chihuahua, the nearest Mexican city to the place where Esequiel was shot, and bordering the town of Presidio, Texas, at the junction of the Concho and Rio Grande rivers. His story profoundly influenced my life, ultimately leading me to pursue a doctoral degree in sociocultural anthropology with a focus on better understanding the spatial, technological, and social assemblages of borders worldwide. I became intrigued by the infrastructure of the border landscape in places beyond the Texas-Chihuahua border, which led me to travel and conduct ethnographic research throughout Honduras, Guatemala, Mexico, and various cities in or near the modern U.S.-Mexico border.

Over the last decade, I have studied practices of border-making,[1] or what I have come to define as the assembling and disassembling of borders. For several years, I conducted research attempting to understand the United States' and Mexico's shifting approaches to the enforcement of unauthorized migration from 2015 to 2020 by accompanying individuals, small groups, and "caravans" of LGBTQ+ Central American and Mexican refugees traveling from southern Mexico to the U.S.-Mexico border, and visiting them for several years during the time they spent in immigration detention in the United States. This research led me to discern that a critical component of borders is how they shape the way people envision their own identity, an idea that is somewhat related to the arguments presented in this chapter.

As Ayuujk (Mixe) scholar Yásnaya Aguilar writes in "The Map and the Territory," "The establishment of a world divided into nation-states, known as countries, is very recent in the history of humanity. . . . The existence of these countries as naturally given entities has been so powerful that it has taken over our imaginations and our identity narratives."[2] In line with Aguilar's argument framing borders as an artificial phenomenon, my work analyzes the border as an assemblage of security and militarization rather than an inherent characteristic of a people's culture and ecology. While borders have real and sometimes fatal consequences for those who are illegalized and those experiencing militarization in their homelands, they do not define the physical landscape or the cultural identity of the people who inhabit these spaces. Instead, borders are part of a larger network of human and nonhuman influences that shape our experiences in these lands.

By juxtaposing the colonial and postcolonial borders with the ancient wame, I can cultivate a nuanced understanding of their temporal dimensions. The wame, a nonlinear and enduring entity that predates contemporary border-control technologies, allows me to shift the focus away from the conventional notion of the "borderland" in relation to the stories we tell about family, territory, and home. My analysis does not elevate the borderland over the homeland; rather, it acknowledges the historical lineage of borders as carceral sites of hypersurveillance, underpinned by the exploitation of displaced individuals through forced labor, enslavement, deportation, and death.

The thousand-year-old wame bush challenges prevailing narratives that seek to define our communities through borders and checkpoints. The wame reminds us to center the natural ecosystems of the land and the cultural diversity that Indigenous peoples, immigrants, and others bring to these places. Examining the history of deportation and bondage of Indigenous people in the Chihuahuan Desert through the Spanish colonial archive reveals the birth of the colonial borderline as a technology of control and as a source of capital for slave hunters and other mercenaries seeking to profit from practices of border-making. This same phenomenon became evident during my time as an ethnographer and human rights advocate conducting research and volunteering along the migrant routes in Mexico and Central America. When displaced people and immigrants are scapegoated, they become accessible targets for employers, gang members, and states, and are often denied basic human rights and dignity.

In this chapter, I engage with the capturing, deportation, and enslavement of Lipan Apache and other Indigenous communities from the early eighteenth century to the beginning of the nineteenth century, or what I refer to as "one hundred years of chains." These approximately one hundred years of chains represent a specific historical period of interaction between the Spanish Crown and the mobile Apache Nation, which, I propose, included some initial historical configurations that rely on the use of a line as a dividing mechanism to produce borders that differentiate distinct conceptions of a "nation" or a self-governing sovereign body. That mechanism is often fueled by forced and enslaved labor. The production of the line, nourished by the capital gained from human enslavement and land theft, often had an end goal for those who refused to be enslaved and for those who remained peaceful. My hope is to provide a better understanding of the impact of the Spanish colonial government and to produce a more systematic approach to its practices of border-making, particularly its policing of the migration of the Ndé (Lipan Apache) and other Natives in the region of Nueva Vizcaya in the Provincias Internas, roughly present-day Chihuahua, as well as parts of present-day Arizona, Sonora, Durango, Coahuila, and Texas. The primary evidence used here is archival work conducted in the summer of 2016 at Mexico's National Archive, or Archivo General de la Nación, located in Mexico City, as well as extensive secondary sources. The questions that I attempt to answer are: What imaginary and physical conception of the Spanish colonial "borderline" was created by means of Native displacement in the 1700s and 1800s in the northern Spanish frontier? What is the relationship between the making of the Spanish borderline and Indigenous mass deportation and transcontinental practices of enslavement? Can this legacy of the borderscape inform how we understand, imagine, and define the border as a component within a homeland?

It is my goal in this chapter to contest the designation of Native communities as merely "prisoners of war" or as "opposing rebels" rather than as peaceful members of a people, a tribe, or a nation who held dogmatic notions of land, territory, and practices of treaty-making.[3] Some clans or bands produced Ndé leaders who became renowned diplomats who negotiated peace with the Spanish, as well as many other colonizing governments such as Mexico and Texas, to safeguard and protect their families as their homelands became more inevitably militarized. The Spanish system of deporting the Apache far away from their homeland can be described as one of the earliest uses of deportation by a governing power to prevent or complicate people's return. In identifying the borderscape, I hope to provide a framework that challenges the normalization and romanticization of our homelands as cultural laboratories of border death. The wame is a reminder that our identities can exist outside of these structures and imaginaries of militarization and death that continue to be imposed on the land. I hope the following archives illustrate everything that the people lost to transnational deportation, forced labor, and enslavement, and ensure that their descendants know their story.

The documents used here were selected from among hundreds of letters between Spanish military officials and the Spanish Crown examined by the author. Each chosen document points to a particular aspect of the uses of language and the military strategies employed by the Spanish Crown to control and demarcate the borderline, followed by the deportation and enslavement of those who became the main target of these military strategies.

The theoretical goal of this chapter is to analytically bifurcate the borderland and the homeland, and to attempt to trace the origins of borders as sites of influx control, enslavement, persecution, deportation, and death. The second task is to examine how the image of the border has become normalized, mobilized, and ingrained in contemporary understandings of sovereignty, cartography, and collective identity in these regions. I do this by writing in opposition to the analytical normalization and, at times, romanticization of present-day homelands located within the bounds of juridical borders and checkpoints. I critique the trope of the “fronteriza/o/e” (from the border) subject, as this misinterprets the homeland and centers the borderland by analyzing “the border” as a place that can only be understood through crossings, as opposed to a place of living where land holds history and memory.

This is not to say that borderlands or “fronterismos” are illegitimate. However, examining the long history of a people and place—in this case, Lipan Apache persecution, enslavement, and deportation—allows us to better grasp the history of the policing of Indigenous people and how it impacts and transforms a place and its people. In writing that the wame is still there, I analyze processes of border-making, not only as a genealogy of the colonial archive or the state, but also through the long-standing spatial presence of the wame.

The Line, the Piece, and the *Collera*

Spanish practices of border-making, spatial control, forced labor, and enslavement in the “northern frontier” began well before the 1700s. The practice of forced unpaid labor and enslavement was documented as early as the 1560s, when the Spanish first attempted to establish a mining town with an adjacent mission in the city of Santa Bárbara, Nueva Vizcaya, located on the Concho River, the homeland of the Tapalcomes, a band of the Concho Nation.[4] The use of Native Americans to work the silver mines came to a halt after various groups rebelled against the Spanish monarchy, influenced by the Tepehuán Revolt of 1617 and the Pueblo Revolt and its aftermath (1680–96) in New Mexico.[5]

By the 1700s, the Concho, Julime, Chiso, and many other communities in La Junta de los Ríos had increasingly become missionized. Others were forced to flee from their traditional villages, often allying and intermarrying with Indigenous communities living in the region. This posed a challenge to the Spanish control of the area for the next few decades, as La Junta natives maintained old alliances and forged new ones with the Lipan Apache by assimilating them into the local culture. For much of the period from the early 1600s to the mid-1700s, the Native American communities of La Junta de los Ríos, such as the Lipan Apache and the People of La Junta, shared customs, language, and ceremonies.[6] One significant ceremony that fostered solidarity across many regions was the peyote medicine ceremony. The People of La Junta, mainly the Julimes, introduced this practice to the Lipan Apache, and it has since spread throughout North America in the beliefs of the Native American Church and other autonomous religious groups. This network of cooperation enabled La Junta's Native communities to preserve customs, language, and millennia-old cultural traditions, which continue among their descendants today.

In the mid-eighteenth century, Spanish colonial policy underwent a significant shift as territorial control became paramount to maintaining colonial stability. Facing Indigenous resistance that had dismantled an older infrastructure of control, the Spanish redefined their approach through the systematic demarcation of an imagined "line" along their proposed colonial borders.[7] This line served as a technique of border-making. It became an emerging and sometimes effective tool for containing Native communities and curbing their seasonal migrations, which were vital for hunting, trade, and the sustenance of Indigenous economies and lifeways.

As evidenced in the recommendations by Hugo O'Conor, a military governor made a "border czar" by the Spanish viceroy in 1767, the Spanish colonial government's main goal between the mid-eighteenth century and the beginning of the nineteenth was to eliminate the Lipan Apache, as recommended by various military officials including Cayetano María Pignatelli Rubí Corbera y Saint Clement, or the Marqués de Rubí, for short.[8] The Marqués de Rubí became instrumental in establishing a modern system of security and control for the Spanish borderlines, which relied on significantly more military control than the previous mission system had. The Marqués de Rubí was tasked with investigating and resolving the "Apache problem." His recommendation was to reorganize New Spain's northern frontier defenses along a cordon of fifteen presidios, each about one hundred miles apart, that would stretch from the Gulf of California to the mouth of the Guadalupe River in Texas, connecting military posts to exert Spanish juridical power over the region more effectively.[9] The organization of this new "bordered" space recommended by Rubí, and later by Croix, included a more peaceful approach to relations with Native peoples in the region.[10] The Spanish would effectively seek to dismantle Native sovereignty, using borders not only as territorial markers but as instruments of suppression and enforced settlement—what could be considered a Spanish infrastructure of borders that relied on placing Native American peoples into colonial reservation-style settlements.

In writing, the Spanish regulations of the eighteenth century occasionally emphasized protecting "peaceful" Apache bands, but in practice, entire families, including young children, were subjected to transnational deportation. By 1780, the term "Apache pieces" in colonial records reflects the commodification of Lipan Apache lives, disregarding diplomatic efforts by leaders like Indio Pascual, an Ndé chief who fostered peace between the Lipan Apache and Spanish authorities. Pascual, followed by Picax Ande Instłe (Strong Arm) or "El Calvo," founded and protected several Ndé rancherías in the Chihuahuan Desert, providing some stability for Indigenous communities amid intensifying colonial aggressions. Yet these peace agreements were systematically violated by the *soldados de cuera*, or the Spanish cavalry, tasked with capturing "criminals" and maintaining Spanish border lines. Initially volunteer units, the soldados de cuera or "leather soldiers" would eventually evolve into paid enforcers, cementing their presence in Spanish campaigns across the U.S. Southwest and repressing many Indigenous efforts at challenging the institution of the borderline.

The first reported deportation of Apache people was documented as early as 1720,[11] and this treatment was made official in the Spanish Regulations of 1737, which were the Spanish colonial government's attempt at establishing a Spanish defense, resulting in the incarceration and deportation of Lipan Apache leader Cabellos Colorados and twenty other leaders to Mexico City.[12] The Spanish Regulations of 1729 would later evolve into the demarcation of a more proper "cordon" or "line" in the Regulations of 1772, which legalized the deportation of *indios bárbaros* (rebellious Natives) to Mexico and the Caribbean. The last documented *collera* (group of chained prisoners) of Apaches deported to Cuba occurred in 1816.[13]

As documented by scholars of the mid- to late nineteenth century, this system was also later challenged by Native solidarity, the shifting mechanisms of forced labor and enslavement, Native warfare, and, later, the birth of the modern nation-state in the nineteenth century.

In *La ruta del horror*, Hernán Maximiliano Venegas Delgado and Carlos Manuel Valdés Dávila write the following:

> The conditions in which the colleras transported and placed in custody in the intermediate places of their long genocidal march implied true horror for their members. The inventory of horror is overwhelming: previous combat wounds poorly cared for after being imprisoned, conditions of intense cold or suffocating heat, inadequate clothing if not the virtual absence of these, absence of shoes, diseases and epidemics suffered in Indian nations. Whether they knew them or they did not know them, deaths or new injuries due to escapes, mistreatment of all kinds, including collars, shackles, handcuffs, etc., poor nutrition, and many other expressions of the Spanish genocidal policy were commonplace. We will then see the conditions in which they were finally enslaved in their main destination: Havana, Cuba, as well as their brave expressions of rebellion there, to avoid the final holocaust of these peoples.[14]

The 1772 regulations included the construction of the San Vicente and San Carlos presidios in the Chihuahuan Desert, which were later relocated to nearby sites as Native migration patterns shifted. Hugo O'Conor was tasked with implementing Rubí's recommendations by establishing a chain of military posts to "maintain the line." In a broader sense, the Regulations of 1772 attempted to simultaneously "reward" Native American allies who supported the persecution and detention of "*indios bárbaros*, pagans, and apostates" who opposed assimilation, and at the same time encourage their total eradication. By 1775, each defense "garrison" had been entirely constructed by its respective presidio, and this arrangement continued until commander-general Teodoro de Croix proposed a new resettlement policy in 1780. Teodoro de Croix reevaluated the relationship between the presidios and local "peaceful" Indigenous communities and implemented a new approach that consisted of aiding the repopulation of these "abandoned frontiers" by using the local Native people to patrol their presidios against Native rebels. Croix would later deactivate the San Vicente and San Carlos presidios, negotiating a peaceful settlement with the Lipan Apache and the Mescalero in 1790 by La Junta de los Ríos, present-day Presidio, Texas, and Ojinaga, Chihuahua.

Environmental challenges such as drought, scarcity, and increased mercenary activity led many Mescalero and Lipan Apache families to relocate. Some migrated to New Mexico, others to South Texas. However, without formal records of all Indigenous prisoners deported to Cuba, estimates suggest that between sixty and one hundred thousand Indigenous people, primarily children and adolescents, endured forced marches from the Provincias Internas to Caribbean servitude.

The Spanish concept of border-making, exemplified in the Marqués de Rubí's 1768 military report to the Crown, echoed this expansionist ethos. His description of the "front of our line" reflects a tactic to solidify their settler-colonial control, exploiting Indigenous territory and bodies for Spanish economic gain in the slave industry. The Rio Grande's designation as a boundary marks an early form of geographical containment predating the nineteenth-century Mexican and American cartographic lines, demonstrating a rhetorical and historical continuity in border creation as a means of subjugation and violence in the same locations as today.

By the late eighteenth century, colonial documents reveal an escalating targeting of Indigenous family systems, with children increasingly being noted in Spanish documents as "Apache pieces." Despite diplomatic efforts by Indigenous leaders, Spanish officials pursued a relentless agenda of maintaining local populations imprisoned in reservation-style practices of border-making. As a result, families who resisted forced resettlement sought refuge along the U.S.-Mexico border in small, iso-

> *Enterado la carta de 26 de octubre . . . La salida del Inspector Hugo O'Connor a la colocación y establecimiento de Presidios . . . construido . . . en el cuidado de atender y cuidar la defensa y resguardo de estos terrenos*
>
> *Dios (¿?) 24 de (¿?) 1773.*

FIGURE 24.1 Unidentified military official, letter to Inspector Hugo O'Conor, 1773. File 41, dossier 7, Chihuahua 1775–86, fs. 300–446 (416–472), Archivo General de la Nación (AGN), Mexico City, Mexico. Fragmentary information about the military situation on the borders of the province of Chihuahua was sent to various viceroys.

El nuevo Reglamento formado por mi antecesor, el señor Marques de Croix, y los demás documentos concernientes al asunto que dispondría el cordón o línea de Presidios proyectada. Para que, de este modo, bien cubiertas las Fronteras de esas Provincias, se remedien las Hostilidades de los Indios, se castique sus delitos y de una vez se logre la deseada tranquilidad.

Abierta la campaña, emprendida las operaciones, procediendo de acuerdo en los movimientos con el teniente coronel Hugo O'Connor y estando a la mira de lo que intentos los Enemigos, no me queda duda en que se conseguirá el feliz éxito que se apetece . . .

FIGURE 24.2 Antonio de Bucarelli y Ursúa, letter to Governor Ugarte, July 1, 1772, Mexico City, 5 pages. Provs. Ints., 24 No. 3, f. 1, Provincias Internas, Archivo General de la Nación (AGN), Mexico City, Mexico. Bucarelli reports on the formation of the Compañía Volante de Chihuahua with three hundred men, and the joint campaign with presidial forces against the "barbarian" Indians, requesting support for Commander Hugo O'Conor.

lated towns like El Mulato, Manuel Benavides (San Carlos), and Barranco Azul, preserving age-old practices amid colonial pressure and persecution. The Spanish insistence on preserving their line continued through increasing militarization and slave-trading policies, establishing a foundation for border dynamics that would persist into the creation of the modern state.

These techniques of line-making by the Spanish military officials not only were common in this area of the Chihuahuan Desert, they also extended to other regions including the Sonoran Desert. For example, in a military report by field marshal Marqués de Rubí in 1768 to the Spanish Crown, he writes the following:

> It must be considered that border enemies of these presidios are the *pápagos* and *piatos* of the northwest and the less-known Nations near the Colorado River, opposite to the Presidio del Altar . . . battered and rejected the Seris in front of our line, were less frequent; owing, while this danger exists, to maintain communication via a detachment . . . to ensure the best safeguarding of the immense [border] entries offered by the wilderness of the area and the frequency of the gullies.[15]

The military line as a juridical boundary became central in the control of Indigenous people caught at the crossroads of these newly instituted techniques of securitization. A line using the Rio Grande as a geographical marker to control Native mobility and nourish slave markets was created before line boundary demarcations and contestations of the nineteenth century,[16] commonly understood as the beginning of the modern configuration of borders in the United States. My argument is not that nineteenth-century cartographers were influenced by the Spanish ideas of border-making, as this is not what is central in the documents I present here. Rather, I propose that the concept of a border and a borderline in these same territories has a specific historical and rhetorical legacy of enslavement and violence in the archive that can be traced to an earlier period, and which is highly documented in military documents.

Pieces	Ages	Daily Assignation	Total
46 17 33	From 1 to 5 . . . years From 6 to 14 . . . From 15 and above . . .	To 1 real . . . , To 1 ½ r(es) . . . To 2 r(es) . . .	402(ps) 4(rs) . . . 223,1,, . . . 577,,4 . . .
96	Totals		1203,,1,, . . .

FIGURE 24.3 Records of the Apache collera led by the lieutenant don Miguel Díaz de Luna, 1790–92. Legajo 142, expediente 14, ff. 437–556, Provincias Internas, Archivo General de la Nación (AGN), Mexico City, Mexico. Includes receipts for supplies acquired from citizens for the prisoners and bureaucratic transportation documentation.

Recibí el 17 de la campaña de voluntarios Don Juan Santonio, diez y ocho pesos . . . de la leña que se ha consumido en cocinar la comida de las piezas Apaches que están en la obra de esta villa a cargo del referido oficial desde el día 24 del mes de Diciembre . . .

Villa de Chiquaqua, 4 de enero de 1780.

FIGURE 24.4 Various accounts of the administration of Nueva Vizcaya. File 71, dossier 1, Nueva Vizcaya, 1776–1780, pp. 1–400, page 84, Provincias Internas, Archivo General de la Nación (AGN), Mexico City, Mexico. Includes details of income and expenditures, particularly the monthly payrolls for the personnel of the new presidios in Durango, Chihuahua, and New Mexico.

Conclusion

In conclusion, this chapter proposes a reimagining of the historical function and contemporary impact of borders by situating them within the broader genealogies of forced migration, labor exploitation, and human enslavement that have shaped Indigenous and displaced communities. Rather than privileging the borderland as a distinct or liminal space, this study reframes the border as an enduring carceral site of hypersurveillance and capital accumulation—one structured by colonial histories of forced labor, enslavement, and displacement. Centering on the concept of wame, the land as an ecosystem of life and memory, this framework challenges dominant border-centric narratives and reclaims the homeland as a space of its own defined by cultural diversity and ecological interdependence, woven together by Indigenous, immigrant, refugee, and other communities alike.

Archival research from Mexico's National Archive reveals how Spanish colonial policies were put in place to systematically surveil and control Indigenous mobility and eliminate Indigenous peoples' access to the bison, particularly that of the Ndé (Lipan Apache) and other neighboring groups. This historical analysis illuminates how the Spanish "borderline" functioned not merely as a boundary but as a capitalist enterprise,

Estimado Señor,

Quedo enterado por la superior orden . . . de 9 de enero que Andrés Nopanan and Pedro Maular están ya en Veracruz destinados por cinco años a la Habana, a las obras de fortificación y me parece conveniente se perpetúen allí por que han sido muy perversos y de cuales quiera parte donde se pongan en este Reino pueden volverse aquí, a levantar otra nueva cuadrilla. Dios guarde . . .

FIGURE 24.5 Apache prisoners of war and their transfer to Havana. No. 3 (44 ff.), MSS 867, CSWR REEL 182, Provincias Internas, Archivo General de la Nación (AGN), Mexico City, Mexico. The document includes a letter dated January 9 regarding the dispatch of Andrés Nopanan and Pedro Maular to Veracruz on the way to five years of work on fortifications in Havana, stating that they were considered too dangerous to be placed elsewhere.

benefiting slave hunters and mercenaries by commodifying Indigenous bodies and enforcing colonial order through violent displacement. The Regulations of 1772, although claiming to offer amnesty to "peaceful" Native groups, in practice criminalized Native populations, fracturing communities and redefining them as threats to colonial power.

The historical lineage of forced migration and fractured family structures established a precedent for later institutionalized forms of displacement and persecution. Both Mexican and U.S. authorities adopted these tactics, solidifying borders as mechanisms of control that disrupted Indigenous sovereignty and contributed to ongoing dispossession. By reinterpreting the border through the lens of wame—as a space of Indigenous cultural memory, resilience, and sovereignty—this analysis calls for a departure from the notion of the border as a mere legal and security construct. Instead, it advocates for an understanding of places remade by borders as inhabited spaces rich in cultural memory and resistance. This approach offers another perspective on land rights, human displacement, and border enforcement, one that acknowledges the living legacy of colonialism and the cultural endurance of Indigenous and displaced communities in the face of historic and modern forms of border exploitation and violence.

NOTES

1. Chiara Brambila, Jussi Laine, and Gianluca Bocchi, *Borderscaping: Imaginations and Practices of Border Making* (London: Routledge, 2015); Valeria Ferraris, "Entangled in the Technology-Driven Borderscape: Border Crossers Rendered to Their Digital Self," *European Journal of Criminology* 20, no. 5 (March 2022), https://doi.org/10.1177/14773708221086717.
2. See Yásnaya Elena Aguilar Gil, "The Map and the Territory," *The Baffler*, October 26, 2020, https://thebaffler.com/latest/the-map-and-the-territory-aguilar-gil.
3. Hernán M. Venegas Delgado, Bárbara O. Venegas Arbolaez, and Israel García Moreno, "Rebeliones de indios apaches y chichimecas en Cuba: Historiografía y realidades (fines del siglo XVIII a inicios del siglo XIX)," *Caravelle*, no. 108 (June 2017): 117–34, https://doi.org/10.4000/caravelle.2320.
4. Diana Hadley et al., *The Presidio and Militia on the Northern Frontier of New Spain: A Documentary History*, vol. 2, part 2, *The Central Corridor and the Texas Corridor, 1700–1765* (Tucson: University of Arizona Press, 1997).
5. Matthew Liebmann and Robert W. Preucel, "The Archaeology of the Pueblo Revolt and the Formation of the Modern Pueblo World," *The Rio Arriba* 73, no. 2 (Winter 2007): 195–217; Hadley et al., *Central Corridor*.
6. The people of La Junta de los Ríos use the term "People of La Junta" to refer to communities that have continuously lived in the area since time immemorial. These include the Julime, Jumano, Concho, Chiso, Puliques, and others.
7. Tracy Duvall, ed., *La revista de presidios por el Marqués de Rubí, 1766–1772* (published by the author, 2020), 89.
8. Dossier 12, file 37—MF Provincias Internas de Oriente, abril–julio 1799, fs 415–57, Archivo General de la Nación, Mexico City, Mexico.
9. Michael R. Hardwick, "Presidios of the Line," Sons of DeWitt Colony, September 2, 1998, http://www.sonsofdewittcolony.org/adp/archives/presidio/presline.html.
10. Duvall, *La revista*; Hadley et al., "Presidio and Militia."
11. Mark Santiago, *The Jar of Severed Hands: Spanish Deportation of Apache Prisoners of War 1770–1810* (Norman: University of Oklahoma Press, 2011).
12. Domingo Cabello (gobernador) to de Croix (comandante general), August 19, 1779, Documentary Relations of the Southwest, University of Arizona.
13. Santiago, *Jar of Severed Hands*.
14. Hernán Maximiliano Venegas Delgado and Carlos Manuel Valdés Dávila, *La ruta del horror* (Mexico City: Plaza y Valdés, 2013), 173–74. All translations from Spanish in this chapter are the author's own, unless otherwise noted.

15. Rubí, quoted in Duvall, *La revista.*
16. Venegas Delgado and Valdés Dávila, *La ruta del horror.*

BIBLIOGRAPHY

Aguilar Gil, Yásnaya Elena. "The Map and the Territory." *The Baffler*, October 26, 2020. https://thebaffler.com/latest/the-map-and-the-territory-aguilar-gil.

Brambilla, Chiara, Jussi Lane, and Gianluca Bocchi. *Borderscaping: Imaginations and Practices of Border Making.* London: Routledge, 2015.

Duvall, Tracy, ed. *La revista de presidios por el Marqués de Rubí, 1766–1772.* Published by the author, 2020.

Ferraris, Valeria. "Entangled in the Technology-Driven Borderscape: Border Crossers Rendered to Their Digital Self." *European Journal of Criminology* 20, no. 5 (March 2022). https://doi.org/10.1177/14773708221086717.

Hadley, Diana, Thomas H. Naylor, Mardith K. Schuetz-Miller, Dale S. Brenneman, Philip E. Coyle, and Osvaldo Barreneche. *The Presidio and Militia on the Northern Frontier of New Spain: A Documentary History.* Vol. 2, part 2, *The Central Corridor and the Texas Corridor, 1700–1765.* Tucson: University of Arizona Press, 1997.

Hardwick, Michael R. "Presidios of the Line." Sons of DeWitt Colony, September 2, 1998. http://www.sonsofdewittcolony.org/adp/archives/presidio/presline.html.

Liebmann, Matthew, and Robert W. Preucel. "The Archaeology of the Pueblo Revolt and the Formation of the Modern Pueblo World." *The Rio Arriba* 73, no. 2 (Winter 2007): 195–217.

Santiago, Mark. *The Jar of Severed Hands: Spanish Deportation of Apache Prisoners of War 1770–1810.* Norman: University of Oklahoma Press, 2011.

Venegas Delgado, Hernán Maximiliano, and Carlos Manuel Valdés Dávila. *La ruta del horror.* Mexico City: Plaza y Valdés, 2013.

Venegas Delgado, Hernán Maximiliano, Bárbara O. Venegas Arbolaez, and Israel García Moreno. "Rebeliones de indios apaches y chichimecas en Cuba: Historiografía y realidades (fines del siglo XVIII a inicios del siglo XIX)." *Caravelle*, no. 108 (June 2017): 117–34. https://doi.org/10.4000/caravelle.2320.

TWENTY-FIVE

Dispossession in El Calaboz and the Ndé Women's Digital Movement

Creating Digital Knowledge Tools Through the Analytical Lenses of Indigenous Feminism and Decolonization

KELLY PANCHYSHYN

I was born and raised in a region known as Kwan Lin or Chū Lin (also known as Whitehorse, Yukon), on the ancestral lands of the Tagish Kwan and the Traditional Territory of the Ta'an Kwäch'än Council and Kwanlin Dün First Nation. To the Indigenous peoples of the area, I am recognized as Guch'an, or "people of the clouds," indicating that I am a White settler in the region. To position myself in relation to colonial borders, I grew up just a two-hour drive from the Alaska-Yukon boundary. In 2021, I completed an interdisciplinary MA from the Community Engagement, Social Change and Equity Program at the University of British Columbia's Okanagan campus, on the unceded lands of the Syilx peoples. It is here, several years earlier, that I came to know and work with Dr. Margo Tamez, while acquiring my BA. My interest in working with Dr. Tamez on her research project, titled "Exploring and Documenting Indigenous Women's Refusals to Leave Indigenous Homelands," first arose from my desire to research the digital constraints faced by so many grassroots researchers and activists in rural communities like my own. I was also drawn to the project's focus on Indigenous women and their resistance to displacement. It is through the El Calaboz project that I received a unique opportunity to recognize and resist my own complacency in ongoing acts of settler patriarchal violence, on the digital front and elsewhere.

Both in my work on the El Calaboz project and in my MA research with and alongside Kwanlin Dün community members, I reflected on the ways in which I found myself walking in multiple worlds. As an interdisciplinary scholar, I blend critical methods and frameworks in a manner that mirrors my complex subjecthood and diverse research interests. This process first began in my undergraduate studies. Between 2011 and 2017, I needed to absorb and understand the massive amounts of important information I received in my academic training from both Indigenous and non-Indigenous scholars in my dual degree in cultural studies and Indigenous studies. This education, and the opportunity to learn from and alongside many Indigenous and non-Indigenous students, helped me to process my own lived experiences, and those of my peers. With the guidance of instructors like Dr. Margo Tamez, I learned to study deep, historical processes and to contextualize my research topics within and through Indigenous and embodied methodologies. Overall, my undergraduate experience taught me to take academic risks and to theorize future imaginaries in which the disruption of oppressive and destructive systems is possible. I also learned about the principles, ethics, and critical analytical lenses that allowed me to develop a unique research approach and offered me the rigorous tools needed to engage with contemporary issues on both a local and global scale. I brought this approach to my work with the El Calaboz research team in 2017 and 2018.

Through blended personal and academic lenses, I explored the power relations embedded in the El Calaboz project, as they related to movements of Indigenous resistance and Indigenous feminism by Ndé (Lipan Apache) women in the Rio Grande Valley. Between 2007 and 2009, Ndé women vehemently refused the United States' border wall construction project, standing against this state-sanctioned dispossession. In the process, they developed significant digital data on multiple platforms and began seeding Indigenous grassroots methodologies inherent to El Calaboz ancestral and historical experiences, oral histories, memory, and cultures. This is the unique standpoint that our team sought to center in digital space, allowing greater access to multiple communities across several borders.

As I mentioned above, in 2017, a decade after *Tamez v. Chertoff* sparked action, Margo Tamez hired me to be a research assistant on her project. This project aimed to "address critical questions informed by Ndé women's current, on-going, and trans-generational histories in which they positioned their memory, history, transgenerational knowledge, laws, and their bodies against the state and settlers in order to protect their lands and to refuse the displacement and dispossession of their villages, many of which defiantly exist today along the Texas-Mexico border."[1] In this chapter, I focus on Ndé (Lipan Apache) women and communities facing an intense border conflict in which many members of their nation have had their traditional land, and historical titles to their lands, diminished by settler governments or violently extinguished by the Secure Fence Act of 2006.[2] As others in this collection discuss in greater depth, the community was actively engaged in challenging the Texas state government and the U.S. federal government over blatant denial of the rights of Indigenous peoples, their ongoing existence and history of anticolonial struggles, and their sovereignty as Indigenous peoples with international rights to free, prior, and informed consent in all matters affecting them.[3] Indigenous women have taken on an integral role in this movement, and our research team has aimed to both learn about and support their actions.

In particular, my task was to organize a multimedia database that could document historical resistance, informing us and the community about ongoing activism in the area. Our hope was that by collecting and curating these documents in a digital space, we could facilitate transnational organizing among and between Indigenous groups in militarized zones of state impunity. Here, I will walk through the creation and implementation of digital knowledge tools informed by Indigenous feminism and decolonial data sovereignty, two theoretical perspectives that have helped me to identify and analyze Ndé resistance to patriarchy, state-sanctioned violence, historical erasure, borders, and colonization.

Indig-ital Feminism: Using Indigenous Feminism as a Framework for Digital Work

My writing about digital resistance is greatly informed by the thinking of Indigenous feminism. As a body of theory, Indigenous feminism interrogates the power relations experienced by Indigenous communities, paying special mind to the gendered nature of settler colonialism.[4] Research guided by this aim seeks to motivate "theoretically informed, politically self-conscious activism" that centers Indigenous women and gender-queer folx, while working toward a decolonized future.[5] By taking up this lens within digital spaces, I explore how patriarchal and colonial modes of domination persist within digital platforms, and, more importantly, how people working on the front lines of digital movements can and do confront such forces. Recognizing Indigenous women's ontological, axiological, and epistemological perspectives is integral to decolonizing research and activism in this field. Many scholars have argued that the exclusion of Indigenous women from such domains reinforces colonial attempts to disempower Indigenous people through the erasure of any form of knowledge and experience that does not reinforce the legitimacy of Western dominance.[6] Given the prominent role digital platforms play in contemporary knowledge production and political organizing, I have chosen to counter this erasure by foregrounding "Indigenous women's ways of being and belonging" in the convergence of digital and physical realms.[7] Doing so makes visible their role "as active producers of knowledge" both on- and offline.[8] In working against the hegemony of Western intellectual imperialism, this project hopes to re-matriate space for the many languages and literacies of Indigenous women.[9] Further, it is a direct acknowledgment of the presence Indigenous women command within digital decolonizing movements, along with the rights and responsibilities they have in their governance. To elucidate this practice further, it is useful to share some of the challenges faced by the project, along with the adaptations our team chose to implement.

Contextualizing the El Calaboz Database Project

During 2017, I assisted Dr. Tamez in her community-engaged, participatory action research with community members in El Calaboz. Learning about her research on Lipan Apache women's refusals to leave their customary homelands was crucial to building my understanding. As other scholars in this collection explain, the Lipan Apache are part of the Ndé peoples, whose larger cultural-spiritual-spatial-historical homelands are connected to the present-day states of Texas, New Mexico, Arizona, and

Colorado, and who are related to the Dene Nation in so-called Canada. The Ndé community in El Calaboz and surrounding communities belong to a larger Indigenous cultural group also known as the Kónìcą̀ą̀hį́į́ Gòkíyàà, or the Big Water Peoples.[10] The community has experienced several waves of historical colonization and is currently confronting the erasure of their presence and denial of their sovereignty and traditional rights under the Texas state and U.S. federal governments. The most recent assault upon their lands stems from the Secure Fence Act of 2006, under which many members of the nation, including Dr. Eloisa García Taméz, had their traditional land title violently extinguished.[11]

Under the act, the Texas-Mexico border wall was built without consent from or consultation with the Lipan Apache, cutting them off from their ancestral lands, family ties, and connections to Indigenous foods, medicines, and sacred sites. This has had a devastating effect on the community's economic, social, and cultural well-being. Despite the lack of state and federal recognition of their struggle and displacement, the people of El Calaboz are determined to assert their rights and actively engage in challenging the authority and control of the nation-state. Ndé women took on an integral role in this movement through organizations like Lipan Apache Women's Defense and the Emilio Institute for Indigenous Research and Rights, a community center where local artists, academics, and activists gather to organize against injustice.

Dr. Margo Tamez and her research team have been working through the Emilio Institute to support the efforts of the Ndé. The community voiced their desire for a tool that would help document their historical resistance and inform ongoing activism. Out of this community-articulated hope emerged the El Calaboz project. I was tasked with supporting this project by organizing a multimedia database that could house content generated both inside and outside of the community. The priority was to develop a knowledge tool that reflected the traditional practices and cultural values of the community, while allowing them access to, and control over, information related to their struggles against the state. The database could also strive to highlight the resistance work of local Indigenous women and connect the community with other Indigenous movements. These priorities led me to consider the following questions in my research and writing:

- *How can we shape the database around the needs of the community?*
- *How can digital tools support Indigenous resistance and decolonization, and how might they undermine it?*
- *How can these tools support an Indigenous feminist methodology unique to El Calaboz?*

Each question relates to the other, and so I have chosen to explore them together in the following section.

Challenges of Indigenous Digital Resistance and Decolonization

While their geographic locations may vary from the high Arctic to the southern U.S. bordered lands, many remote Indigenous communities in colonial North America face intense social and environmental issues, which stem from ongoing acts of colonization. Digital tools have become a significant part of Indigenous grassroots efforts to address these challenges. This Indigenous-led use of technology, in pushing back against colonial oppression and in reinforcing decolonization, is an expression of digital resistance. Digital resistance is part of a larger historical trend of adapting colonial tools for Indigenous purposes.[12] Building on similar ideas, Tagish Tlingit art historian Candice Hopkins emphasizes that digital tools do not threaten tradition, but rather allow for the continuation and adaptation of Indigenous knowledge systems.[13] An excellent example of those who practice digital resistance is the Inuit of Rigolet, who are using video and animation to capture their oral history and to better understand and articulate the effects of climate change on their vitality.[14] In this case, digital tools offer a new avenue for maintaining valuable traditional knowledge, which can then be used to protect Inuit lands and communities.

The El Calaboz project emerges from the Tamez family's own history of digital resistance. In the early 2000s, while conducting research for her doctoral thesis at Washington State University, Margo Tamez worked with WSU research technology support teams who trained her in Web 2.0 Google juice methods of keyword linking across the vast spatial constellations of the internet. At the behest of Eloisa García Taméz, she used this method to capture all major keywords used in the testimonies of Ndé peoples on the harms caused by wall construction and the government's refusal to address them. She then sought to foreground these words in their media production and interactions with search engines like Google. Margo Tamez's influence in Google word-search "juicing" concentrated the "pulp" results she sought. Within a three-month period, the term "border fence" used by the U.S. government and mainstream media would be supplanted by "border wall," a term that more accurately conveyed the severity of the intrusion. As Tamez orally recollects:

> My goals to elevate the Indigenous peoples' experience-based perspectives and lived reality of the megaproject and gulag-style architecture of construction, and its psychosocial effects on their mental health, demanded that the rather passive terms of reference that the nation was utilizing at the time—"border fence"—be adjusted to the experience that Indigenous peoples actually felt and knew based on a national and political intent to subject them to a colossal carceral architecture. My goal was "border wall"—and in a relatively short time, "border wall" reached the summit of the number-one spot as the top search result on Google. This is the actual history of how we—all of us today, on a global level—use the term "border wall" and how eventually the mainstream media had to change their terminology as well.[15]

What I took away from the oral history of her doctoral research was her hands-on approach to digital intervention. Though geographically separated from her community while at university, Tamez joined the standoff between her mother Eloisa and the U.S. government. Adapting the digital tools accessible to her, she participated in the ongoing struggle over the protection of her homelands, creating a new pathway for deep engagement in Indigenous efforts against state-sanctioned violence.

While the American government and corporate- and state-controlled media continued to refer to the project as a "border fence," the Tamez women sought to push back against this erasure by amplifying Indigenous voices in their use of the term "border wall." The two believed "wall" would also invoke greater public comprehension of the project's human rights violations. To influence public perception, Dr. Tamez began creating strategic web pages and word associations, and persistently edited Wiki pages to successfully "educate the public on the importance of language, accuracy, and new literacies from sites of state violence which deserved new analytics and new languages which accurately reflect the terms of usage from those impacted by state violence."[16] The use of the phrase "border wall" over "border fence" demonstrates how digital resources can offer a platform for Indigenous resistance through the promotion of Indigenous language, knowledge, and autonomy. However, this method does not come without challenges.

Rising out of digital resistance is the larger question of Indigenous digital self-determination, meaning the ability for Indigenous peoples to control the policy and infrastructure surrounding digital resources and the role of those resources in the community. Digital self-determination is quickly becoming an integral part of Indigenous self-determination overall, yet it remains difficult to achieve in rural communities.[17] These Indigenous communities are trapped within the digital divide—a term widely used to describe the uneven distribution of essential digital infrastructure in marginalized communities. Consequently, the lack of access to digital networks continues to undermine Indigenous people's overall self-determination and ability to exercise their rights as both Indigenous people and citizens of the nation-state. While the COVID-19 pandemic has radically shifted the way in which we can conduct community-based face-to-face research online, this level of knowledge, skill, and university infrastructure was nonexistent for Dr. Tamez in 2017.

Traversing the Digital Divide: The Twenty-First-Century Border Wall

Along the Rio Grande, Ndé communities experience an intense digital divide. Historically, some of the lowest rates of computer ownership and internet access in the United States have been found in the Texas border region.[18] In many cases, state and corporate solutions have been harmful or have fallen woefully short of community needs. While our research team did not have the resources to tackle the digital divide, we had to consider how we might work within it. The first major challenge was to confront the reality that many members of the community do not have access to computers or the internet. We had to take careful steps to navigate these limitations. Another key consideration taken was the theoretical and practical limits of using digital tools to host a project grounded in an Indigenous worldview. Cree-Métis media artist Loretta Todd explains that the capitalist foundation of the digital industry influences which ideologies are emphasized in digital spaces.[19] For this reason, Western frameworks are inherently linked to many digital platforms, and thus it can be difficult to modify them in a way that is conducive to Indigenous values. Indigenous communities are tasked with adapting tools to counter the colonial, patriarchal, and capitalist values embedded in them. This is particularly difficult in rural settings, where digital resources are limited and there are few opportunities to build tools from scratch.

Due to the resource limitations of the El Calaboz project, we had to use a prefabricated database software. Unfortunately, our database license could only support a limited number of access points, meaning that a small number of individuals or computers were able to view and shape content. Such a restriction hindered our ability to uphold our commitment to ensure widespread access for Indigenous women, people with disabilities, Two-Spirit, trans-Indigiqueer, and LGBTQIA+ people, low-income workers, and other marginalized people within the community. In other words, the prefabricated resources prohibited us from making the database accessible to all or reflective of our project values. This felt like moving into a house where the rooms and doors were uncomfortably set to narrow dimensions for the previous owner. The program's limitations and the inadequate research training support to help bridge this gap also impeded our ability to train and to compensate community members in a respectful manner, and to collaboratively interpret community-generated materials in a way that could meaningfully address their digital literacy levels. This conflicted greatly with the project's intent to make the database a collaborative effort, and to make the final product available to the community.

To move around the furniture and widen the doorways of our new home, we enacted the rigorous Ndé research principles and protocols that Dr. Tamez embedded in the project's methodology and ethics. Before the project's term expired, we found a way to share the database, without exhausting our financial resources or overextending our license.

After assembling the foundation of the database on the UBC Okanagan campus, our team installed it on the computers of the Emilio Institute, in El Calaboz. This fit within the restriction of our license and granted members of the community a chance to interact with the database on shared computers. Further, the Lipan Apache government designated the Women and Elders' Leadership Circle to oversee the use of the database at the Institute's center in El Calaboz, meaning that access to the database would be overseen by those most often excluded by digital projects. In order to gain access, Indigenous and non-Indigenous community members and visitors had to establish a relationship with these knowledge keepers. My hope is that this approach will transform one of the project's limitations into an opportunity to follow Ndé knowledge practices. While the installation of the database at the Emilio Institute is not a perfect solution, it allowed us to maintain the forward momentum we would need to face the challenges ahead.

Our team initially planned to include the oral accounts of Elders in the database; however, the terms of software meant we could not protect these testimonies from misuse. Anything we uploaded could be collected in the databases of other users without our knowledge, something that made the community deeply uncomfortable. Similarly, the funding we received (from a Texas-based archival center) to record and preserve the testimonies required participants to sign away rights to their stories using a "deed of gift" contract. Although Dr. Tamez spent months in conversation with the funding agency, institutional rules prevailed. As a result, our team declined the oral history digitization award and shifted our focus to documenting these barriers along with our proposed solutions. It became clear that our use of digital tools risked creating yet another platform for the colonization of Indigenous space and knowledge.[20] Anything that removes ownership of knowledge from Indigenous peoples is not conducive to an Ndé model of Indigenous feminism. Nevertheless, our research team was intent on adapting the database, or at least the context in which it is used, to suit the community. Each time we faced a new hurdle, we returned to the Tamez women and the Ndé cultural protocols to map out a new path.

Despite the problems outlined above, the El Calaboz project has had success. For example, the community struggles with outside media outlets and researchers that produce content concerning the Lipan Apache but consistently do not provide them with access to the final product. This database has been extremely helpful in facilitating the retrieval of such documents. Moreover, users can compile and contrast data on the legal, demographic, and statistical realities of El Calaboz. From here it is possible to build stronger representation for local issues or identify gaps in information. Thus, local scholars and community leaders can use this collection to establish priority areas, guide local projects, and make informed decisions.

Thankfully, in documenting our challenges and adaptations, the team has supported Dr. Tamez in her "decolonizing the archive" discussions with historians and archivists. Both professions are necessary and valued actors in the struggle to combat injustices against Indigenous rights and intellectual traditions. Establishing positive and anti-oppressive working arrangements with such experts will be key to the long-term success of the project and others like it. Led by Dr. Tamez, we drew upon our experience to educate potential partners on Ndé research principles and protocols, setting the tone for future collaborations. The aim is still to have oral histories housed in a digital archive, protected and curated by the Ndé in El Calaboz, accompanied by the Ndé protocols, and open to Ndé communities and the general public when appropriate. While much work remains, the current database captures the crucial work done by Ndé women scholars and land protectors. It is vital that we continue to develop a digital footprint of Ndé land protection and refusal for current and future generations of Indigenous peoples and non-Indigenous peoples who honor Ndé laws.

I believe our most notable achievement has been to keep Ndé women at the heart of this digital project: they have shaped its creation, are the primary feature of its content, and are the stewards of its legacy. The hope is that this database will continue to support the ongoing efforts of Ndé feminism and address the imposition of colonial patriarchy along the Texas-Mexico border. While the tool does not escape these systems of oppression entirely, it makes an honest effort to depart from them. In a small way, it decentralizes the control of knowledge by placing it in the hands of Ndé women, rather than institutional databases and libraries that are governed by the values of White authority.

Re-circling My Learning: My Journey from El Calaboz to Yukon

Six years have passed since my role in the El Calaboz project. In that time, I partnered with Kwanlin Dün First Nations staff to research the inclusion of women and the practice of plant harvest in land planning.[21] Together we aimed to create interventions that enabled women and the practice of plant harvest to be included in the region's upcoming planning process for the Łu Zil Män area. When we were on the verge of launching our community engagement in the early spring of 2020, the COVID-19 pandemic hit. As a result, we had to drastically revamp our approach. In navigating community- and land-centric research amid fluctuating restrictions, I once again had to reflect on the use of digital tools within contemporary circles of knowledge production and activism.

Like El Calaboz, Yukon struggles with access to affordable and functional digital infrastructure along with inconsistent levels of trust and literacy in such resources. Yet in 2020 and 2021 many of my interactions with community partners and participants had to move online. Our research team had to contend with the fact that the format in which knowledge was being gathered for the project felt so distant from the manner in which knowledge of plant harvesting was typically shared and created—through on-the-land gatherings with community members, young and old. However, delaying the project would mean forgoing our chance to influence the Łu Zil Män Local Area Plan. Like the El Calaboz project, delays risked further disenfranchisement. And so my research with Kwanlin Dün First Nation moved forward, as has the work of the El Calaboz research team. My ongoing correspondence with the Tamez family has indicated that the pandemic, political unrest, and the rolling electrical blackouts experienced by the El Calaboz region between 2020 and 2023 have only exacerbated both the digital divide and the need to confront it. We have an opportunity here to continue our critical engagement with the digital spaces we inhabit by exchanging knowledge and building on our shared experiences. Our greatest test will be to incorporate the theoretical ideals of digital decolonization while working within the limitations of the effects of transgenerational trauma; institutional, structural, and systemic racism; and deep economic, legal, and access-to-justice divides in our communities. With each step of the project, we must strive to balance our short-term efforts toward digital inclusion with more radical attempts at digital inventions and interventions.[22] Using the metaphor of living in a house, we will need to find ways of changing the paint in the short term, while drawing up future renovation plans for greater inclusion.

The Lipan Apache are eager to take on this challenge. While initial adaptations to the database may be small, more ambitious forms of digital resistance will follow. Each hurdle along the way will inform a grassroots digital research policy that embodies traditional and contemporary Ndé knowledge-sharing protocols. Given our own team's struggles with data ownership, we are motivated to create tools that assist Lipan in the governance of their digital research materials.

As we move forward in a post-pandemic digital environment, our team would like to see the adaptation of the existing database into one that stands apart from its original software and incorporates Ndé language and oral history. We would also like to push further by creating digital tools that align with Ndé languages and aesthetics. As of yet, there are no restrictions on the goals we can establish for our work in digital decolonization. However, as our use of digital tools rapidly increases, so too does the necessity for us to engage critically with them. No matter how small, projects like this provide a launching point for the disruption of the divide and offer another stepping-stone on the path toward digital self-determination. Regardless, the El Calaboz team will continue to keep asking difficult questions of our work, like: How might we connect digital tools to the land? Or, How might we learn to see these tools through the eyes of both future generations and those who came before us? We hope you will join in the conversation.

NOTES

1. Margo Tamez, "Restoring Lipan Apache Women's Laws, Lands, and Strength in El Calaboz Ranchería at the Texas-Mexico Border," *Signs: Journal of Women in Culture and Society* 35, no. 3 (2010): 559.
2. Tamez, "Restoring."
3. Tamez, "Restoring," 566.
4. Joyce Green, "Taking More Account of Indigenous Feminism: An Introduction," in *Making Space for Indigenous Feminism*, 2nd ed., ed. Joyce Green (Halifax: Fernwood Publishing, 2017), 16; Maile Arvin, Eve Tuck, and Angie Morrill, "De-

colonizing Feminism: Challenging Connections Between Settler Colonialism and Heteropatriarchy," *Feminist Formations* 25, no. 1 (2013): 9.

5. Green, "Taking More Account," 16–17.
6. Aileen Moreton-Robinson, *White Possessive* (Minneapolis: University of Minnesota Press, 2015), 165–68; Aileen Moreton-Robinson, "Tellin' It Straight: Self-Presentation Within Indigenous Women's Life Writing," in *Talkin' Up to the White Women* (Brisbane: University of Queensland Press, 2000), 1–31; Audra Simpson, "The Chief's Two Bodies: Theresa Spence and the Gender of Settler Sovereignty; Unsettling Conversations" (keynote presentation at R.A.C.E. Conference, Edmonton, Alberta, October 2014), https://vimeo.com/110948627; Cassidy Acheson, "Reawakening Memory and Refusing Erasure: Sqilxw Legacies of Resistance Through Familial Stories of Mary Ann and Mary Terese" (MA thesis, University of British Columbia, 2022), 142–62; Jody Pepion, "Aawaatowapsiiksi 'Those People That Have Sacred Ceremonies' Indigenous Women's Bodies: Recovering the Sacred, Restoring Our Lands, Decolonization" (PhD diss., Washington State University, 2009), 80; Linda Tuhiwai Smith, *Decolonizing Methodologies*, 3rd ed. (London: Zed Books, 2021), 9, 173–74; Nathalie Kermoal and Isabel Altamirano-Jiménez, "Introduction," in *Living on the Land: Indigenous Women's Understanding of Place*, ed. Nathalie Kermoal and Isabel Altamirano-Jiménez (Athabasca: Athabasca University Press, 2016), 12.
7. Aileen Moreton-Robinson and Maggie Walter, "Indigenous Methodologies in Social Research," in *Social Research Methods*, ed. Maggie Walter (Oxford: Oxford University Press, 2009), 5.
8. Kermoal and Altamirano-Jiménez, "Introduction," 4.
9. Kermoal and Altamirano-Jiménez, "Introduction," 11.
10. Margo Tamez, "The Texas-Mexico Border Wall and Ndé Memory: Confronting Genocide and State Criminality, Beyond the Guise of 'Impunity,'" in *Beyond Walls and Cages*, ed. Jenna M. Loyd, Matt Mitchelson, and Andrew Burridge (Athens: University of Georgia Press, 2012), 57–58.
11. Denise Gilman, "Seeking Breaches in the Wall: An International Human Rights Law Challenge to the Texas-Mexico Border Wall," *Texas International Law Journal* 46, no. 2 (2011): 272–93.
12. Greg Younging, "The Indigenous Tradition / New Technology Interface," in *Transference, Tradition, Technology: Native New Media Exploring Visual and Digital Culture*, ed. Danna Claxton (Banff: Walter Phillips Gallery Editions, 2005), 180–84.
13. Candice Hopkins, "Interventions in Digital Territories: Narrative in Native New Media," in Claxton, *Transference, Tradition, Technology*, 130.
14. Ashlee Consolo Willox, Sherilee L. Harper, and Victoria L. Edge, "Storytelling in a Digital Age: Digital Storytelling as an Emerging Narrative Method for Preserving and Promoting Indigenous Oral Wisdom," *Qualitative Research* 13, no. 2 (2012): 130–32.

15. Margo Tamez, "Oral History of the Legitimation of the Keywords 'Border Wall' in the Ndé LAW-Defense Web 2.0 Digital Land Protection Project" (lecture, February 24, 2021).
16. Tamez, "Oral History."
17. Rob McMahon, "The Institutional Development of Indigenous Broadband Infrastructure in Canada and the United States: Two Paths to 'Digital Self-Determination,'" *Canadian Journal of Communication* 36, no. 1 (2011): 115–40.
18. Jordana Barton, *Closing the Digital Divide: A Framework for Meeting CRA Obligations* (El Paso: Southwest Border Colonias, 2016); Kelvin Pollard and Matthew Martinez, "Digital Divide in High-Speed Internet Leaves Rural Area Behind," Population Reference Bureau, December 15, 2021, accessed August 30, 2023, https://www.prb.org/articles/digital-divide-in-high-speed-internet-access-leaves-rural-areas-behind/.
19. Loretta Todd, "Narratives in Cyberspace," in Claxton, *Transference, Tradition, Technology*, 154–55.
20. Dallas Hunt and Shaun A. Stevenson, "Decolonizing Geographies of Power: Indigenous Digital Counter-mapping Practices on Turtle Island," *Settler Colonial Studies* 7, no. 3 (2017): 372–92.
21. Kelly Panchyshyn, "Collaborative and Creative Land Planning in Canada's North: Supporting Wild Plant Harvest Through Participatory Action Research in Whitehorse, Yukon" (MA thesis, University of British Columbia, 2021).
22. Rob McMahon, "Co-developing Digital Inclusion Policy and Programming with Indigenous Partners: Interventions from Canada," *Internet Policy Review* 9, no. 2 (2020).

BIBLIOGRAPHY

Acheson, Cassidy. "Reawakening Memory and Refusing Erasure: Sqilxw Legacies of Resistance Through Familial Stories of Mary Ann and Mary Terese." MA thesis, University of British Columbia, 2022. https://dx.doi.org/10.14288/1.0417550.

Arvin, Maile, Eve Tuck, and Angie Morrill. "Decolonizing Feminism: Challenging Connections Between Settler Colonialism and Heteropatriarchy." *Feminist Formations* 25, no. 1 (2013): 8–34. https://doi.org/10.1353/ff.2013.0006.

Barton, Jordana. *Closing the Digital Divide: A Framework for Meeting CRA Obligations.* El Paso: Southwest Border Colonias, 2016. https://www.dallasfed.org/~/media/documents/cd/pubs/digitaldivide.pdf.

Consolo Willox, Ashlee, Sherilee L. Harper, and Victoria L. Edge. "Storytelling in a Digital Age: Digital Storytelling as an Emerging Narrative Method for Preserving and Promoting Indigenous Oral Wisdom." *Qualitative Research* 13, no. 2 (2012): 130–32. https://doi.org/10.1177/1468794112446105.

Gilman, Denise. "Seeking Breaches in the Wall: An International Human Rights Law Challenge to the Texas-Mexico Border Wall." *Texas International Law Journal* 46, no. 2 (2011): 257–94.

Green, Joyce. "Taking More Account of Indigenous Feminism: An Introduction." In *Making Space for Indigenous Feminism*, 2nd ed., edited by Joyce Green, 1–20. Halifax: Fernwood Publishing, 2017.

Hopkins, Candice. "Interventions in Digital Territories: Narrative in Native New Media." In *Transference, Tradition, Technology: Native New Media Exploring Visual and Digital Culture*, edited by Danna Claxton. Banff: Walter Phillips Gallery Editions, 2005.

Hunt, Dallas, and Shaun A. Stevenson. "Decolonizing Geographies of Power: Indigenous Digital Counter-mapping Practices on Turtle Island." *Settler Colonial Studies* 7, no. 3 (2017): 372–92. https://doi.org/10.1080/2201473X.2016.1186311.

Kermoal, Nathalie, and Isabel Altamirano-Jiménez. "Introduction." In *Living on the Land: Indigenous Women's Understanding of Place*, edited by Nathalie Kermoal and Isabel Altamirano-Jiménez, 3–17. Athabasca: Athabasca University Press, 2016.

McMahon, Rob. "Co-developing Digital Inclusion Policy and Programming with Indigenous Partners: Interventions from Canada." *Internet Policy Review* 9, no. 2 (2020): 1–26. https://doi.org/10.14763/2020.2.1478.

McMahon, Rob. "The Institutional Development of Indigenous Broadband Infrastructure in Canada and the United States: Two Paths to 'Digital Self-Determination.'" *Canadian Journal of Communication* 36, no. 1 (2011): 115–40. https://policyreview.info/articles/analysis/co-developing-digital-inclusion-policy-and-programming-indigenous-partners.

Moreton-Robinson, Aileen. "Tellin' It Straight: Self-Presentation Within Indigenous Women's Life Writing." In *Talkin' Up to the White Women*, 1–31. Brisbane: University of Queensland Press, 2000.

Moreton-Robinson, Aileen. *White Possessive*. Minneapolis: University of Minnesota Press, 2015.

Moreton-Robinson, Aileen, and Maggie Walter. "Indigenous Methodologies in Social Research." In *Social Research Methods*, edited by Maggie Walter, 1–18. Oxford: Oxford University Press, 2009.

Panchyshyn, Kelly. "Collaborative and Creative Land Planning in Canada's North: Supporting Wild Plant Harvest Through Participatory Action Research in Whitehorse, Yukon." MA thesis, University of British Columbia, 2021. https://dx.doi.org/10.14288/1.0401786.

Pepion, Jody. "Aawaatowapsiiksi 'Those People That Have Sacred Ceremonies' Indigenous Women's Bodies: Recovering the Sacred, Restoring Our Lands, Decolonization." PhD dissertation, Washington State University, 2009.

Pollard, Kelvin, and Matthew Martinez. "Digital Divide in High-Speed Internet Leaves Rural Area Behind." Population Reference Bureau, December 15, 2021. Accessed August 30, 2023. https://www.prb.org/articles/digital-divide-in-high-speed-internet-access-leaves-rural-areas-behind/.

Simpson, Audra. "The Chief's Two Bodies: Theresa Spence and the Gender of Settler Sovereignty; Unsettling Conversations." Keynote presentation at the R.A.C.E. Conference, Edmonton, Alberta, October 2014. https://vimeo.com/110948627.

Smith, Linda Tuhiwai. *Decolonizing Methodologies: Research and Indigenous Peoples.* 3rd ed. London: Zed Books, 2021.

Tamez, Margo. "Oral History of the Legitimation of the Keywords 'Border Wall' in the Ndé LAW-Defense Web 2.0 Digital Land Protection Project." Lecture, February 24, 2021.

Tamez, Margo. "Restoring Lipan Apache Women's Laws, Lands, and Strength in El Calaboz Ranchería at the Texas-Mexico Border." *Signs: Journal of Women in Culture and Society* 35, no. 3 (2010): 558–69. https://doi.org/10.1086/649053.

Tamez, Margo. "The Texas-Mexico Border Wall and Ndé Memory: Confronting Genocide and State Criminality, Beyond the Guise of 'Impunity.'" In *Beyond Walls and Cages*, edited by Jenna M. Loyd, Matt Mitchelson, and Andrew Burridge, 57–73. Athens: University of Georgia Press, 2012.

Todd, Loretta. "Narratives in Cyberspace." In *Transference, Tradition, Technology: Native New Media Exploring Visual and Digital Culture*, edited by Danna Claxton. Banff: Walter Phillips Gallery Editions, 2005.

Younging, Greg. "The Indigenous Tradition / New Technology Interface." In *Transference, Tradition, Technology: Native New Media Exploring Visual and Digital Culture*, edited by Danna Claxton, 180–84. Banff: Walter Phillips Gallery Editions, 2005.

TWENTY-SIX

Coyotl Interventions

Chicanx Indigenous Decolonial Research Methods

ROSALVA RESENDIZ AND RAMÓN RESENDIZ

On the Texas-Mexico borderlands we grew up knowing that there were two types of coyotes. One coyote is the human smuggler who both guides and exploits migrants crossing the border from Mexico into the United States, a necessity that grew out of the Anglo settler conquest of Indigenous Mexican lands in 1848. The other coyote is our friendly and secretive wild *Canis,* who has managed to survive at the edges of human settlements as it lost its hunting grounds. In understanding this violently intersecting binary of criminality and dispossession imposed by settlers over Indigenous bodies and lands, we are forced to ask: Why do we call human smugglers coyotes? Where does the word *coyote* come from?

Coyotes have been demonized as predators, and yet they are revered in Indigenous cosmologies. Etymologically the word *coyote* derives from *coyotl,* the Nahuatl word for this sacred being. This knowledge is important, because Nahuatl is the classical Mexica language, thus reminding us of the ancestral relational significance that we as racialized Mexicans—mythopoetically, the descendants of the Mexicas, "the Aztecs"—hold in this word. In Mexica cosmology the god Huehuecoyotl, "very old coyote," is depicted as a dancing coyote with human hands and feet and is the god of the arts, lord of music and ceremonial dance, guide of adulthood and adolescence, a gender-fluid/bisexual shapeshifter, a storyteller, and god(dess) of deception.

More broadly, in Indigenous mythologies, coyotes may symbolize astuteness, worldly wisdom, pragmatism, storytelling, and the roles of both teacher and trickster. There are many faces to the coyote: those who adapted to living close to humans, in cities and parks, as they lost their land; those who subvert border surveillance and militarization; and those who subvert modernity through their ongoing resistance and survival. It is at these intersections/crossroads that we find ourselves as Indigenous academics. Very much like the coyotl, we have survived in the margins, yet we have crossed into Western Eurocentric academia in an effort to resist the attacks on our indigeneity, as well as the continued dispossession by imperialism.

Much like the notorious *coyotl trickster/guide*, in this chapter we introduce the concept of *coyotl interventions* as a Chicanx decolonial research methodology—as a methodology that centers our place in the borderlands and also deconstructs the Eurocentric paradigms that attempt to erase our Indigenous ontologies and epistemologies. Our methodology mirrors the border coyote smuggler, as well as the divine coyotl of Indigenous cosmology. As Chicanx feminists we have learned to use the colonial archive and the academy's disciplining "epistemological" tools to co-construct Indigenous research frameworks that transgress and disrupt Eurocentric positivism by centering Indigenous epistemologies, relationalities, and methodologies. In this vein, the coyotl reminds us of our connection to these lands and honors the teachings of our ancestors as we negotiate, adapt to, and subvert the settler-colonial project.

On the Surface of *El Muro*: Centering Indigenous Resistance

In 2014 Ramón began his graduate studies at the University of Washington's Native Voices documentary film master's program, which sought to center Indigenous approaches to filmmaking and documentary media production. It was a moment of excitement for our family, because we knew one of us would finally get to make documentaries that foregrounded our histories of survival and resistance on the borderlands. This was the beginning of what would eventually become *El Muro | The Wall* (2017), and it was also a critical flashpoint in foregrounding the existing gaps in "Indigenous"-centered research in the world of media production. At the time, Indigenous studies was reduced to an Anglocentric definition of indigeneity as something predominantly synonymous with the ethnographic and colonial history of federally recognized tribes in the United States.[1] The program did not address what being Mexican American or Chicanx entailed—a categorical silencing of the identities of dispossessed Indigenous and detribalized peoples, and an erasure of the multifaceted colonial experience of Indigenous peoples under Spain and Mexico. It was a major encounter by our family with the ways the United States had defined indigeneity by conflating it with federal recognition. One goal of the film was to open space for recognizing indigeneity outside the federal paradigm, and within the borderlands.

The purpose of the film was to document the *forgotten archive of the colonial encounter*, which "narrates multiple stories of contestation and its discomfiting other, complicity," for the purposes of questioning the deployment of nationalistic postcolonial dichotomies.[2] We sought to document the Indigenous resistance and struggle of Dr. Eloisa G. Taméz, a Lipan Apache Elder, fighting against the United States Department of Homeland Security, which had used eminent domain to dispossess her of a portion of her ancestral lands in El Calaboz Ranchería in order to build the border wall along the Rio Grande River / Río Bravo. El Calaboz was part of the San Pedro de Carricitos Land Grant, which was granted by the Spanish Crown in 1761. In 1745, Spanish colonization of what was to be called Nuevo Santander began with the excursions and settlements of José de Escandón, a recognized Indian killer.[3] Eloisa Taméz was not simply fighting for her land; she was also fighting for her people. The unjust seizure of her land impacted their own Lipan Apache cultural traditions, since their lives are connected to the land and the river, and such violations were a breach of the United Nations Declaration on the Rights of Indigenous Peoples.

Our Background

As Chicanx individuals, we grew up knowing that we were Mexican with various Indigenous ancestries. We were raised with the knowledge that being Mexican meant we were "mestizos," the detribalized bastard children of the colonizer Hernán Cortés and Malintzin or "La Malinche," a Spanish conquistador and the raped Indian slave.[4] We knew that our family had lived and traversed the Rio Grande River / Río Bravo for many generations. Much like the coyote, we were from both Mexico and the United States. We had always been here, but colonial forces had separated us from our relatives—dispersing us from our lands through violence. As academics, we both have had to temporarily forget our past, to *learn* social science—"the master's tools"—to deconstruct the myths surrounding our people. It would have been much easier to forget, but our desire to reclaim our lands/space/place has always brought us back to trace back *the forgotten archive of the colonial encounter*.[5] As such, it has been our purpose to engage in decolonizing *the archive*, by *writing back* against the colonial erasures, mythologies, and imaginaries perpetrated by the epistemic apparatuses of European imperialism and colonization.[6]

We both left the Rio Grande Valley or "the colony" / *la colonia* at eighteen. And we both attended the University of North Texas during different decades, but the outcome was similar. Academia gave us the tools to critically analyze and deconstruct the structures of power that have subjugated, fractured, and attempted to historically suppress our peoples and erase our Indigenous identities. Much like W. E. B. Du Bois and Anzaldúa, our experiences in higher education provided us an entry point to contest the methods that boxed us into neat labels and hid our complex experiences on the border.[7] As Mexican Americans in the United States, we were racialized as Mexicans but not Indigenous. As Brown mestizos in Mexico, we were racialized as Indigenous, marked by our dark skin and Indigenous features—black straight hair, curved noses, short stature, and poverty. In the United States, we were not Native Americans, because we were detribalized by the geopolitical forces of Mexico and the United States, yet we were indeed Indigenous—but not Indian enough.[8]

The eugenic thinking underneath notions of racial purity has been utilized as a settler-colonial method of regulating and erasing Indigenous peoples and communities, rendering them abstract populations throughout the Americas. In the United States this was executed by the imposition of blood quantums and the carceral reservation system. In New Spain, criollos established a caste system in which the purity of European ancestry set a racial standard of White superiority against the inferiority of the "savage Indian" and/or African, the dark-skinned Black or Brown person.[9] These same criollo elites, however, eventually deployed the notion of "*mestizaje*" as a way to legitimate their own ancestral land claims to the Americas, consolidating land and power under the Porfirio Díaz regime—all while continuing a White supremacist subjection of racialization; that is, the *coloniality of power*.[10] In the United States these systems of eugenicist biopolitical control were used to dispose of and erase the indigeneity of Mexican/Chicanx peoples, labeling them as "Hispanic" immigrants in their own lands.

Methodological Concerns

As Chicanx feminist scholars, we knew that our people—Indigenous, Black, Brown, dispossessed, and detribalized—were always subjects of academic exploitation by White scholars. We understood what it meant to be rendered as an *ethnic population* under the gaze of scientists. We did not want to replicate the exploitative and binary methods of positivism, which Du Bois had debated/discounted in *Dusk of Dawn: An Essay Toward an Autobiography of a Race Concept*.[11] Building from this understanding, we applied this consciousness to our collaboration with the Tamez family. We wanted to respect their story and their people, not as subjects, but as co-creators. Their story was also ours, as we were the descendants of Indians who had been dispossessed and stripped of our lands, identity, and history—this was our own *coyotl intervention*.

For us the border is not just a "representational space in the colonial and national imaginaries of both Mexico and the United States"; it is a place of settler-colonial violence: of land theft, death, erasure, and discomfiting histories of Indigenous resistance against colonization.[12] It has crossed over our flesh and deeply over our minds. It is a place of Hispanic and Anglo settler *coloniality* and *racial geographies* in which "the spatial practices of early colonial settlement and of U.S. expansionism conjoined with the representation of space in historiography, literature, and film to produce a shared set of conventions for envisioning" the border.[13]

As Saldaña-Portillo and Philip Deloria have articulated, the creation of these nation-states was intrinsically reliant on the construction of the Indian, *el indio*, to create a hierarchy of White supremacy and subjugation.[14] The processes by which this was achieved entailed the creation of national imaginaries of Indigenous peoples as savage, noble and ignoble, assimilated to a point of nonrecognition, vanishing, racially inferior, and ultimately existing only in the past. The trope of the vanishing Indian in modernity was achieved through the western film genre and salvage ethnography, what Fatimah Tobing Rony has termed an *ethnographic taxidermy* in which "Indigenous peoples were assumed to be already dying if not dead, [in which] the ethnographic 'taxidermist' turned to artifice, seeking an image more true to the posited original."[15] The colonial image-making practices of misrepresenting Indigenous peoples and their indigeneity permeate the history of ethnographic documentary media production and structure the way the history of the United States is visualized, obfuscated, and rendered invisible. Cognizant of the structuring processes of settler colonialism, we endeavored to make a decolonial didactic document(ary) that exposed the discomfiting histories of the colonial archive, while avoiding the reproduction of taxidermic, ethnographic, essentialist misrepresentations of Indigenous peoples.[16]

In these respects, *El Muro | The Wall* was our way of "writing back" against settler colonialism: in our case, we "shot back" with the camera.[17] Working on the documentary with Dr. Eloisa Taméz brought up many memories of resistance and survival in our own families—providing us with some healing and strength. Dr. Eloisa Taméz's story of resistance intersects with history in the archives, but also intersects with the oral history of resistance by Indigenous peoples under colonization, including our own family. Settler colonialism has left us a legacy of trauma, which has been hidden by myths of the cosmic race of mestizos/as, and in this respect, we sought to decolonize these discourses through the documentary act of speaking truth to power, especially in the face of the militarization represented by the U.S. border wall.

Framing the Border: Narratives of Erasure

In 2005, the U.S. Congress began enacting legislation to build a physical fence along its border with Mexico, which would cover 700 out of the 1,954 miles of the international boundary. By January 2010, the construction of the border fence was deemed complete, with 651 miles along the U.S. side of the border, at a taxpayer cost of roughly $2.8 million per mile.[18]

The construction of the border wall was a coercive process, with the human rights and freedoms of local landowners and border inhabitants forfeited under the pretext of national security. In 2005, when the U.S. Congress passed the Real ID Act, it gave the government the power to build the border wall without consulting the affected communities, many of which were Indigenous. Hence, this entailed the discriminatory disregard of Indigenous peoples' ancestral land claims, as well as the Spanish land-grant protection provisions of the 1848 Treaty of Guadalupe Hidalgo. In 2006, Congress passed the Secure Fence Act, which gave DHS the power to waive thirty-six state and federal laws that might interfere with the building of the wall.[19]

In 2014, there was a surge of asylum-seeking unaccompanied minors, leading to a recentering of the border as a key rhetorical point for the upcoming 2016 election.[20] Inevitably, immigration and the border became a mobilization tool for nationalist right-wing amnesia, revitalized by Donald Trump's first press conference, in which he called for the building of a border wall.[21] In 2016, Trump won the presidency with his infamous chant of "build the wall," conveniently forgetting that one already existed, but using it as a right-wing nationalist propaganda tool. In early 2017, the Trump administration began sending out condemnation letters to landowners whose property was located on sites where the construction of the U.S. border fence was planned.[22] As the Department of Homeland Security intensified its aggressive eminent domain land grab of private and Indigenous lands, it cut across historic cemeteries, wildlife refuges, and the Organ Pipe Cactus National Monument, a sacred burial ground of the Tohono O'odham Nation as well as a UNESCO biosphere reserve.[23]

Six months before Trump called for the building of a wall, we had begun our journey toward the making of an archival documentary film that sought to foreground the "forgotten" and purposely "erased" histories of settler-colonial violence against Indigenous presence in the U.S.-Mexico borderlands. We envisioned a collaborative project that would serve as a decolonial didactic tool by foregrounding the history of South Texas / northern Mexico—prior to its annexation by the United States, before the Texas Revolution, before Mexico called the region Coahuila y Tejas, and before the Spanish came to call the region Nuevo Santander, or even El Seno Mexicano (which translates to "the Mexican Womb"). The documentary was produced for the purpose of disavowing settler-colonial imaginings/narratives of terra nullius (a no-man's-land), of which the Texas creation myth is emblematic.

After the Texas Revolution, this myth was reproduced to erase the history of many peoples by claiming that Tejas was a wasteland of untamable wild Indians who had to be conquered/placated/killed/erased. As Tejas became Texas, Anglo settlers created a narrative of heroism and triumph over nature, yet the truth of their "revolution" was their desire to maintain a slave economy.[24] The Texas creation myth informs some of the key theoretical and material stakes present in the context of the settler-colonial state of Texas, and by extension the United States, both of which depend on the constitutive redeployment of nationalistic rebordering practices.[25] Through our documentary, we demonstrate that contested space has been a social and historical fact, involving multiple, layered identities and numerous internal conflicts.[26] And as such, the borderlands have been imagined and reimagined by Aboriginal, colonial, and imperial agents.

Chicana feminists have led in contesting "the terms of capitalist spatial formation" and the narratives used "to naturalize violent racial, gender, sexual, and class ideologies."[27] Narratives form and conceptualize traditions, myths, and definitions in particular spaces; and it is through narratives/propaganda that nation-states reproduce their borders. Therefore, there has to be "border amnesia" in order to maintain the nation-state, which strategically and violently erases cultures, identities, and differences while creating systems of domination.[28] It is our goal to demonstrate that the borderlands are in a process of continued contestation and that such processes continue in the "postcolonial" era, in which an imperialist paradigm imposes its will on the region.

"In the Beginning": *Operación Ocelotl*

On February 22, 2008, the *Texas Observer Magazine* published Melissa del Bosque's article titled "Holes in the Wall."[29] Del Bosque, an investigative journalist, wrote the first article to critically look at the U.S. border fence in South Texas, which was the last place to be seized by the Department of Homeland Security (DHS). Land seizures by the DHS began in the autumn of 2007, and she was the first journalist to ask what the determinants in the placing of the U.S. border fence were, and to report the coercive methods employed by the DHS.

Almost seven years after Melissa del Bosque's article, Ramón met with Dr. Eloisa G. Taméz on January 3, 2015, to discuss the possibility of collaborating on a documentary in which she could share her story of resistance. Professor Taméz's case was unique in that it involved the intersection of various identities that reflected the complicated discourses of the borderlands. She was a U.S. citizen, a tribal Elder of the Lipan Apache Band of Texas, a retired colonel of the U.S. Army Medical Corps, and a full professor at the University of Texas Rio Grande Valley. She embodied intersectionality, and her story exemplified the multiple layers of history and identities of the Texas-Mexico borderlands and mirrored the stories of survival and resistance of Indigenous people.[30]

Initially, Ramón envisioned an environmental justice film focusing on historical resistance movements against colonialism and imperialism, but as we came to know the Tamez family, the documentary organically changed as a result of our respectful collaboration. We listened. In the first meeting, Professor Taméz mentioned that she had spoken to many journalists over the years but at times she felt that her story was exploited. And she said that she would be willing to participate in a project, provided we listen to her on her own terms. For us, this meant we needed to honor and respect her story, as we knew that traditional Western research had a tendency to be exploitative.[31]

Ramón's second meeting with Professor Taméz was in August 2015, when he delivered a rough draft of the proposal for the film and asked if it would be possible to employ the Rio Grande River as one of the key storytellers of the film. She beamed and said that would be wonderful, because the river was a sacred source of life. Eloisa suggested Ramón contact her daughter, Dr. Margo Tamez, as feedback from Margo would be of critical importance in being able to responsibly produce the film. Margo's doctoral dissertation had been about the border wall and the violent erasures it entailed to the lives of the Lipan Apache.[32] It was at this point that Ramón asked Dr. Rosalva Resendiz, his paternal aunt, to join this collaborative decolonial project.

The proposal contained an expansive theorization regarding the role of boundaries, borders, and the river, along with some of the environmental considerations inherent to the Texas-Mexico borderlands. The original working title of the film was *Operación Ocelotl*, a reference to the now critically endangered native feline that once freely roamed the area that has been walled. The word is Indigenous and derived from the Nahuatl *ocelotl*, a reminder of the erasure of our language, but also our survival.

Tribal Board Review of *Operación Ocelotl*

Ramón received a warm reply from Margo, but she noted that he must follow the proper protocols for engaging in conversation with members of the Lipan Apache Band of Texas. Ramón met with Margo the following week via Skype, and we were provided with a set of community guidelines to abide by: "Ndé Guidelines and Principles for Respectful Partnerships with Government, Law (Advocacy), Energy, Environment, Policy, Academia (Advocacy)."[33] Margo and Ramón went through the proposal together before submitting it for a full tribal board review. At the time, there were no stipulations except that we conduct all inquiries and communication pertaining to the film and any/all potential Lipan Apache participants through her. Margo would be our liaison until the tribal board's Committee on the Protection of Ndé (Lipan Apache) Knowledge and Cultural Property finished their review, and, more importantly, she would become a significant collaborator on and producer of the film.

Fortunately, the working proposal was largely in compliance with the stipulated guidelines. The key element that the guidelines helped us address was naming the Emilio Institute for Indigenous Research and Rights as the entity to whom we would provide all of the raw materials gathered from the production process.

In November 2015, Rosalva met with Margo and Eloisa for the first time. Margo was visiting from British Columbia and requested a meeting to discuss the production and the direction of the film. We all agreed on wanting to do a documentary that would center an Indigenous matriarch, and in doing so, we enacted a matriarchal discourse of production. Using a feminist matriarch-centered approach, we centered an Indigenous ontology that contested the patriarchal nature of Eurocentric research paradigms. This meeting solidified our objectives and set forth a collaborative Indigenous project. On March 16, 2016, after six months of anxiously waiting, we received notice that our project had been fully approved by the Committee on the Protection of Ndé (Lipan Apache) Knowledge and Cultural Property, with no stipulations other than that we continue to remain respectful.

The selection of participants was a collaborative effort, with Dr. Eloisa Taméz and Dr. Margo Tamez as leads; they also assisted in identifying other participants who had been significant in their case *Tamez v. Chertoff*. Margo was pivotal in organizing and mobilizing the efforts against the wall leading up to the federal court case in 2009, as well as taking their case to the Organization of American States (OAS) and the United Nations Committee on Ending Racial Discrimination (UNCERD). These two latter instances would involve the help of the UT Austin School of Law's Human Rights and Immigration Clinic, headed by Denise Gilman and Ariel Dulitzky, who were featured in the film. The film ultimately featured seven participants: three members of the Lipan Apache Band of Texas, one member of the Lipan Apache Tribe of Texas, and three additional individuals who had been of critical importance in raising awareness of the issues posed by the border wall—namely, Denise Gilman, Ariel Dulitzky, and Melissa del Bosque.

In addition to these methodological procedures, we purposefully honored a decolonial perspective centering Indigenous research and epistemology. We sought only to give a platform to those who had been deemed allies or had aided in the case. In working toward this end, no agent aligned with or sympathetic to the colonial/imperial goals of CBP, or agent from the DHS, was to receive a platform, especially since the political intent of the film was to redress asymmetric colonial injustices. To provide a space for the colonizer would have been a breach of trust on our end and would have also been counterproductive with regard to our decolonial goals.

Methodological Interventions

In developing an Indigenous theoretical and methodological framework, we derived most of the key provisions and theoretical interventions from

Linda Tuhiwai Smith's *Decolonizing Methodologies* (1999), Jay Ruby's *Picturing Culture* (2000), Fatimah Tobing Rony's *The Third Eye* (1996), and Philip Deloria's *Indians in Unexpected Places* (2004), as well as some of the filmmaking conventions pioneered by John Marshall and Timothy Asch.[34] Furthermore, we honored the four key principles of respect, relevance, reciprocity, and responsibility as prescribed in "Ndé: Guidelines and Principles for Respectful Partnerships with Government, Law (Advocacy), Energy, Environment, Policy, Academia (Advocacy)."[35]

In honoring an Indigenous research framework, we were guided by seven interventions that intersected with the four principles of respect, relevance, reciprocity, and responsibility. First and foremost, consent was to be respected throughout the process. We would honor and respect free, prior, and informed consent (FPIC) on an ongoing procedural basis, which would allow participants to withdraw from the project at any point in the process. Second, the editing of the film would be done in consultation with all participants about their respective portrayal. Participants were to review every edited cut of the film in order to provide feedback. Third, we would have to receive full approval from all participants before disseminating the final cut of the film. Fourth, to honor relevancy and responsibility, there would be a free mass and public dissemination of the final film, as its political intent was and still is to keep it in circulation for didactic purposes and to raise awareness of the ongoing issues along the U.S.-Mexico border. Fifth, the film would be co-owned between the filmmakers and the key participant Dr. Eloisa G. Taméz. Sixth, reciprocity would be honored by providing the Emilio Institute for Indigenous Research and Rights with a hard drive including all of the unedited footage gathered throughout the production of the film, which would contribute to their ongoing efforts to create an archive of their own. Finally—and this was largely inspired by a larger epistemic and imaginative political perspective—we committed to employing an open disclosure and acknowledgment of the co-construction entailed by the project at all times. This spoke directly against the lasting legacy of the stereotypical portrayal of Indigenous peoples as not contemporaneous with (post)modernity.[36]

This last point addresses Indigenous erasure created by "salvage ethnography," which was perpetrated by ethnographers such as Robert Flaherty, Franz Boas, and Margaret Mead. The myth of *the vanishing Indian* was based on the belief that "Indians" would vanish due to their inability to survive colonization and modernity.[37] Addressing this taxidermic process of erasure was of critical importance in the making of our documentary and informed the archival and aesthetic nature of the film. First, we had to honor our agreement and do justice to Prof. Taméz's story of resistance. Second, we were committed to utilizing the same colonial archive (maps, documents, architecture) to disavow the Texas creation myth, while drawing attention to the forgotten archive of the colonial encounter.[38] And finally, our guiding principle was to create a decolonizing document that would *write back* against the colonial erasures that have been perpetrated by ethnographic documentaries and by the misrepresentation of Indigenous peoples in cinematic film.[39]

(Post)production of *El Muro | The Wall*: Relational Relevancy

After our first interview with Eloisa Taméz on May 20, 2016, the film remained in production through July 29, 2016, when the final interview was conducted with Chief Daniel Castro Romero, Lipan Apache tribal chairman. At his request we filmed the interview in front of the Alamo in San Antonio, Texas, where the Texas creation myth had its beginnings. And with that backdrop, we recorded the truth of Indigenous dispossession and the assault on the borderlands.

At the suggestion of Dr. Margo Tamez, our first public community screening was done through the Research Exchange Symposium in May 2017, in an effort to share our work with the Lipan Apache Band of Texas, as well as to engage with the local community, including those in the academic community interested in decolonial approaches. We received positive feedback, as well as suggestions that we received respectfully, honoring the exchange. At the time, we were still calling the film *Operación Ocelotl*, but we knew it was time to create a new title in consultation with the Tamez family. By November 2017, Ramón showcased the film in Seattle, Washington, at the Native Voices Film Festival. Then, on Thursday, February 14, 2018, we screened the film in a premiere at the historic Cine El Rey Theater in McAllen, Texas, with the Tamez family in attendance, as well as many of our contributors.

As a decolonial archival tool, *El Muro | The Wall* presents a single case against the coercive power of the nation-state and historic colonial erasures. But it also documents a case study in the use of decoloniality and Indigenous knowledge production that talks back against the material and imaginative archive used to reproduce and stabilize the bordering processes of settler colonialism. The film itself addresses the continued assault on Indigenous peoples, who are an unsettling reminder of the illegitimacy with which Anglo settlers came to occupy the Americas and continue to dispossess Indigenous peoples through coercive legal and extralegal means. In regard to the action of "writing back," as expounded upon by Linda Smith's *Decolonizing Methodologies*, we hope that by producing a film of this kind, we may begin to ameliorate the violence enacted by colonial mythologies. And in doing so, we hope that we have situated Indigenous research within the academy.[40]

In the end, the film led us to travel the vast majority of the Mexica/Coahuiltecan-Tejas border, as well as to visit the unceded territory of the Syilx Okanagan People (British Columbia, Canada). Like the coyotl, we crossed the imagined borders of colonialism. This would itself become a small distance compared to the extent of circulation of the film, which has been publicly screened on three continents, at various film festivals, and in many academic conferences. Honoring relevancy and reciprocity, the film continues to be available for public viewing online, subtitled in English and Spanish.[41] And very much like the coyotl, which survived linguistic erasure to become known as coyote both in Spanish and English, we have traversed ontological and epistemic academic borders in an effort to ensure the survival of our knowledge and culture.

NOTES

1. María Josefina Saldaña-Portillo, *Indian Given: Racial Geographies Across Mexico and the United States* (Durham, N.C.: Duke University Press, 2016).
2. Leela Gandhi, *Postcolonial Theory: A Critical Introduction*, 2nd ed. (New York: Columbia University Press, 2019), 4–5.
3. Hubert J. Miller, *José de Escandón: Colonizer of Nuevo Santander* (Edinburg, Tex.: The New Santander Press, 1980).
4. Emma Pérez, *The Decolonial Imaginary: Writing Chicanas into History* (Bloomington: Indiana University Press, 1999).
5. Audre Lorde, *Sister Outsider: Essays and Speeches* (Berkeley: Crossing Press, 1984); Gandhi, *Postcolonial Theory*.

6. Gandhi, *Postcolonial Theory*; Linda Tuhiwai Smith, *Decolonizing Methodologies* (London: Zed Books, 1999).
7. W. E. B. Du Bois, *Dusk of Dawn: An Essay Toward an Autobiography of a Race Concept* (New Brunswick: Transaction Publishers, 1994); Gloria Anzaldúa, *Borderlands / La Frontera: The New Mestiza* (San Francisco: Aunt Lute Books, 1987).
8. María Eugenia Cotera and María Josefina Saldaña-Portillo, "Indigenous but Not Indian? Chicana/os and the Politics of Indigeneity," in *The World of Indigenous North America*, ed. Robert Warrior (London: Taylor & Francis Group, 2014), 549–68.
9. Martha Menchaca, *Recovering History, Constructing Race: The Indian, Black, and White Roots of Mexican Americans* (Austin: University of Texas Press, 2001); Saldaña-Portillo, *Indian Given*.
10. Enrique Krauze, *Mexico: Biography of Power; A History of Modern Mexico, 1810–1996* (New York: HarperCollins, 1997); Aníbal Quijano, "Coloniality of Power, Eurocentrism, and Latin America," *Nepantla: Views from South* 1, no. 3 (2000): 533.
11. Du Bois, *Dusk of Dawn*.
12. Quote from Saldaña-Portillo, *Indian Given*, 23. See also Ramón Resendiz, Rosalva Resendiz, and Irene Klaver, "Colonialism and Imperialism: Indigenous Resistance on the US/Mexico Border," *Perspectives on Global Development and Technology* 16 (2017): 15–33; Patrick Wolfe, "Settler Colonialism and the Elimination of the Native," *Journal of Genocide Research* 8, no. 4 (2006): 387–409.
13. Saldaña-Portillo, *Indian Given*, 23.
14. Saldaña-Portillo, *Indian Given*; Philip Joseph Deloria, *Indians in Unexpected Places* (Lawrence: University Press of Kansas, 2004).
15. Fatimah Tobing Rony, *The Third Eye: Race, Cinema, and Ethnographic Spectacle* (Durham, N.C.: Duke University Press, 1996), 102.
16. Gandhi, *Postcolonial Theory*; Faye Ginsberg, "Archival Exposure: Disability, Documentary, and the Making of Counternarratives," in *Documenting the World: Film, Photography, and the Scientific Record*, ed. Gregg Mitman and Kelley Wilder (Chicago: University of Chicago Press, 2016); Rony, *Third Eye*.
17. Smith, *Decolonizing Methodologies*.
18. Michelle Guzman and Zachary Hurwitz, "Violations on the Part of the United States Government of Indigenous Rights Held by Members of the Lipan Apache, Kickapoo, and Ysleta del Sur Tigua Tribes of the Texas-Mexico Border" (briefing paper, Working Group on Human Rights and the Border Wall, University of Texas at Austin, June 2008, revised October 18, 2008), 2–4, https://law.utexas.edu/humanrights/borderwall/analysis/briefing-violations-of-indigenous-rights.pdf.
19. These included key provisions of the Environmental Protection Act of 1986, the Clean Water Act of 1972, the Clean Air Act of 1963, the Endangered Species Act of 1973, and the Native American Graves Protection and Repatriation Act of 1990. See Nicole Miller, "How Property Rights Are Affected by the Texas-

Mexico Border Fence: A Failure Due to Insufficient Procedure," *Texas International Law Journal* 45, no. 3 (2010): 631–54.

20. Sural Shah, "The Crisis in Our Own Backyard: United States Response to Unaccompanied Minor Children from Central America," *Harvard Public Health Review* 9 (2016), http://harvardpublichealthreview.org/the-crisis-in-our-own-backyard-united-states-response-to-unaccompanied-minor-children-from-central-america/.
21. Jose A. DelReal, "Donald Trump Announces a Presidential Bid," *The Washington Post*, June 16, 2015, https://www.washingtonpost.com/news/post-politics/wp/2015/06/16/donald-trump-to-announce-his-presidential-plans-today/?noredirect=on&utm_term=.5633d4ffde4e.
22. Melissa del Bosque, "Texans Receive First Notices of Land Condemnation for Trump's Border Wall," *Texas Observer Magazine*, March 14, 2017, https://www.texasobserver.org/texas-border-wall-mexico-condemnation-letter/.
23. Erik Ortiz, "Ancient Native American Burial Site Blasted for Trump Border Wall Construction," *NBC News*, February 12, 2020, https://www.nbcnews.com/news/us-news/ancient-native-american-burial-site-blasted-trump-border-wall-construction-n1135906.
24. Brian DeLay, "Independent Indians and the U.S.-Mexican War," *The American Historical Review* 112, no. 1 (2007): 35.
25. The processes are noted by both Gandhi, in *Postcolonial Thought*, and Benedict Anderson, in *Imagined Communities: Reflections on the Origin and Spread of Nationalism* (New York: Verso, 2006); they note the necessity of deploying amnesiac colonial practices for the purpose of creating nationalistic mythologies in the postcolony.
26. Doreen Massey, *Space, Place, and Gender* (Minneapolis: University of Minnesota Press, 1994).
27. Mary Pat Brady, *Extinct Lands, Temporal Geographies: Chicano Literature and the Urgency of Space* (Durham, N.C.: Duke University Press, 2002), 6.
28. Brady, *Extinct Lands*, 60.
29. Melissa del Bosque, "Holes in the Wall," *Texas Observer Magazine*, February 22, 2008, https://www.texasobserver.org/2688-holes-in-the-wall/.
30. Patricia Hill Collins, *Black Feminist Thought: Knowledge, Consciousness and the Politics of Empowerment* (New York: Routledge, Chapman & Hall, 1990); Patricia Hill Collins, *Fighting Words: Black Women and the Search for Justice* (Minneapolis: University of Minnesota Press, 1998).
31. Smith, *Decolonizing Methodologies*.
32. Margo Tamez, "Returning Lipan Apache Women's Laws, Lands and Power in El Calaboz Rancheria, Texas-Mexico Border" (PhD diss., Washington State University, 2010), ProQuest.
33. Margo Tamez et al., "Ndé: Guidelines and Principles for Respectful Partnerships with Government, Law (Advocacy), Energy, Environment, Policy, Aca-

demia (Advocacy)" (unpublished manuscript, Emilio Institute for Indigenous Research and Rights, El Calaboz, 2013).

34. Smith, *Decolonizing Methodologies*; Jay Ruby, *Picturing Culture: Explorations of Film and Anthropology* (Chicago: University of Chicago Press, 2000); Rony, *Third Eye*; Deloria, *Indians in Unexpected Places*.
35. Tamez et al., "Guidelines and Principles."
36. Deloria, *Indians in Unexpected Places*; Rony, *Third Eye*; Smith, *Decolonizing Methodologies*.
37. Robert Flaherty is credited with making the first ethnographic documentary, *Nanook of the North* (1922), in which he employed fictional reconstructions to portray what was held as an ethnographic past. Rony notes, "When Flaherty stated, 'One often has to distort a thing to catch its true spirit,' he was not just referring to his own artistry but to the preconditions for the effective, 'true' representation of so-called vanishing culture." Rony, *Third Eye*, 102. See also Deloria, *Indians in Unexpected Places*.
38. DeLay, "Independent Indians"; Gandhi, *Postcolonial Theory*.
39. Philip Joseph Deloria, *Playing Indian* (New Haven: Yale University Press, 1998); Smith, *Decolonizing Methodologies*.
40. To watch the full film, please visit ElMuroTheWall.DocumentaryWorlds.com.
41. Thanks to Miguel Aguilar Dorado, a doctoral candidate at the National Autonomous University of Mexico, who translated the film's subtitles into Spanish free of charge.

BIBLIOGRAPHY

Anderson, Benedict. *Imagined Communities: Reflections on the Origin and Spread of Nationalism*. New York: Verso, 2006.

Anzaldúa, Gloria. *Borderlands / La Frontera: The New Mestiza*. San Francisco: Aunt Lute Books, 1987.

Brady, Mary Pat. *Extinct Lands, Temporal Geographies: Chicano Literature and the Urgency of Space*. Durham, N.C.: Duke University Press, 2002.

Collins, Patricia Hill. *Black Feminist Thought: Knowledge, Consciousness, and the Politics of Empowerment*. New York: Routledge, Chapman & Hall, 1980.

Collins, Patricia Hill. *Fighting Words: Black Women and the Search for Justice*. Minneapolis: University of Minnesota Press, 1998.

Cotera, María Eugenia, and María Josefina Saldaña-Portillo. "Indigenous but Not Indian? Chicana/os and the Politics of Indigeneity." In *The World of Indigenous North America*, edited by Robert Warrior, 549–68. London: Taylor & Francis Group, 2014.

DeLay, Brian. "Independent Indians and the U.S.-Mexican War." *American Historical Review* 112, no. 1 (2007): 35–68.

del Bosque, Melissa. "Holes in the Wall." *Texas Observer Magazine*, February 22, 2008. https://www.texasobserver.org/2688-holes-in-the-wall/.

del Bosque, Melissa. "Texans Receive First Notices of Land Condemnation for Trump's Border Wall." *Texas Observer Magazine*, March 14, 2017. https://www.texasobserver.org/texas-border-wall-mexico-condemnation-letter/.

Deloria, Philip Joseph. *Indians in Unexpected Places*. Lawrence: University Press of Kansas, 2004.

Deloria, Philip Joseph. *Playing Indian*. New Haven: Yale University Press, 1998.

DelReal, Jose A. "Donald Trump Announces a Presidential Bid." *The Washington Post*, June 16, 2015. https://www.washingtonpost.com/news/post-politics/wp/2015/06/16/donald-trump-to-announce-his-presidential-plans-today/?noredirect=on&utm_term=.5633d4ffde4e.

Du Bois, W. E. B. *Dusk of Dawn: An Essay Toward an Autobiography of a Race Concept*. New Brunswick: Transaction Publishers, 1994.

Gandhi, Leela. *Postcolonial Theory: A Critical Introduction*. 2nd ed. New York: Columbia University Press, 2019.

Ginsberg, Faye. "Archival Exposure: Disability, Documentary, and the Making of Counternarratives." In *Documenting the World: Film, Photography, and the Scientific Record*, edited by Gregg Mitman and Kelley Wilder. Chicago: University of Chicago Press, 2016.

Guzman, Michelle, and Zachary Hurwitz. "Violations on the Part of the United States Government of Indigenous Rights Held by Members of the Lipan Apache, Kickapoo, and Ysleta del Sur Tigua Tribes of the Texas-Mexico Border." Briefing paper, Working Group on Human Rights and the Border Wall, University of Texas at Austin, June 2008, revised October 18, 2008. https://law.utexas.edu/humanrights/borderwall/analysis/briefing-violations-of-indigenous-rights.pdf.

Krauze, Enrique. *Mexico: Biography of Power; A History of Modern Mexico, 1810–1996*. New York: HarperCollins, 1997.

Lorde, Audre. *Sister Outsider: Essays and Speeches*. Berkeley: Crossing Press, 1984.

Massey, Doreen. *Space, Place, and Gender*. Minneapolis: University of Minnesota Press, 1994.

Menchaca, Martha. *Recovering History, Constructing Race: The Indian, Black, and White Roots of Mexican Americans*. Austin: University of Texas Press, 2001.

Miller, Hubert J. *José de Escandón: Colonizer of Nuevo Santander*. Edinburg, Tex.: The New Santander Press, 1980.

Miller, Nicole. "How Property Rights Are Affected by the Texas-Mexico Border Fence: A Failure Due to Insufficient Procedure." *Texas International Law Journal* 45, no. 3 (2010): 631–54.

Ortiz, Erik. "Ancient Native American Burial Site Blasted for Trump Border Wall Construction." *NBC News*, February 12, 2020. https://www.nbcnews.com/news/us-news/ancient-native-american-burial-site-blasted-trump-border-wall-construction-n1135906.

Pérez, Emma. *The Decolonial Imaginary: Writing Chicanas into History*. Bloomington: Indiana University Press, 1999.

Quijano, Aníbal. "Coloniality of Power, Eurocentrism, and Latin America." *Nepantla: Views from South* 1, no. 3 (2000): 533–80.

Resendiz, Ramón, Rosalva Resendiz, and Irene Klaver. "Colonialism and Imperialism: Indigenous Resistance on the US/Mexico Border." *Perspectives on Global Development and Technology* 16 (2017): 15–33.

Rony, Fatimah Tobing. *The Third Eye: Race, Cinema, and Ethnographic Spectacle*. Durham, N.C.: Duke University Press, 1996.

Ruby, Jay. *Picturing Culture: Explorations of Film and Anthropology*. Chicago: University of Chicago Press, 2000.

Saldaña-Portillo, María Josefina. *Indian Given: Racial Geographies Across Mexico and the United States*. Durham, N.C.: Duke University Press, 2016.

Shah, Sural. "The Crisis in Our Own Backyard: United States Response to Unaccompanied Minor Children from Central America." *Harvard Public Health Review* 9 (2016). http://harvardpublichealthreview.org/the-crisis-in-our-own-backyard-united-states-response-to-unaccompanied-minor-children-from-central-america/.

Smith, Linda Tuhiwai. *Decolonizing Methodologies*. London: Zed Books, 1999.

Tamez, Margo. "Returning Lipan Apache Women's Laws, Lands and Power in El Calaboz Rancheria, Texas-Mexico Border." PhD diss., Washington State University, 2010. ProQuest.

Tamez, Margo, et al. "Ndé: Guidelines and Principles for Respectful Partnerships with Government, Law (Advocacy), Energy, Environment, Policy, Academia (Advocacy)." Unpublished manuscript, Emilio Institute for Indigenous Research and Rights, El Calaboz, 2013.

Wolfe, Patrick. "Settler Colonialism and the Elimination of the Native." *Journal of Genocide Research* 8, no. 4 (2006): 387–409.

TWENTY-SEVEN

Settler-Colonial Visions, Texas Mythmaking, and Indigenous Resistance to "the Wall"

JEFFREY P. SHEPHERD

It should come as no surprise that one of the most prominent challenges to the militarization of the U.S.-Mexico border came from an Apache woman. Dr. Eloisa Taméz, a professor of nursing at the University of Texas Rio Grande Valley and a veteran of the U.S. Army Nurse Corps, refused to submit to federal pressure and forfeit her land along the Rio Grande in South Texas. Taméz, who is Lipan Apache, filed a lawsuit against Michael Chertoff, secretary of the Department of Homeland Security (DHS), as the point person for the Bush administration and its implementation of the 2006 Secure Fence Act. In her lawsuit, she refused condemnation of lands that have belonged to the Tamez family for centuries. Born in 1935, Eloisa came from a long line of strong Apache women who struggled to fend off attempts at land theft and dispossession under the flags of Spain, Mexico, Texas, and the United States. Considering this history of resistance and perseverance, Dr. Taméz was following the footsteps of her grandmothers, who maintained deep ties to the land and the river that informed their culture, history, and identity.

As an activist historian with brief and tenuous ties to Texas and the borderlands, my position as a White settler colonist commenting on Apache resistance seems suspect. I was born in New York City and raised in Florida and Nebraska, and I live in New Mexico (but teach in Texas), so why should I be writing about the Tamez family and a struggle that is the most recent iteration of centuries of fighting against nation-state oppression? Considering the legacy of non-Native academics contributing to the silencing of Indigenous histories, it is important to establish my positionality and be transparent about my intentions. My entrance into this conversation, and my relationship with the Tamez family, reflects an academic, activist, and pedagogical orientation toward the histories and contemporary realities of Indigenous peoples in the Southwest and greater borderlands region. I have worked with the Hualapai in Arizona; Ysleta del Sur Pueblo in El Paso, Texas; Blackfoot/Blood peoples along the U.S.-Canada borderlands; the Mescalero Tribe in New Mexico; and non–federally recognized groups in Texas and New Mexico.

In this essay, however, I want to situate the El Calaboz Gathering and the Tamez lawsuit within multiple layers of physical violence, representational erasure, and settler-colonial mythmaking. I divide the essay into several sections: First, I explain my relationship with the Tamez family and how I became involved with their case; second, I explain the ways in which stereotypes about Indigenous identity in Texas complicated their land claims case; third, I summarize Texas "Indian policy" in the nineteenth century and then segue into a narrative that explains the "submergence" of Indigenous identities in Texas due to anti-Indian violence. I then shift to a discussion of representational violence perpetrated by historians and marketers of the Texas myth, which erased Indigenous histories in the public historical imagination. Finally, I provide context for the "resurgence" of Indigenous identities and activism along the border and comment on how the Lipan fight against militarization is both cause and consequence of a larger Indigenous movement against racism and oppression in the borderlands. My positionality as an academic and witness-participant in these Indigenous struggles for twenty-five years influences the structure, form, and tone of this chapter, which is not a strictly "academic piece." It is a personal reflection emerging from my research and advocacy, as well as my relationship with the Tamez family.

I began working with the Tamez family in 2007, when Dr. Margo Tamez, the daughter of Eloisa, reached out to me because she saw my PowerPoint lectures and a conference talk posted online. I had been reading articles about Indigenous groups in the borderlands "reemerging" to claim their rightful place in historical narratives and contemporary discussions about the militarization of the border. Although federally recognized and unrecognized groups have been struggling to survive the economic, social, political, and ecological pressures of life along the international boundary for generations, the post-9/11 spike in military presence accelerated the actions of Native groups from Corpus Christi to Tijuana. Indigenous peoples saw their ability to cross the border truncated by Border Patrol and customs officials, and they were distraught at the destruction of ecosystems and the pollution of water sources due to construction of "the wall." Their traditions of moving throughout their homelands have particularly come under assault since the passage of NAFTA in 1994 and the border control policies called Operations Hold the Line and Gatekeeper.[1] The U.S. reaction to the destruction of the World Trade Center on 9/11, resulting in the largest militarization of the border in modern history, offers a direct throughline to the Bush-era assault upon Indigenous lands and people in the borderlands.

When Margo and I began talking, she explained the basic contours of what her family was facing and she provided a summary of her family history, including the land grant they received from Spain that was threatened by the Secure Fence Act. She explained that the Department of Homeland Security was pressuring residents to sell their land so that the federal government could build a wall to prohibit people from "unlawfully" entering the United States. Landowners reacted variously with refusal, apprehension, and willing participation. However, DHS was pressuring some people more than others, and this reflected biases against impoverished communities of color. In particular, she shared that her mother refused to sell her land and that she was beginning a lawsuit against the secretary of the Department of Homeland Security, Michael Chertoff. Later I joined a phone conference between her, Eloisa, Denise Gilman, Peter Schey, and others involved with the lawsuit. As they struggled to reframe the case as one of Aboriginal land rights and the violation of the rights of Indigenous peoples, I thought about the historical context of this particular case brought by a Lipan family, and the larger narratives of violence, dispossession, and silencing of Indigenous histories in the borderlands.[2]

It was clear that the militarization of the border after 9/11 and the Secure Fence Act of 2006 were disproportionately impacting Indigenous peoples, and that they were protesting this assault upon their lands, histories, and cultures. Just as the Tamez lawsuit against Chertoff and DHS brought the history of the Lipan Apache into public awareness in South Texas, the increased policing of people of color, anti-immigrant rhetoric, and White supremacist movement were accelerating an Indigenous reaction throughout the borderlands. In direct defiance of these waves of violence, Indigenous peoples from South Texas to San Diego were using social media and grassroots organizing to amplify their voices. As they worked assiduously against the border wall, an increased Border Patrol presence, the destruction of ecosystems, and the evisceration of federal laws protecting sacred sites in the present, they simultaneously fought to reframe the histories of their peoples in the public imagination. Resisting the border wall and militarization required Indigenous peoples to explain—and in some cases justify—their historical presence in the region. This twin struggle over land and rights in the present, and over reenvisioning the Indigenous past, made the Lipan case important for all Indigenous peoples.[3]

While the Tamez family litigated the case against DHS, few people understood that the histories of Indigenous peoples in Texas had been largely erased across most public spaces and state institutions. Residents of Texas may have been familiar with the colonial-era land grants, and they may have thought they knew something about "Apaches" during the nineteenth century. But very few understood that a Lipan family still held a grant, and that an Apache woman in her seventies was suing the secretary of the Department of Homeland Security. There was an epistemological gulf between the dominant tropes of savage Apaches in the nineteenth century and a highly educated Lipan woman suing the federal government in the twenty-first century. These erasures made it difficult for the Tamez family to make their case, because Texas is particularly notorious for a deeply entrenched set of myths and metanarratives that privilege settler-colonial perspectives and silence Indigenous histories. Thus, as the Tamez family litigated their case, several racist narratives had to be deconstructed and replaced with accurate representations of Native people—particularly the Lipan Apache—in Texas.

Several factors contributed to the White supremacist assumptions about alleged Native disappearance in Texas. First, Texas history during the mid-nineteenth century contained a pernicious mix of Southern anti-Blackness that included chattel slavery and lynching; "Western" tropes about Manifest Destiny, frontier violence, and anti-Indianism; and borderlands animosities toward Mexican-origin peoples. Texas embodied these trends, and it responded violently to the non-White populations within the state. As Gary Clayton Anderson notes in *The Conquest of Texas*, between 1825 and 1875 Anglo Texans resolved differences with non-White peoples through perpetual racialized warfare. This mixture of violence, grievance, racism, and toxic masculinity structured the uprisings against Mexico in the 1830s that led to the creation of the independent Republic of Texas, it fueled the U.S. annexation of Texas, and it propelled the subsequent invasion of Mexico. Moreover, the post–Civil War disfranchisement of people of color, a decades-long spike in the lynching of Black and Mexican people, repeated filibusters into Mexico, the hardening of the border, and warfare against Indians defined violence in Texas.[4]

Several critical decisions in Texas caused tremendous damage to Native people in the new state. First, in 1845, upon annexation by the United States, Texas retained control of land within its boundaries, rather than the federal government, as was the case in New Mexico, for instance. The new state was also bankrupt and had a very high debt load. To resolve its financial problems and to "settle" the region with non-Indians, Texas initiated a terribly pernicious process of selling off "state lands" to private individuals and corporations. These sales for relatively little triggered a chain reaction of non-Indians flooding into the public lands and purchasing them as private property. This placed Native peoples such as the Apache in the direct crosshairs of capitalists and settler colonists purchasing the land and wanting to exploit it. Vigilante groups, militias, the Texas Rangers, and the U.S. military facilitated this process.[5]

Racialized violence and militarized removal were practically inevitable. The second problem for Native people flowed out of the first one: the state of Texas generally oversaw Indian affairs, rather than the Department of War. The Department of the Interior was created after Texas was annexed, and after the U.S. invasion of Mexico and the signing of the Treaty of Guadalupe Hidalgo, so Texas came into the union before the Office of Indian Affairs could establish itself in Texas. Thus there was no check on the expansion of Anglos into Apache land—in fact, the state promoted it, protecting Anglos, while blaming Indians and taking their land.[6] The second governor of Texas, Mirabeau Buonaparte Lamar, even employed the rhetoric of extermination and genocide as a basis of his Indian policy.

The antebellum westward push for land to support chattel slavery worked in combination with Indian hating and Indian hunting. The two were part of the same settler-colonial, racial capitalistic system: make warfare against Native people and take their land to expand chattel slavery, and then require more enslaved peoples to work new plantations. Simultaneously, Texas and the United States expanded the string of military forts established during the U.S. invasion of Mexico, to serve a dual purpose of militarizing the border and launching expeditions against Native groups. After the Civil War, the military used the forts to stop the cross-border movement of Native peoples and to destroy Apache communities north of the border. In addition to campaigns by the army, a few decades earlier Texas had conjured up its own uniquely brutal police force in the Texas Rangers. Ranger groups led by John Baylor, Sul Ross, and others hunted Native people in the name of protecting White families along the Texas frontier.[7]

After the Civil War, Ranger forces and military troops pursued Apaches, Comanches, and Kiowas to near extinction. The brief experiment with reservations in Texas ended because covetous Anglos attacked Native families, and the anemic Indian Bureau relocated the groups north to Indian Territory. Indeed, by the 1870s, many tribal groups had been driven north or sought refuge in Mexico. Popularized battles at Palo Duro Canyon and Adobe Walls marked the end of militarized resistance by the Comanche in 1874 and 1875, while the final stand of Victorio—after he crisscrossed the border between Texas, Chihuahua, and New Mexico—ended with his death at the hands of Mexican forces in 1880. Lesser known than these encounters was "Mackenzie's Raid" in 1875 and the murder of Lipan men, women, and children across the border in Mexico. These violent attacks upon the Lipan characterized their history for the rest of the nineteenth century.[8]

While the blatant physical violence against the Lipan somewhat subsided in the early twentieth century, several intersecting developments unfolded to cause ongoing harm against Natives in Texas. First, vigilante groups continued using racial violence to divest people of color of land, power, and status. Anglos assaulted and hanged Mexicans, Indians, and Blacks throughout Texas. Local law enforcement participated in and facilitated the extralegal violence. This violence reached near-genocidal levels in the decades following the Mexican Revolution, as evidenced in the massacre in El Polvo, West Texas, known as "La Matanza." Mobs of racist Anglos attacked Mexicans who they claimed were "invading" the United States by illegally crossing the border, and they shot and hanged longtime residents in expressions of violence designed to strengthen racial and class hierarchies. Some of these victims were Indigenous people.[9]

As this physical violence unfolded, two related forms of epistemic violence continued. Many Native peoples in the borderlands were claiming a Mexican identity with greater frequency. For various reasons, including the influence of the Catholic Church giving Native people Spanish surnames, groups like the Lipan could reasonably "hide in plain sight" as Mexicans, rather than Apaches. While this practice was clearly a means of survival in the face of intimidation and harassment, it carried with it a unique epistemological violence that caused many Indigenous peoples to submerge their traditional cultures from the public gaze. Many families with Indigenous ancestry feared sharing this information with grandchildren, so within a few generations, many "Mexicans" knew little about their Apache ancestry.

Second, dominant narratives of Texas history extolled a particular exceptionalism that erased these patterns of violence, or they inverted the violence of Anglos as a defensive measure against aggressive Mexicans and Indians. Combined with the trope of the dangerous and unstable border prone to drugs, deviance, and violence, the Southern imaginary of violent Black uprising, and the salacious stories of the wild Texas "frontier" inhabited by savage Indians, the popular narratives of Texas history included a triple threat to White settler-colonial hegemony.[10]

A full analysis of the historiography of Texas exceptionalism and how it framed anti-Indianism is beyond the scope of this chapter, but a few central themes have defined Texas identity and its sense of superiority. One thread of historical production promotes the Southern "Lost Cause" narrative in which the antebellum South was characterized by noble plantation owners providing for their Black workers until an overzealous Northern federal government stripped them of their rights and freedoms in the Civil War. This Lost Cause narrative framed Texans as aggrieved patriots defending states' rights. A second strand of historiography situates Texas history within the epic westward movement of frontiersmen battling Indians and conquering the wilderness. This strand drew heavily upon the tropes of American innocence, Manifest Destiny, and indomitable White male courage. This narrative claimed that Texans were at the vanguard of fighting Indians to open the West for Anglo settlement. The third strand is steeped in anti-Mexican racism rooted in the Black Legend of Spanish excess, and, alternatively, claims of Mexican sloth, violence, criminality, and racial inferiority. The anti-Mexican "scholarship" offers justifications for the U.S. invasion of Mexico, categorizes Mexicans as second-class citizens after the war, eviscerates land grants in the nineteenth century, and consigns Mexicans to the most dangerous jobs in the labor system of the twentieth century. Tied to these stereotypes are the tropes of the perpetual Mexican foreigner invading the United States and taking American jobs. This anti-Mexican narrative buttressed the trope of the violent, permeable border characterized by vice and criminality. Braided together, these historiographical strands have defined Texas exceptionalism and settler-colonial narratives of White supremacy, and have made invisible the Indigenous presence in Texas.[11]

A few books have had an outsized influence on the exclusionary historical memory and state-sponsored narratives of Texas. First, John Wesley Wilbarger's racist book *Indian Depredations in Texas* (1889) offered a synthesis of the fears of Indian-on-white violence on the Texas frontier. This tome, reprinted numerous times, confirmed White victimhood with its assertions that Native people were guilty of "depredations" against innocent White settlers. It ensconced the notion that the federal government facilitated Native recalcitrance due to its coddling of Native people.[12] A generation later, Walter Prescott Webb became one of the most well-known historians in Texas, and his scholarship fundamentally shaped narratives of Texas exceptionalism. Webb received his PhD from the University of Texas at Austin and was a president of the Texas State Historical Association, where he started the *Handbook of Texas*, the precursor to the online handbook. His work influenced thousands of historians, schoolteachers, and politicians, as well as the general public. His two most noteworthy books, *The Great Plains* (1931) and *The Texas Rangers: A Century of Frontier Defense* (1935), offered the most significant history of the near-mythological police force and its heroic protection of the White settler-citizen against the Mexican and Indian threats surrounding him.[13]

Another highly influential author is T. R. Fehrenbach, whose *Lone Star: A History of Texas and the Texans* has cast a long shadow over Texas historiography since its publication in 1968. An author of more than twenty books, Fehrenbach was a columnist for *The San Antonio Express-News* and the director of the Texas Historical Commission. Academic historians were not particularly impressed with Fehrenbach's portrayal of non-White male Texans, but the book became widely popular, and it stands as one of the most influential portrayals of the state. These authors bear responsibility for deeply entrenching the Anglo-centric narratives of frontier heroics, White settler innocence, and masculine individualism at the core of Texas exceptionalism. These narrative tropes saturated textbooks used in history classes; they formed the touchstone for state-supported commemorative sites, museum exhibits, monuments, and memorials, and nearly all representations of the Texas past in the public realm. Indeed, the Texas myth of exceptionalism has become history, and this imagined past has become fact.[14]

This multilayered history of violence clouded conversations about Indigenous land rights, historical memory, land claims, and the lawsuit against the DHS. The Tamez family had to fight on multiple fronts, beyond the legal system. They faced racism and a highly toxic form of masculinity in the Lower Rio Grande Valley, promoted by both Anglo and Hispanic-identifying men. They had to deconstruct the notion that they were "only" Hispanic or Mexican American, and this put them sometimes at odds with people in those communities. They had to contend with ubiquitous displays of American patriotism, as their lawsuit and refusal to forfeit their land made them enemies of the state in the eyes of an ultranationalistic faction of society that grew after 9/11. Their refusal to forfeit their land was wrapped up in xenophobic rhetoric that lumped them together with the ideas of the "Muslim threat" and the "Mexican menace" promulgated by anti-immigrant nativists.

As I became more involved with the Tamez case, I reflected upon how their struggles overlapped with Apache and Indigenous resurgence throughout the borderlands. The physical violence, hiding of identities, erasures of history, and modern revitalization movements of the past few decades mirrored what I had witnessed over the previous decades. In 1999 I met with Yoeme (Yaqui) citizens who talked about their diasporic histories, their successful campaign for federal recognition, and their ties with relatives throughout Mexico. In early 2001 I talked with Tohono O'odham members about their relatives in Sonora and their plans for a card that ensured their border-crossing rights and reflected their claims to triple citizenship. In 2006, I visited museums in southern Chihuahua that held objects belonging to Apaches and emphasized their presence south of the international boundary. In 2007 I attended a meeting of the International Indigenous Treaty Council in Arizona on the Tohono O'odham reservation with representatives from dozens of Indigenous communities in Mexico, the United States, and Canada as they discussed cross-border movement and their strategies for surviving increased militarization. Citizens of the Haudenosaunee Nation talked with Yoeme/Yaqui, Apache, O'odham, Kumeyaay, and other peoples about how the nation-state borders undermined access to traditional sites and cultural landscapes.

These experiences contextualized conversations with the Tamez family, which led to our participation in the Lipan Apache gathering in El Calaboz during 2011. By this time I had conducted preliminary research into Lipan history, learning some of the reasons for submergence of their identities in Texas. I talked with Jumano Apache elder Enrique Madrid at a conference sponsored by the Center for Big Bend Studies at Sul Ross State University in Alpine, Texas. I had found an earlier article that quoted Enrique in which he critiqued the militarization of his village in Redford, Texas. Enrique and his wife Ruby ran a library and school for the community, and they knew Esequiel Hernández, the teenage boy shot by the military in 1997. Enrique was quoted in a 2006 article talking about the militarization of the border, in which Ignacio Menchaca de la Luz explained why it seemed like Apaches had disappeared from Texas. Proving the trend that Apaches sometimes claimed to be Mexican, the article offered the quote "If you said you were a Jumano Apache, you were a dead Jumano Apache." This article stuck in my head, and when I talked with Margo about it, she told me to talk with Enrique and Ruby, thus leading to the conference in Alpine. That conversation opened my eyes to the complex racial dynamics of West Texas and helped me think critically about people who said they were Mexican, when in fact they could have been Indigenous. These experiences better prepared me for the El Calaboz Gathering.[15]

The 2011 gathering represented a long-standing form of traditional gathering along the river. It was also a twenty-first-century reaction to racism and patriarchy, settler-colonial violence, capitalist extraction, militarization, and land theft. As this collection emerged from the gathering and thus encapsulates its diverse and multilayered impact, the gathering itself was a consequence of the forces mentioned above, and a catalyst for transnational Indigenous rights movements. It strengthened kin-based familial ties, brought together Lipan and non-Lipan Indigenous rights activists, and affirmed bonds between elders and youth, academics, legal theorists, lawyers, and allies. This gathering accelerated actions tied to the Tamez lawsuit and its legal challenges to the jurisdiction of nation-states over Indigenous lands on the border. It foregrounded Aboriginal territorial claims along the river, exposed land appropriation, revealed environmental degradation, and offered paths forward for the rights of non–federally recognized Indigenous groups. The ensuing briefs, testimonies, and reports delivered at the United Nations, in particular, punctuated the globally significant claims made by the Tamez family and Indigenous communities along the border.

It is difficult to summarize all of my reactions to the El Calaboz Gathering and its long-term legacy, but a few things come to mind. Women such as Margo and Eloisa were more than organizers behind the scenes: they were on the "front lines" of the legal case, speaking with human rights attorneys, judges, and the media. Second, the community relationship with the land and the river anchored conversations about environmental justice, territorial claims, and the future of youth in attendance. Third, the disregard for Indigenous land rights and centuries-old traditions of land use was manifest with the construction of the wall on the Tamez property. Fourth, the Lower Rio Grande Valley was a highly militarized space, as evidenced by a ubiquitous system of policing, military bases, Border Patrol agents, and razor wire and fencing along the border. And finally, as we drove throughout the region during the gathering, and beforehand as we followed the border southward, we witnessed historical misrepresentation and the erasure of the Indigenous presence in public space. Knowing the long history of Indigenous peoples in "the borderlands," it was shocking to observe the near-total lack of awareness about Native peoples. Aside from the Kickapoo reservation to the northwest in Eagle Pass, and an occasional Spanish mission, one would not have known that the Lower Rio Grande Valley was once a vibrant hub of Indigenous life.

The El Calaboz Gathering was a Lipan Apache reaction to the layers of historical violence, marginalization, and misremembering in the borderlands that impacted nearly all Indigenous groups. Related gatherings throughout the borderlands were impressive because of the multiple levels of violence and erasure they had confronted. Ndé and all Indigenous groups had to overcome the historical legacy of war and physical violence, policies of assimilation and extermination, ideologies of erasure, and historical representations of disappearance. Nineteenth- and early twentieth-century policies on both sides of the border accelerated the alleged disappearance of Apaches—and other Indigenous groups—sparked by Spanish policies of congregation, assimilation, and enslavement during the colonial era. Generations of baptisms, weddings, and burials as semi-citizens under colonial Spain, as well as forced labor in mines, capture by raiding Native groups or Spaniards, the loss of land, and other measures, challenged Indigenous identities. During the Mexican era, the national government conferred citizenship upon everyone in the country and eliminated race as a legal category. These decisions paved the way for the liberal state to weaken the protection of Indian lands and institute various programs that assaulted the collective lands and identities of Native people. Similar processes of disappearance and erasure happened in the United States: vigilante violence, military expeditions, and concentration on reservations removed Apaches from many of their traditional cultural places. The expansion of mining and ranching, large-scale agriculture, railroads, and incredibly disruptive water and dam projects further displaced Apache families, pushed them off their lands, and pulled them into a precarious wage-labor force in the Southwest.[16]

Alongside these physical assaults upon Indigenous lands and communities, ideologies of assimilation caused epistemic violence to Native people. The Mexican decision to erase racial categories in its constitution, combined with its ideologies of "*la raza cósmica*" and *mestizaje*, contributed to the official, bureaucratic erasure of Indigenous peoples like the Apache. Rather than recognizing a multiracial republic with independent Indigenous communities, the Mexican state promoted the notion that everyone in Mexico had Indigenous and Spanish ancestry. This ideology of unity erased "special protections" for Indigenous lands and undermined Native autonomy. In the United States, assimilation programs targeting Native land, culture, and identity weakened the sovereign claims of tribes tentatively preserved in treaties and executive orders. For nonreservation communities, ideologies of assimilation and Americanization further eroded Indigenous difference. New rules regarding the way in which the U.S. Census categorized off-reservation Indians as "White"—which sometimes meant "Mexican" in the borderlands—made them invisible to the twentieth-century racial state. Thus, by the mid-twentieth century, many Apache people living off reservations or in Mexico had allegedly disappeared and assimilated into the larger "Hispanic" population on both sides of the border.

Considering this incomplete summary of the very broad trends of the alleged disappearance and the erasure of Native peoples, it is all the more impressive that people on both sides of the border began to reconnect in the late twentieth century, denounce militarization, and revitalize their identities and cultures. This resurgence occurred throughout Texas, particularly among Indigenous peoples that predated Spanish entrance into the region. Coahuiltecans, long thought to have "disappeared" by the nineteenth century, organized in small community groups to raise awareness about their past. The Tāp Pīlam Nation of Coahuiltecans has been problematizing the misrepresentation of their history and the false claim that they went extinct by holding public gatherings, organizing dance groups, and maintaining a vibrant presence in cities such as San Antonio.[17] The Tonkawas were also reestablishing community and kinship bonds after generations of subsuming their identities in public for fear of racist reprisals. Their resurgence has been particularly remarkable considering the well-funded and vicious campaigns of genocide against them in the eighteenth and nineteenth centuries. Moreover, Tonkawas were victims of one of the most pervasive and pernicious of stereotypes, which claimed they were giant cannibals. Thus, like many other Native groups that are Indigenous to Texas, the Tonkawas assumed an outward-facing identity as Mexican while maintaining internal relations and identities as Indigenous people.[18]

Indigenous groups in the Sonoran borderlands, whether Yoeme, Cucopa, Pai Pai, or O'odham, challenged militarization, nativism, and anti-Indigenous policies that targeted their people in their own homelands for centuries. Groups like Alianza Indígena Sin Fronteras advocated for multiethnic, cross-border collaboration between federally recognized and unrecognized groups as well as Chicana/o activists. Tohono O'odham youth were particularly important in these movements, as they utilized social media tools and online platforms to magnify their networks. This pattern of resisting militarization while strengthening cultural bonds across the border unfolded among the Kumeyaay and groups in Baja and Alta California. Indeed, whether in rural spaces, urban community events, formal meetings with settler-state officials, or even online, Indigenous peoples were gathering together to secure their rights, improve their representation, and reconfigure relations of power in the borderlands.[19]

As seen in the Gathering in El Calaboz, evidence abounded for the "reemergence" of Apaches throughout the borderlands. The Chihene Nde of southwest New Mexico sponsored powwows in Silver City for the first time in the early 2000s. One of the groups of Chiricahuas not on a reservation, the Chihene Nde were holding annual gatherings and rekindling family ties. With members in the diaspora, they held the long-term goal of federal rerecognition. Similarly, Lipan Apache groups throughout Texas made increasingly prominent demands for attention from the state of Texas and the United States. The Lipan Apache Band of Texas, which is Margo's band, and the Lipan Apache Tribe of Texas sponsored annual gatherings and advocated to raise awareness of their presence. In the early 2010s, Lipan Apache Band leader Daniel Castro Romero Jr. engaged with the historic missions in San Antonio to stress the importance of including Lipan voices and perspectives throughout their public representations of Spanish colonial history in the historic sites. He and vice-chairman Richard Gonzalez traveled across the state to various historical commemorations to stress the contributions of Lipan Apaches in Texas history.

Ndé peoples have been rebuilding ties and connections across the U.S.-Mexico international boundary. Apaches claim one of the largest territories of any Indigenous group in North America. Starting in the Sonoran Desert and going east to the Gulf of Mexico, and starting at the New Mexico–Colorado border and going to the southern borders of Sonora and Chihuahua, Apaches continued to live across this vast expanse even after the 1853 Treaty of La Mesilla finalized the border at its present location. Although Apache peoples kept cultural and even familial ties intact after the "Indian Wars" of the late nineteenth century and the heightened border militarization after 1924, the growing circuits of blockading the border made it difficult to rejuvenate these relationships.[20]

For instance, some of the most public and high-profile gatherings of Ndé communities across the border were organized during the late 2010s with the aid of social media platforms on the internet. Meetings in the summer of 2017 in Ojinaga, Chihuahua, brought groups together to reestablish cultural ties, share stories, confirm identities, and assert kinship lineages. Representatives from the Lipan Apache Band and Tribe, along with members from Mescalero, San Carlos, and White Mountain in the United States, met with relatives in Chihuahua and Sonora who had been furthering a cultural revitalization movement of their own for several years. This cross-border organizing to rekindle old cultural ties and publicly express an Ndé/Apache identity is an astonishing example of Indigenous persistence and Native survival in the face of systemic racism, land theft, historical erasure, and nation-state boundary making.

As a settler colonist living in the heart of Apachería, I have witnessed and participated in nearly two decades' worth of Indigenous resurgence in what many people refer to as the borderlands. This bordered land is Indigenous land, and Native groups from the Pacific Ocean to the Gulf of Mexico have been fighting against dispossession, violence, erasure, and marginalization. Settler colonists have tried taking the land and criminalizing their existence through assimilationist ideologies, while simultaneously forcing them onto reservations or segregating them in poverty-stricken urban barrios. Anglo historians have penned self-serving narratives that erased real-world violence against Native people, thus engaging in representational and epistemological violence against the memories and histories of Native people. Ignoring contemporary poverty and marginalization, these scholars rewrote their history to justify conquest as an inevitable "clash of cultures." Despite generations of multiple forms of violence and erasure, Indigenous groups like the Apache have fought tirelessly to retain their lands, cultures, and identities. The fact that Eloisa Tamez, a Lipan grandmother, a professor of nursing, and a veteran of the U.S. Army Nurse Corps, filed suit against the U.S. government to protect her 275-year-old land grant speaks to this vitality.

Situated within this longer and larger time frame, the El Calaboz Gathering in 2011 is all the more impressive and inspirational. Organized by Lipan women, the gathering in southern Cameron County, in the Lower Rio Grande Valley, marked a turning point in the history of Indigenous rights activism and campaigns against militarization. Women between the ages of eight and eighty not only prepared food, they also prepared legal analyses in defense of Indigenous land claims and human rights. Situated not in a conference center or a hotel, we met in a community center and on the Tamez family land where the wall blocked access to the Rio Grande. Participants came from across the country, followed Indigenous protocols, and testified to the impact of militarization in their communities. Some talked about harassment by officials at the local, state, and national level. Although Native people have constantly fought against racism, violence, and dispossession, the post-9/11 political regime in the United States posed an existential threat to Indigenous communities in the borderlands, as evidenced by the testimonies shared in El Calaboz. Thus the gathering was critical because it was a result of women's activism and it served as a catalyst against the Secure Fence Act of 2006 and the militarization of the border coordinated by the Department of Homeland Security and the state of Texas.

In conclusion, the El Calaboz Gathering was a pivotal moment in time, when Indigenous women and families came together to speak truth to their memories and experiences of dispossession, to take a stand against the destructive wall and its impact on the land and their cultures, and to accelerate the larger Indigenous protest against settler-colonial violence and erasure.

NOTES

1. Eileen Luna-Firebaugh, "The Border Crossed Us: Border Crossing Issues of the Indigenous Peoples of the Americas," *Wicazo Sa Review* 17, no. 1 (Spring 2002): 159–81.
2. Melissa del Bosque, "Holes in the Wall," *The Texas Observer*, February 22, 2008, https://www.texasobserver.org/2688-holes-in-the-wall/.
3. Ned Norris Jr., "Stop the Destruction of Tohono O'odham Lands," *High Country News*, October 30, 2020, https://www.hcn.org/issues/52.12/indigenous-affairs-borderlands-stop-the-destruction-of-tohono-oodham-lands.
4. Gary Clayton Anderson, *The Conquest of Texas: Ethnic Cleansing in the Promised Land, 1820–1875* (Norman: University of Oklahoma Press, 2004), 7; Ty Cashion, *Lone Star Mind: Reimagining Texas History* (Norman: University of Oklahoma Press, 2018).
5. Aldon S. Lang and Berte R. Haigh, "Public Lands," *Handbook of Texas*, Texas State Historical Association, last modified August 3, 2017, https://www.tshaonline.org/handbook/entries/public-lands.
6. Anderson, *Conquest of Texas*.

7. Anderson, *Conquest of Texas.*
8. David La Vere, *The Texas Indians* (College Station: Texas A&M Press, 2004), 197.
9. Benjamin H. Johnson, *Revolution in Texas: How a Forgotten Rebellion and Its Bloody Suppression Turned Mexicans into Americans* (New Haven: Yale University Press, 2003), 3; Monica Muñoz Martinez, *The Injustice Never Leaves You: Anti-Mexican Violence in Texas* (Cambridge, Mass.: Harvard University Press, 2018).
10. Martha Menchaca, *Recovering History, Constructing Race: The Indian, Black, and White Roots of Mexican Americans* (Austin: University of Texas Press, 2001).
11. Cashion, *Lone Star Mind,* 25.
12. John Wesley Wilbarger, *Indian Depredations in Texas* (Austin: Hutchings Printing House, 1889).
13. Walter Prescott Webb, *The Great Plains* (Boston: Ginn and Company, 1931); Walter Prescott Webb, *The Texas Rangers: A Century of Frontier Defense* (Boston: Houghton Mifflin, 1935).
14. T. R. Fehrenbach, *Lone Star: A History of Texas and the Texans* (New York: Macmillan, 1968).
15. Geoff Folsom, "Redford Revisited," *The Odessa American,* July 2, 2006, 1.
16. David Weber, *The Spanish Frontier in North America* (New Haven: Yale University Press, 1992).
17. Homepage of the Tāp Pīlam Coahuiltecan Nation website, accessed March 15, 2023, https://tappilam.org/.
18. La Vere, *Texas Indians,* 187.
19. Luna-Firebaugh, "Border Crossed Us."
20. Matthew Babcock, *Apache Adaptation to Hispanic Rule* (New York: Oxford University Press, 2017).

BIBLIOGRAPHY

Anderson, Gary Clayton. *The Conquest of Texas: Ethnic Cleansing in the Promised Land, 1820–1875.* Norman: University of Oklahoma Press, 2004.

Babcock, Matthew. *Apache Adaptation to Hispanic Rule.* New York: Oxford University Press, 2017.

Cashion, Ty. *Lone Star Mind: Reimagining Texas History.* Norman: University of Oklahoma Press, 2018.

del Bosque, Melissa. "Holes in the Wall." *The Texas Observer,* February 22, 2008. https://www.texasobserver.org/2688-holes-in-the-wall/.

Fehrenbach, T. R. *Lone Star: A History of Texas and the Texans.* New York: Macmillan, 1968.

Folsom, Geoff. "Redford Revisited." *The Odessa American,* July 2, 2006.

Johnson, Benjamin H. *Revolution in Texas: How a Forgotten Rebellion and Its Bloody Suppression Turned Mexicans into Americans.* New Haven: Yale University Press, 2003.

Lang, Aldon S., and Berte R. Haigh. "Public Lands." *Handbook of Texas*, Texas State Historical Association, last modified August 3, 2017. https://www.tshaonline.org/handbook/entries/public-lands.

La Vere, David. *The Texas Indians*. College Station: Texas A&M Press, 2004.

Luna-Firebaugh, Eileen. "The Border Crossed Us: Border Crossing Issues of the Indigenous Peoples of the Americas." *Wicazo Sa Review* 17, no. 1 (Spring 2002): 159–81.

Martinez, Monica Muñoz. *The Injustice Never Leaves You: Anti-Mexican Violence in Texas*. Cambridge, Mass.: Harvard University Press, 2018.

Menchaca, Martha. *Recovering History, Constructing Race: The Indian, Black, and White Roots of Mexican Americans*. Austin: University of Texas Press, 2001.

Norris Jr., Ned. "Stop the Destruction of Tohono O'odham Lands." *High Country News*, October 30, 2020. https://www.hcn.org/issues/52.12/indigenous-affairs-borderlands-stop-the-destruction-of-tohono-oodham-lands.

Tāp Pīlam Coahuiltecan Nation (website). Accessed March 15, 2023. https://tappilam.org/.

Webb, Walter Prescott. *The Great Plains*. Boston: Ginn and Company, 1931.

Webb, Walter Prescott. *The Texas Rangers: A Century of Frontier Defense*. Boston: Houghton Mifflin, 1935.

Weber, David. *The Spanish Frontier in North America*. New Haven: Yale University Press, 1992.

Wilbarger, John Wesley. *Indian Depredations in Texas*. Austin: Hutchings Printing House, 1889.

Conclusion

Ha'dée áíńzi̱? What Do You Think?

Why end this collection with a question, when conclusions by their very nature are supposed to wrap things up and address lingering concerns? As editors, we thought long and hard about how to "conclude" this collection, waiting until the very last moment to put our thoughts to paper. In part, this has been one of the most difficult aspects of editing this collection: What do we want people to think about everything? What should they take away from this story? Where do we begin? End? We agreed that the story we curate here began, essentially, when Dr. Eloisa Taméz sued Michael Chertoff, but even that starting point seemed problematic because the court case grew out of the struggles of Indigenous peoples in the bordered lands dating back centuries. Additionally, we failed to see an end to the struggles and resistance efforts associated with antimilitarization resistance activism in Indigenous peoples' homelands throughout the U.S.-Mexico bordered lands, including Indigenous communities across the longest part of the bordered lands—the Texas-Mexico border—and also U.S. federally recognized tribes' reserved lands. As editors we understand that a standard conclusion is not necessarily consonant with an end to the injustices epitomized by the border separation wall and anti-Indigenous violence, but we nonetheless found ourselves grasping for obvious benchmarks ushering us toward a sound "end" to the collection.

In short, to some degree, words failed us when we began drafting this conclusion. We do not see an end to the mechanics of dispossession and the technologies of erasure. Emotions such as despair, frustration, anger, and loss have been intimately intertwined with the intellectual process and painstaking labor of compiling this collection. As scholars, community members, activists, border dwellers, Indigenous youth, Native elders, witnesses, and allies, we are overcome with rage and anger at the ongoing assault upon Aboriginal homelands. That said, this has not been a negative experience: in fact, it has been the opposite. Writing these chapters, compiling the archives, curating the documents, and foregrounding the artwork and poetry has been spiritually and emotionally cathartic because it highlights Indigenous knowledge, action, voices, and epistemologies in resistance to deeply anti-Indigenous, misogynist militarized violation of Ndé peoples' inherent and inalienable rights as Ndé peoples, and their international rights to resist all threats to their existence and survival in occupied homelands.

Many authors expressed a profound sense of relief—even empowerment—in narrating their own stories and having their voices heard, some for the first time. Indeed, we found hope in their words. For some, these essays were their last words to be documented in the English language. During the early days of the El Calaboz Elders' resistances against Michael Chertoff's aggression, U.S. government attorneys were sent to the community without community consent or invitation and drilled them for information about their land's forced acquisition. We recall that one Elder who had joined the class action with Eloisa against the government was literally on his deathbed when they held discussions with him. His vulnerability at that moment of the crisis, as retold by Eloisa, was devastating to hear. Our entire network of people who were supporting the family in their journeys in national and international legal systems was enraged at the persistent pattern of dehumanizing degradation the family and community endured. Americans predominantly had little interest in or empathy for the human toll exacted in resisting settler-colonial physical violence at this scale. There had been no precedent of a wall constructed across the continent in the history of the Americas. The burden of refusing and of insisting on continuing Indigenous legal independence outside of the U.S. "Indian recognition" apparatus fell upon a small number of Indigenous peoples, in reality and fact. We placed urgency on the four actions of documenting, remembering, preserving, and mobilizing. Our insistence on recognizing these actions was rooted in Margo's expertise in genocidal erasures predating the wall period, which she documented extensively in her 2010 dissertation. Because the primary events described in this collection coincided with her doctoral studies, and because that study was shelved repeatedly due to the physical, psychological, and emotional pressures caused by her responsibility to combat the government's attempts to destroy her mother's and community's resistance, the publishing of this collection was urgent and took priority. In this spirit, remembering and documenting has been our central wish: that *Gathering Together, We Decide* can offer an inspirational model for future scholarship and activism within Indigenous communities facing similar challenges and oppressions.

While we were compiling this collection, the tensions between hope and despair threatened the viability of the project, as contributors faced life-altering and, in some cases, life-ending tragedies. Colleagues faced economic precarity, they had to relocate homes several times, and many of them lived in diaspora, dislocated from their homelands. Many of these kinds of traumatic challenges are hidden behind a thin veneer of "professionalism" that silences the painful truths of human emotion in the context of this work we do in physical, mental, emotional, and spiritual solidarity with and alongside Indigenous peoples of these lands (and who are the land), where we live alongside them. As editors, friends, and family members, we watched as our collaborators (also friends and family members) passed away due to a lifelong exposure to toxic chemicals, complications associated with diabetes, and the crushing weight of poverty. Indeed, many of the contributors lacked access to email and the internet, and a few barely had cell phone service. Some community members lived in such remote areas that they did not have reliable electricity and running water. Two of them could not even afford the cost of standard word-processing software. Many did not have computers. The realities that our friends, family members, and colleagues faced directly shatters the stereotypical image of the academic author, the lone scholar assiduously typing away on their university-purchased computer. Many of the voices included in this collection are those of grassroots community members on the front lines of border militarization, state violence, anti-Indigenous racism, and environmental degradation, and we thank them for lending their words to this collection.

Despite the challenges in curating this collection, and the ongoing traumas faced by Indigenous communities in the border region, we do nonetheless have four critical reflections that engage with the question "What do you think?" First, Ndé women have led a centuries-long campaign to protect their lands, cultures, families, rights, and identities. Henrique Maestas reminds us about the deep roots of Ndé matrilineal and matriarchal traditions through his scholarly work and conversations with women relatives. Similarly, Eloisa Taméz and María de Jesús García Atkinson (Eloisa's sister) offer personal memories of their experiences growing up with proud matriarchs around them. Indeed, they are the strong women that we wanted to (re)center in narratives about survival and resistance in violent and settler-militarized spaces. These Elders gifted their wisdom, voice, and power to Margo Tamez, who has worked assiduously to defend Lipan Apache homelands and customary territory from the United States' efforts to condemn and appropriate their ancestral place, which is vast and filled with stories and knowledge systems shared with many related Indigenous peoples. Working at the local, national, and international levels, she has met with human rights tribunals and myriad agencies dedicated to protecting Indigenous rights. Through her scholarship, poetry, and activism, she has been an unwavering voice not only for Lipan land rights but more broadly for the rights of all Indigenous peoples of the world.

A second point that is related to the first: we have tried to emphasize and analyze how the Tamez case and the gathering in El Calaboz created a space for Indigenous remembering, archiving, documenting, and storytelling. Contributors such as Jeffrey P. Shepherd, Annette Portillo, Koyana Flotte, Rosalva Resendiz, and Cynthia Bejarano deconstruct racist mythologies tied to hegemonic narratives extolling Texas exceptionalism. These contributors conclude that the cultural landscape and historical imaginary of Texas is saturated with tropes of Indigenous savagery, settler-colonial conquest, and violent masculinities that collectively silence Indigenous voices and perspectives. Excavating these deeply entrenched untruths, the collection then shifts to the ways in which Ndé and other Indigenous storytellers have archived their memories through paper documentation and family historical recollection. The legal documents, *testimonios*, digital footprints, and other remembrances undermine the systematic erasure of Indigenous viewpoints and voices from the past and present. In doing so, the collection paves the way for Indigenous youth to express their ways of knowing, being, and living in these highly volatile border spaces and militarized places.

Third, this collection makes an important series of arguments—some implicit, some explicit—regarding dominant and widespread notions of indigeneity. The modern U.S. system of federal recognition, also known as federal acknowledgment, is based on critical historical relationships between Indigenous peoples and the U.S. nation-state, a contested polity because, internationally, the United States is understood to be a significant example of a settler-colonial nation, despite the fact that, domestically, this international legal understanding is confronted by the ruling class's aggressive denialism and defensiveness. These relationships reflected the inherent nationhood of Indigenous groups dating back millennia before the arrival of Europeans and their violent implementation of the Doctrine of Discovery to justify dispossession and genocide. In the U.S. context, what is popularly known as "American Indian law" gains traction from the important though contradictory bundle of rulings collectively known as the "Marshall Trilogy," articulated in the first third of the nineteenth century. These rulings grew out of the constitutionally based view that Indian nations were external to the U.S. body politic, and that because of that, nation-to-nation treaty making would structure relations between Native peoples and the United States. Though the Marshall rulings echoed, and to some extent weakened, these early understandings of Native sovereignty, they further ingrained the process of "recognizing" and "acknowledging" Indigenous groups as semi-separate political nations with distinct legal traditions, statuses, and rights.

This system of treaty making between Indian nations and the United States ended in 1871, but the federal government continued to "recognize" Native peoples through executive orders and other mechanisms. During the process of land allotment and the creation of tribal rolls, the federal government ironically legitimized some groups as Indigenous polities. Similarly, the Indian New Deal programs and the Indian Reorganization Act of the 1930s further ensconced tribal political identities and thereby encompassed more Native groups within the federal recognition process. And finally, the creation of the Office of Federal Acknowledgment in the 1970s, which came at the tail end of the Indian Claims Commission (ICC) and termination legislation, formalized the process of recognition. A painful legacy of this era was the impact of the ICC on many groups, but specifically the Lipan peoples, whose documented claim to vast territory throughout Texas and southeastern New Mexico was used to benefit the Mescalero and a small number of Lipan Apaches in that reservation, rather than the much larger numbers of Lipan Apaches inhabiting traditional and customary places across the state of Texas. A thorough analysis of this issue goes beyond the scope of this collection, but Docket 22, *Lipan Apache Tribe v. U.S.* (1971), relied on Lipan land title, which was recognized by Spain, Mexico, the Republic of Texas, and the United States. Unfortunately, the leverage enjoyed by the federally recognized Mescalero Apache Tribe resulted in a significant dispersal of money, none of which the Lipan bands in Texas ever received. Collectively, these official actions constituted the architecture of what we now understand as federal recognition or federal acknowledgment, which many Indigenous peoples find deeply problematic at best, and racist at worst.

The case *Tamez v. Chertoff* and the Gathering in El Calaboz opened a window onto these processes of acknowledgment for several reasons, and especially generated an appreciation of the severely undertheorized and misunderstood area of still-independent Indigenous peoples, meaning those who have not experienced being legally enclosed by treaties with colonial powers, or ever having their homelands severed legally by way of treaties or other legal mechanisms with colonial powers. Ndé peoples in the broader, larger homelands in current-day Texas, Tamaulipas, Coahuila, and other parts of Mexico did not experience formal, legal severing and disposal of their Indigenous lands. Nor did their descendants, Indigenous peoples still surviving on lands determined through processes emanating from Ndé diplomacies with Spain and Mexico.

First, the Tamez case and the El Calaboz Gathering were happening along the U.S.-Mexico border, where Indigenous identities have been shaped by centuries of interactions with Spain and Mexico. These formative experiences placed Indigenous peoples within a very specific though fluid set of relationships with the Spanish Empire, the Republic of Mexico, the Republic of Texas, and the United States. With those relationships came a litany of institutions, rules, laws, and pressures that forced Indigenous people to make difficult decisions about how they prayed, what religions they embraced, what languages they spoke, how they dressed, what people they married, and what labors they engaged in. Conversion to Catholicism, forced usage of Spanish, new legal codes, the transformation of their economies, the impact of disease, and the traumatic system of slave trading and captive taking placed immense pressures on Indigenous peoples in what some scholars now refer to as "the borderlands."

By the time Texas entered the union in 1845, groups such as the Lipan had signed several treaties with Spain and Mexico, but their livelihoods were threatened by drastic changes around them. For instance, because Texas was previously an independent republic, it entered the United States with total control over all its land. The federal government owned practically nothing. Similarly, the state of Texas controlled nearly all its policies toward Indigenous peoples, and the Treaty of Guadalupe Hidalgo did not apply to it because Texas was a state before the war with Mexico began. These pivotal developments extinguished treaties with Lipan and all Indigenous peoples, according to both the state and the federal government. At that moment, the acknowledgment of Lipan peoples as sovereign landholders began to diminish, only to disappear in the minds of the U.S. settler state in coming decades. Similar pressures continued after the Civil War, when the Union passed punitive measures against the ex-Confederate states and all Native sympathizers. Finally, by the end of the nineteenth century, Texas Rangers, vigilante groups, and the U.S. military waged genocidal campaigns against Comanche, Kiowa, and Apache groups trying to remain in the state. Lacking reservation lands or even the most nominal protection by the Office of Indian Affairs, groups like the Lipan in Texas struggled to survive on the margins of a racist state that regularly used violence to punish people of color. Some of them fled to Mexico, a few found refuge on the Mescalero reservation, and a few stalwart families remained in the state and hid in the shadows, sometimes claiming to be "Mexican." Others proudly retained a Lipan identity. Ultimately, however, this combination of violence, erasure of Lipan land title, rejection of treaties, policies of ethnic cleansing, and practices of genocide cumulatively resulted in the nonrecognition of Lipan peoples in Texas.

Fast-forwarding to the Tamez case, the El Calaboz Gathering, and the ensuing years of activism against the border wall, the "reemergence," which was of course a more critical resurgence and upsurgence of Lipan communities in South Texas, surprised observers around the world. Their presence in Texas raised important questions about history, identity, and erasure. Moreover, their claims to the land bisected by the international boundary foregrounded their long relationships with Spain and Mexico, which resulted in the Crown land grant to Indigenous peoples that Eloisa fought to preserve when she sued Michael Chertoff. Their enduring presence in the U.S.-Mexico bordered lands in general, and along the Texas-Mexico border specifically, opened a range of questions tied to federal recognition and the common, though wholly mistaken, belief that the federal government retains the right to grant Indigenous identity to people claiming it. The Lipan case, echoing the contemporaneous ethnic revitalization of tribal peoples such as the Tonkawa and Coahuiltecan groups, punctuated the hidden yet vitally important histories of the independent Indigenous peoples in Texas. Their histories revealed the unique dimensions of Texas anti-Indian policies and the lingering impact of Spanish and Mexican laws and racial ideologies upon Indigenous groups presently living in the U.S.-Mexico bordered lands.

By actively asserting their rights to the land as Indigenous peoples broadly, and as Lipan Apache / Ndé specifically, the community members included in this collection help us rethink the present-day ideologies and processes that constitute federal recognition in the twenty-first century. We do not argue against federally recognized nations, nor do we question their identities or status as sovereignty-claiming peoples. Rather, the authors in this collection seek to foreground a diverse range of identities and forms of self-recognition that acknowledge indigeneity within complex landscapes characterized by Indigenous power, Indigenous rights, Indigenous self-determination, and Indigenous cultural pluralism and heterogeneity. In short, the Lipan and other Indigenous groups in the so-called borderlands are who they say they are, and that says a lot about their voice, self-determination, and survival. It is necessary to resist the epistemological violence of, on the one hand, "borderland" history and its ethnographic and hagiographic erasures, and, on the other, the persistent tendency of the field of Texas history to address Lipan Apaches in monolithic terms and solely as "Indians" of the past, while remaining silent about its own role in marginalizing Lipan historians of and from Texas in the present. Rejecting the overtly colonial and disrespectful authenticity gaze that has privileged how anthropologists and ethnographers interpreted and represented Lipan Apaches, rather than emphasize who they are—which is the Ndé peoples' story to tell, as Margo enunciated in her chapter—we, like others in this collection, are much more interested in how they are doing. Especially because in rethinking Indigenous pluri-legalism, we have been pushed to consider that we ought to be applying our analytical lenses and skill sets, not to perpetuating epistemological violence upon Indigenous peoples in this region, but rather to shifting and transitioning our inquiry to the root of the problems. Ongoing coloniality and daily threats to well-being in areas targeted for state-sanctioned militarized violence are normalized to various extents by those not living in bordered and walled conditions, but it is natural to resist such unacceptable conditions of existence. In the twenty-first century Ndé scholars have delineated the harrowing history that the Ndé people have been forced to suffer and tolerate for more than a century: genocide as a necropolitical order. And yet Ndé have retained what the first Europeans who encountered them had always known: that "Apaches" are a nation and an empire all at once. The Europeans, in truth, did not have a parallel legal concept that could specifically conceptualize the category of nation-empire that peoples like the Dene (Athapaskan), who had spread across the hemisphere by the fifteenth century, looked like in reality, until they met them and labeled them as such: La Gran Apachería, vast as a decentralized geopolitical region, and more autonomous and nuanced than an empire. Therefore, any further attempts to perpetuate academic imperialism upon Ndé, in terms of fixing or forcing them into some antiquated ethnographic methodology wholly irrelevant to their social, historical, and political trajectories, must end.

Moreover, their voices, their analysis of pluri-Indigenous convergences over generations, and their couplings with peoples-in-solidarity who are also in resistance to colonization have been a robust form of Indigenous and Ndé cultural and gender-based resistance to Euro-American hegemony and patriarchal violence, which also raises important questions about the prevalence of Latinx, Hispanic, and Chicanx identities. U.S. White supremacy places value upon a racial hierarchy that has the inherent intention to fragment and to erase the indigeneity of colonized others; it attempts to accomplish this through broad othering categories, invented by political and economic elites, that delegitimize Indigenous, Brown, and Black identities to such an extent that people claiming a Mexican American or Hispanic identity sometimes, perhaps strategically, sometimes unconsciously, reject their Indigenous roots. That has been the intention all along. Theory and methodology, therefore, need rethinking. How decolonial and decolonizing are we, or can we claim to be, if we are also perpetuating, through our silences or our passive neutrality, the anti-Indigenous colonial systems and structures that prop up anti-Indigenous agendas in this region? We need to question why and where we give a pass to the fragmenting typologies invented and perpetuated uncritically in academic institutions, which have been major drivers of, and have performed the genocidal intent of, White settler erasure to procure more lands for profit-making industry in this region.

That is, the settler imperative, to take control of the land and to destroy the groups resisting violent occupation, understands quite well who and what stands between the settlers and the land coveted. Taking control of Indigenous people's identities and minds became part and parcel of the process. That is, settlers' theft, through violence, of Indigenous peoples' capacity of world-making left Indigenous peoples with the bare-life scraps of the oppressed, obscured, and distorted, a design by the settler occupiers that reinvented the past and rescripted the present—the perfect, invisible crime. In order to understand the continuing anticolonial and antiviolence struggles, which we cannot fully address, as they are ever growing and intensifying in this region, it is important to state that what we do know is that this ongoing and ever-complicated settler-colonial legacy of Texas is a root determinant. While some people employing the terms "Hispanic," "Mexican American," "Chicanx," and "Latinx" may indeed have roots solely connecting them to Europe, most do not, and the projected Eurocentric anxieties of racial purity erase Native ancestry. Chicanx identity functions differently in that it embraces indigeneity and offers flexible pathways for engaging with those complex ancestries. That said, some Chicanx indigeneity focuses more on groups in central Mexico, particularly those groups that are popularly known as the Aztecs—that is, the Mexicas or Nahuas—rather than the local Indigenous groups with deep ties to the bordered region. This is not universally the case, but this identification with nonregional groups raises questions about how these frameworks erase local Indigenous peoples who may, in some cases, constitute the indigeneity that is part of the *mestizaje* at the root of Chicanx identities. Importantly, Lipan and related Indigenous peoples of the region do not disavow the real or possible mixed Indigenous, Basque, Irish, Scottish, British, African, Arab, and other ancestries that define their families' pasts. They engage with those genealogies by embracing the pluricultural and pluri-legal indigeneity that the expansive Ndé and Dene worldview provides them, based in understanding, accepting, and celebrating, rather than disavowing, devaluing, and diminishing these identities. The important Ndé framework of pluri-Indigenous cultural, ceremonial, legal, and anticolonial community protection and collective solidarity resistance legacies has been around for millennia. Dene Athapaskan peoples' ways of being and existing far and wide across the hemisphere prior to European invasion and occupation laid down foundations for examining how borders, racism, nationalism, and cultural authenticity colonized Indigenous peoples and caused them to doubt and question themselves. For the Ndé, plurality kept them adaptable in resistance against common oppressors, which is specific to their local-regional land-based and antigenocide struggles. They also point to the documents and legal claims that anchor their rights to specific Aboriginal territories, making their identities much more enriching, empowering, and nuanced than the accumulation of settler-colonial racialized thinking that has sought to erase the pluri-legal worldviews and systems of La Gran Apachería, which awed and amazed the first Europeans due to their uniquely broad effectiveness in land, water, food, and military governance, based on keeping peace for all and rejecting war.

Therefore, it is important to dismantle the myths and social constructions of the purported foreignness of Indigenous peoples of the region, and to think more critically about how and why terms such as "Mexican American," "Hispanic," and "Latino" were invented. These terms served to impose an unnatural "minority" status on a majority Indigenous population of diverse peoples colonized and forcibly assimilated. These artificial and imposed identities are fragments that are products of settler-colonial occupation. Many of these communities have unique histories and ongoing processes of anticolonial resistance and decolonization that are specific to local Indigenous and settler dynamics. The region's history of intensified policing and militarization of their communities is a product of the underlying settler-colonial impulse to control the psychology of the colonized, to remind the colonized that the colonizers are in control, and to suppress Indigenous peoples' legitimate determination to liberate themselves from those colonizers' control. Meanwhile, settlers and other groups—who experience anxiety and discomfort with Ndé and other Indigenous peoples of the region as they challenge settlers' suppositions of superiority, and who may not be willing to acknowledge these histories, processes, and realities—are determined to undermine, suppress, and obstruct this region's Indigenous peoples. This does not, however, alter the fact that these realities have existed for generations. They are persistent self-determination processes of this region's Indigenous peoples, which mirror the decolonization across the hemisphere and the global south from settler-colonial tyranny and injustices.

These struggles over identity and the sometimes violent histories that shaped them emerge repeatedly in this collection as they manifest themselves in the U.S./Texas-Mexico bordered lands. Contributors talk about family histories that are scarred by the violence of Texas Rangers during the late nineteenth and early twentieth centuries, which often caused them to claim a Mexican (national) identity rather than declare an Indigenous identity at the very site of genocidal incitement, threat, or enactment. Yet the land objectives of settlers in South Texas collapsed Mexican nationality as a race and class upon local Indigenous peoples, thereby erasing indigeneity in the Rio Grande River region in Texas north of Mexico. In South Texas and the Rio Grande River region, Indigenous people and multiracial Indigenous-origin people were, and still continue to be, a majority. These survival tactics continued through much of the twentieth century, particularly when settler laws and social relations devalued indigeneity through suppression, erasure, and discrimination and structured the administrative incentivization of Indigenous peoples' self-representation as Mexican, Mexican American, or Hispanic in vital records (birth, marriage, death) and related institutions. These trends of forced disavowing of one's Native past while foregrounding a Hispanic—that is, White—identity afforded some people a degree of political, social, and cultural cache in a predominantly White state. However, the majority of racialized Indigenous-rooted peoples in southern Texas are critically aware of the nefarious detribalizing impacts and the destruction of cultural, linguistic, intellectual, and material heritage caused by the imposed systems of "Mexican American" and "Hispanic" as weaponized by White settler power. Most recently, in a region of the United States where the investment in Whiteness among some Latinx communities has revealed itself in anti-immigrant rhetoric and pro–border wall policies, the conscious embrace of indigeneity by migrant Indigenous peoples who are categorically lumped within the term "Latinos" by the ruling class can be jarring, even revolutionary to mainstream society. Thus, the Tamez case and the El Calaboz Gathering, along with the activism that unfolded afterward, introduced many people to the hidden Indigenous histories of Texas and to these complexities and nuances.

The fourth point that we hope readers will think about is how this collection foregrounds Indigenous youth empowerment through art, language, and popular culture across international borders, in diaspora, across the twenty-first century. Many of the youth included in this collection are members of the Tamez family, and they have experienced trauma both directly and secondarily via their relationships with ancestors. The Tamez youth participated fully in the gathering, as they cooked food, set up camp, made artwork, and offered their own testimonios. Their perspectives are an important part of this collection for many reasons, not the least of which is their unique understanding of how the border wall and militarization impacted the land, plants, animals, and water of the region. Moreover, they astutely diagnosed the long-term and multigenerational impacts that the wall would have on the lands and cultures they will inherit far into the future. Their expressions in artwork, storytelling, video recordings, and, much later, the tattoos on their bodies offered important insights, lessons, and perspectives for this collection. We doubt that there is any more profound legacy of the activism that this collection documents than the ongoing visionary commitment of the youth who are included in these pages.

These youth voices also included individuals from other tribes in the United States and Canada, particularly those individuals who participated directly in the gathering or who were impacted by militarization and border wall construction during the ensuing years. Youth from the Akimel and Tohono O'odham, Yaqui, Diné (Navajo), and several Apache nations joined the gathering and expressed solidarity with the Lipan youth. These individuals shared their stories of militarization and racial violence from other parts of the U.S.-Mexico borderlands, and then they shared stories from El Calaboz with their families back home. Similarly, young Indigenous and non-Indigenous adults living in Canada and working with Margo as student researchers and community activists shared their experiences of militarization and surveillance in the north. Their stories critique and deconstruct Canadian national mythologies of benevolent relationships with First Nations peoples by highlighting the ongoing health challenges, economic disparities, and environmental impacts facing Indigenous peoples on and off the reserves. In the same way, their testimonies mirrored many of the issues of state-sanctioned and state-imposed attempts to suppress and erase Indigenous identity, culture, belonging, and personhood of First Nations peoples. We learned how Canada attacked and suppressed Indigenous peoples, invented methods to unground them from their indigeneity, and had convinced multitudes, through administrative genocidal processes similar to those in Texas, that they were not Indigenous to their own homelands, and/or that they could "improve" their lives through enfranchisement in Canadian society by legally and administratively disclaiming indigeneity. Through a wide variety of methods and mediums, from poetry to artwork to the increasingly popular, revitalized, rigorous tradition of Indigenous-based tattooing, these youth offer global voices responding to the challenges of young Indigenous adults in the U.S.-Mexico bordered lands.

To return to the question posed at the beginning of this conclusion—"What do you think?"—we ask that readers indeed think deeply about the significance of the Tamez case and the Gathering in El Calaboz. While contemplating this significance, we also ask that readers reflect upon the life and contributions of warrior women such as Teresa Leal, the Mayo-Ópata environmental and Indigenous rights activist whom many of us drew inspiration from during and after the El Calaboz Gathering. Long before many of us contemplated such issues, Teresa fought against militarization of the border and state-supported racial violence against Indigenous communities in Mexico. We similarly encourage people to learn about Enrique Madrid, the Jumano Apache intellectual and human rights activist who lives in Redford, Texas, directly on the border. For decades he and his wife Ruby have provided food, shelter, education, and inspiration for youth in far western Texas and northern Mexico. Enrique introduced the world to Esequiel Hernández, the Jumano youth shot by U.S. Marines on May 20, 1997, during a major border policing operation.

And finally, we hope that you will find inspiration in the words and deeds of allies such as April Cotte, a White settler activist who devoted her life to helping Enrique and Ruby, along with the larger cause of Jumano Apache and Lipan families, as well as the pathbreaking documentary film work of Ramón and Rosalva Resendiz, and the cultural preservation efforts of tattoo artist and activist Dion Kaszas (Nlaka'pamux, Métis, and Hungarian). These are just a few of the people whom we hope that you carry with you after you put down this book, think about what it means, and move into a world of despair and suffering, as well as hope and inspiration.

Contributors

Margo Tamez (she/her), Ndé Dene (Lipan Apache, Dene [Athapaskan] Peoples), is a poet and historian. Born in Kónìcą̀ą̀hį́į́ Gòkíyàà (Big Water Peoples' Country; southern and southwestern Texas and northeastern Mexico), she is the award-winning author of *FATHER | GENOCIDE* (2021), *Raven Eye* (2007), *Naked Wanting* (2003), and *Alleys & Allies* (1991). Tamez has led and co-led significant legal briefs and legal interventions at several convention bodies of the United Nations and the Organization of American States' Inter-American Commission on Human Rights documenting the U.S. border separation wall's construction and many violations of international law, Indigenous rights, and human rights (land dispossession, forced displacement, cultural and ecological destruction, economic and political rights violations, heritage systems destruction, burial site desecrations, and religious rights violations). Tamez's international activism and award-winning scholarship has contributed to understanding the implications of the magnitude of human rights violations against the Ndé peoples specifically, and Dene (Athapaskan) peoples—in lands divided by Canadian, U.S., and Mexican borders—broadly. Her interventions have mobilized international experts to interrogate Indigenous nonrecognition and related erasures in the United States as a settler-colonial system in violation of international human rights. She is an associate professor appointed in the Indigenous Studies Program in the Faculty of Arts and Social Sciences and an affiliated faculty member in the MFA (Poetry) Creative Writing Program at the University of British Columbia (Okanagan), in the unceded Syilx territory.

Cynthia Bejarano is a Regents Professor in gender and sexuality studies and the College of Arts and Sciences Stan Fulton Chair at New Mexico State University. Her scholarship and advocacy center on the U.S.-Mexico border. She authored *¿Qué Onda? Urban Youth Culture and Border Identity* (2005), and co-edited *Terrorizing Women: Feminicides in the Americas* with Rosa Linda Fregoso (2010) and *Frontera Madre(hood): Brown Mothers Challenging Oppression and Transborder Violence at the U.S.-Mexico Border* with Maria Cristina Morales (2024).

Jeffrey P. Shepherd is a professor of history at the University of Texas at El Paso. His research interests include Indigenous peoples in North America, particularly the Apache/Ndé and Native groups in the U.S.-Mexico borderlands; environmental history; and the history of extremist groups. He is the author of *We Are an Indian Nation: A History of the Hualapai People*, published in 2010 by the University of Arizona Press, and *The Guadalupe Mountains National Park: An Environmental History of the Southwest Borderlands*, published in 2019 with the University of Massachusetts Press. He is also the co-editor, with Dr. Myla Vicenti Carpio, of the book series Critical Issues in Indigenous Studies, from the University of Arizona Press. He has received grants from the National Park Service, the American Philosophical Society, the Andrew W. Mellon Foundation, the Charles Redd Center at Brigham Young University, and Texas Tech University.

María Jesús (García) Atkinson was born on December 3, 1936, at El Calaboz, Texas, to Lydia Esparza García and José Cavazos García. She enjoyed joining her father at the farmland at the Rio Grande River's edge. María attended La Encantada Elementary School and San Benito High School, and graduated from Brownsville High School in 1954. She earned a degree in education and a master's in bilingual education from Pan American College. On December 23, 1956, she married Gilberto Federico Atkinson, and they raised seven children. María taught second grade at Longoria Elementary for four decades. She enjoyed seeing her former students as adults as they warmly greeted her, remembering her kindness and how each was special to her. She joined her students for the Charro Days Fiesta children's parades, in traditional dress and always beautiful. She passed away on August 29, 2024, and we are so deeply honored and forever grateful that she generously shared her stories and knowledge with us all.

Mia Boccella is a filmmaker and photographer who spent ten years working on feature films in Santa Fe, New Mexico, and Los Angeles, California. In 2005 she founded Boccella Productions and produced, directed, and edited two feature-length documentary films. In 2019 she was invited to photograph at the inauguration of the first two Native American congresswomen at the U.S. Capitol in Washington, D.C. Mia was a 2022 recipient of the Getty Images Disability Community Grant and won second prize for her proposal about the Blind Equestrian Community, of which she is a founding member. Mia's films have been screened and broadcast internationally and have also been used as educational tools by thousands in schools, universities, treatment and rehabilitation centers, prisons, and Indigenous communities. Another source of her joy comes from intentional allyship with Indigenous communities and respectful advocacy for their cultural preservation. She has a relationship with Diné (Navajo) and Pueblo tribes of New Mexico that spans over thirty years.

Melanie Cervantes (Xicanx) holds a BA in ethnic studies from the University of California, Berkeley, and has never lived far from the California coast. Born in Harbor City, California, and raised in a small city in the South Bay of Los Angeles, Melanie now makes her home in the San Francisco Bay Area, where she creates visual art that is inspired by the people around her and her communities' desire for radical social transformation. Melanie's intention is to create a visual lexicon of resistance to multiple oppressions that will inspire curiosity, raise consciousness, and inspire solidarities among communities of struggle. In 2007 she co-founded Dignidad Rebelde, a graphic arts collaboration that produces screen prints, political posters, and multimedia projects grounded in Third World and Indigenous movements that build people's power to transform the conditions of fragmentation, displacement, and loss of culture resulting from histories of colonialism, patriarchy, genocide, and exploitation. Dignidad Rebelde's purpose is to illustrate stories of struggle, resistance, and triumph in artwork that can be put back into the hands of the communities who inspire it. Melanie has exhibited extensively across the United States, including at the Yerba Buena Center for the Arts and the San Francisco Museum of Modern Art (San Francisco), the National Museum of Mexican Art (Chicago), and the Museum of Modern Art (New York, NY), and internationally at the Musée d'Aquitaine (Bordeaux, France), Galerija Alkatraz (Ljubljana, Slovenia), and the Museo Franz Mayer (Mexico City, Mexico). Her work is in the permanent collections of the Center for the Study of Political Graphics, the Latin American Collection of the Green Library at Stanford, the Rauner Special Collections Library at Dartmouth College, and the Library of Congress, as well as various other public and private collections throughout the United States.

April Cotte self-identified as a settler American activist based out of Redford, Texas, where she worked closely with and alongside Jumano Apache and Lipan Apache peoples living under the U.S. militarization of their traditional communities, lands, traditional river crossings, traditional food systems, cultural practices, education, family rituals and practices, and everyday lives in the La Junta region in the Big Bend. She was forty-nine when she traveled on to the spirit world on January 25, 2018. She taught Earth-awareness skills as an outdoor educator to young people and adults and was a passionate and fierce advocate for girls, women, queer people, and the Indigenous communities along the Texas-Mexico border. April wrote feature articles for *Reclaiming Quarterly* magazine, such as "Descending Bruja Canyon: An Initiatory Journey" and "Resisting the Wall: Working for a World Without Borders." In 2021, her family and friends posthumously published *April's Book of Games: Creative Exercises for Classes, Camps, and Communities*, which is a collection of and tribute to her legacy dedicated to grassroots teaching. April divided her time between her home in Pacifica, California, and Redford, Texas, in the Big Bend.

Koyana Flotte has a PhD in sociocultural anthropology from Harvard University. She is a lineal descendant of the Aboriginal People of La Junta de los Ríos (Julime/Concho), present-day Presidio, Texas. She is also an enrolled member of the Lipan Apache Tribe of Texas (Tall Grass Band). In 2023, she became a consultant and founded Flotte Consulting LLC.

Arnoldo García is originally from the deep south of Texas. He lives in the San Francisco Bay Area and combines visual arts, music, spoken word, and poetry. His work has been featured in online literary spaces and cultural and political gatherings, as well as opening the international forum "Defending the Displaced: Border Justice and Migrant Rights" convened by UC Berkeley's Othering and Belonging Institute. Arnoldo's poetry is featured in the groundbreaking anthology *Painting the Streets: Oakland Uprising in a Time of Rebellion*, documenting Oakland's antiracist art and cultural explosion in the wake of the police murder of George Floyd. Arnoldo co-founded editorial Xingao, publishing Chicano, Xicana, Palestinian, Black, Asian, and Indigenous poets. Xingao just published the new poetry and art broadside *La comuna*. You can read Arnoldo's poetry in the blogs *La carpa del FEO: Fandango in East Oakland* and *Art of the Commune*.

Denise Gilman is on the faculty of the University of Texas School of Law, where she co-directs the Immigration Clinic and teaches Refugee Law and Policy. Professor Gilman received her undergraduate degree with honors from Northwestern University and her law degree from Columbia University Law School, where she served on the *Columbia Law Review*. Professor Gilman has extensive research and practice experience in the human rights and migrants' rights fields. Her recent publications include "Making Protection Unexceptional: A Reconceptualization of the U.S. Asylum System," in the *Loyola University Chicago Law Journal* (2023); and "Immigration Detention, Inc.," in the *Journal on Migration and Human Security* (2018). She has been interviewed by the BBC, CNN, C-SPAN, and the *New York Times*, among others.

Dion Kaszas is a Nlaka'pamux ancestral skin marker, podcaster, and born-again Coyote. He has been at the forefront of reviving Indigenous tattooing in Canada since 2012. Within this role, he trains, mentors, and teaches the next wave of revivalists. He has curated two major exhibitions highlighting Indigenous ancestral skin markers and ancestral practices: *Body Language: Reawakening Cultural Tattooing of the Northwest* at the Bill Reid Gallery, and *Truly Tribal: Contemporary Expressions of Ancestral Tattoo Practices* at the Museum of Vancouver. In January 2024, the *Transformative Marks* podcast launched. It journeys through the world of Indigenous tattooing, amplifying the voices of ancestral skin markers and Indigenous tattoo artists, as well as those who wear the marks. In 2019, he began developing Nlaka'pamux Blackwork, a contemporary customary practice rooted in his ancestors' visual language and worldview, and his understanding of ceremonies that celebrate and enhance the lives of all human beings.

María Teresa Leal (Ópata-Mayo) was born in Navojoa, Sonora, Mexico, and formally trained as a social anthropologist. She was an internationally renowned Indigenous rights, feminist, environmental justice, labor rights, political rights, migration, and human rights activist, networker, and social movement organizer extraordinaire. She coined the phrase "seres puente" ("human bridge") within the transborder Indigenous campesino movement in the context of intersectional social-justice solidarity building between and across physical, social, class-based, race-based, sex-based, gender-based, and geopolitical structural barriers and ignorance. Leal taught the "seres puente" and circle organization method as a social model for understanding Indigenous knowledge systems at the root of Indigenous activism, community organizing, liberatory education, and decolonization. She was a longtime volunteer and key contributor to community-based archive protection at the Nogales Historical Society Museum, located in the old city hall in downtown Nogales, Sonora, Mexico. She oversaw the summer program for local youth, educating them about the Society's collections and historical consciousness, and emphasizing the literacy of place, Indigenous cultures, and the environment. Deeply committed to Indigenous socialist and egalitarian methodologies, she was a mother and grandmother who stressed the importance of community-based education and mentorship informed by Indigenous women's leadership in Nogales's sixty-plus campesino/a/x colonias. Teresa walked to the spirit world on May 1, 2016.

Diana Lucas is an Indigenous healer and community activist, and has dedicated her life to advocating for the rights and well-being of Indigenous peoples since 1965. Born in Brownsville, Texas, in 1960, she now resides in Navajo tribal territory, where she continues her work as a Native American anti-alcoholism specialist. A mother of six, grandmother, and great-grandmother, Diana's commitment to her family and community is unwavering. She is a motivational speaker, emphasizing the importance of unity and support among marginalized communities, particularly migrants. As a fierce advocate for Indigenous rights, she has been instrumental in various initiatives, serving as a peacekeeper and champion for social justice. With a background in college life at Navajo Community College and the University of Texas, Brownsville, Diana envisions a future where Indigenous voices are celebrated and represented, including seeing a woman in the White House.

Enrique Madrid (Jumano Apache) is a renowned community-based historian, scholar, and activist from Redford, Texas. His activist research on the U.S. Joint Task Force Six operation in Redford that resulted in the murder of Esequiel Hernández (Jumano Apache youth) on May 20, 1997, by a U.S. Marine has been the subject of numerous articles, documentaries, films, and public investigations into the role of U.S. media and politicians in manufacturing and weaponizing "drug-war" propaganda against Texas border Indigenous communities. He is the author of "The Lost Mission of El Polvo: Searching for the History of a State Archaeological Landmark," in *Journal of Big Bend Studies* (2003); "Expedition to La Junta de los Rios, 1747–1748: Captain Commander Joseph de Ydoiaga's Report to the Viceroy of New Spain, Office of the Viceroy of New Spain," in *Special Report 33*, Texas Historical Commission, Austin (1992); and "Architectural Details of San Antonio de los Puliques Mission, El Polvo Site (41PS21), Redford, Texas," in *The Cache.*

Henrique Maestas is Ndé through mothers and grandmothers from land between Red River above Taos and the Rio Grande. Dr. Henrique Maestas sees himself as an unapologetic savage and an unshackled academic with over twenty years of college teaching experience in urban and rural U.S. institutions using antiracist tactics to effect structural change. Henrique is a scribe chosen by elders of his family, the Danza Azteca, Lipan Apache in Texas, the Lipan Apache Elders Council, and Indigenous communities in the Great Apache Homeland and in Mexico. Henrique makes sacred offerings at the Yampa River and holds solstice, equinox, and other ceremony, as he has for over forty years. Henrique is an Ndé Native Foods and Field Guide gardening and foraging elder in the Yampa Valley of Colorado. Dr. Maestas is part of the family and community of the Texas Tribal Buffalo Project and Lipan Apache Women Legal Defense. Still Here! Land Back! Anti-Genocide!

Hawk Mendoza (he/him) is an enrolled member of the Lipan Apache Band of Texas, was born in Phoenix, Arizona, and attended public schools in Maricopa (Arizona), Tucson (Arizona), Pullman (Washington), Rutland (British Columbia), and Vernon (British Columbia) prior to studying and working for four years at the University of British Columbia, Faculty of Critical and Creative Studies (Theatre), in the ancestral and unceded territory of the Syilx Okanagan Nation. While a resident in Canada he worked to support his studies in various roles in local restaurants and in local performing arts theaters, and actively participated in comedy and poetry performance collectives. He currently lives and works in Austin, Texas, as a freelance audio-video technology contractor and hangs out with the buffalo in his spare time.

Milpa Mendoza (she/her) is an enrolled member of the Lipan Apache Band of Texas, was born in Casa Grande, Arizona, and attended public schools in Maricopa (Arizona), Tucson (Arizona), Pullman (Washington), Lake Country (British Columbia), and Vernon (British Columbia) prior to studying and working for six years at the University of British Columbia (Okanagan campus), Faculty of Health Sciences, in the ancestral and unceded territory of the Syilx Okanagan Nation. While a resident in Canada, she worked to support her studies in various part-time positions in locally owned businesses, including as a camp leader at a daycare on the Okanagan Indian Band reserve, a barista at a coffeehouse, a laundry attendant at a resort, and a bakery assistant and cashier in a family-owned grocery store on a local First Nation reserve, where she resided. She currently lives in Logan, Utah, and works for a locally owned and operated specialty grocery store. In her spare time, she can be found watering her plants, camping, and hanging out with her dog, Palouse, and her cats, Pinto and Billy.

Kelly Panchyshyn (they/she) grew up as a settler on the lands of the Ta'an Kwach'an and the Kwanlin Dün, in Whitehorse, Yukon. Kelly first connected with Dr. Margo Tamez and the El Calaboz project while studying at the University of British Columbia's Okanagan campus on Syilx lands. They now live on Gadigal lands, in Sydney, Australia, where they are undertaking a PhD in film studies at the University of Sydney. Kelly's current research explores the historical and contemporary significance of teen television through queer, feminist, and anticolonial frameworks.

Annette Portillo is a mama-scholar-activist whose research is grounded in ethnic and women's studies, with an emphasis in Chicana and Indigenous literature, history, and culture. She was born in the borderlands of San Diego, California, and Baja California, Mexico, where she attended San Diego State University and the University of California, San Diego (BA 1996). She received her MA and PhD from Cornell University (2005). Her scholarly work is directly informed by her life experiences as a working-class first-generation woman of color. Her interdisciplinary research focuses on life stories and oral histories by women of color. She is the author of *Sovereign Stories and Blood Memories: Native American Women's Autobiography* and has taught comparative ethnic studies courses at Cornell University, Mount Holyoke College, Oberlin College, and Nevada State College. After thirty years in academia she has learned that what matters most is *always speaking truth to power.*

Dr. Ramón Resendiz is a Xicanx documentary filmmaker and media anthropologist from Cameron Park in deep South Texas. His research interrogates the material and imaginary intersections of national borders, memory, visual culture, systemic violence, and settler colonialism. He investigates the erasure of Indigenous peoples, how modern nation-states are visualized by archival institutions across the South Texas / United States and northern Mexico border landscapes, and the ways visual documentary producers contest and render visible these erasures. He has produced multiple collaborative documentaries including *Voces del Norte: Mariachi Quinto Sol de UW* (2016), *El Muro | The Wall* (2017), and *Migrant: A Reflection from Thundercloud* (2019). He holds a PhD in media, culture, and communication from New York University and a master's in communication from the Native Voices Documentary Program at University of Washington, and is an assistant professor of anthropology at the University of Oregon.

Rosalva Resendiz holds a PhD in sociology from Texas Woman's University and is currently an associate professor in the Department of Criminal Justice at the University of Texas Rio Grande Valley, previously known as the University of Texas–Pan American. Dr. Resendiz's research interests focus on social justice, critical criminology, decoloniality, postcolonial studies, Chicanx feminism, and Mexican American / border studies. She has published the scholarly textbooks *Criminology Throughout History: Critical Readings* (2021) and *Gender, Crime and Justice: Critical and Feminist Perspectives, 2nd Edition* (2021). She is lead author of a book chapter in *BIPOC Alliances: Building Communities and Curricula* (2022), titled "Reclaiming Our Indigeneity: Deconstructing Settler Myths through Micro-activism." Most recently she published "Indigenizing the Tejas/Mexico Borderlands: A Pedagogy of Acknowledgements" in *Sociological Imagination* (2024). She also co-directed/produced the documentary *El Muro | The Wall* (2017) with her nephew Dr. Ramón Resendiz.

Lori Riddle (Akimel O'odham) is the director and co-founder of the Gila River Alliance for a Clean Environment (GRACE), a grassroots tribal member organization on the Gila River Indian Community reservation in Arizona working on environmental, sacred site, and cultural protection. Lori was a leader in the fights that closed the Romic toxic waste plant and the Stericycle incinerator on the reservation. Lori and her family were poisoned by living on a site contaminated by pesticides.

Madeline Newman Ríos is an ATA-certified translator and Spanish court interpreter, certified by the State of California and the Administrative Office of the United States Courts. Ríos holds a master of arts degree in Spanish translation and interpreting and is a former university instructor of business, legal, and technical translation. She specializes in Spanish-to-English legal and technical translations, which are always translated and/or edited in-house. Her translation firm, Ríos Translations, specializes in Spanish-to-English legal and technical translations, particularly in the fields of contracts and case law, energy and mining, telecommunications, and environmental expert reports, and also provides services from English into Spanish in these fields.

Shannon Speed is a citizen of the Chickasaw Nation. She is the Paula Gunn Allen Chair and a professor of American Indian studies, gender studies, and anthropology at UCLA, where she also serves as director of the American Indian Studies Center and special advisor to the chancellor on Native American and Indigenous affairs. Her books include the award-winning *Incarcerated Stories: Indigenous Women Migrants and Violence in the Settler Capitalist State* (2020) and the co-edited volume, with Dr. Lynn Stephen, *Heightened States of Injustice: Activist Research on Indigenous Women and Violence* (2021). Her current book project is entitled "Chickasaw Spring: Law and Resurgent Sovereignty in a Native Nation." She is a recipient of the President's Award from the American Anthropological Association and the Chickasaw Dynamic Woman of the Year award from the Chickasaw Nation. She served as the president of the Native American and Indigenous Studies Association (NAISA) from 2018 to 2021.

Eloisa G. Taméz, RN, PhD, MSCJ, FAAN, is a professor and the Associate Dean of Student Success and Engagement in the School of Nursing (SON) at the University of Texas Rio Grande Valley, where she formerly was chief nursing administrator and associate dean of student affairs. She joined academia following years in service in the private sector and the Department of Veterans Affairs (DVA). In academia, she has held faculty and leadership positions and founded the Psychiatric Mental Health Nurse Practitioner Post-Master's Certificate Program. Dr. Taméz, among many awards, is a recipient of a Frederick Douglass 200 (FD200), was inducted as Fellow of the Academy of Nursing, and is a recipient of the "A" Proficiency Designator. As a retired colonel of the United States Army and former Chief Nurse Executive in the DVA, Taméz was appointed to the National Advisory Committee for Disability and Compensation by the secretary of the DVA. She is of Lipan Apache and Mexican descent.

Maura Tamez (she/her) is a multidisciplinary Ndé (Lipan Apache, Southern Plains Dene) artist whose practice centers on Ndé aesthetics, sciences, histories, and ways of being. She lives on the unceded territories of the xʷməθkʷəy̓əm (Musqueam), Sḵwx̱wú7mesh (Squamish), and səlilwətaɬ (Tsleil-Waututh) nations and is a 2022 graduate of the University of British Columbia Okanagan, holding a bachelor of fine arts degree. Tamez received the Norma and Jack Aitkens Prize in Visual Arts in 2022 and is a 2023 recipient of a Canada Council Research and Creation Grant. She has been featured in several exhibitions at galleries such as the 2024 Biennale d'art contemporain autochtone, the Polygon Art Gallery, the Alternator Centre for Contemporary Art, the Kelowna Art Gallery, the Lake Country Art Gallery, and the Vernon Art Gallery. Her work engages themes of belonging, story, and history. Her cultural legacy of ancestral border violence, removal, erasure, and surveillance is generously represented in her practice in sculpture and metal. This material energizes Ndé knowledge and asserts the Ndé peoples as current—time—place. Something present and formidable.

Myst Tamez-Hrabovsky writes, "I am twenty-one years old as of October 2024. I am an enrolled member of the Lipan Apache Band of Texas, and we are related to the larger Dene (Athapaskan) peoples. I currently live in the unceded Okanagan territory of the Syilx peoples, living with my partner on the Okanagan Indian Band No. 1 reserve near Vernon, British Columbia. I am currently working on a few personal beaded art projects, aiming to officially start my beadwork/sewing business in winter 2025. During my elementary school years, I attended the Okanagan language immersion school, named nkmaplqs isnmamayatn klsqilxwtet. I graduated from Seaton High School in Vernon, British Columbia, and I am a published poet. My poetry appears in *The Night's Voice: Anthology of Creative Writing—Young Writers of Canada* (2017) and *Catch the Whispers: Anthology of Verse—Young Writers of Canada* (2018)."

Aurora Vasquez is a former community-based civil rights attorney with proven experience managing teams of staff and volunteers in matters of racial, social, and economic justice, employing a human rights lens. She has also designed and implemented a number of creative and successful campaigns, programs, and projects in the education equity, voting rights, economic justice, and immigrant justice sectors. Aurora transitioned her skills into the gun violence prevention sector after her youngest niece was murdered while a sophomore in college. Particularly known for her diplomacy and ability to build, sustain, and resource diverse coalitions, Aurora has had extensive success helping communities pressure decision-makers—including agency leaders and elected officials at the local, state, and national levels—into adopting more equitable laws, policies, and practices.

Monica Villarreal studied typography at Symbiosis International University in India and holds an MA in digital media studies from the University of Houston–Clear Lake. She is an interdisciplinary artist and grassroots organizer whose work explores themes of ethnic identity, gender roles, migration, land sovereignty, and environmental justice. A recipient of grants from the BIPOC Arts Network and Fund, Houston Endowment, Houston Arts Alliance, and the Idea Fund, her art has been showcased at venues such as DiversWorks, Project Row Houses, Art League Houston, and Santa Fe Arts Institute. Monica co-founded Creative Women Unite (2007), a feminist arts collective, and Danza Azteca Taxcayolotl (2012), a traditional Indigenous dance group where she serves as First Palabra. Most recently, she established Xochipilli Collective, an Indigenous organization dedicated to promoting arts, sustainability, and culture. Monica is a mother and works full-time at the University of Houston–Downtown, where she also serves on the Sustainability Council.

Index

Note: Page numbers for photographs, artwork, maps, and other images are indicated with *italics*. References to contributor profiles are indicated in **bold**. Items appearing in the notes are indicated using page and note numbers, e.g., 303n4.